Data Parallel C++

Programming Accelerated Systems Using C++ and SYCL

Second Edition

James Reinders
Ben Ashbaugh
James Brodman
Michael Kinsner
John Pennycook
Xinmin Tian

Foreword by Erik Lindahl, GROMACS and Stockholm University

Apress
open

Data Parallel C++: Programming Accelerated Systems Using C++ and SYCL, Second Edition

James Reinders
Beaverton, OR, USA

Ben Ashbaugh
Folsom, CA, USA

James Brodman
Marlborough, MA, USA

Michael Kinsner
Halifax, NS, Canada

John Pennycook
San Jose, CA, USA

Xinmin Tian
Fremont, CA, USA

ISBN-13 (pbk): 978-1-4842-9690-5
ISBN-13 (electronic): 978-1-4842-9691-2
https://doi.org/10.1007/978-1-4842-9691-2

Managing Director, Apress Media LLC: Welmoed Spahr
Acquisitions Editor: Susan McDermot
Development Editor: James Markham
Coordinating Editor: Jessica Vakili

Distributed to the book trade worldwide by Springer Science+Business Media New York, 1 NY Plaza, New York, NY 10004. Phone 1-800-SPRINGER, fax (201) 348-4505, e-mail orders-ny@springer-sbm.com, or visit https://www.springeronline.com. Apress Media, LLC is a California LLC and the sole member (owner) is Springer Science + Business Media Finance Inc (SSBM Finance Inc). SSBM Finance Inc is a **Delaware** corporation.

For information on translations, please e-mail booktranslations@springernature.com; for reprint, paperback, or audio rights, please e-mail bookpermissions@springernature.com.

Apress titles may be purchased in bulk for academic, corporate, or promotional use. eBook versions and licenses are also available for most titles. For more information, reference our Print and eBook Bulk Sales web page at https://www.apress.com/bulk-sales.

Any source code or other supplementary material referenced by the author in this book is available to readers on the Github repository: https://github.com/Apress/Data-Parallel-CPP. For more detailed information, please visit https://www.apress.com/gp/services/source-code.

Paper in this product is recyclable

Table of Contents

About the Authors

James Reinders is an Engineer at Intel Corporation with more than four decades of experience in parallel computing and is an author/coauthor/editor of more than ten technical books related to parallel programming. James has a passion for system optimization and teaching. He has had the great fortune to help make contributions to several of the world's fastest computers (#1 on the TOP500 list) as well as many other supercomputers and software developer tools.

Ben Ashbaugh is a Software Architect at Intel Corporation where he has worked for over 20 years developing software drivers and compilers for Intel graphics products. For the past ten years, Ben has focused on parallel programming models for general-purpose computation on graphics processors, including SYCL and the DPC++ compiler. Ben is active in the Khronos SYCL, OpenCL, and SPIR working groups, helping define industry standards for parallel programming, and he has authored numerous extensions to expose unique Intel GPU features.

James Brodman is a Principal Engineer at Intel Corporation working on runtimes and compilers for parallel programming, and he is one of the architects of DPC++. James has a Ph.D. in Computer Science from the University of Illinois at Urbana-Champaign.

Michael Kinsner is a Principal Engineer at Intel Corporation developing parallel programming languages and compilers for a variety of architectures. Michael contributes extensively to spatial architectures and programming models and is an Intel representative within The Khronos Group where he works on the SYCL and OpenCL industry standards for parallel programming. Mike has a Ph.D. in Computer Engineering from McMaster University and is passionate about programming models that cross architectures while still enabling performance.

John Pennycook is a Software Enabling and Optimization Architect at Intel Corporation, focused on enabling developers to fully utilize the parallelism available in modern processors. John is experienced in optimizing and parallelizing applications from a range of scientific domains, and previously served as Intel's representative on the steering committee for the Intel eXtreme Performance User's Group (IXPUG). John has a Ph.D. in Computer Science from the University of Warwick. His research interests are varied, but a recurring theme is the ability to achieve application "performance portability" across different hardware architectures.

Xinmin Tian is an Intel Fellow and Compiler Architect at Intel Corporation and serves as Intel's representative on the OpenMP Architecture Review Board (ARB). Xinmin has been driving OpenMP offloading, vectorization, and parallelization compiler technologies for Intel architectures. His current focus is on LLVM-based OpenMP offloading, SYCL/DPC++ compiler optimizations for CPUs/GPUs, and tuning HPC/AI application performance. He has a Ph.D. in Computer Science from Tsinghua University, holds 27 US patents, has published over 60 technical papers with over 1300+ citations of his work, and has coauthored two books that span his expertise.

Preface

If you are new to parallel programming that is okay. If you have never heard of SYCL or the DPC++ compilerthat is also okay

Compared with programming in CUDA, C++ with SYCL offers portability beyond NVIDIA, and portability beyond GPUs, plus a tight alignment to enhance modern C++ as it evolves too. C++ with SYCL offers these advantages without sacrificing performance.

C++ with SYCL allows us to accelerate our applications by harnessing the combined capabilities of CPUs, GPUs, FPGAs, and processing devices of the future without being tied to any one vendor.

SYCL is an industry-driven Khronos Group standard adding advanced support for data parallelism with C++ to exploit accelerated (heterogeneous) systems. SYCL provides mechanisms for C++ compilers that are highly synergistic with C++ and C++ build systems. DPC++ is an open source compiler project based on LLVM that adds SYCL support. All examples in this book should work with any C++ compiler supporting SYCL 2020 including the DPC++ compiler.

If you are a C programmer who is not well versed in C++, you are in good company. Several of the authors of this book happily share that they picked up much of C++ by reading books that utilized C++ like this one. With a little patience, this book should also be approachable by C programmers with a desire to write modern C++ programs.

Second Edition

With the benefit of feedback from a growing community of SYCL users, we have been able to add content to help learn SYCL better than ever.

This edition teaches C++ with SYCL 2020. The first edition preceded the SYCL 2020 specification, which differed only slightly from what the first edition taught (the most obvious changes for SYCL 2020 in this edition are the header file location, the device selector syntax, and dropping an explicit *host device*).

Important resources for updated SYCL information, including any known book errata, include the book GitHub (`https://github.com/Apress/data-parallel-CPP`), the Khronos Group SYCL standards website (`www.khronos.org/sycl`), and a key SYCL education website (`https://sycl.tech`).

Chapters 20 and 21 are additions encouraged by readers of the first edition of this book.

We added Chapter 20 to discuss backend interoperability. One of the key goals of the SYCL 2020 standard is to enable broad support for hardware from many vendors with many architectures. This required expanding beyond the OpenCL-only backend support of SYCL 1.2.1. While generally "it just works," Chapter 20 explains this in more detail for those who find it valuable to understand and interface at this level.

For experienced CUDA programmers, we have added Chapter 21 to explicitly connect *C++ with SYCL* concepts to *CUDA* concepts both in terms of approach and vocabulary. While the core issues of expressing heterogeneous parallelism are fundamentally similar, C++ with SYCL offers many benefits because of its multivendor and multiarchitecture approach. Chapter 21 is the only place we mention CUDA terminology; the rest of this book teaches using C++ and SYCL terminology with its open multivendor, multiarchitecture approaches. In Chapter 21, we strongly encourage looking at the open source tool "SYCLomatic" (`github.com/oneapi-src/SYCLomatic`), which helps automate migration of CUDA code. Because it is helpful, we recommend it as the preferred first step in migrating code. Developers using C++ with SYCL have been reporting strong results on NVIDIA, AMD, and Intel GPUs on both codes that have been ported from CUDA and original C++ with SYCL code. The resulting C++ with SYCL offers portability that is not possible with NVIDIA CUDA.

The evolution of C++, SYCL, and compilers including DPC++ continues. Prospects for the future are discussed in the Epilogue, after we have taken a journey together to learn how to create programs for heterogeneous systems using C++ with SYCL.

It is our hope that this book supports and helps grow the SYCL community and helps promote data-parallel programming in C++ with SYCL.

Structure of This Book

This book takes us on a journey through what we need to know to be an effective programmer of accelerated/heterogeneous systems using C++ with SYCL.

Chapters 1–4: Lay Foundations

Chapters 1–4 are important to read in order when first approaching C++ with SYCL.

Chapter 1 lays the first foundation by covering core concepts that are either new or worth refreshing in our minds.

Chapters 2–4 lay a foundation of understanding for data-parallel programming in C++ with SYCL. When we finish reading Chapters 1–4, we will have a solid foundation for data-parallel programming in C++. Chapters 1–4 build on each other and are best read in order.

Chapters 5–12: Build on Foundations

With the foundations established, Chapters 5–12 fill in vital details by building on each other to some degree while being easy to jump between as desired. All these chapters should be valuable to all users of C++ with SYCL.

Chapters 13–21: Tips/Advice for SYCL in Practice

These final chapters offer advice and details for specific needs. We encourage at least skimming them all to find content that is important to your needs.

Epilogue: Speculating on the Future

The book concludes with an Epilogue that discusses likely and potential future directions for C++ with SYCL, and the Data Parallel C++ compiler for SYCL.

We wish you the best as you learn to use C++ with SYCL.

Foreword

SYCL 2020 is a milestone in parallel computing. For the first time we have a modern, stable, feature-complete, and portable open standard that can target all types of hardware, and the book you hold in your hand is the premier resource to learn SYCL 2020.

Computer hardware development is driven by our needs to solve larger and more complex problems, but those hardware advances are largely useless unless programmers like you and me have languages that allow us to implement our ideas and exploit the power available with reasonable effort. There are numerous examples of amazing hardware, and the first solutions to use them have often been proprietary since it saves time not having to bother with committees agreeing on standards. However, in the history of computing, they have eventually always ended up as vendor lock-in—unable to compete with open standards that allow developers to target any hardware and share code—because ultimately the resources of the worldwide community and ecosystem are far greater than any individual vendor, not to mention how open software standards drive hardware competition.

Over the last few years, my team has had the tremendous privilege of contributing to shaping the emerging SYCL ecosystem through our development of GROMACS, one of the world's most widely used scientific HPC codes. We need our code to run on every supercomputer in the world as well as our laptops. While we cannot afford to lose performance, we also depend on being part of a larger community where other teams invest effort in libraries we depend on, where there are open compilers available, and where we can recruit talent. Since the first edition of this book, SYCL has matured into such a community; in addition to several vendor-provided compilers, we now have a major community-driven implementation[1] that targets all hardware, and there are thousands of developers worldwide sharing experiences, contributing to training events, and participating in forums. The outstanding power of open source—whether it is an application, a compiler, or an open standard—is that we can peek under the hood to learn, borrow, and extend. Just as we repeatedly learn from the code in the Intel-led LLVM implementation,[2] the community-driven implementation from Heidelberg University, and several other codes, you can use our public repository[3] to compare CUDA and SYCL implementations in a large production codebase or borrow solutions for your needs—because when you do so, you are helping to further extend our community.

Perhaps surprisingly, data-parallel programming as a paradigm is arguably far easier than classical solutions such as message-passing communication or explicit multithreading—but it poses special challenges to those of us who have spent decades in the old paradigms that focus on hardware and explicit data placement. On a small scale, it was trivial for us to explicitly decide how data is moved between a handful of processes, but as the problem scales to thousands of units, it becomes a nightmare to manage the complexity without introducing bugs or having the hardware sit idle waiting for data. Data-parallel programming with SYCL solves this by striking the balance of primarily asking us to explicitly *express the inherent parallelism of our algorithm*, but once we have done that, the compiler and drivers will mostly handle the data locality and scheduling over tens of thousands of functional units. To be successful in data-parallel programming, it is important not to think of a computer as a single unit executing one program, but as a collection of units working independently

---

[1] Community-driven implementation from Heidelberg University: `tinyurl.com/HeidelbergSYCL`

[2] DPC++ compiler project: `github.com/intel/llvm`

[3] GROMACS: `gitlab.com/gromacs/gromacs/`

to solve parts of a large problem. As long as we can express our problem as an algorithm where each part does not have dependencies on other parts, it is in theory straightforward to implement it, for example, as a parallel for-loop that is executed on a GPU through a device queue. However, for more practical examples, our problems are frequently not large enough to use an entire device efficiently, or we depend on performing tens of thousands of iterations per second where latency in device drivers starts to be a major bottleneck. While this book is an outstanding introduction to performance-portable GPU programming, it goes far beyond this to show how both throughput and latency matter for real-world applications, how SYCL can be used to exploit unique features both of CPUs, GPUs, SIMD units, and FPGAs, but it also covers the caveats that for good performance we need to understand and possibly adapt code to the characteristics of each type of hardware. Doing so, it is not merely a great tutorial on data-parallel programing, but an authoritative text that anybody interested in programming modern computer hardware in general should read.

One of SYCL's key strengths is the close alignment to modern C++. This can seem daunting at first; C++ is not an easy language to fully master (I certainly have not), but Reinders and coauthors take our hand and lead us on a path where we only need to learn a handful of C++ concepts to get started and be productive in actual data-parallel programming. However, as we become more experienced, SYCL 2020 allows us to combine this with the extreme generality of C++17 to write code that can be dynamically targeted to different devices, or relying on heterogeneous parallelism that uses CPU, GPU, and network units in parallel for different tasks. SYCL is not a separate bolted-on solution to enable accelerators but instead holds great promise to be the general way we express data parallelism in C++. The SYCL 2020 standard now includes several features previously only available as vendor extensions, for example, Unified Shared Memory, sub-groups, atomic operations, reductions, simpler accessors, and many other concepts that make code cleaner, and facilitates both development as well as porting from standard C++17 or CUDA to have your code target more diverse hardware. This book provides a wonderful and accessible introduction to all of them, and you will also learn how SYCL is expected to evolve together with the rapid development C++ is undergoing.

This all sounds great in theory, but how portable is SYCL in practice? Our application is an example of a codebase that is quite challenging to optimize since data access patterns are random, the amount of data to process in each step is limited, we need to achieve thousands of iterations per second, and we are limited both by memory bandwidth, floating-point, and integer operations—it is an extreme opposite of a simple data-parallel problem. We spent over two decades writing assembly SIMD instructions and native implementations for several GPU architectures, and our very first encounters with SYCL involved both pains with adapting to differences and reporting performance regressions to driver and compiler developers. However, as of spring 2023, our SYCL kernels can achieve 80–100% of native performance on all GPU architectures not only from a single codebase but even a single precompiled binary.

SYCL is still young and has a rapidly evolving ecosystem. There are a few things not yet part of the language, but SYCL is unique as the only performance-portable standard available that successfully targets all modern hardware. Whether you are a beginner wanting to learn parallel programming, an experienced developer interested in data-parallel programming, or a maintainer needing to port 100,000 lines of proprietary API code to an open standard, this second edition is the only book you will need to become part of this community.

Erik Lindahl
Professor of Biophysics
Dept. Biophysics & Biochemistry
Science for Life Laboratory
Stockholm University

Acknowledgments

We have been blessed with an outpouring of community input for this second edition of our book. Much inspiration came from interactions with developers as they use SYCL in production, classes, tutorials, workshops, conferences, and hackathons. SYCL deployments that include NVIDIA hardware, in particular, have helped us enhance the inclusiveness and practical tips in our teaching of SYCL in this second edition.

The SYCL community has grown a great deal—and consists of engineers implementing compilers and tools, and a much larger group of users that adopt SYCL to target hardware of many types and vendors. We are grateful for their hard work, and shared insights.

We thank the Khronos SYCL Working Group that has worked diligently to produce a highly functional specification. In particular, Ronan Keryell has been the SYCL specification editor and a longtime vocal advocate for SYCL.

We are in debt to the numerous people who gave us feedback from the SYCL community in all these ways. We are also deeply grateful for those who helped with the first edition a few years ago, many of whom we named in the acknowledgement of that edition.

The first edition received feedback via GitHub,[1] which we did review but we were not always prompt in acknowledging (imagine six coauthors all thinking "*you* did that, right?"). We did benefit a great deal from that feedback, and we believe we have addressed all the feedback in the samples and text for this edition. Jay Norwood was the most prolific at commenting and helping us—a big thank you to Jay from all the authors!

[1] `github.com/apress/data-parallel-CPP`

Other feedback contributors include Oscar Barenys, Marcel Breyer, Jeff Donner, Laurence Field, Michael Firth, Piotr Fusik, Vincent Mierlak, and Jason Mooneyham. Regardless of whether we recalled your name here or not, we thank everyone who has provided feedback and helped refine our teaching of C++ with SYCL.

For this edition, a handful of volunteers tirelessly read draft manuscripts and provided insightful feedback for which we are incredibly grateful. These reviewers include Aharon Abramson, Thomas Applencourt, Rod Burns, Joe Curley, Jessica Davies, Henry Gabb, Zheming Jin, Rakshith Krishnappa, Praveen Kundurthy, Tim Lewis, Eric Lindahl, Gregory Lueck, Tony Mongkolsmai, Ruyman Reyes Castro, Andrew Richards, Sanjiv Shah, Neil Trevett, and Georg Viehöver.

We all enjoy the support of our family and friends, and we cannot thank them enough. As coauthors, we have enjoyed working as a team challenging each other and learning together along the way. We appreciate our collaboration with the entire Apress team in getting this book published.

We are sure that there are more than a few people whom we have failed to mention explicitly who have positively impacted this book project. We thank all who helped us.

As you read this second edition, please do provide feedback if you find any way to improve it. Feedback via GitHub can open up a conversation, and we will update the online errata and book samples as needed.

Thank you all, and we hope you find this book invaluable in your endeavors.

CHAPTER 1

Introduction

We have undeniably entered the age of accelerated computing. In order to satisfy the world's insatiable appetite for more computation, accelerated computing drives complex simulations, AI, and much more by providing greater performance *and* improved power efficiency when compared with earlier solutions.

Heralded as a "New Golden Age for Computer Architecture,"[1] we are faced with enormous opportunity through a rich diversity in compute devices. We need portable software development capabilities that are not tied to any single vendor or architecture in order to realize the full potential for accelerated computing.

SYCL (pronounced *sickle*) is an industry-driven Khronos Group standard adding advanced support for data parallelism with C++ to support accelerated (heterogeneous) systems. SYCL provides mechanisms for C++ compilers to exploit accelerated (heterogeneous) systems in a way that is highly synergistic with modern C++ and C++ build systems. SYCL is not an acronym; SYCL is simply a name.

---

[1] *A New Golden Age for Computer Architecture* by John L. Hennessy, David A. Patterson; Communications of the ACM, February 2019, Vol. 62 No. 2, Pages 48-60.

J. Reinders et al., *Data Parallel C++*, https://doi.org/10.1007/978-1-4842-9691-2_1

ACCELERATED VS. HETEROGENEOUS

These terms go together. *Heterogeneous* is a technical description acknowledging the combination of compute devices that are programmed differently. *Accelerated* is the motivation for adding this complexity to systems and programming. There is no guarantee of acceleration ever; programming heterogeneous systems will only accelerate our applications when we do it right. This book helps teach us how to do it right!

Data parallelism in C++ with SYCL provides access to all the compute devices in a modern accelerated (heterogeneous) system. A single C++ application can use any combination of devices—including GPUs, CPUs, FPGAs, and application-specific integrated circuits (ASICs)—that are suitable to the problems at hand. No proprietary, single-vendor, solution can offer us the same level of flexibility.

This book teaches us how to harness accelerated computing using data-parallel programming using C++ with SYCL and provides practical advice for balancing application performance, portability across compute devices, and our own productivity as programmers. This chapter lays the foundation by covering core concepts, including terminology, which are critical to have fresh in our minds as we learn how to accelerate C++ programs using data parallelism.

Read the Book, Not the Spec

No one wants to be told "Go read the spec!"—specifications are hard to read, and the SYCL specification (`www.khronos.org/sycl/`) is no different. Like every great language specification, it is full of precision but is light on motivation, usage, and teaching. This book is a "study guide" to teach C++ with SYCL.

No book can explain *everything at once*. Therefore, this chapter does what no other chapter will do: the code examples contain programming constructs that go unexplained until future chapters. We should not get hung up on understanding the coding examples completely in Chapter 1 and trust it will get better with each chapter.

SYCL 2020 and DPC++

This book teaches C++ with SYCL 2020. The first edition of this book preceded the SYCL 2020 specification, so this edition includes updates including adjustments in the header file location (`sycl` instead of `CL`), device selector syntax, and removal of an explicit host device.

DPC++ is an open source compiler project based on LLVM. It is our hope that SYCL eventually be supported by default in the LLVM community and that the DPC++ project will help make that happen. The DPC++ compiler offers broad heterogeneous support that includes GPU, CPU, and FPGA. All examples in this book work with the DPC++ compiler and should work with any C++ compiler supporting SYCL 2020.

Important resources for updated SYCL information, including any known book errata, include the book GitHub (`github.com/Apress/data-parallel-CPP`), the Khronos Group SYCL standards website (`www.khronos.org/sycl`), and a key SYCL education website (`sycl.tech`).

As of publication time, no C++ compiler claims full conformance or compliance with the SYCL 2020 specification. Nevertheless, the code in this book works with the DPC++ compiler and should work with other C++ compilers that have most of SYCL 2020 implemented. We use only standard C++ with SYCL 2020 excepting for a few DPC++-specific extensions that are clearly called out in Chapter 17 (Programming for FPGAs) to a small degree, Chapter 20 (Backend Interoperability) when connecting to Level Zero backends, and the Epilogue when speculating on the future.

Why Not CUDA?

Unlike CUDA, SYCL supports data parallelism in C++ for all vendors and all types of architectures (not just GPUs). CUDA is focused on NVIDIA GPU support only, and efforts (such as HIP/ROCm) to reuse it for GPUs by other vendors have limited ability to succeed despite some solid success and usefulness. With the explosion of accelerator architectures, only SYCL offers the support we need for harnessing this diversity and offering a multivendor/multiarchitecture approach to help with portability that CUDA does not offer. To more deeply understand this motivation, we highly recommend reading (or watching the video recording of their excellent talk) "A New Golden Age for Computer Architecture" by industry legends John L. Hennessy and David A. Patterson. We consider this a must-read article.

Chapter 21, in addition to addressing topics useful for migrating code from CUDA to C++ with SYCL, is valuable for those experienced with CUDA to bridge some terminology and capability differences. The most significant capabilities beyond CUDA come from the ability for SYCL to support multiple vendors, multiple architectures (not just GPUs), and multiple backends even for the same device. This flexibility answers the question "Why not CUDA?"

SYCL does not involve any extra overhead compared with CUDA or HIP. It is not a compatibility layer—it is a generalized approach that is open to all devices regardless of vendor and architecture while simultaneously being in sync with modern C++. Like other open multivendor and multiarchitecture techniques, such as OpenMP and OpenCL, the ultimate proof is in the implementations including options to access hardware-specific optimizations when absolutely needed.

Why Standard C++ with SYCL?

As we will point out repeatedly, every program using SYCL is first and foremost a C++ program. SYCL does not rely on any language changes to C++. SYCL does take C++ programming places it cannot go without SYCL. We have no doubt that all programming for accelerated computing will continue to influence language standards including C++, but we do not believe the C++ standard should (or will) evolve to displace the need for SYCL any time soon. SYCL has a rich set of capabilities that we spend this book covering that extend C++ through classes and rich support for new compiler capabilities necessary to meet needs (already existing today) for multivendor and multiarchitecture support.

Getting a C++ Compiler with SYCL Support

All examples in this book compile and work with all the various distributions of the DPC++ compiler and should compile with other C++ compilers supporting SYCL (see "SYCL Compilers in Development" at `www.khronos.org/sycl`). We are careful to note the very few places where extensions are used that are DPC++ specific at the time of publication.

The authors recommend the DPC++ compiler for a variety of reasons, including our close association with the DPC++ compiler. DPC++ is an open source compiler project to support SYCL. By using LLVM, the DPC++ compiler project has access to backends for numerous devices. This has already resulted in support for Intel, NVIDIA, and AMD GPUs, numerous CPUs, and Intel FPGAs. The ability to extend and enhance support openly for multiple vendors and multiple architecture makes LLVM a great choice for open source efforts to support SYCL.

There are distributions of the DPC++ compiler, augmented with additional tools and libraries, available as part of a larger project to offer broad support for heterogeneous systems, which include libraries, debuggers, and other tools, known as the oneAPI project. The oneAPI tools, including the DPC++ compiler, are freely available (`www.oneapi.io/implementations`).

```
1.  #include <iostream>
2.  #include <sycl/sycl.hpp>
3.  using namespace sycl;
4.
5.  const std::string secret{
6.      "Ifmmp-!xpsme\"\012J(n!tpssz-!Ebwf/!"
7.      "J(n!bgsbje!J!dbo(u!ep!uibu/!.!IBM\01"};
8.
9.  const auto sz = secret.size();
10.
11. int main() {
12.   queue q;
13.
14.   char* result = malloc_shared<char>(sz, q);
15.   std::memcpy(result, secret.data(), sz);
16.
17.   q.parallel_for(sz, [=](auto& i) {
18.      result[i] -= 1;
19.    }).wait();
20.
21.   std::cout << result << "\n";
22.   free(result, q);
23.   return 0;
24. }
```

EXAMPLE
IS KNOWN TO HAVE ELEMENTS NOT TAUGHT UNTIL FUTURE CHAPTERS. EXAMINE AT YOUR OWN RISK OF CONFUSION.

Figure 1-1. *Hello data-parallel programming*

Hello, World! and a SYCL Program Dissection

Figure 1-1 shows a sample SYCL program. Compiling and running it results in the following being printed:

`Hello, world!` (and some additional text left to experience by running it)

We will completely understand this example by the end of Chapter 4. Until then, we can observe the single include of `<sycl/sycl.hpp>` (line 2) that is needed to define all the SYCL constructs. All SYCL constructs live inside a namespace called `sycl`.

- Line 3 lets us avoid writing `sycl::` over and over.
- Line 12 instantiates a queue for work requests directed to a particular device (Chapter 2).
- Line 14 creates an allocation for data shared with the device (Chapter 3).
- Line 15 copies the secret string into device memory, where it will be processed by the kernel.
- Line 17 enqueues work to the device (Chapter 4).
- Line 18 is the only line of code that will run on the device. All other code runs on the host (CPU).

Line 18 is the *kernel* code that we want to run on devices. That kernel code decrements a single character. With the power of `parallel_for()`, that kernel is run on each character in our secret string in order to decode it into the `result` string. There is no ordering of the work required, and it is run asynchronously relative to the main program once the `parallel_for` queues the work. It is critical that there is a `wait` (line 19) before looking at the result to be sure that the kernel has completed, since in this example we are using a convenient feature (Unified Shared Memory, Chapter 6). Without the wait, the output may occur before all the characters have been decrypted. There is more to discuss, but that is the job of later chapters.

Queues and Actions

Chapter 2 discusses queues and actions, but we can start with a simple explanation for now. Queues are the only connection that allows an application to direct work to be done on a device. There are two types of actions that can be placed into a queue: (a) code to execute and (b) memory operations. Code to execute is expressed via either `single_task` or `parallel_for` (used in Figure 1-1). Memory operations perform copy operations between host and device or fill operations to initialize memory. We only need to use memory operations if we seek more control than what is done automatically for us. These are all discussed later in the book starting with Chapter 2. For now, we should be aware that queues are the connection that allows us to command a device, and we have a set of actions available to put in queues to execute code and to move around data. It is also very important to understand that requested actions are placed into a queue without waiting. The host, after submitting an action into a queue, continues to execute the program, while the device will eventually, and asynchronously, perform the action requested via the queue.

QUEUES CONNECT US TO DEVICES

We submit actions into queues to request computational work and data movement.

Actions happen asynchronously.

It Is All About Parallelism

Since programming in C++ for data parallelism is all about parallelism, let's start with this critical concept. The goal of parallel programming is to compute something faster. It turns out there are two aspects to this: *increased throughput* and *reduced latency*.

Throughput

Increasing throughput of a program comes when we get more work done in a set amount of time. Techniques like pipelining may stretch out the time necessary to get a single work-item done, to allow overlapping of work that leads to more work-per-unit-of-time being done. Humans encounter this often when working together. The very act of sharing work involves overhead to coordinate that often slows the time to do a single item. However, the power of multiple people leads to more throughput. Computers are no different—spreading work to more processing cores adds overhead to each unit of work that likely results in some delays, but the goal is to get more total work done because we have more processing cores working together.

Latency

What if we want to get one thing done faster—for instance, analyzing a voice command and formulating a response? If we only cared about throughput, the response time might grow to be unbearable. The concept of latency reduction requires that we break up an item of work into pieces that can be tackled in parallel. For throughput, image processing might assign whole images to different processing units—in this case, our goal may be optimizing for images per second. For latency, image processing might assign each pixel within an image to different processing cores—in this case, our goal may be maximizing pixels per second from a single image.

Think Parallel

Successful parallel programmers use both techniques in their programming. This is the beginning of our quest to *Think Parallel*.

We want to adjust our minds to think first about where parallelism can be found in our algorithms and applications. We also think about how different ways of expressing the parallelism affect the performance we ultimately achieve. That is a *lot* to take in all at once. The quest to *Think Parallel* becomes a lifelong journey for parallel programmers. We can learn a few tips here.

Amdahl and Gustafson

Amdahl's Law, stated by the supercomputer pioneer Gene Amdahl in 1967, is a formula to predict the theoretical maximum speed-up when using multiple processors. Amdahl lamented that the maximum gain from parallelism is limited to `(1/(1-p))` where `p` is the fraction of the program that runs in parallel. If we only run two-thirds of our program in parallel, then the most that program can speed up is a factor of 3. We definitely need that concept to sink in deeply! This happens because no matter how fast we make that two-thirds of our program run, the other one-third still takes the same time to complete. Even if we add 100 GPUs, we will only get a factor of 3 increase in performance.

For many years, some viewed this as proof that parallel computing would not prove fruitful. In 1988, John Gustafson wrote an article titled "Reevaluating Amdahl's Law." He observed that parallelism was not used to speed up fixed workloads, but it was used to allow work to be scaled up. Humans experience the same thing. One delivery person cannot deliver a single package faster with the help of many more people and trucks. However, a hundred people and trucks can deliver one hundred packages more quickly than a single driver with a truck. Multiple drivers will definitely increase throughput and will also generally reduce latency for package deliveries. Amdahl's Law tells us that a single driver cannot deliver one package faster by adding ninety-nine more drivers with their own trucks. Gustafson noticed the opportunity to deliver one hundred packages faster with these extra drivers and trucks.

This emphasizes that parallelism is most useful because the size of problems we tackle keep growing in size year after year. Parallelism would not nearly as important to study if year after year we only wanted to run the same size problems faster. This quest to solve larger and larger problems fuels our interest in exploiting data parallelism, using C++ with SYCL, for the future of computer (heterogeneous/accelerated systems).

Scaling

The word "scaling" appeared in our prior discussion. Scaling is a measure of how much a program speeds up (simply referred to as "speed-up") when additional computing is available. Perfect speed-up happens if one hundred packages are delivered in the same time as one package, by simply having one hundred trucks with drivers instead of a single truck and driver. Of course, it does not reliably work that way. At some point, there is a bottleneck that limits speed-up. There may not be one hundred places for trucks to dock at the distribution center. In a computer program, bottlenecks often involve moving data around to where it will be processed. Distributing to one hundred trucks is similar to having to distribute data to one hundred processing cores. The act of distributing is not instantaneous. Chapter 3 starts our journey of exploring how to distribute data to where it is needed in a heterogeneous system. It is critical that we know that data distribution has a cost, and that cost affects how much scaling we can expect from our applications.

Heterogeneous Systems

For our purposes, a heterogeneous system is any system which contains multiple types of computational devices. For instance, a system with both a central processing unit (CPU) and a graphics processing unit (GPU) is a heterogeneous system. The CPU is often just called a processor, although that can be confusing when we speak of all the processing units in a heterogeneous system as compute processors. To avoid this confusion, SYCL refers to processing units as *devices*. An application always runs on a *host* that in turn sends work to *devices*. Chapter 2 begins the discussion of how our main application (*host* code) will steer work (computations) to particular *devices* in a heterogeneous system.

A program using C++ with SYCL runs on a *host* and issues kernels of work to *devices*. Although it might seem confusing, it is important to know that the host will often be able to serve as a device. This is valuable for two key reasons: (1) the host is most often a CPU that will run a kernel if no accelerator is present—a key promise of SYCL for application portability is that a kernel can always be run on any system even those without accelerators—and (2) CPUs often have vector, matrix, tensor, and/or AI processing capabilities that are accelerators that kernels map well to run upon.

Host code invokes code on *devices*. The capabilities of the *host* are very often available as a *device* also, to provide both a back-up device and to offer any acceleration capabilities the host has for processing kernels as well. Our *host* is most often a CPU, and as such it may be available as a *CPU device*. There is no guarantee by SYCL of a *CPU device*, only that there is at least one device available to be the default device for our application.

While heterogeneous describes the system from a technical standpoint, the reason to complicate our hardware and software is to obtain higher performance. Therefore, the term *accelerated computing* is popular for marketing heterogeneous systems or their components. We like to emphasize that there is no guarantee of acceleration. Programming of heterogeneous systems will only accelerate our applications when we do it right. This book helps teach us how to do it right!

GPUs have evolved to become high-performance computing (HPC) devices and therefore are sometimes referred to as general-purpose GPUs, or GPGPUs. For heterogeneous programming purposes, we can simply assume we are programming such powerful GPGPUs and refer to them as GPUs.

Today, the collection of devices in a heterogeneous system can include CPUs, GPUs, FPGAs (field-programmable gate arrays), DSPs (digital signal processors), ASICs (application-specific integrated circuits), and AI chips (graph, neuromorphic, etc.).

The design of such devices will involve duplication of compute processors (multiprocessors) and increased connections (increased bandwidth) to data sources such as memory. The first of these, multiprocessing, is particularly useful for raising throughput. In our analogy, this was done by adding additional drivers and trucks. The latter of these, higher bandwidth for data, is particularly useful for reducing latency. In our analogy, this was done with more loading docks to enable trucks to be fully loaded in parallel.

Having multiple types of devices, each with different architectures and therefore different characteristics, leads to different programming and optimization needs for each device. That becomes the motivation for C++ with SYCL and the majority of what this book has to teach.

SYCL was created to address the challenges of C++ data-parallel programming for heterogeneous (accelerated) systems.

Data-Parallel Programming

The phrase "data-parallel programming" has been lingering unexplained ever since the title of this book. Data-parallel programming focuses on parallelism that can be envisioned as a bunch of data to operate on in parallel. This shift in focus is like Gustafson vs. Amdahl. We need one hundred packages to deliver (effectively lots of data) in order to divide up the work among one hundred trucks with drivers. The key concept comes down to what we should divide. Should we process whole images or process them in smaller tiles or process them pixel by pixel? Should we analyze a collection of objects as a single collection or a set of smaller groupings of objects or object by object?

Choosing the right division of work and mapping that work onto computational resources effectively is the responsibility of any parallel programmer using C++ with SYCL. Chapter 4 starts this discussion, and it continues through the rest of the book.

Key Attributes of C++ with SYCL

Every program using SYCL is first and foremost a C++ program. SYCL does not rely on any language changes to C++.

C++ compilers with SYCL support will optimize code based on built-in knowledge of the SYCL specification as well as implement support so heterogeneous compilations "just work" within traditional C++ build systems.

Next, we will explain the key attributes of C++ with SYCL: *single-source* style, host, devices, kernel code, and asynchronous task graphs.

Single-Source

Programs are single-source, meaning that the same translation unit[2] contains both the code that defines the compute kernels to be executed on devices and also the host code that orchestrates execution of those compute kernels. Chapter 2 begins with a more detailed look at this capability. We can still divide our program source into different files and translation units for host and device code if we want to, but the key is that we don't have to!

---

[2] We could just say "file," but that is not entirely correct here. A translation unit is the actual input to the compiler, made from the source file after it has been processed by the C preprocessor to inline header files and expand macros.

Host

Every program starts by running on a host, and most of the *lines* of code in a program are usually for the host. Thus far, hosts have always been CPUs. The standard does not require this, so we carefully describe it as a host. This seems unlikely to be anything other than a CPU because the host needs to fully support C++17 in order to support all C++ with SYCL programs. As we will see shortly, devices (accelerators) do not need to support all of C++17.

Devices

Using multiple devices in a program is what makes it heterogeneous programming. That is why the word *device* has been recurring in this chapter since the explanation of heterogeneous systems a few pages ago. We already learned that the collection of devices in a heterogeneous system can include GPUs, FPGAs, DSPs, ASICs, CPUs, and AI chips, but is not limited to any fixed list.

Devices are the targets to gain acceleration. The idea of offloading computations is to transfer work to a device that can accelerate completion of the work. We have to worry about making up for time lost moving data—a topic that needs to constantly be on our minds.

Sharing Devices

On a system with a device, such as a GPU, we can envision two or more programs running and wanting to use a single device. They do not need to be programs using SYCL. Programs can experience delays in processing by the device if another program is currently using it. This is really the same philosophy used in C++ programs in general for CPUs. Any system can be overloaded if we run too many active programs on our CPU (mail, browser, virus scanning, video editing, photo editing, etc.) all at once.

On supercomputers, when nodes (CPUs + all attached devices) are granted exclusively to a single application, sharing is not usually a concern. On non-supercomputer systems, we can just note that the performance of a program may be impacted if there are multiple applications using the same devices at the same time.

Everything still works, and there is no programming we need to do differently.

Kernel Code

Code for a device is specified as kernels. This is a concept that is not unique to C++ with SYCL: it is a core concept in other offload acceleration languages including OpenCL and CUDA. While it is distinct from loop-oriented approaches (such as commonly used with OpenMP target offloads), it may resemble the body of code within the innermost loop without requiring the programmer to write the loop nest explicitly.

Kernel code has certain restrictions to allow broader device support and massive parallelism. The list of features *not* supported in kernel code includes dynamic polymorphism, dynamic memory allocations (therefore no object management using new or delete operators), static variables, function pointers, runtime type information (RTTI), and exception handling. No virtual member functions, and no variadic functions, are allowed to be called from kernel code. Recursion is not allowed within kernel code.

VIRTUAL FUNCTIONS?

While we will not discuss it further in this book, the DPC++ compiler project does have an experimental extension (visible in the open source project, of course) to implement some support for virtual functions within kernels. Thanks to the nature of offloading to accelerator efficiently, virtual functions cannot be supported well without some restrictions, but many users have expressed interest in seeing SYCL offer such support even with some restrictions. The beauty of open source, and the open SYCL specification, is the opportunity to participate in experiments that can inform the future of C++ and SYCL specifications. Visit the DPC++ project (github.com/intel/llvm) for more information.

Chapter 3 describes how memory allocations are done before and after kernels are invoked, thereby making sure that kernels stay focused on massively parallel computations. Chapter 5 describes handling of exceptions that arise in connection with devices.

The rest of C++ is fair game in a kernel, including functors, lambda expressions, operator overloading, templates, classes, and static polymorphism. We can also share data with the host (see Chapter 3) and share the read-only values of (non-global) host variables (via lambda expression captures).

Kernel: Vector Addition (DAXPY)

Kernels should feel familiar to any programmer who has worked on computationally complex code. Consider implementing DAXPY, which stands for "double-precision A times X Plus Y." A classic for decades. Figure 1-2 shows DAXPY implemented in modern Fortran, C/C++, and SYCL. Amazingly, the computation lines (line 3) are virtually identical. Chapters 4 and 10 explain kernels in detail. Figure 1-2 should help remove any concerns that kernels are difficult to understand—they should feel familiar even if the terminology is new to us.

```
! Fortran loop
do i = 1, n
  z(i) = alpha * x(i) + y(i)
end do

// C/C++ loop
for (int i=0;i<n;i++) {
  z[i] = alpha * x[i] + y[i];
}

// SYCL kernel
q.parallel_for(range{n},[=](id<1> i) {
  z[i] = alpha * x[i] + y[i];
}).wait();
```

EXAMPLE

IS KNOWN TO HAVE ELEMENTS NOT TAUGHT IN THIS BOOK AT ALL. PLEASE ENJOY THIS FORTRAN, SADLY THERE IS NO MORE IN THIS BOOK.

Figure 1-2. *DAXPY computations in Fortran, C/C++, and SYCL*

Asynchronous Execution

The asynchronous nature of programming using C++ with SYCL must *not* be missed. Asynchronous programming is critical to understand for two reasons: (1) proper use gives us better performance (better scaling), and (2) mistakes lead to parallel programming errors (usually race conditions) that make our applications unreliable.

The asynchronous nature comes about because work is transferred to devices via a "queue" of requested actions. The host program submits a requested action into a queue, and the program continues without waiting for any results. This *no waiting* is important so that we can try to keep computational resources (devices and the host) busy all the time. If we had to wait, that would tie up the host instead of allowing the host to do useful work. It would also create serial bottlenecks when the device finished, until we queued up new work. Amdahl's Law, as discussed earlier, penalizes us for time spent not doing work in parallel. We need to construct our programs to be moving data to and from devices while the devices are busy and keep all the computational power of the devices and host busy any time work is available. Failure to do so will bring the full curse of Amdahl's Law upon us.

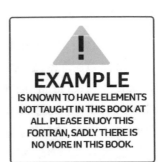

Chapter 3 starts the discussion on thinking of our program as an asynchronous task graph, and Chapter 8 greatly expands upon this concept.

Race Conditions When We Make a Mistake

In our first code example (Figure 1-1), we specifically did a "`wait`" on line 19 to prevent line 21 from writing out the value from `result` before it was available. We must keep this asynchronous behavior in mind. There is another subtle thing done in that same code example—line 15 uses `std::memcpy` to load the input. Since `std::memcpy` runs on the host, line 17 and later do not execute until line 15 has completed. After reading Chapter 3, we could be tempted to change this to use `q.memcpy` (using SYCL). We have done exactly that in Figure 1-3 on line 7. Since that is a queue submission, there is no guarantee that it will execute before line 9. This creates a *race condition*, which is a type of parallel programming bug. A race condition exists when two parts of a program access the same data without coordination. Since we expect to write data using line 7 and then read it in line 9, we do not want a race that might have line 9 execute before line 7 completes! Such a race condition would make our program unpredictable—our program could get different results on different runs and on different systems. A fix for this would be to explicitly wait for `q.memcpy` to complete before proceeding by adding `.wait()` to the end of line 7. That is not the best fix. We could have used event dependences to solve this (Chapter 8). Creating the queue as an ordered queue would also add an implicit dependence between the `memcpy` and the `parallel_for`. As an alternative, in Chapter 7, we will see how a buffer and accessor programming style can be used to have SYCL manage the dependences and waits automatically for us.

```
// ...we are changing one line from Figure 1-1
char* result = malloc_shared<char>(sz, q);

// Introduce potential data race!  We don't define a
// dependence to ensure correct ordering with later
// operations.
q.memcpy(result, secret.data(), sz);

q.parallel_for(sz, [=](auto& i) {
   result[i] -= 1;
 }).wait();

// ...
```

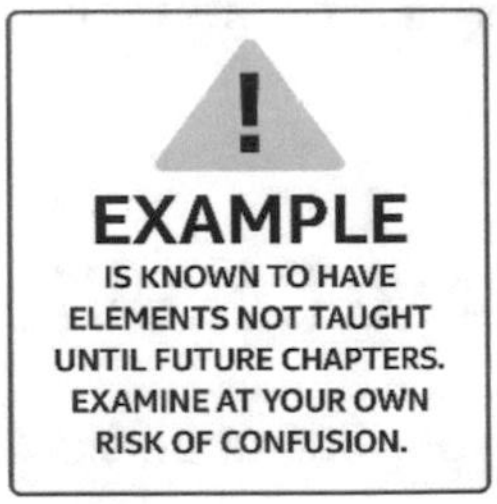

!
EXAMPLE
IS KNOWN TO HAVE ELEMENTS NOT TAUGHT UNTIL FUTURE CHAPTERS. EXAMINE AT YOUR OWN RISK OF CONFUSION.

Figure 1-3. *Adding a race condition to illustrate a point about being asynchronous*

RACE CONDITIONS DO NOT ALWAYS CAUSE A PROGRAM TO FAIL

An astute reader noticed that the code in Figure 1-3 did not fail on every system they tried. Using a GPU with `partition_max_sub_devices==0` did not fail because it was a small GPU not capable of running the `parallel_for` until the `memcpy` had completed. Regardless, the code is flawed because the race condition exists even if it does not universally cause a failure at runtime. We call it a race—sometimes we win, and sometimes we lose. Such coding flaws can lay dormant until the right combination of compile and runtime environments lead to an observable failure.

Adding a `wait()` forces host synchronization between the `memcpy` and the kernel, which goes against the previous advice to keep the device busy all the time. Much of this book covers the different options and trade-offs that balance program simplicity with efficient use of our systems.

OUT-OF-ORDER QUEUES VS. IN-ORDER QUEUES

We will use out-of-order queues in this book because of their potential performance benefits, but it is important to know that support for in-order queues does exist. In-order is simply an attribute we can request when creating a queue. CUDA programmers will know that CUDA streams are unconditionally *in-order*. SYCL queues instead are *out-of-order* by default but may optionally be in-order by passing the `in_order` queue property when the SYCL queue is created (refer to Chapter 8). Chapter 21 provides information on this and other considerations for programmers coming from using CUDA.

For assistance with detecting data race conditions in a program, including kernels, tools such as Intel Inspector (available with the oneAPI tools mentioned previously in "Getting a DPC++ Compiler") can be helpful. The sophisticated methods used by such tools often do not work on all devices. Detecting race conditions may be best done by having all the kernels run on a CPU, which can be done as a debugging technique during development work. This debugging tip is discussed as Method#2 in Chapter 2.

TO TEACH THE CONCEPT OF *DEADLOCK*, THE DINING PHILOSOPHERS PROBLEM IS A CLASSIC ILLUSTRATION OF A SYNCHRONIZATION PROBLEM IN COMPUTER SCIENCE

Imagine a group of philosophers sitting around a circular table, with a single chopstick placed between each philosopher. Every philosopher needs two chopsticks to eat their meal, and they always pick up chopsticks one at a time. Regrettably, if all philosophers first grab the chopstick to their left and then hold it waiting for the chopstick from their right, we have a problem if they all get hungry at the same time. Specifically, they will end up all waiting for a chopstick that will never be available.

Poor algorithm design (grab left, then wait until grab right) in this case can result in deadlock and all the philosophers starving to death. That is sad. Discussing the numerous ways to design an algorithm that starves fewer philosophers to death, or hopefully is fair and feeds them all (none starve), is a topic that is fun to consider and has been written about many times.

Realizing how easy it is to make such programming errors, looking for them when debugging, and gaining a feel for how to avoid them are all essential experiences on the journey to become an effective parallel programmer.

Deadlock

Deadlocks are bad, and we will emphasize that understanding concurrency vs. parallelism (see last section of this chapter) is essential to understanding how to avoid deadlock.

Deadlock occurs when two or more actions (processes, threads, kernels, etc.) are blocked, each waiting for the other to release a resource or complete a task, resulting in a standstill. In other words, our application will never complete. Every time we use a wait, synchronization, or lock, we can create deadlocks. Lack of synchronization can lead to deadlock, but more often it manifests as a race condition (see prior section).

Deadlocks can be difficult to debug. We will revisit this in the "Concurrency vs. Parallelism" section at the end of this chapter.

Chapter 4 will tell us "lambda expressions not considered harmful." We should be comfortable with lambda expressions in order to use DPC++, SYCL, and modern C++ well.

C++ Lambda Expressions

A feature of modern C++ that is heavily used by parallel programming techniques is the lambda expression. Kernels (the code to run on a device) can be expressed in multiple ways, the most common one being a lambda expression. Chapter 10 discusses all the various forms that a kernel can take, including lambda expressions. Here we have a refresher on C++ lambda expressions plus some notes regarding use to define kernels. Chapter 10 expands on the kernel aspects after we have learned more about SYCL in the intervening chapters.

The code in Figure 1-3 has a lambda expression. We can see it because it starts with the very definitive `[=]`. In C++, lambdas start with a square bracket, and information before the closing square bracket denotes how to *capture* variables that are used within the lambda but not explicitly passed to it as parameters. For kernels in SYCL, the capture must be *by value* which is denoted by the inclusion of an equals sign within the brackets.

Support for lambda expressions was introduced in C++11. They are used to create anonymous function objects (although we can assign them to named variables) that can capture variables from the enclosing scope. The basic syntax for a C++ lambda expression is

```
[ capture-list ] ( params ) -> ret { body }
```

where

- *`capture-list`* is a comma-separated list of captures. We capture a variable by value by listing the variable name in the capture-list. We capture a variable by reference by prefixing it with an ampersand, for example, &v. There are also shorthands that apply to all in-scope automatic variables: `[=]` is used to capture all automatic variables used in the body by value and the current object by reference, `[&]` is used to capture all automatic variables used in the body as well as the current object by reference, and `[]` captures nothing. With SYCL, `[=]` is always used because no variable is allowed to be captured by reference for use in a kernel. Global variables are *not* captured in a lambda, per the C++ standard. Non-global static variables *can* be used in a kernel but *only* if they are `const`. The few restrictions noted here allow kernels to behave consistently across different device architectures and implementations.

- *`params`* is the list of function parameters, just like for a named function. SYCL provides for parameters to identify the element(s) the kernel is being invoked to process: this can be a unique `id` (one-dimensional) or a 2D or 3D `id`. These are discussed in Chapter 4.
- *`ret`* is the return type. If `->ret` is not specified, it is inferred from the return statements. The lack of a return statement, or a return with no value, implies a return type of `void`. SYCL kernels must *always* have a return type of `void`, so we should not bother with this syntax to specify a return type for kernels.
- *body* is the function body. For a SYCL kernel, the contents of this kernel have some restrictions (see earlier in this chapter in the "Kernel Code" section).

Figure 1-4 shows a C++ lambda expression that captures one variable, i, by value and another, j, by reference. It also has a parameter k0 and another parameter l0 that is received by reference. Running the example will result in the output shown in Figure 1-5.

```
int i = 1, j = 10, k = 100, l = 1000;

auto lambda = [i, &j](int k0, int& l0) -> int {
  j = 2 * j;
  k0 = 2 * k0;
  l0 = 2 * l0;
  return i + j + k0 + l0;
};

print_values(i, j, k, l);
std::cout << "First call returned " << lambda(k, l)
          << "\n";
print_values(i, j, k, l);
std::cout << "Second call returned " << lambda(k, l)
          << "\n";
print_values(i, j, k, l);
```

Figure 1-4. *Lambda expression in C++ code*

```
i == 1
j == 10
k == 100
l == 1000
First call returned 2221
i == 1
j == 20
k == 100
l == 2000
Second call returned 4241
i == 1
j == 40
k == 100
l == 4000
```

Figure 1-5. *Output from the lambda expression demonstration code in Figure 1-4*

We can think of a lambda expression as an instance of a function object, but the compiler creates the class definition for us. For example, the lambda expression we used in the preceding example is analogous to an instance of a class as shown in Figure 1-6. Wherever we use a C++ lambda expression, we can substitute it with an instance of a function object like the one shown in Figure 1-6.

Whenever we define a function object, we need to assign it a name (Functor in Figure 1-6). Lambda expressions expressed inline (as in Figure 1-4) are anonymous because they do not need a name.

```
class Functor {
 public:
  Functor(int i, int &j) : my_i{i}, my_jRef{j} {}

  int operator()(int k0, int &l0) {
    my_jRef = 2 * my_jRef;
    k0 = 2 * k0;
    l0 = 2 * l0;
    return my_i + my_jRef + k0 + l0;
  }

 private:
  int my_i;
  int &my_jRef;
};
```

Figure 1-6. *Function object instead of a lambda expression (more on this in Chapter 10)*

Functional Portability and Performance Portability

Portability is a key objective for using C++ with SYCL; however, nothing can guarantee it. All a language and compiler can do is to make portability a little easier for us to achieve in our applications when we want to do so. It is true that higher-level (more abstract) programming—such as domain-specific languages, libraries, and frameworks—can offer more portability in large part because they allow less prescriptive programming. Since we are focused on *data-parallel* programming in C++ in this book, we assume a desire to have more control and with that comes more responsibility to understand how our coding affects portability.

Portability is a complex topic and includes the concept of *functional portability* as well as *performance portability*. With functional portability, we expect our program to compile and run equivalently on a wide variety of platforms. With performance portability, we would like our program to get reasonable performance on a wide variety of platforms. While that is a pretty soft definition, the converse might be clearer—we do not want to write a program that runs superfast on one platform only to find that it is unreasonably slow on another. In fact, we would prefer that it got the most out of any platform upon which it is run. Given the wide variety of devices in a heterogeneous system, performance portability requires nontrivial effort from us as programmers.

Fortunately, SYCL defines a way to code that can improve performance portability. First of all, a generic kernel can run everywhere. In a limited number of cases, this may be enough. More commonly, several versions of important kernels may be written for different types of devices. Specifically, a kernel might have a generic GPU *and* a generic CPU version. Occasionally, we may want to specialize our kernels for a specific device such as a specific GPU. When that occurs, we can write multiple versions and specialize each for a different GPU model. Or we can parameterize one version to use attributes of a GPU to modify how our GPU kernel runs to adapt to the GPU that is present.

While we are responsible for devising an effective plan for performance portability ourselves as programmers, SYCL defines constructs to allow us to implement a plan. As mentioned before, capabilities can be layered by starting with a kernel for all devices and then gradually introducing additional, more specialized kernel versions as needed. This sounds great, but the overall flow for a program can have a profound impact as well because data movement and overall algorithm choice matter. Knowing that gives insight into why no one should claim that C++ with SYCL (or other programming solution) solves performance portability. However, it is a tool in our toolkit to help us tackle these challenges.

Concurrency vs. Parallelism

The terms *concurrent* and *parallel* are not necessarily equivalent, although they are sometimes misconstrued as such. Any discussion of these terms is further complicated by the fact that various sources rarely agree on the same definitions.

Consider these definitions from the Sun Microsystems *Multithreaded Programming Guide*:[3]

- **Concurrency**: A condition that exists when at least two threads are making progress
- **Parallelism**: A condition that exists when two threads are executing simultaneously

To fully appreciate the difference between these concepts, we need to seek an intuitive understanding of what matters here. The following observations can help us gain that understanding:

- **Executing simultaneously can be faked**: Even without hardware support for doing more than one thing at a time, software can fake doing multiple things at once by multiplexing. Multiplexing is a good example of concurrency without parallelism.

[3] The authors are fans of this programming guide's coverage of the fundamentals that never go away. It is online at docs.oracle.com/cd/E19253-01/816-5137/816-5137.pdf.

- **Hardware resources are limited**: Hardware is never infinitely "wide" because hardware always has a finite number of execution resources (e.g., processors, cores, execution units). When hardware can execute each of our threads using dedicated resources, we have both concurrency and parallelism.

When we as programmers say, "do X, Y and Z at the same time," we often do not actually care whether hardware provides concurrency or parallelism. We probably do not want our program (with three tasks) to fail to launch on a machine that can only run two of them simultaneously. We would prefer that as many tasks as possible are processed in parallel, repeatedly stepping through batches of tasks until they are all complete.

But sometimes, we *do* care. And mistakes in our thinking can have disastrous effects (like "deadlock"). Imagine that our example from the last paragraph was modified such that the last thing a task (X, Y, or Z) does is "wait until *all* the tasks are done." Our program will run just fine if the number of tasks never exceeds the limits of the hardware. But if we break our tasks into batches, a task in our first batch will wait forever. Unfortunately, that means our application never finishes.

This is a common mistake that is easy to make, which is why we are emphasizing these concepts. Even expert programmers must focus to try to avoid this—and we all find that we will need to debug issues when we miss something in our thinking. These concepts are not simple, and the C++ specification includes a lengthy section detailing the precise conditions in which threads are guaranteed to make progress. All we can do in this introductory section is highlight the importance of understanding these concepts as much as we can.

Developing an intuitive grasp of these concepts is important for effective programming of heterogeneous and accelerated systems. We all need to give ourselves time to gain such intuition—it does not happen all at once.

Summary

This chapter provided terminology needed for understanding C++ with SYCL and provided refreshers on key aspects of parallel programming and C++ that are critical to SYCL. Chapters 2, 3, and 4 expand on three keys to data-parallel programming while using C++ with SYCL: devices need to be given work to do (send code to run on them), be provided with data (send data to use on them), and have a method of writing code (kernels).

CHAPTER 2

Where Code Executes

Parallel programming is not really about driving in *the* fast lane. It is actually about driving fast in *all* the lanes. This chapter is all about enabling us to put our code everywhere that we can. We choose to enable all the compute resources in a heterogeneous system whenever it makes sense. Therefore, we need to know where those compute resources are hiding (find them) and put them to work (execute our code on them).

We can control *where* our code executes—in other words, we can control which devices are used for which kernels. C++ with SYCL provides a framework for heterogeneous programming in which code can execute on a mixture of a host CPU and devices. The mechanisms which determine where code executes are important for us to understand and use.

This chapter describes where code can execute, when it will execute, and the mechanisms used to control the locations of execution. Chapter 3 will describe how to manage data so it arrives where we are executing our code, and then Chapter 4 returns to the code itself and discusses the writing of kernels.

Single-Source

C++ with SYCL programs are single-source, meaning that the same translation unit (typically a source file and its headers) contains both the code that defines the compute kernels to be executed on SYCL devices and

J. Reinders et al., *Data Parallel C++*, https://doi.org/10.1007/978-1-4842-9691-2_2

also the host code that orchestrates execution of those kernels. Figure 2-1 shows these two code paths graphically, and Figure 2-2 provides an example application with the host and device code regions marked.

Combining both device and host code into a single-source file (or translation unit) can make it easier to understand and maintain a heterogeneous application. The combination also provides improved language type safety and can lead to more compiler optimizations of our code.

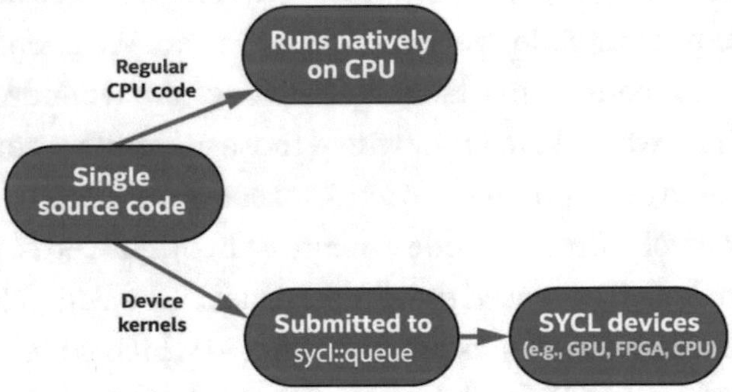

***Figure 2-1.** Single-source code contains both host code (runs on CPU) and device code (runs on SYCL devices)*

```
#include <array>
#include <iostream>
#include <sycl/sycl.hpp>
using namespace sycl;

int main() {
  constexpr int size = 16;
  std::array<int, size> data;

  // Create queue on implementation-chosen default device
  queue q;

  // Create buffer using host allocated "data" array
  buffer B{data};

  q.submit([&](handler& h) {

    accessor A{B, h};
    h.parallel_for(size, [=](auto& idx) {
      A[idx] = idx;
    });
  });

  // Obtain access to buffer on the host
  // Will wait for device kernel to execute to generate data
  host_accessor A{B};
  for (int i = 0; i < size; i++)
    std::cout << "data[" << i << "] = " << A[i] << "\n";

  return 0;
}
```

Host code

Device code

Host code

Figure 2-2. *Simple SYCL program*

Host Code

Applications contain C++ host code, which is executed by the CPU(s) on which the operating system has launched the application. Host code is the backbone of an application that defines and controls assignment of work to available devices. It is also the interface through which we define the data and dependences that should be managed by the SYCL runtime.

Host code is standard C++ augmented with SYCL-specific constructs and classes that may be implementable as a C++ library. This makes it easier to reason about what is allowed in host code (anything that is allowed in C++) and can simplify integration with build systems.

The host code in an application orchestrates data movement and compute offload to devices but can also perform compute-intensive work itself and can use libraries like any C++ application.

Device Code

Devices correspond to accelerators or processors that are conceptually independent from the CPU that is executing host code. An implementation may also expose the host processor as a device, as described later in this chapter, but the host processor and devices should be thought of as logically independent from each other. The host processor runs native C++ code, while devices run device code which includes some additional features and restrictions.

Queues are the mechanism through which work is submitted to a device for future execution. There are three important properties of device code to understand:

1. **It executes asynchronously from the host code.** The host program submits device code to a device, and the runtime tracks and starts that work only when all dependences for execution are satisfied (more on this in Chapter 3). The host program execution carries on before the submitted work is started on a device, providing the property that

execution on devices is asynchronous to host program execution, unless we explicitly tie the two together. As a side effect of this asynchronous execution, work on a device isn't guaranteed to start until the host program forces execution to begin through various mechanisms that we cover in later chapters, such as host accessors and blocking queue wait operations.

2. **There are restrictions on device code** to make it possible to compile and achieve performance on accelerator devices. For example, dynamic memory allocation and runtime type information (RTTI) are not supported within device code, because they would lead to performance degradation on many accelerators. The small set of device code restrictions is covered in detail in Chapter 10.

3. **Some functions and queries defined by SYCL are available only within device code**, because they only make sense there, for example, work-item identifier queries that allow an executing instance of device code to query its position in a larger data-parallel range (described in Chapter 4).

In general, we will refer to work that is submitted to queues as *actions*. Actions include execution of device code on a device, but in Chapter 3 we will learn that actions also include memory movement commands. In this chapter, since we are concerned with the device code aspect of actions, we will be specific in mentioning device code much of the time.

Choosing Devices

To explore the mechanisms that let us control where device code will execute, we'll look at five use cases:

> **Method#1**: Running device code *somewhere* when we don't care which device is used. This is often the first step in development because it is the simplest.
>
> **Method#2**: Explicitly running device code on a CPU device, which is often used for debugging because most development systems have an accessible CPU. CPU debuggers are also typically very rich in features.
>
> **Method#3**: Dispatching device code to a GPU or other accelerator.
>
> **Method#4**: Dispatching device code to a heterogeneous set of devices, such as a GPU and an FPGA.
>
> **Method#5**: Selecting specific devices from a more general class of devices, such as a specific type of FPGA from a collection of available FPGA types.

Developers will typically debug their code as much as possible with Method#2 and only move to Methods #3–#5 when code has been tested as much as is practical with Method#2.

Method#1: Run on a Device of Any Type

When we don't care where our device code will run, it is easy to let the runtime pick for us. This automatic selection is designed to make it easy to start writing and running code, when we don't yet care about what device is chosen. This device selection does *not* take into account the code to be run, so should be considered an arbitrary choice which likely won't be optimal.

Before talking about choice of a device, even one that the implementation has selected for us, we should first cover the mechanism through which a program interacts with a device: the *queue*.

Queues

A queue is an abstraction to which actions are submitted for execution on a single device. A simplified definition of the queue class is given in Figures 2-3 and 2-4. Actions are usually the launch of data-parallel compute, although other commands are also available such as manual control of data motion for when we want more control than the automatic movement provided by the SYCL runtime. Work submitted to a queue can execute after prerequisites tracked by the runtime are met, such as availability of input data. These prerequisites are covered in Chapters 3 and 8.

```
class queue {
 public:
  // Create a queue associated with a default
  // (implementation chosen) device.
  queue(const property_list & = {});

  queue(const async_handler &, const property_list & = {});

  // Create a queue using a DeviceSelector.
  // A DeviceSelector is a callable that ranks
  // devices numerically. There are a few SYCL-defined
  // device selectors available such as
  // cpu_selector_v and gpu_selector_v.
  template <typename DeviceSelector>
  explicit queue(const DeviceSelector &deviceSelector,
                 const property_list &propList = {});

  // Create a queue associated with an explicit device to
  // which the program already holds a reference.
  queue(const device &, const property_list & = {});

  // Create a queue associated with a device in a specific
  // SYCL context. A device selector may be used in place
  // of a device.
  queue(const context &, const device &,
        const property_list & = {});
};
```

Figure 2-3. *Simplified definition of some constructors of the queue class*

```
class queue {
 public:
  // Submit a command group to this queue.
  // The command group may be a lambda expression or
  // function object. Returns an event reflecting the status
  // of the action performed in the command group.
  template <typename T>
  event submit(T);

  // Wait for all previously submitted actions to finish
  // executing.
  void wait();

  // Wait for all previously submitted actions to finish
  // executing. Pass asynchronous exceptions to an
  // async_handler function.
  void wait_and_throw();
};
```

Figure 2-4. *Simplified definition of some key member functions in the queue class*

A queue is bound to a single device, and that binding occurs on construction of the queue. It is important to understand that work submitted to a queue is executed on the single device to which that queue is bound. Queues cannot be mapped to collections of devices because that would create ambiguity on which device should perform work. Similarly, a queue cannot spread the work submitted to it across multiple devices. Instead, there is an unambiguous mapping between a queue and the device on which work submitted to that queue will execute, as shown in Figure 2-5.

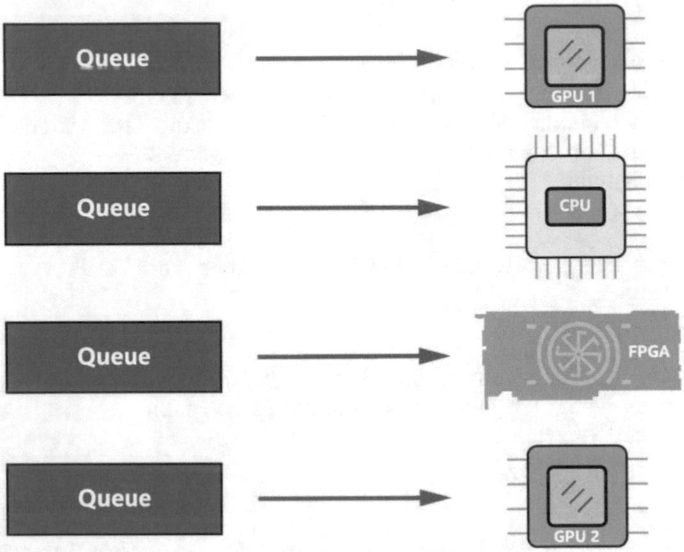

Figure 2-5. *A queue is bound to a single device. Work submitted to the queue executes on that device*

Multiple queues may be created in a program, in any way that we desire for application architecture or programming style. For example, multiple queues may be created to each bind with a different device or to be used by different threads in a host program. Multiple different queues can be bound to a single device, such as a GPU, and submissions to those different queues will result in the combined work being performed on the device. An example of this is shown in Figure 2-6. Conversely, as we mentioned previously, a queue cannot be bound to more than one device because there must not be any ambiguity on where an action is being requested to execute. If we want a queue that will load balance work across multiple devices, for example, then we can create that abstraction in our code.

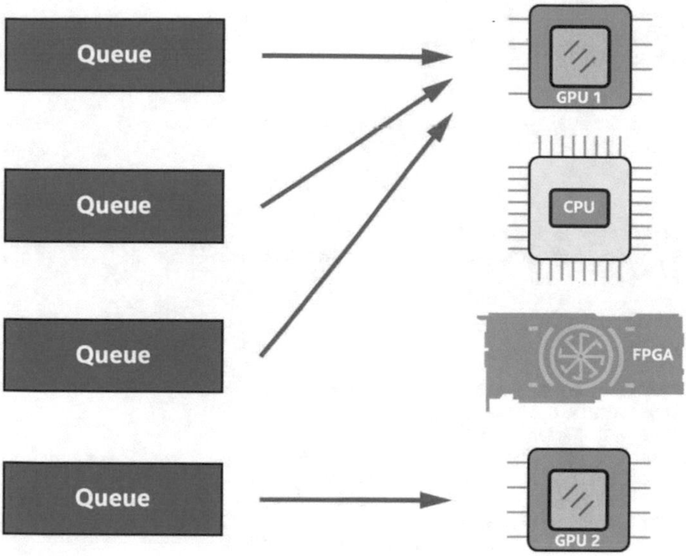

Figure 2-6. *Multiple queues can be bound to a single device*

Because a queue is bound to a specific device, queue construction is the most common way in code to choose the device on which actions submitted to the queue will execute. Selection of the device when constructing a queue is achieved through a device selector abstraction.

Binding a Queue to a Device When Any Device Will Do

Figure 2-7 is an example where the device that a queue should bind to is not specified. The default queue constructor that does not take any arguments (as in Figure 2-7) simply chooses some available device behind the scenes. SYCL guarantees that at least one device will always be available, so some device will always be selected by this default selection mechanism. In many cases the selected device may happen to be a CPU which is also executing the host program, although this is not guaranteed.

```
#include <iostream>
#include <sycl/sycl.hpp>
using namespace sycl;

int main() {
  // Create queue on whatever default device that the
  // implementation chooses. Implicit use of
  // default_selector_v
  queue q;

  std::cout << "Selected device: "
            << q.get_device().get_info<info::device::name>()
            << "\n";

  return 0;
}

Sample Outputs (one line per run depending on system):
Selected device: NVIDIA GeForce RTX 3060
Selected device: AMD Radeon RX 5700 XT
Selected device: Intel(R) Data Center GPU Max 1100
Selected device: Intel(R) FPGA Emulation Device
Selected device: AMD Ryzen 5 3600 6-Core Processor
Selected device: Intel(R) UHD Graphics 770
Selected device: Intel(R) Xeon(R) Gold 6128 CPU @ 3.40GHz
Selected device: 11th Gen Intel(R) Core(TM) i9-11900KB @ 3.30GHz
many more possible… these are only examples
```

Figure 2-7. *Implicit default device selector through default construction of a queue*

Using the trivial queue constructor is a simple way to begin application development and to get device code up and running. More control over selection of the device bound to a queue can be added as it becomes relevant for our application.

Method#2: Using a CPU Device for Development, Debugging, and Deployment

A CPU device can be thought of as enabling the host CPU to act as if it was an independent device, allowing our device code to execute regardless of the accelerators available in a system. We always have some processor running the host program, so a CPU device is therefore usually available to our application (very occasionally a CPU might not be exposed as a SYCL device by an implementation, for a variety of reasons). Using a CPU device for code development has a few advantages:

1. **Development of device code** on less capable systems that don't have any accelerators: One common use is development and testing of device code on a local system, before deploying to an HPC cluster for performance testing and optimization.

2. **Debugging of device code** with non-accelerator tooling: Accelerators are often exposed through lower-level APIs that may not have debug tooling as advanced as is available for host CPUs. With this in mind, a CPU device often supports debugging using standard tools familiar to developers.

3. **Backup** if no other devices are available, to guarantee that device code can be executed functionally: A CPU device may not have performance as a primary goal, or may not match the architecture for which kernel code was optimized, but can often be considered as a functional backup to ensure that device code can always execute in any application.

It should not be a surprise to find that multiple CPU devices are available to a SYCL application, with some aimed at ease of debugging while others may be focused on execution performance. Device aspects can be used to differentiate between these different CPU devices, as described later in this chapter.

When considering use of a CPU device for development and debugging of device code, some consideration should be given to differences between the CPU and a target accelerator architecture (e.g., GPU). Especially when optimizing code performance, and particularly when using more advanced features such as sub-groups, there can be some differences in functionality and performance across architectures. For example, the sub-group size may change when moving to a new device. Most development and debugging can typically occur on a CPU device, sometimes followed by final tuning and debugging on the target device architecture.

A CPU device is functionally like a hardware accelerator in that a queue can bind to it and it can execute device code. Figure 2-8 shows how the CPU device is a peer to other accelerators that might be available in a system. It can execute device code, in the same way that a GPU or FPGA is able to, and can have one or more queues constructed that bind to it.

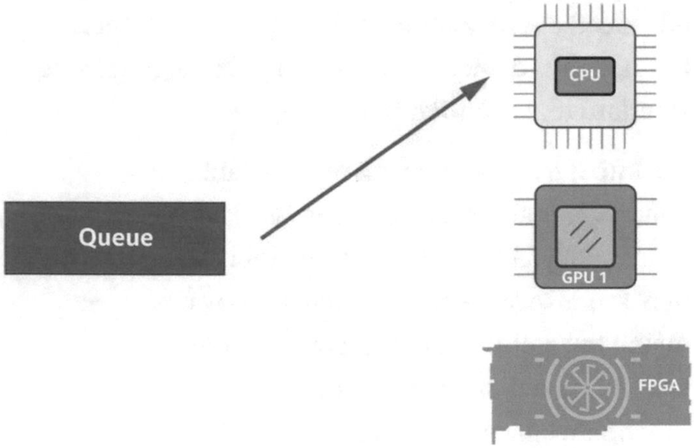

Figure 2-8. *A CPU device can execute device code like any accelerator*

An application can choose to create a queue that is bound to a CPU device by explicitly passing `cpu_selector_v` to a queue constructor, as shown in Figure 2-9.

```
#include <iostream>
#include <sycl/sycl.hpp>
using namespace sycl;

int main() {
  // Create queue to use the CPU device explicitly
  queue q{cpu_selector_v};

  std::cout << "Selected device: "
            << q.get_device().get_info<info::device::name>()
            << "\n";
  std::cout
      << " -> Device vendor: "
      << q.get_device().get_info<info::device::vendor>()
      << "\n";

  return 0;
}

Example Output:
Selected device: Intel(R) Xeon(R) Gold 6128 CPU @ 3.40GHz
 -> Device vendor: Intel(R) Corporation
```

Figure 2-9. *Selecting the host device using the* `cpu_selector_v`

Even when not specifically requested (e.g., using `cpu_selector_v`), the CPU device might happen to be chosen by the default selector as occurred in the output in Figure 2-7.

A few variants of device selectors are defined to make it easy for us to target a type of device. The `cpu_selector_v` is one example of these selectors, and we'll get into others in the coming sections.

Method#3: Using a GPU (or Other Accelerators)

GPUs are showcased in the next example, but any type of accelerator applies equally. To make it easy to target common classes of accelerators, devices are grouped into several broad categories, and SYCL provides built-in selector classes for them. To choose from a broad category of device type such as "any GPU available in the system," the corresponding code is very brief, as described in this section.

Accelerator Devices

In the terminology of the SYCL specification, there are a few broad groups of accelerator types:

1. CPU devices.
2. GPU devices.
3. Accelerators, which capture devices that don't identify as either a CPU device or a GPU. This includes FPGA and DSP devices.

A device from any of these categories is easy to bind to a queue using built-in selectors, which can be passed to queue (and some other class) constructors.

Device Selectors

Classes that must be bound to a specific device, such as the queue class, have constructors that can accept a `DeviceSelector`. A `DeviceSelector` is a callable taking a const reference to a device, and which ranks it numerically so that the runtime can choose a device with the highest ranking. For example, one queue constructor which accepts a `DeviceSelector` is `queue(const DeviceSelector &deviceSelector, const property_list &propList = {});`

There are four built-in selectors for the broad classes of common devices.

`default_selector_v`	Any device of the implementation's choosing
`cpu_selector_v`	Select a device that identifies itself as a CPU in device queries
`gpu_selector_v`	Select a device that identifies itself as a GPU in device queries
`accelerator_selector_v`	Select a device that identifies itself as an "accelerator," which includes FPGAs

One additional selector included in DPC++ (not available in SYCL) is available by including the header "`sycl/ext/intel/fpga_extensions.hpp`".

`ext::intel::fpga_selector_v`	Select a device that identifies itself as an FPGA

A queue can be constructed using one of the built-in selectors, such as

```
queue myQueue{ gpu_selector_v{} };
```

Figure 2-10 shows a complete example using the GPU selector, and Figure 2-11 shows the corresponding binding of a queue with an available GPU device.

Figure 2-12 shows an example using a variety of built-in selectors and demonstrates use of device selectors with another class (`device`) that accepts a device selector on construction.

```
#include <iostream>
#include <sycl/sycl.hpp>
using namespace sycl;

int main() {
  // Create queue bound to an available GPU device
  queue q{gpu_selector_v};

  std::cout << "Selected device: "
            << q.get_device().get_info<info::device::name>()
            << "\n";
  std::cout
      << " -> Device vendor: "
      << q.get_device().get_info<info::device::vendor>()
      << "\n";

  return 0;
}

Example Output:
Selected device: AMD Radeon RX 5700 XT
 -> Device vendor: AMD Corporation
```

Figure 2-10. *GPU device selector example*

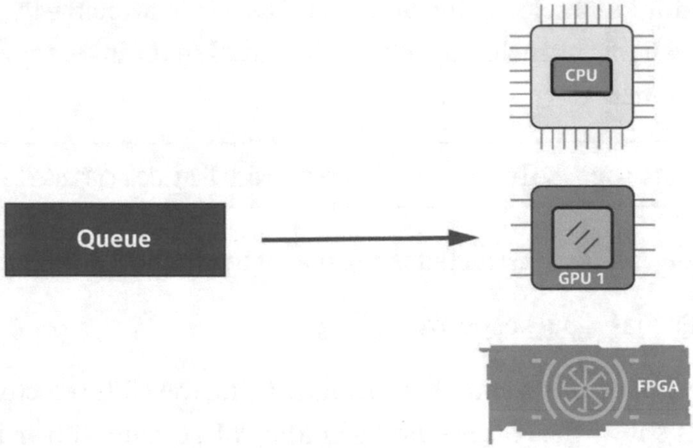

Figure 2-11. *Queue bound to a GPU device available to the application*

```
#include <iostream>
#include <string>
#include <sycl/ext/intel/fpga_extensions.hpp>  // For fpga_selector_v
#include <sycl/sycl.hpp>
using namespace sycl;

void output_dev_info(const device& dev,
                     const std::string& selector_name) {
  std::cout << selector_name << ": Selected device: "
            << dev.get_info<info::device::name>() << "\n";
  std::cout << "                  -> Device vendor: "
            << dev.get_info<info::device::vendor>() << "\n";
}

int main() {
  output_dev_info(device{default_selector_v},
                  "default_selector_v");
  output_dev_info(device{cpu_selector_v}, "cpu_selector_v");
  output_dev_info(device{gpu_selector_v}, "gpu_selector_v");
  output_dev_info(device{accelerator_selector_v},
                  "accelerator_selector_v");
  output_dev_info(device{ext::intel::fpga_selector_v},
                  "fpga_selector_v");

  return 0;
}

Example Output:
default_selector_v: Selected device: Intel(R) UHD Graphics [0x9a60]
                  -> Device vendor: Intel(R) Corporation
cpu_selector_v: Selected device: 11th Gen Intel(R) Core(TM) i9-11900KB @ 3.30GHz
                  -> Device vendor: Intel(R) Corporation
gpu_selector_v: Selected device: Intel(R) UHD Graphics [0x9a60]
                  -> Device vendor: Intel(R) Corporation
accelerator_selector_v: Selected device: Intel(R) FPGA Emulation Device
                  -> Device vendor: Intel(R) Corporation
fpga_selector_v: Selected device: pac_a10 : Intel PAC Platform (pac_ee00000)
                  -> Device vendor: Intel Corp
```

Figure 2-12. *Example device identification output from various classes of device selectors and demonstration that device selectors can be used for construction of more than just a queue (in this case, construction of a device class instance)*

When Device Selection Fails

If a GPU selector is used when creating an object such as a queue and if there are no GPU devices available to the runtime, then the selector throws a `runtime_error` exception. This is true for all device selector classes in that if no device of the required class is available, then a `runtime_error` exception is thrown. It is reasonable for complex applications to catch that error and instead acquire a less desirable (for the application/algorithm) device class as an alternative. Exceptions and error handling are discussed in more detail in Chapter 5.

Method#4: Using Multiple Devices

As shown in Figures 2-5 and 2-6, we can construct multiple queues in an application. We can bind these queues to a single device (the sum of work to the queues is funneled into the single device), to multiple devices, or to some combination of these. Figure 2-13 provides an example that creates one queue bound to a GPU and another queue bound to an FPGA. The corresponding mapping is shown graphically in Figure 2-14.

```
#include <iostream>
#include <sycl/ext/intel/fpga_extensions.hpp>  // For fpga_selector_v
#include <sycl/sycl.hpp>
using namespace sycl;

int main() {
  queue my_gpu_queue(gpu_selector_v);
  queue my_fpga_queue(ext::intel::fpga_selector_v);

  std::cout << "Selected device 1: "
            << my_gpu_queue.get_device()
                   .get_info<info::device::name>()
            << "\n";

  std::cout << "Selected device 2: "
            << my_fpga_queue.get_device()
                   .get_info<info::device::name>()
            << "\n";

  return 0;
}

Example Output:
Selected device 1: Intel(R) UHD Graphics [0x9a60]
Selected device 2: pac_a10 : Intel PAC Platform (pac_ee00000)
```

Figure 2-13. *Creating queues to both GPU and FPGA devices*

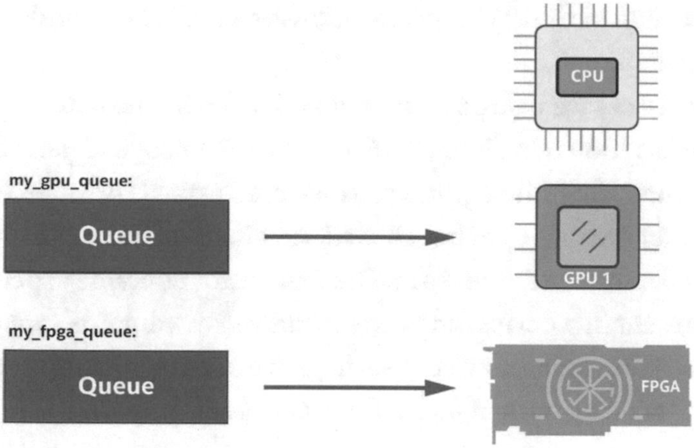

***Figure 2-14.** GPU + FPGA device selector example: One queue is bound to a GPU and another to an FPGA*

Method#5: Custom (Very Specific) Device Selection

We will now look at how to write a custom selector. In addition to examples in this chapter, there are a few more examples shown in Chapter 12. The built-in device selectors are intended to let us get code up and running quickly. Real applications usually require specialized selection of a device, such as picking a desired GPU from a set of GPU types available in a system. The device selection mechanism is easily extended to arbitrarily complex logic, so we can write whatever code is required to choose the device that we prefer.

Selection Based on Device Aspects

SYCL defines properties of devices known as *aspects*. For example, some aspects that a device might exhibit (return true on aspect queries) are `gpu`, `host_debuggable`, `fp64`, and `online_compiler`. Please refer to the "Device

Aspects" section of the SYCL specification for a full list of standard aspects, and their definitions.

To select a device using aspects defined in SYCL, the `aspect_selector` can be used as shown in Figure 2-15. In the form of `aspect_selector` taking a comma-delimited group of aspects, all aspects must be exhibited by a device for the device to be selected. An alternate form of `aspect_selector` takes two `std::vectors`. The first vector contains aspects that must be present in a device, and the second vector contains aspects that must not be present in a device (lists negative aspects). Figure 2-15 shows an example of using both of these forms of `aspect_selector`.

```
#include <iostream>
#include <sycl/sycl.hpp>
using namespace sycl;

int main() {
  // In the aspect_selector form taking a comma seperated
  // group of aspects, all aspects must be present for a
  // device to be selected.
  queue q1{aspect_selector(aspect::fp16, aspect::gpu)};

  // In the aspect_selector form that takes two vectors, the
  // first vector contains aspects that a device must
  // exhibit, and the second contains aspects that must NOT
  // be exhibited.
  queue q2{aspect_selector(
      std::vector{aspect::fp64, aspect::fp16},
      std::vector{aspect::gpu, aspect::accelerator})};

  std::cout
      << "First selected device is: "
      << q1.get_device().get_info<info::device::name>()
      << "\n";

  std::cout
      << "Second selected device is: "
      << q2.get_device().get_info<info::device::name>()
      << "\n";

  return 0;
}

Example Output:
First selected device is: Intel(R) UHD Graphics [0x9a60]
Second selected device is: 11th Gen Intel(R) Core(TM) i9-11900KB @ 3.30GHz
```

Figure 2-15. *Aspect selector*

Some aspects may be used to infer performance characteristics of a device. For example, any device with the `emulated` aspect may not perform as well as a device of the same type, which is not emulated, but may instead exhibit other aspects related to improved debuggability.

Selection Through a Custom Selector

When existing aspects aren't sufficient for selection of a specific device, a custom device selector may be defined. Such a selector is simply a C++ callable (e.g., a function or lambda) that takes a `const Device&` as a parameter and that returns an integer score for the specific device. The SYCL runtime invokes the selector on all available root devices that can be found and chooses the device for which the selector returned the highest score (which must be nonnegative for selection to occur).

In cases where there is a tie for the highest score, the SYCL runtime will choose one of the tied devices. No device for which the selector returned a negative number will be chosen by the runtime, so returning a negative number from a selector guarantees that the device will not be selected.

Mechanisms to Score a Device

We have many options to create an integer score corresponding to a specific device, such as the following:

1. Return a positive value for a specific device class.

2. String match on a device name and/or device vendor strings.

3. Compute anything that we can imagine leading to an integer value, based on device or platform queries.

For example, one possible approach to select a specific Intel Arria FPGA accelerator board is shown in Figure 2-16.

```
int my_selector(const device &dev) {
  if (dev.get_info<info::device::name>().find("pac_a10") !=
          std::string::npos &&
      dev.get_info<info::device::vendor>().find("Intel") !=
          std::string::npos) {
    return 1;
  }
  return -1;
}

Example Output:
Selected device is: pac_a10 : Intel PAC Platform (pac_ee00000)
```

Figure 2-16. *Custom selector for a specific Intel Arria FPGA accelerator board*

Chapter 12 has more discussion and examples for device selection and discusses the `get_info` method in more depth.

Creating Work on a Device

Applications usually contain a combination of both host code and device code. There are a few class members that allow us to submit device code for execution, and because these work dispatch constructs are the only way to submit device code, they allow us to easily distinguish device code from host code.

The remainder of this chapter introduces some of the work dispatch constructs, with the goal to help us understand and identify the division between device code and host code that executes natively on the host processor.

Introducing the Task Graph

A fundamental concept in the SYCL execution model is a graph of nodes. Each node (unit of work) in this graph contains an action to be performed on a device, with the most common action being a data-parallel device kernel invocation. Figure 2-17 shows an example graph with four nodes, where each node can be thought of as a device kernel invocation.

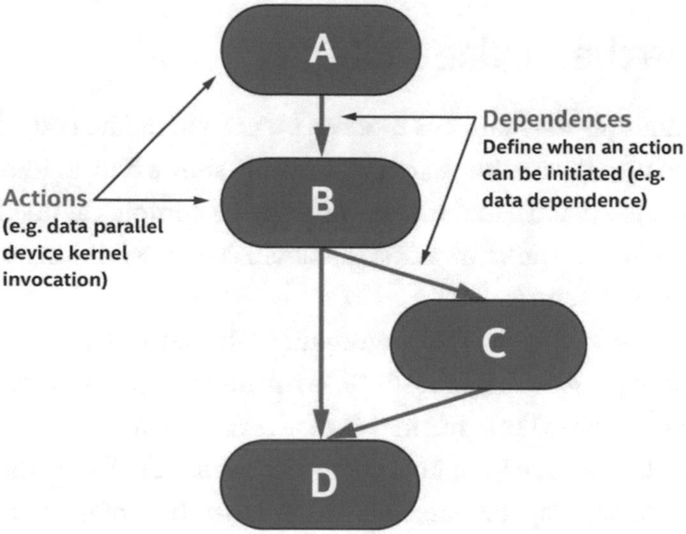

***Figure 2-17.** The task graph defines actions to perform (asynchronously from the host program) on one or more devices and also dependences that determine when an action is safe to execute*

The nodes in Figure 2-17 have dependence edges defining when it is legal for a node's work to begin execution. The dependence edges are most commonly generated automatically from data dependences, although there are ways for us to manually add additional custom dependences when we want to. Node B in the graph, for example, has a dependence edge from node A. This edge means that node A must complete execution, and most likely (depending on specifics of the dependence) make generated data available on the device where node B will execute before node B's action is started. The runtime controls resolution of dependences and triggering of node executions completely asynchronously from the host program's execution. The graph of nodes defining an application will be referred to in this book as the task graph and is covered in more detail in Chapter 3.

Where Is the Device Code?

There are multiple mechanisms that can be used to define code that will be executed on a device, but a simple example shows how to identify such code. Even if the pattern in the example appears complex at first glance, the pattern remains the same across all device code definitions so quickly becomes second nature.

The code passed as the final argument to the `parallel_for`, defined as a lambda expression in Figure 2-18, is the device code to be executed on a device. The `parallel_for` in this case is the construct that lets us distinguish device code from host code. The `parallel_for` is one of a small set of device dispatch mechanisms, all members of the `handler` class, that define the code to be executed on a device. A simplified definition of the `handler` class is given in Figure 2-19.

```
q.submit([&](handler& h) {
  accessor acc{B, h};

  h.parallel_for(size,
                 [=](auto& idx) { acc[idx] = idx; });
});
```

Device code

Command group

Figure 2-18. *Submission of device code*

```
class handler {
 public:
  // Specify event(s) that must be complete before the action
  // defined in this command group executes.
  void depends_on(std::vector<event> & events);

  // Guarantee that the memory object accessed by the accessor
  // is updated on the host after this action executes.
  template <typename AccessorT>
  void update_host(AccessorT acc);

  // Submit a memset operation writing
  // to the specified pointer.
  // Return an event representing this operation.
  event memset(void *ptr, int value, size_t count);

  // Submit a memcpy operation copying from src to dest.
  // Return an event representing this operation.
  event memcpy(void *dest, const void *src, size_t count);

  // Copy to/from an accessor and host memory.
  // Accessors are required to have appropriate correct
  // permissions. Pointer can be a raw pointer or
  // shared_ptr.
  template <typename SrcAccessorT, typename DestPointerT>
  void copy(SrcAccessorT src, DestPointerT dest);

  template <typename SrcPointerT, typename DestAccessorT>
  void copy(SrcPointerT src, DestAccessorT dest);

  // Copy between accessors.
  // Accessors are required to have appropriate correct
  // permissions.
  template <typename SrcAccessorT, typename DestAccessorT>
  void copy(SrcAccessorT src, DestAccessorT dest);

  // Submit different forms of kernel for execution.
  template <typename KernelName, typename KernelType>
  void single_task(KernelType kernel);

  template <typename KernelName, typename KernelType,
            int Dims>
  void parallel_for(range<Dims> num_work_items,
                    KernelType kernel);

  template <typename KernelName, typename KernelType,int Dims>
  void parallel_for(nd_range<Dims> execution_range,
                    KernelType kernel);

  template <typename KernelName, typename KernelType, int Dims>
  void parallel_for_work_group(range<Dims> num_groups,
                               KernelType kernel);

  template <typename KernelName, typename KernelType, int Dims>
  void parallel_for_work_group(range<Dims> num_groups,
                               range<Dims> group_size,
                               KernelType kernel);
};
```

Figure 2-19. *Simplified definition of member functions in the `handler` class*

In addition to calling members of the `handler` class to submit device code, there are also members of the queue class that allow work to be submitted. The queue class members shown in Figure 2-20 are shortcuts that simplify certain patterns, and we will see these shortcuts used in future chapters.

```
class queue {
 public:
  // Submit a memset operation writing to the specified
  // pointer. Return an event representing this operation.
  event memset(void* ptr, int value, size_t count);

  // Submit a memcpy operation copying from src to dest.
  // Return an event representing this operation.
  event memcpy(void* dest, const void* src, size_t count);

  // Submit different forms of kernel for execution.
  // Return an event representing the kernel operation.
  template <typename KernelName, typename KernelType>
  event single_task(KernelType kernel);

  template <typename KernelName, typename KernelType,
            int Dims>
  event parallel_for(range<Dims> num_work_items,
                     KernelType kernel);

  template <typename KernelName, typename KernelType,
            int Dims>
  event parallel_for(nd_range<Dims> execution_range,
                     KernelType kernel);

  // Submit different forms of kernel for execution.
  // Wait for the specified event(s) to complete
  // before executing the kernel.
  // Return an event representing the kernel operation.
  template <typename KernelName, typename KernelType>
  event single_task(const std::vector<event>& events,
                    KernelType kernel);

  template <typename KernelName, typename KernelType,
            int Dims>
  event parallel_for(range<Dims> num_work_items,
                     const std::vector<event>& events,
                     KernelType kernel);

  template <typename KernelName, typename KernelType,
            int Dims>
  event parallel_for(nd_range<Dims> execution_range,
                     const std::vector<event>& events,
                     KernelType kernel);
};
```

Figure 2-20. *Simplified definition of member functions in the queue class that act as shorthand notation for equivalent functions in the `handler` class*

Actions

The code in Figure 2-18 contains a `parallel_for`, which defines work to be performed on a device. The `parallel_for` is within a command group (CG) submitted to a queue, and the queue defines the device on which the work is to be performed. Within the command group, there are two categories of code:

1. **Host code** that sets up dependences defining when it is safe for the runtime to start execution of the work defined in (2), such as creation of accessors to buffers (described in Chapter 3)

2. **At most one call to an action** that either queues device code for execution or performs a manual memory operation such as `copy`

The handler class contains a small set of member functions that define the action to be performed when a task graph node is executed. Figure 2-21 summarizes these actions.

Work Type	Actions (handler class methods)	Summary
Device code execution	`single_task`	Execute a single instance of a device function.
	`parallel_for`	Multiple forms are available to launch device code with different combinations of work sizes.
Explicit memory operation	`copy`	Copy data between locations specified by accessor, pointer, and/or `shared_ptr`. The copy occurs as part of the SYCL task graph (described later), including dependence tracking.
	`update_host`	Trigger update of host data backing of a buffer object.
	`fill`	Initialize data in a buffer to a specified value.

Figure 2-21. *Actions that invoke device code or perform explicit memory operations*

At most one action from Figure 2-21 may be called within a command group (it is an error to call more than one), and only a single command group can be submitted to a queue per `submit` call. The result of this is that a single (or potentially no) operation from Figure 2-21 exists per task graph node, to be executed when the node dependences are met and the runtime determines that it is safe to execute.

A command group must have at most one action within it, such as a kernel launch or explicit memory operation.

The idea that code is executed asynchronously in the future is the critical difference between code that runs on the CPU as part of the host program and device code that will run in the future when dependences are satisfied. A command group usually contains code from each category, with the code that defines dependences running as part of the host program (so that the runtime knows what the dependences are) and device code running in the future once the dependences are satisfied.

There are three classes of code in Figure 2-22:

1. **Host code**: Drives the application, including creating and managing data buffers and submitting work to queues to form new nodes in the task graph for asynchronous execution.

2. **Host code within a command group**: This code is run on the processor that the host code is executing on and executes immediately, before the `submit` call returns. This code sets up the node dependences by creating accessors, for example. Any arbitrary CPU code can execute here, but best practice is to restrict it to code that configures the node dependences.

3. **An action**: Any action listed in Figure 2-21 can be included in a command group, and it defines the work to be performed asynchronously in the future when node requirements are met (set up by (2)).

```
#include <array>
#include <iostream>
#include <sycl/sycl.hpp>
using namespace sycl;

int main() {
  constexpr int size = 16;
  std::array<int, size> data;
  buffer B{data};

  queue q{};  // Select any device for this queue

  std::cout << "Selected device is: "
            << q.get_device().get_info<info::device::name>()
            << "\n";

  q.submit([&](handler& h) {
    accessor acc{B, h};
    h.parallel_for(size,
                   [=](auto& idx) { acc[idx] = idx; });
  });

  return 0;
}
```

Host code

Immediate code to set up task graph node.

Device code runs in the future when dependences are met.

Host code

Figure 2-22. *Submission of device code*

To understand when code in an application will run, note that *anything* passed to an action listed in Figure 2-21 that initiates device code execution, or an explicit memory operation listed in Figure 2-21, will execute *asynchronously* in the future when the SYCL task graph (described later) node dependences have been satisfied. All other code runs as part of the host program *immediately*, as expected in typical C++ code.

It is important to note that although device code *can* start running (asynchronously) when task graph node dependences have been met, device code is not *guaranteed* to start running at that point. The only way to be sure that device code will start executing is to have the host program wait for (block on) results from the device code execution, through mechanisms such as host accessors or queue wait operations, which we cover in later chapters. Without such host blocking operations, the SYCL and lower-level runtimes make decisions on when to start execution of device code, possibly optimizing for objectives other than "run as soon as possible" such as optimizing for power or congestion.

Host tasks

In general, the code executed by an action submitted to a queue (such as through `parallel_for`) is device code, following a few language restrictions that allow it to run efficiently on many architectures. There is one important deviation, though, which is accessed through a `handler` method named `host_task`. This method allows arbitrary C++ code to be submitted as an action in the task graph, to be executed on the host once any task graph dependences have been satisfied.

Host tasks are important in some programs for two reasons:

1. Arbitrary C++ can be included, even `std::cout` or `printf`. This can be important for easy debugging, interoperability with lower-level APIs such as OpenCL, or for incrementally enabling the use of accelerators in existing code.

2. Host tasks execute asynchronously as part of the task graph, instead of synchronously with the host program. Although a host program can launch additional threads or use other task parallelism approaches, host tasks integrate with the dependence tracking mechanisms of the SYCL runtime. This can be very convenient and may result in higher performance when device and host code need to be interspersed.

```
#include <array>
#include <iostream>
#include <sycl/sycl.hpp>
using namespace sycl;
constexpr int N = 4;

int main() {
  queue q;
  int* A = malloc_shared<int>(N, q);

  std::cout << "Selected device: "
            << q.get_device().get_info<info::device::name>()
            << "\n";

  // Initialize values in the shared allocation
  auto eA = q.submit([&](handler& h) {
    h.parallel_for(N, [=](auto& idx) { A[idx] = idx; });
  });

  // Use a host task to output values on the host as part of
  // task graph.  depends_on is used to define a dependence
  // on previous device code having completed. Here the host
  // task is defined as a lambda expression.
  q.submit([&](handler& h) {
    h.depends_on(eA);
    h.host_task([=]() {
      for (int i = 0; i < N; i++)
        std::cout << "host_task @ " << i << " = " << A[i]
                  << "\n";
    });
  });

  // Wait for work to be completed in the queue before
  // accessing the shared data in the host program.
  q.wait();

  for (int i = 0; i < N; i++)
    std::cout << "main @ " << i << " = " << A[i] << "\n";

  free(A, q);

  return 0;
}

Example Output:
Selected device: NVIDIA GeForce RTX 3060
host_task @ 0 = 0
host_task @ 1 = 1
host_task @ 2 = 2
host_task @ 3 = 3
main @ 0 = 0
main @ 1 = 1
main @ 2 = 2
main @ 3 = 3
```

Figure 2-23. *A simple host_task*

Figure 2-23 demonstrates a simple host task, which outputs text using `std::cout` when the task graph dependences have been met. Remember that the host task is executed asynchronously from the rest of the host program. This is a powerful part of the task graph mechanism in which the SYCL runtime schedules work when it is safe to do so, without interaction from the host program which may instead continue with other work. Also note that the code body of the host task does not need to follow any restrictions that are imposed on device code (described in Chapter 10).

The example in Figure 2-23 is based on events (described in Chapter 3) to create a dependence between the device code submission and a later host task, but host tasks can also be used with accessors (also covered in Chapter 3) through a special accessor template parameterization of `target::host_task` (Chapter 7).

Summary

In this chapter we provided an overview of queues, selection of the device with which a queue will be associated, and how to create custom device selectors. We also overviewed the code that executes on a device asynchronously when dependences are met vs. the code that executes as part of the C++ application host code. Chapter 3 describes how to control data movement.

CHAPTER 3

Data Management

Supercomputer architects often lament the need to "feed the beast." The phrase "feed the beast" refers to the "beast" of a computer we create when we use lots of parallelism and feeding data to it becomes a key challenge to solve.

Feeding a SYCL program on a heterogeneous machine requires some care to ensure data is where it needs to be when it needs to be there. In a large program, that can be a lot of work. In a preexisting C++ program, it can be a nightmare just to sort out how to manage all the data movements needed.

We will carefully explain the two ways to manage data: Unified Shared Memory (USM) and buffers. USM is pointer based, which is familiar to C++ programmers. Buffers offer a higher-level abstraction. Choice is good.

We need to control the movement of data, and this chapter covers options to do exactly that.

In Chapter 2, we studied how to control where code executes. Our code needs data as input and produces data as output. Since our code may run on multiple devices and those devices do not necessarily share memory, we need to manage data movement. Even when data is shared, such as with USM, synchronization and coherency are concepts we need to understand and manage.

A logical question might be "Why doesn't the compiler just do everything automatically for us?" While a great deal can be handled for us automatically, performance is usually suboptimal if we do not assert

J. Reinders et al., *Data Parallel C++*, https://doi.org/10.1007/978-1-4842-9691-2_3

ourselves as programmers. In practice, for best performance, we will need to concern ourselves with code placement (Chapter 2) and data movement (this chapter) when writing heterogeneous programs.

This chapter provides an overview of managing data, including controlling the ordering of data usage. It complements the prior chapter, which showed us how to control where code runs. This chapter helps us efficiently make our data appear where we have asked the code to run, which is important not only for correct execution of our application but also to minimize execution time and power consumption.

Introduction

Compute is nothing without data. The whole point of accelerating a computation is to produce an answer more quickly. This means that one of the most important aspects of data-parallel computations is how they access data and introducing accelerator devices into a machine further complicates the picture. In traditional single-socket CPU-based systems, we have a single memory. Accelerator devices often have their own attached memories that cannot be directly accessed from the host. Consequently, parallel programming models that support discrete devices must provide mechanisms to manage these multiple memories and move data between them.

In this chapter, we present an overview of the various mechanisms for data management. We introduce Unified Shared Memory and the buffer abstractions for data management and describe the relationship between kernel execution and data movement.

The Data Management Problem

Historically, one of the advantages of shared memory models for parallel programming is that they provide a single, shared view of memory. Having this single view of memory simplifies life. We are not required to do anything special to access memory from parallel tasks (aside from proper synchronization to avoid data races). While some types of accelerator devices (e.g., integrated GPUs) share memory with a host CPU, many discrete accelerators have their own local memories separate from that of the CPU as seen in Figure 3-1.

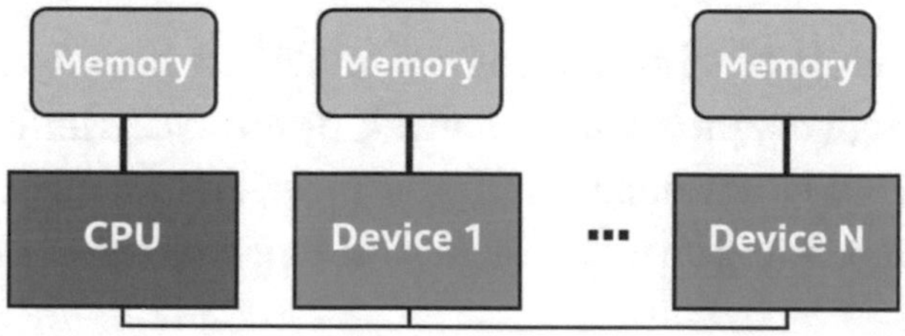

Figure 3-1. *Multiple discrete memories*

Device Local vs. Device Remote

Programs running on a device generally perform better when reading and writing data using memory attached directly to the device rather than remote memories. We refer to accesses to a directly attached memory as *local* accesses. Accesses to another device's memory are *remote* accesses. Remote accesses tend to be slower than local accesses because they must travel over data links with lower bandwidth and/or higher latency. This means that it is often advantageous to colocate both a computation and the data that it will use. To accomplish this, we must somehow ensure that data is copied or migrated between different memories in order to move it closer to where computation occurs.

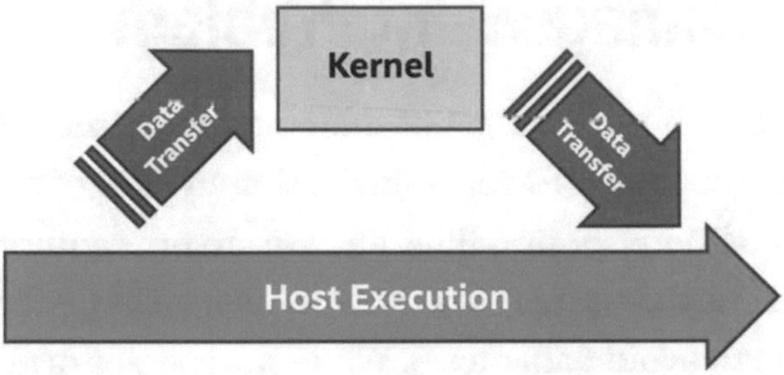

Figure 3-2. *Data movement and kernel execution*

Managing Multiple Memories

Managing multiple memories can be accomplished, broadly, in two ways: *explicitly* through our program or *implicitly* by the SYCL runtime library. Each method has its advantages and drawbacks, and we may choose one or the other depending on circumstances or personal preference.

Explicit Data Movement

One option for managing multiple memories is to explicitly copy data between different memories. Figure 3-2 shows a system with a discrete accelerator where we must first copy any data that a kernel will require from the host memory to accelerator memory. After the kernel computes results, we must copy these results back to the host before the host program can use that data.

The primary advantage of explicit data movement is that we have full control over when data is transferred between different memories. This is important because overlapping computation with data transfer can be essential to obtain the best performance on some hardware.

The drawback of explicit data movement is that specifying all data movements can be tedious and error prone. Transferring an incorrect amount of data or not ensuring that all data has been transferred before a kernel begins computing can lead to incorrect results. Getting all of the data movement correct from the beginning can be a very time-consuming task.

Implicit Data Movement

The alternative to program-controlled explicit data movements are implicit data movements controlled by a parallel runtime or driver. In this case, instead of requiring explicit copies between different memories, the parallel runtime is responsible for ensuring that data is transferred to the appropriate memory before it is used.

The advantage of implicit data movement is that it requires less effort to get an application to take advantage of faster memory attached directly to the device. All the heavy lifting is done automatically by the runtime. This also reduces the opportunity to introduce errors into the program since the runtime will automatically identify both when data transfers must be performed and how much data must be transferred.

The drawback of implicit data movement is that we have less or no control over the behavior of the runtime's implicit mechanisms. The runtime will provide functional correctness but may not move data in an optimal fashion that ensures maximal overlap of computation with data transfer, and this could have a negative impact on program performance.

Selecting the Right Strategy

Picking the best strategy for a program can depend on many different factors. Different strategies might be appropriate for different phases of program development. We could even decide that the best solution is to mix and match the explicit and implicit methods for different pieces of the program. We might choose to begin using implicit data movement to simplify porting an application to a new device. As we begin tuning the application for performance, we might start replacing implicit data movement with explicit in performance-critical parts of the code. Future chapters will cover how data transfers can be overlapped with computation in order to optimize performance.

USM, Buffers, and Images

There are three abstractions for managing memory: Unified Shared Memory (USM), buffers, and images. USM is a pointer-based approach that should be familiar to C/C++ programmers. One advantage of USM is easier integration with existing C++ code that operates on pointers. Buffers, as represented by the `buffer` template class, describe one-, two-, or three-dimensional arrays. They provide an abstract view of memory that can be accessed on either the host or a device. Buffers are not directly accessed by the program and are instead used through `accessor` objects. Images act as a special type of buffer that provides extra functionality specific to image processing. This functionality includes support for special image formats, reading of images using sampler objects, and more. Buffers and images are powerful abstractions that solve many problems but rewriting all interfaces in existing code to accept buffers or accessors can be time-consuming. Since the interface for buffers and images is largely the same, the rest of this chapter will only focus on USM and buffers.

Unified Shared Memory

USM is one tool available to us for data management. USM is a pointer-based approach that should be familiar to C and C++ programmers who use `malloc` or `new` to allocate data. USM simplifies life when porting existing C/C++ code that makes heavy use of pointers. Devices that support USM support a unified virtual address space. Having a unified virtual address space means that any pointer value returned by a USM allocation routine on the host will be a valid pointer value on the device. We do not have to manually translate a host pointer to obtain the "device version"—we see the same pointer value on both the host and device.

A more detailed description of USM can be found in Chapter 6.

Accessing Memory Through Pointers

Since not all memories are created equal when a system contains both host memory and some number of device-attached local memories, USM defines three different types of allocations: `device`, `host`, and `shared`. All types of allocations are performed on the host. Figure 3-3 summarizes the characteristics of each allocation type.

Allocation Type	Description	Accessible on host?	Accessible on device?	Located on
device	Allocations in device memory	✗	✓	device
host	Allocations in host memory	✓	✓	host
shared	Allocations shared between host and device	✓	✓	can migrate back and forth

Figure 3-3. *USM allocation types*

A `device` allocation occurs in device-attached memory. Such an allocation can be read from and written to on a device but is not directly accessible from the host. We must use explicit copy operations to move data between regular allocations in host memory and `device` allocations.

A `host` allocation occurs in host memory that is accessible both on the host and on a device. This means the same pointer value is valid both in host code and in device kernels. However, when such a pointer is accessed, the data always comes from host memory. If it is accessed on a device, the data does not migrate from the host to device-local memory. Instead, data is typically sent over a bus, such as PCI Express (PCI-E), that connects the device to the host.

A `shared` allocation is accessible on both the host and the device. In this regard, it is very similar to a host allocation, but it differs in that data can now migrate between host memory and device-local memory. This means that accesses on a device, after the migration has occurred, happen from much faster device-local memory instead of remotely accessing host memory though a higher-latency connection. Typically, this is accomplished through mechanisms inside the runtime and lower-level drivers that are hidden from us.

USM and Data Movement

USM supports both explicit and implicit data movement strategies, and different allocation types map to different strategies. Device allocations require us to explicitly move data between host and device, while host and shared allocations provide implicit data movement.

Explicit Data Movement in USM

Explicit data movement with USM is accomplished with `device` allocations and a special `memcpy()` found in the queue and handler classes. We enqueue `memcpy()` operations (actions) to transfer data either from the host to the device or from the device to the host.

Figure 3-4 contains one kernel that operates on a device allocation. Data is copied between `host_array` and `device_array` before and after the kernel executes using `memcpy()` operations. Calls to `wait()` on the queue ensure that the copy to the device has completed before the kernel executes and ensure that the kernel has completed before the data is copied back to the host. We will learn how we can eliminate these calls later in this chapter.

```
#include <array>
#include <sycl/sycl.hpp>
using namespace sycl;
constexpr int N = 42;

int main() {
  queue q;

  std::array<int, N> host_array;
  int *device_array = malloc_device<int>(N, q);

  for (int i = 0; i < N; i++) host_array[i] = N;

  // We will learn how to simplify this example later
  q.submit([&](handler &h) {
    // copy host_array to device_array
    h.memcpy(device_array, &host_array[0], N * sizeof(int));
  });
  q.wait();

  q.submit([&](handler &h) {
    h.parallel_for(N, [=](id<1> i) { device_array[i]++; });
  });
  q.wait();

  q.submit([&](handler &h) {
    // copy device_array back to host_array
    h.memcpy(&host_array[0], device_array, N * sizeof(int));
  });
  q.wait();

  free(device_array, q);
  return 0;
}
```

Figure 3-4. *USM explicit data movement*

Implicit Data Movement in USM

Implicit data movement with USM is accomplished with `host` and `shared` allocations. With these types of allocations, we do not need to explicitly insert copy operations to move data between host and device. Instead, we simply access the pointers inside a kernel, and any required data movement is performed automatically without programmer intervention (as long as your device supports these allocations). This greatly simplifies porting of existing codes: at most we need to simply replace any malloc or new with the appropriate USM allocation functions (as well as the calls to free to deallocate memory), and everything should just work.

```
#include <sycl/sycl.hpp>
using namespace sycl;
constexpr int N = 42;

int main() {
  queue q;
  int *host_array = malloc_host<int>(N, q);
  int *shared_array = malloc_shared<int>(N, q);

  for (int i = 0; i < N; i++) {
    // Initialize host_array on host
    host_array[i] = i;
  }

  // We will learn how to simplify this example later
  q.submit([&](handler &h) {
    h.parallel_for(N, [=](id<1> i) {
      // access shared_array and host_array on device
      shared_array[i] = host_array[i] + 1;
    });
  });
  q.wait();

  for (int i = 0; i < N; i++) {
    // access shared_array on host
    host_array[i] = shared_array[i];
  }

  free(shared_array, q);
  free(host_array, q);
  return 0;
}
```

Figure 3-5. *USM implicit data movement*

In Figure 3-5, we create two arrays, host_array and shared_array, that are host and shared allocations, respectively. While both host and shared allocations are directly accessible in host code, we only initialize `host_array` here. Similarly, it can be directly accessed inside the kernel, performing remote reads of the data. The runtime ensures that `shared_array` is available on the device before the kernel accesses it and that it is moved back when it is later read by the host code, all without programmer intervention.

Buffers

The other abstraction provided for data management is the buffer object. Buffers are a data abstraction that represent one or more objects of a given C++ type. Elements of a buffer object can be a scalar data type (such as an `int`, `float`, or `double`), a vector data type (Chapter 11), or a user-defined class or structure. SYCL 2020 defines a new notion, *device copyable*, that expands upon the notion of trivially copyable with additions to the set of permissible types. In particular, if the templated types in common C++ classes such as `std::array`, `std::pair`, `std::tuple`, or `std::span` are themselves device copyable, then those C++ class specializations built using those types are also device copyable. Take care that your data types are device copyable before using them with buffers!

While a buffer itself is a single object, the C++ type encapsulated by the buffer could be an array that contains multiple objects. Buffers represent data objects rather than specific memory addresses, so they cannot be directly accessed like regular C++ arrays. Indeed, a buffer object might map to multiple different memory locations on several different devices, or even on the same device, for performance reasons. Instead, we use *accessor* objects to read and write to buffers.

A more detailed description of buffers can be found in Chapter 7.

Creating Buffers

Buffers can be created in a variety of ways. The simplest method is to simply construct a new buffer with a range that specifies the size of the buffer. However, creating a buffer in this fashion does not initialize its data, meaning that we must first initialize the buffer through other means before attempting to read useful data from it.

Buffers can also be created from existing data on the host. This is done by invoking one of the several constructors that take either a pointer to an existing host allocation, a set of `InputIterators`, or a container that has certain properties. Data is copied during buffer construction from the existing host allocation into the buffer object's host memory. A buffer may also be created from a backend-specific object using SYCL interoperability features (e.g., from an OpenCL `cl_mem` object). See the chapter on interoperability for more details on how to do this.

Accessing Buffers

Buffers may not be directly accessed by the host and device (except through advanced and infrequently used mechanisms not described here). Instead, we must create accessors in order to read and write to buffers. Accessors provide the runtime with information about how we plan to use the data in buffers, allowing it to correctly schedule data movement.

```
#include <array>
#include <sycl/sycl.hpp>
using namespace sycl;
constexpr int N = 42;

int main() {
  std::array<int, N> my_data;
  for (int i = 0; i < N; i++) my_data[i] = 0;

  {
    queue q;
    buffer my_buffer(my_data);

    q.submit([&](handler &h) {
      // create an accessor to update
      // the buffer on the device
      accessor my_accessor(my_buffer, h);

      h.parallel_for(N, [=](id<1> i) { my_accessor[i]++; });
    });

    // create host accessor
    host_accessor host_accessor(my_buffer);

    for (int i = 0; i < N; i++) {
      // access myBuffer on host
      std::cout << host_accessor[i] << " ";
    }
    std::cout << "\n";
  }

  // myData is updated when myBuffer is
  // destroyed upon exiting scope
  for (int i = 0; i < N; i++) {
    std::cout << my_data[i] << " ";
  }
  std::cout << "\n";
}
```

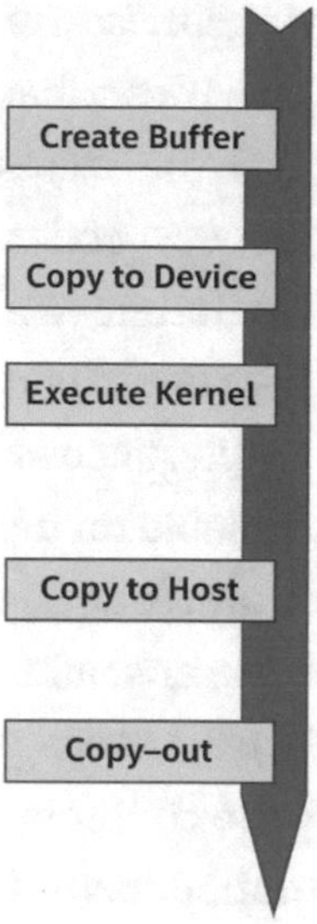

***Figure 3-6.** Buffers and accessors*

Access Mode	Description
`read`	Read-only access.
`write`	Write-only access. Previous contents are not discarded in case of partial writes.
`read_write`	Read and write access.

***Figure 3-7.** Buffer access modes*

Access Modes

When creating an accessor, we can inform the runtime how we are going to use it to provide more information for optimizations. We do this by specifying an *access mode*. Access modes are defined in the `access_mode` enum class described in Figure 3-7. In the code example shown in Figure 3-6, the accessor `my_accessor` is created with the default access mode, `access_mode::read_write`. This lets the runtime know that we intend to both read and write to the buffer through `my_accessor`. Access modes are how the runtime is able to optimize implicit data movement. For example, `access_mode::read` tells the runtime that the data needs to be available on the device before this kernel can begin executing. If a kernel only reads data through an accessor, there is no need to copy data back to the host after the kernel has completed as we haven't modified it. Likewise, `access_mode::write` lets the runtime know that we will modify the contents of a buffer and may need to copy the results back after computation has ended.

Creating accessors with the proper modes gives the runtime more information about how we use data in our program. The runtime uses accessors to order the uses of data, but it can also use this data to optimize scheduling of kernels and data movement. The access modes and optimization tags are described in greater detail in Chapter 7.

Ordering the Uses of Data

Kernels can be viewed as asynchronous tasks that are submitted for execution. These tasks must be submitted to a queue where they are scheduled for execution on a device. In many cases, kernels must execute in a specific order so that the correct result is computed. If obtaining the correct result requires task A to execute before task B, we say that a *dependence*[1] exists between tasks A and B.

However, kernels are not the only form of task that must be scheduled. Any data that is accessed by a kernel needs to be available on the device before the kernel can start executing. These data dependences can create additional tasks in the form of data transfers from one device to another. Data transfer tasks may be either explicitly coded copy operations or more commonly implicit data movements performed by the runtime.

If we take all the tasks in a program and the dependences that exist between them, we can use this to visualize the information as a graph. This task graph is specifically a directed acyclic graph (DAG) where the nodes are the tasks and the edges are the dependences. The graph is *directed* because dependences are one-way: task A must happen before task B. The graph is *acyclic* because it cannot contain any cycles or paths from a node that lead back to itself.

In Figure 3-8, task A must execute before tasks B and C. Likewise, B and C must execute before task D. Since B and C do not have a dependence between each other, the runtime is free to execute them in any order (or even in parallel) as long as task A has already executed. Therefore, the possible legal orderings of this graph are A ⇒ B ⇒ C ⇒ D, A ⇒ C ⇒ B ⇒ D, and even A ⇒ `{B,C}` ⇒ D if B and C can concurrently execute.

[1] Note that you may see "dependence" and "dependences" sometimes spelled "dependency" and "dependencies" in other texts. They mean the same thing, but we are favoring the spelling used in several important papers on data flow analysis. See `https://dl.acm.org/doi/pdf/10.1145/75277.75280` and `https://dl.acm.org/doi/pdf/10.1145/113446.113449`.

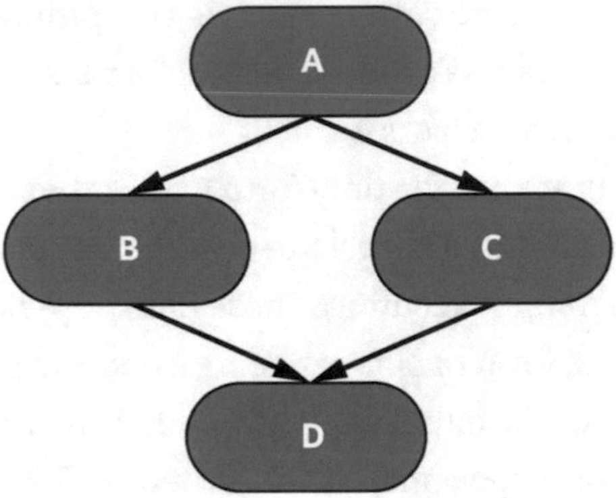

Figure 3-8. *Simple task graph*

Tasks may have a dependence with a subset of all tasks. In these cases, we only want to specify the dependences that matter for correctness. This flexibility gives the runtime latitude to optimize the execution order of the task graph. In Figure 3-9, we extend the earlier task graph from Figure 3-8 to add tasks E and F where E must execute before F. However, tasks E and F have no dependences with nodes A, B, C, and D. This allows the runtime to choose from many possible legal orderings to execute all the tasks.

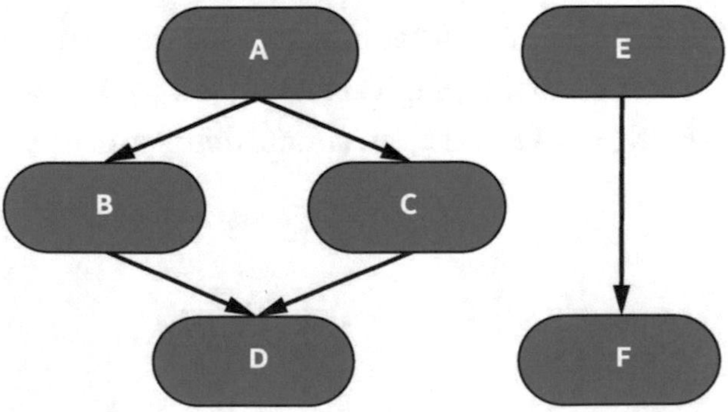

Figure 3-9. *Task graph with disjoint dependences*

There are two different ways to model the execution of tasks, such as a launch of a kernel, in a queue: the queue could either execute tasks in the order of submission, or it could execute tasks in *any* order subject to any dependences that we define. There are several mechanisms for us to define the dependences needed for correct ordering.

In-order Queues

The simplest option to order tasks is to submit them to an in-order queue object. An in-order queue executes tasks in the order in which they were submitted as seen in Figure 3-10. Their intuitive task ordering means that in-order queues an advantage of simplicity but a disadvantage of serializing tasks even if no dependences exist between independent tasks. In-order queues are useful when bringing up applications because they are simple, intuitive, deterministic on execution ordering, and suitable for many codes.

```
#include <sycl/sycl.hpp>
using namespace sycl;
constexpr int N = 4;

int main() {
  queue q{property::queue::in_order()};

  q.submit([&](handler& h) {
    h.parallel_for(N, [=](id<1> i) { /*...*/ });  // Task A
  });
  q.submit([&](handler& h) {
    h.parallel_for(N, [=](id<1> i) { /*...*/ });  // Task B
  });
  q.submit([&](handler& h) {
    h.parallel_for(N, [=](id<1> i) { /*...*/ });  // Task C
  });

  return 0;
}
```

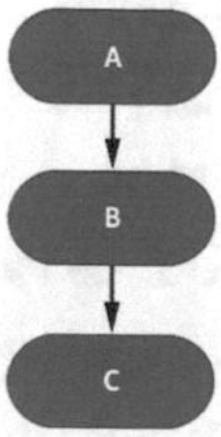

Figure 3-10. *In-order queue usage*

Out-of-Order Queues

Since `queue` objects are out-of-order queues (unless created with the `in-order` queue property), they must provide ways to order tasks submitted to them. Queues order tasks by letting us inform the runtime of dependences between them. These dependences can be specified, either explicitly or implicitly, using *command groups*. We will consider them separately in the following sections.

A command group is an object that specifies a task and its dependences. Command groups are typically written as C++ lambda expressions passed as an argument to the `submit()` method of a queue object. This lambda's only parameter is a reference to a `handler` object. The handler object is used inside the command group to specify actions, create accessors, and specify dependences.

Explicit Dependences with Events

Explicit dependences between tasks look like the examples we have seen (Figure 3-8) where task A must execute before task B. Expressing dependences in this way focuses on explicit ordering based on the computations that occur rather than on the data accessed by the computations. Note that expressing dependences between computations is primarily relevant for codes that use USM since codes that use buffers express most dependences via accessors. In Figures 3-4 and 3-5, we simply tell the queue to wait for all previously submitted tasks to finish before we continue. Instead, we can express task dependences through *event* objects. When submitting a command group to a queue, the `submit()` method returns an event object. These events can then be used in two ways.

First, we can synchronize through the host by explicitly calling the `wait()` method on an event. This forces the runtime to wait for the task that generated the event to finish executing before host program execution may continue. Explicitly waiting on events can be very useful for debugging an application but `wait()` can overly constrain the asynchronous execution of tasks since it halts all execution on the host thread. Similarly, one could also call `wait()` on a queue object, which would block execution on the host until all enqueued tasks have completed. This can be a useful tool if we do not want to keep track of all the events returned by enqueued tasks.

This brings us to the second way that events can be used. The handler class contains a method named `depends_on()`. This method accepts either a single event or a vector of events and informs the runtime that the command group being submitted requires the specified events to complete before the action within the command group may execute. Figure 3-11 shows an example of how `depends_on()` may be used to order tasks.

```
#include <sycl/sycl.hpp>
using namespace sycl;
constexpr int N = 4;

int main() {
  queue q;

  auto eA = q.submit([&](handler &h) {
    h.parallel_for(N, [=](id<1> i) { /*...*/ });  // Task A
  });
  eA.wait();
  auto eB = q.submit([&](handler &h) {
    h.parallel_for(N, [=](id<1> i) { /*...*/ });  // Task B
  });
  auto eC = q.submit([&](handler &h) {
    h.depends_on(eB);
    h.parallel_for(N, [=](id<1> i) { /*...*/ });  // Task C
  });
  auto eD = q.submit([&](handler &h) {
    h.depends_on({eB, eC});
    h.parallel_for(N, [=](id<1> i) { /*...*/ });  // Task D
  });

  return 0;
}
```

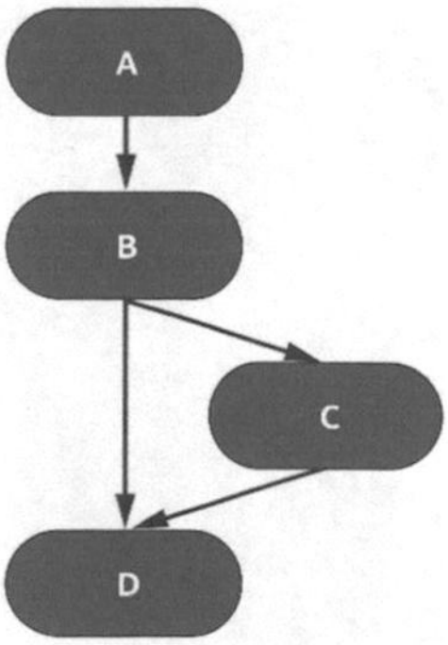

Figure 3-11. *Using events and depends_on*

Implicit Dependences with Accessors

Implicit dependences between tasks are created from data dependences. Data dependences between tasks take three forms, shown in Figure 3-12.

Dependence Type	Description
Read-after-Write (RAW)	Occurs when task B needs to read data computed by task A.
Write-after-Read (WAR)	Occurs when task B writes over data after it has been read by task A.
Write-after-Write(WAW)	Occurs when task B also writes over data written by task A.

Figure 3-12. *Three forms of data dependences*

Data dependences are expressed to the runtime in two ways: accessors and program order. Both must be used for the runtime to properly compute data dependences. This is illustrated in Figures 3-13 and 3-14.

```
#include <array>
#include <sycl/sycl.hpp>
using namespace sycl;
constexpr int N = 42;

int main() {
  std::array<int, N> a, b, c;
  for (int i = 0; i < N; i++) {
    a[i] = b[i] = c[i] = 0;
  }

  queue q;

  // We will learn how to simplify this example later
  buffer a_buf{a};
  buffer b_buf{b};
  buffer c_buf{c};

  q.submit([&](handler &h) {
    accessor a(a_buf, h, read_only);
    accessor b(b_buf, h, write_only);
    h.parallel_for(  // computeB
        N, [=](id<1> i) { b[i] = a[i] + 1; });
  });

  q.submit([&](handler &h) {
    accessor a(a_buf, h, read_only);
    h.parallel_for(  // readA
        N, [=](id<1> i) {
          // Useful only as an example
          int data = a[i];
        });
  });

  q.submit([&](handler &h) {
    // RAW of buffer B
    accessor b(b_buf, h, read_only);
    accessor c(c_buf, h, write_only);
    h.parallel_for(  // computeC
        N, [=](id<1> i) { c[i] = b[i] + 2; });
  });

  // read C on host
  host_accessor host_acc_c(c_buf, read_only);
  for (int i = 0; i < N; i++) {
    std::cout << host_acc_c[i] << " ";
  }
  std::cout << "\n";
  return 0;
}
```

Figure 3-13. *Read-after-Write*

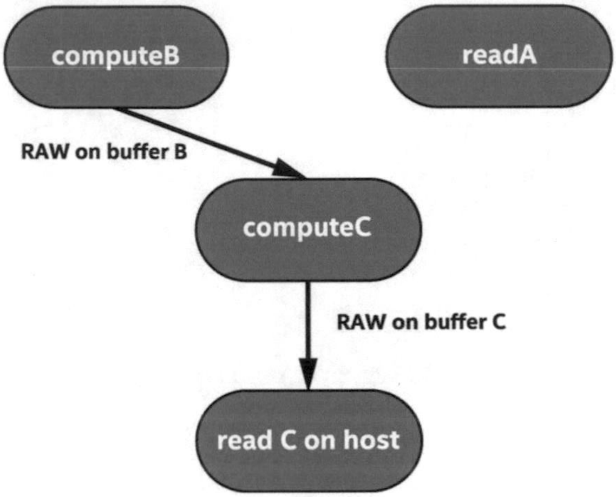

Figure 3-14. *RAW task graph*

In Figures 3-13 and 3-14, we execute three kernels—`computeB`, `readA`, and `computeC`—and then read the final result back on the host. The command group for kernel `computeB` creates two accessors, `a` and `b`. These accessors use access tags `read_only` and `write_only` for optimization to specify that we do not use the default access mode, `access_mode::read_write`. We will learn more about access tags in Chapter 7. Kernel `computeB` reads buffer `a_buf` and writes to buffer `b_buf`. Buffer `a_buf` must be copied from the host to the device before the kernel begins execution.

Kernel `readA` also creates a read-only accessor for buffer `a_buf`. Since kernel `readA` is submitted after kernel `computeB`, this creates a Read-after-Read (RAR) scenario. However, RARs do not place extra restrictions on the runtime, and the kernels are free to execute in any order. Indeed, a runtime might prefer to execute kernel `readA` before kernel `computeB` or even execute both at the same time. Both require buffer `a_buf` to be copied to the device, but kernel `computeB` also requires buffer `b_buf` to be copied in case any existing values are not overwritten by `computeB` and which might be used by later kernels. This means that the runtime could execute kernel `readA` while the data transfer for buffer `b_buf` occurs and also shows that even if a kernel will only write to a buffer, the original content of the buffer may still be moved to the device because there is no guarantee that all values in the buffer will be written by a kernel (see Chapter 7 for tags that let us optimize in these cases).

Kernel computeC reads buffer b_buf, which we computed in kernel computeB. Since we submitted kernel computeC after we submitted kernel computeB, this means that kernel computeC has a RAW data dependence on buffer b_buf. RAW dependences are also called true dependences or flow dependences, as data needs to flow from one computation to another in order to compute the correct result. Finally, we also create a RAW dependence on buffer c_buf between kernel computeC and the host since the host wants to read C after the kernel has finished. This forces the runtime to copy buffer c_buf back to the host. Since there were no writes to buffer a_buf on devices, the runtime does not need to copy that buffer back to the host because the host has an up-to-date copy already.

```
#include <array>
#include <sycl/sycl.hpp>
using namespace sycl;
constexpr int N = 42;

int main() {
  std::array<int, N> a, b;
  for (int i = 0; i < N; i++) {
    a[i] = b[i] = 0;
  }

  queue q;
  buffer a_buf{a};
  buffer b_buf{b};

  q.submit([&](handler &h) {
    accessor a(a_buf, h, read_only);
    accessor b(b_buf, h, write_only);
    h.parallel_for(  // computeB
        N, [=](id<1> i) { b[i] = a[i] + 1; });
  });

  q.submit([&](handler &h) {
    // WAR of buffer A
    accessor a(a_buf, h, write_only);
    h.parallel_for(  // rewriteA
        N, [=](id<1> i) { a[i] = 21 + 21; });
  });

  q.submit([&](handler &h) {
    // WAW of buffer B
    accessor b(b_buf, h, write_only);
    h.parallel_for(  // rewriteB
        N, [=](id<1> i) { b[i] = 30 + 12; });
  });

  host_accessor host_acc_a(a_buf, read_only);
  host_accessor host_acc_b(b_buf, read_only);
  for (int i = 0; i < N; i++) {
    std::cout << host_acc_a[i] << " " << host_acc_b[i]
              << " ";
  }
  std::cout << "\n";
  return 0;
}
```

Figure 3-15. *Write-after-Read and Write-after-Write*

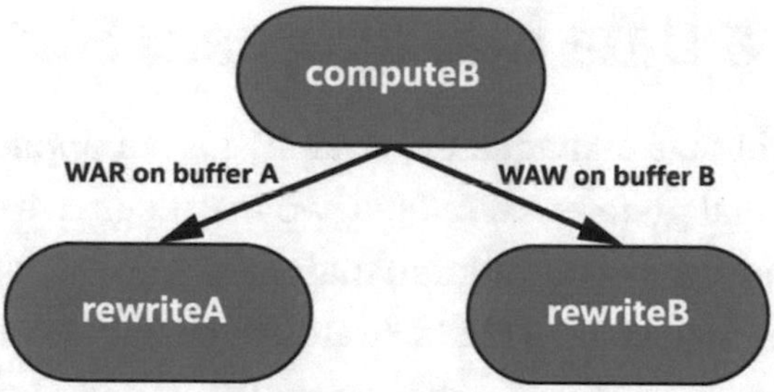

Figure 3-16. *WAR and WAW task graph*

In Figures 3-15 and 3-16, we again execute three kernels: `computeB`, `rewriteA`, and `rewriteB`. Kernel `computeB` once again reads buffer `a_buf` and writes to buffer `b_buf`, kernel `rewriteA` writes to buffer `a_buf`, and kernel `rewriteB` writes to buffer `b_buf`. Kernel `rewriteA` could theoretically execute earlier than kernel `computeB` since less data needs to be transferred before the kernel is ready, but it must wait until after kernel `computeB` finishes since there is a WAR dependence on buffer `a_buf`.

In this example, kernel `computeB` requires the original value of A from the host, and it would read the wrong values if kernel `rewriteA` executed before kernel `computeB`. WAR dependences are also called anti-dependences. RAW dependences ensure that data properly flows in the correct direction, while WAR dependences ensure existing values are not overwritten before they are read. The WAW dependence on buffer `b_buf` found in kernel rewrite functions similarly. If there were any reads of buffer `b_buf` submitted in between kernels `computeB` and `rewriteB`, they would result in RAW and WAR dependences that would properly order the tasks. However, there is an implicit dependence between kernel `rewriteB` and the host in this example since the final data must be written back to the host. We will learn more about what causes this writeback in Chapter 7. The WAW dependence, also called an output dependence, ensures that the final output will be correct on the host.

Choosing a Data Management Strategy

Selecting the right data management strategy for our applications is largely a matter of personal preference. Indeed, we may begin with one strategy and switch to another as our program matures. However, there are a few useful guidelines to help us to pick a strategy that will serve our needs.

The first decision to make is whether we want to use explicit or implicit data movement since this greatly affects what we need to do to our program. Implicit data movement is generally an easier place to start because all the data movement is handled for us, letting us focus on expression of the computation.

If we decide that we'd rather have full control over all data movement from the beginning, then explicit data movement using USM device allocations is where we want to start. We just need to be sure to add all the necessary copies between host and devices!

When selecting an implicit data movement strategy, we still have a choice of whether to use buffers or USM host or shared pointers. Again, this choice is a matter of personal preference, but there are a few questions that could help guide us to one over the other. If we're porting an existing C/C++ program that uses pointers, USM might be an easier path since most code won't need to change. If data representation hasn't guided us to a preference, another question we can ask is how we would like to express our dependences between kernels. If we prefer to think about data dependences between kernels, choose buffers. If we prefer to think about dependences as performing one computation before another and want to express that using an in-order queue or with explicit events or waiting between kernels, choose USM.

When using USM pointers (with either explicit or implicit data movement), we have a choice of which type of queue we want to use. In-order queues are simple and intuitive, but they constrain the runtime and may limit performance. Out-of-order queues are more complex, but they give the runtime more freedom to reorder and overlap execution. The out-of-order queue class is the right choice if our program will have complex dependences between kernels. If our program simply runs many kernels one after another, then an in-order queue will be a better option for us.

Handler Class: Key Members

We have shown a number of ways to use the `handler` class. Figures 3-17 and 3-18 provide a more detailed explanation of the key members of this very important class. We have not yet used all these members, but they will be used later in the book. This is as good a place as any to lay them out.

A closely related class, the `queue` class, is similarly explained at the end of Chapter 2.

```
class handler {
  ...
      // Specifies event(s) that must be complete before the
      // action defined in this command group executes.
      void depends_on({event / std::vector<event> & });

  // Enqueues a memcpy from Src to Dest.
  // Count bytes are copied.
  void memcpy(void* Dest, const void* Src, size_t Count);

  // Enqueues a memcpy from Src to Dest.
  // Count elements are copied.
  template <typename T>
  void copy(const T* Src, T* Dest, size_t Count);

  // Enqueues a memset operation on the specified pointer.
  // Writes the first byte of Value into Count bytes.
  void memset(void* Ptr, int Value, size_t Count)

      // Enques a fill operation on the specified pointer.
      // Fills Pattern into Ptr Count times.
      template <typename T>
      void fill(void* Ptr, const T& Pattern, size_t Count);

  // Submits a kernel of one work-item for execution.
  template <typename KernelName, typename KernelType>
  void single_task(KernelType KernelFunc);

  // Submits a kernel with NumWork-items work-items for
  // execution.
  template <typename KernelName, typename KernelType,
            int Dims>
  void parallel_for(range<Dims> NumWork - items,
                    KernelType KernelFunc);

  // Submits a kernel for execution over the supplied
  // nd_range.
  template <typename KernelName, typename KernelType,
            int Dims>
  void parallel_for(nd_range<Dims> ExecutionRange,
                    KernelType KernelFunc);
  ...
};
```

***Figure 3-17.** Simplified definition of the non-accessor members of the handler class*

```
class handler {
  ...
  // Specifies event(s) that must be complete before the
  // action. Copy to/from an accessor.
  // Valid combinations:
  // Src: accessor,   Dest: shared_ptr
  // Src: accessor,   Dest: pointer
  // Src: shared_ptr  Dest: accessor
  // Src: pointer     Dest: accessor
  // Src: accesssor   Dest: accessor
  template <typename T_Src, typename T_Dst, int Dims,
            access::mode AccessMode,
            access::target AccessTarget,
            access::placeholder IsPlaceholder =
                access::placeholder::false_t>
  void copy(accessor<T_Src, Dims, AccessMode,
                     AccessTarget, IsPlaceholder> Src,
            shared_ptr_class<T_Dst> Dst);
  void copy(shared_ptr_class<T_Src> Src,
            accessor<T_Dst, Dims, AccessMode, AccessTarget,
                     IsPlaceholder>
                Dst);
  void copy(accessor<T_Src, Dims, AccessMode, AccessTarget,
                     IsPlaceholder> Src,
            T_Dst *Dst);
  void copy(const T_Src *Src,
            accessor<T_Dst, Dims, AccessMode, AccessTarget,
                     IsPlaceholder> Dst);
  template <typename T_Src, int Dims_Src,
            access::mode AccessMode_Src,
            access::target AccessTarget_Src, typename T_Dst,
            int Dims_Dst, access::mode AccessMode_Dst,
            access::target AccessTarget_Dst,
            access::placeholder IsPlaceholder_Src =
                access::placeholder::false_t,
            access::placeholder IsPlaceholder_Dst =
                access::placeholder::false_t>
  void copy(accessor<T_Src, Dims_Src, AccessMode_Src,
                     AccessTarget_Src, IsPlaceholder_Src> Src,
            accessor<T_Dst, Dims_Dst, AccessMode_Dst,
                     AccessTarget_Dst, IsPlaceholder_Dst> Dst);

  // Provides a guarantee that the memory object accessed by
  // the accessor is updated on the host after this action
  // executes.
  template <typename T, int Dims, access::mode AccessMode,
            access::target AccessTarget,
            access::placeholder IsPlaceholder =
                access::placeholder::false_t>
  void update_host(accessor<T, Dims, AccessMode,
                            AccessTarget, IsPlaceholder> Acc);
  ...
};
```

Figure 3-18. *Simplified definition of the accessor members of the handler class*

Summary

In this chapter, we have introduced the mechanisms that address the problems of data management and how to order the uses of data. Managing access to different memories is a key challenge when using accelerator devices, and we have different options to suit our needs.

We provided an overview of the different types of dependences that can exist between the uses of data, and we described how to provide information about these dependences to queues so that they properly order tasks.

This chapter provided an overview of Unified Shared Memory and buffers. We explore all the modes and behaviors of USM in greater detail in Chapter 6. Chapter 7 explores buffers more deeply, including all the different ways to create buffers and control their behavior. Chapter 8 revisits the scheduling mechanisms for queues that control the ordering of kernel executions and data movements.

CHAPTER 4

Expressing Parallelism

We already know how to place code (Chapter 2) and data (Chapter 3) on a device—all we must do now is engage in the art of deciding what to do with it. To that end, we now shift to fill in a few things that we have conveniently left out or glossed over so far. This chapter marks the transition from simple teaching examples toward real-world parallel code and expands upon details of the code samples we have casually shown in prior chapters.

Writing our first program in a new parallel language may seem like a daunting task, especially if we are new to parallel programming. Language specifications are not written for application developers and often assume some familiarity with terminology; they do not contain answers to questions like these:

- Why is there more than one way to express parallelism?
- Which method of expressing parallelism should I use?
- How much do I really need to know about the execution model?

This chapter seeks to address these questions and more. We introduce the concept of a data-parallel kernel, discuss the strengths and weaknesses of the different kernel forms using working code examples, and highlight the most important aspects of the kernel execution model.

J. Reinders et al., *Data Parallel C++*, https://doi.org/10.1007/978-1-4842-9691-2_4

Parallelism Within Kernels

Parallel kernels have emerged in recent years as a powerful means of expressing data parallelism. The primary design goals of a kernel-based approach are *portability* across a wide range of devices and high programmer *productivity*. As such, kernels are typically not hard-coded to work with a specific number or configuration of hardware resources (e.g., cores, hardware threads, SIMD [single instruction, multiple data] instructions). Instead, kernels describe parallelism in terms of abstract concepts that an implementation (i.e., the combination of compiler and runtime) can then map to the hardware parallelism available on a specific target device. Although this mapping is implementation-defined, we can (and should) trust implementations to select a mapping that is sensible and capable of effectively exploiting hardware parallelism.

Exposing a great deal of parallelism in a hardware-agnostic way ensures that applications can scale up (or down) to fit the capabilities of different platforms, but...

Guaranteeing functional portability is not the same as guaranteeing high performance!

There is a significant amount of diversity in the devices supported, and we must remember that different architectures are designed and optimized for different use cases. Whenever we hope to achieve the highest levels of *performance* on a specific device, we should always expect that some additional manual optimization work will be required—regardless of the programming language we are using! Examples of such device-specific optimizations include blocking for a particular cache size, choosing a work grain size that amortizes scheduling overheads, making use of specialized instructions or hardware units, and, most importantly, choosing an appropriate algorithm. Some of these examples will be revisited in Chapters 15, 16, and 17.

Striking the right balance between performance, portability, and productivity during application development is a challenge that we must all face—and a challenge that this book cannot address in its entirety. However, we hope to show that C++ with SYCL provides all the tools required to maintain both generic portable code and optimized target-specific code using a single high-level programming language. The rest is left as an exercise to the reader!

Loops vs. Kernels

An iterative loop is an inherently serial construct: each iteration of the loop is executed sequentially (i.e., in order). An optimizing compiler may be able to determine that some or all iterations of a loop can execute in parallel, but it must be conservative—if the compiler is not smart enough or does not have enough information to prove that parallel execution is always safe, it must preserve the loop's sequential semantics for correctness.

```
for (int i = 0; i < N; ++i) {
  c[i] = a[i] + b[i];
}
```

Figure 4-1. *Expressing a vector addition as a serial loop*

Consider the loop in Figure 4-1, which describes a simple vector addition. Even in a simple case like this, proving that the loop can be executed in parallel is not trivial: parallel execution is only safe if `c` does not overlap `a` or `b`, which in the general case cannot be proven without a runtime check! In order to address situations like this, languages have added features enabling us to provide compilers with extra information that may simplify analysis (e.g., asserting that pointers do not overlap with `restrict`) or to override all analysis altogether (e.g., declaring that all iterations of a loop are independent or defining exactly how the loop should be scheduled to parallel resources).

The exact meaning of a *parallel loop* is somewhat ambiguous—due to overloading of the term by different parallel programming languages and runtimes—but many common parallel loop constructs represent compiler transformations applied to sequential loops. Such programming models enable us to write sequential loops and only later provide information about how different iterations can be executed safely in parallel. These models are very powerful, integrate well with other state-of-the-art compiler optimizations, and greatly simplify parallel programming, but do not always encourage us to think about parallelism at an early stage of development.

A parallel kernel is not a loop and does not have iterations. Rather, a kernel describes a single operation, which can be instantiated many times and applied to different input data; when a kernel is launched in parallel, multiple instances of that operation may be executed simultaneously.

```
launch N kernel instances {
  int id =
      get_instance_id();  // unique identifier in [0, N)
  c[id] = a[id] + b[id];
}
```

Figure 4-2. *Loop rewritten (in pseudocode) as a parallel kernel*

Figure 4-2 shows our simple loop example rewritten as a kernel using pseudocode. The opportunity for parallelism in this kernel is clear and explicit: the kernel can be executed in parallel by any number of instances, and each instance independently applies to a separate piece of data. By writing this operation as a kernel, we are asserting that it is safe to run in parallel (and that it ideally should be run in parallel).

In short, kernel-based programming is not a way to retrofit parallelism into existing sequential codes, but a methodology for writing explicitly parallel applications.

The sooner that we can shift our thinking from parallel loops to kernels, the easier it will be to write effective parallel programs using C++ with SYCL.

Multidimensional Kernels

The parallel constructs of many other languages are one-dimensional, mapping work directly to a corresponding one-dimensional hardware resource (e.g., number of hardware threads). Parallel kernels in SYCL are a higher-level concept than this, and their dimensionality is more reflective of the problems that our codes are typically trying to solve (in a one-, two-, or three-dimensional space).

However, we must remember that the multidimensional indexing provided by parallel kernels is a programmer convenience that may be implemented on top of an underlying one-dimensional space. Understanding how this mapping behaves can be an important part of certain optimizations (e.g., tuning memory access patterns).

One important consideration is which dimension is *contiguous* or *unit-stride* (i.e., which locations in the multidimensional space are next to each other in a one-dimensional mapping). All multidimensional quantities related to parallelism in SYCL use the same convention: dimensions are numbered from 0 to N-1, where dimension N-1 corresponds to the contiguous dimension. Wherever a multidimensional quantity is written as a list (e.g., in constructors) or a class supports multiple subscript operators, this numbering applies left to right (starting with dimension 0 on the left). This convention is consistent with the behavior of multidimensional arrays in standard C++.

An example of mapping a two-dimensional space to a linear index using the SYCL convention is shown in Figure 4-3. We are of course free to break from this convention and adopt our own methods of linearizing indices, but must do so carefully—breaking from the SYCL convention may have a negative performance impact on devices that benefit from stride-one accesses.

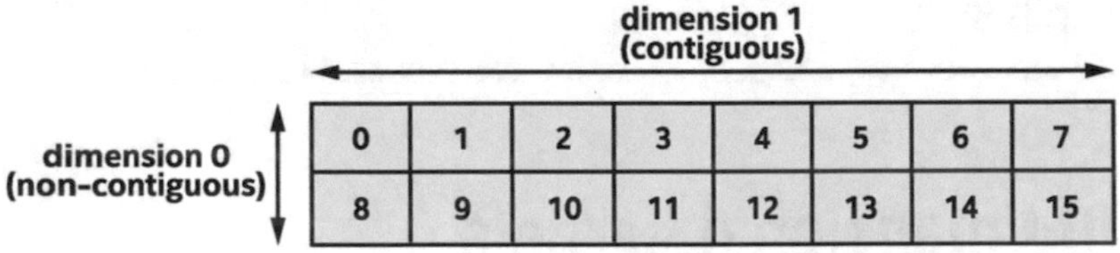

Figure 4-3. *Two-dimensional range of size (2, 8) mapped to linear indices*

If an application requires more than three dimensions, we must take responsibility for mapping between multidimensional and linear indices manually, using modulo arithmetic or other techniques.

Overview of Language Features

Once we have decided to write a parallel kernel, we must decide what type of kernel we want to launch and how to represent it in our program. There are a multitude of ways to express parallel kernels, and we need to familiarize ourselves with each of these options if we want to master the language.

Separating Kernels from Host Code

We have several alternative ways to separate host and device code, which we can mix and match within an application: C++ lambda expressions or function objects, kernels defined via an interoperability interface (e.g., OpenCL C source strings), or binaries. Some of these options were already covered in Chapter 2, and the others will be covered in detail in Chapters 10 and 20.

The fundamental concepts of expressing parallelism are shared by all these options. For consistency and brevity, all the code examples in this chapter express kernels using C++ lambda expressions.

LAMBDA EXPRESSIONS NOT CONSIDERED HARMFUL

There is no need to fully understand everything that the C++ specification says about lambda expressions in order to get started with SYCL—all we need to know is that the body of the lambda expression represents the kernel and that variables captured (by value) will be passed to the kernel as arguments.

There is no performance impact arising from the use of lambda expressions instead of more verbose mechanisms for defining kernels. A C++ compiler with SYCL support always understands when a lambda expression represents the body of a parallel kernel and can optimize for parallel execution accordingly.

For a refresher on C++ lambda expressions, with notes about their use in SYCL, see Chapter 1. For more specific details on using lambda expressions to define kernels, see Chapter 10.

Different Forms of Parallel Kernels

There are three different kernel forms in SYCL, supporting different execution models and syntax. It is possible to write portable kernels using any of the kernel forms, and kernels written in any form can be tuned to achieve high performance on a wide variety of device types. However, there will be times when we may want to use a specific form to make a specific parallel algorithm easier to express or to make use of an otherwise inaccessible language feature.

The first form is used for *basic* data-parallel kernels and offers the gentlest introduction to writing kernels. With basic kernels, we sacrifice control over low-level features like scheduling to make the expression of the kernel as simple as possible. How the individual kernel instances are mapped to hardware resources is controlled entirely by the implementation, and so as basic kernels grow in complexity, it becomes harder and harder to reason about their performance.

The second form extends basic kernels to provide access to low-level performance-tuning features. This second form is known as *ND-range* (N-dimensional range) data parallel for historical reasons, and the most important thing to remember is that it enables certain kernel instances to be grouped together, allowing us to exert some control over data locality and the mapping between individual kernel instances and the hardware resources that will be used to execute them.

The third form offers an experimental alternative syntax for expressing ND-range kernels using syntax similar to nested parallel loops. This third form is referred to as *hierarchical* data parallel, referring to the hierarchy of the nested constructs that appear in user source code. Compiler support for this syntax is still immature, and many SYCL implementations do not implement hierarchical data-parallel kernels as efficiently as the other two forms. The syntax is also incomplete, in the sense that there are many performance-enabling features of SYCL that are incompatible with or inaccessible from hierarchical kernels. Hierarchical parallelism in SYCL is in the process of being updated, and the SYCL specification includes a note recommending that new codes refrain from using hierarchical parallelism until the feature is ready; in keeping with the spirit of this note, the remainder of this book teaches only basic and ND-range parallelism.

We will revisit how to choose between the different kernel forms again at the end of this chapter once we have discussed their features in more detail.

Basic Data-Parallel Kernels

The most basic form of parallel kernel is appropriate for operations that are *embarrassingly parallel* (i.e., operations that can be applied to every piece of data completely independently and in any order). By using this form, we give an implementation complete control over the scheduling of work. It is thus an example of a *descriptive* programming construct—we *describe* that the operation is embarrassingly parallel, and all scheduling decisions are made by the implementation.

Basic data-parallel kernels are written in a single program, multiple data (SPMD) style—a single "program" (the kernel) is applied to multiple pieces of data. Note that this programming model still permits each instance of the kernel to take different paths through the code, because of data-dependent branches.

One of the greatest strengths of a SPMD programming model is that it allows the same "program" to be mapped to multiple levels and types of parallelism, without any explicit direction from us. Instances of the same program could be pipelined, packed together and executed with SIMD instructions, distributed across multiple hardware threads, or a mix of all three.

Understanding Basic Data-Parallel Kernels

The execution space of a basic parallel kernel is referred to as its execution *range*, and each instance of the kernel is referred to as an *item*. This is represented diagrammatically in Figure 4-4.

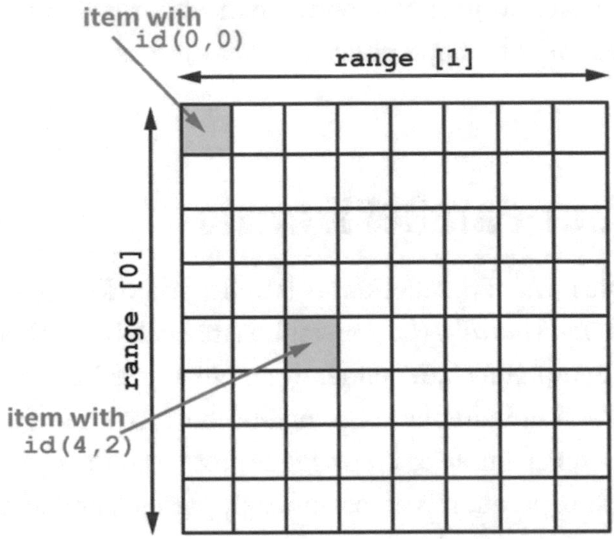

Figure 4-4. *Execution space of a basic parallel kernel, shown for a 2D range of 64 items*

The execution model of basic data-parallel kernels is very simple: it *allows* for completely parallel execution but does not *guarantee* or *require* it. Items can be executed in any order, including sequentially on a single hardware thread (i.e., without any parallelism)! Kernels that assume that all items will be executed in parallel (e.g., by attempting to synchronize items) could therefore very easily cause programs to hang on some devices.

However, to guarantee correctness, we must always write our kernels under the assumption that they *could* be executed in parallel. For example, it is our responsibility to ensure that concurrent accesses to memory are appropriately guarded by atomic memory operations (see Chapter 19) to prevent race conditions.

Writing Basic Data-Parallel Kernels

Basic data-parallel kernels are expressed using the `parallel_for` function. Figure 4-5 shows how to use this function to express a vector addition, which is our take on "Hello, world!" for parallel accelerator programming.

```
h.parallel_for(range{N}, [=](id<1> idx) {
  c[idx] = a[idx] + b[idx];
});
```

Figure 4-5. *Expressing a vector addition kernel with `parallel_for`*

The function only takes two arguments: the first is a `range` (or integer) specifying the number of items to launch in each dimension, and the second is a kernel function to be executed for each index in the range. There are several different classes that can be accepted as arguments to a kernel function, and which should be used depends on which class exposes the functionality required—we'll revisit this later.

Figure 4-6 shows a very similar use of this function to express a matrix addition, which is (mathematically) identical to vector addition except with two-dimensional data. This is reflected by the kernel—the only difference between the two code snippets is the dimensionality of the `range` and `id` classes used! It is possible to write the code this way because a SYCL `accessor` can be indexed by a multidimensional `id`. As strange as it looks, this can be very powerful, enabling us to write generic kernels templated on the dimensionality of our data.

```
h.parallel_for(range{N, M}, [=](id<2> idx) {
  c[idx] = a[idx] + b[idx];
});
```

Figure 4-6. *Expressing a matrix addition kernel with `parallel_for`*

It is more common in C/C++ to use multiple indices and multiple subscript operators to index multidimensional data structures, and this explicit indexing is also supported by accessors. Using multiple indices in this way can improve readability when a kernel operates on data of different dimensionalities simultaneously or when the memory access patterns of a kernel are more complicated than can be described by using an item's `id` directly.

For example, the matrix multiplication kernel in Figure 4-7 must extract the two individual components of the index in order to be able to describe the dot product between rows and columns of the two matrices. In the authors' opinion, consistently using multiple subscript operators (e.g., `[j][k]`) is more readable than mixing multiple indexing modes and constructing two-dimensional `id` objects (e.g., `id(j,k)`), but this is simply a matter of personal preference.

The examples in the remainder of this chapter all use multiple subscript operators, to ensure that there is no ambiguity in the dimensionality of the buffers being accessed.

```
h.parallel_for(range{N, N}, [=](id<2> idx) {
  int j = idx[0];
  int i = idx[1];
  for (int k = 0; k < N; ++k) {
    c[j][i] +=
        a[j][k] * b[k][i];  // or c[idx] += a[id(j,k)]
                            // * b[id(k,i)];
  }
});
```

Figure 4-7. *Expressing a naïve matrix multiplication kernel for square matrices, with* `parallel_for`

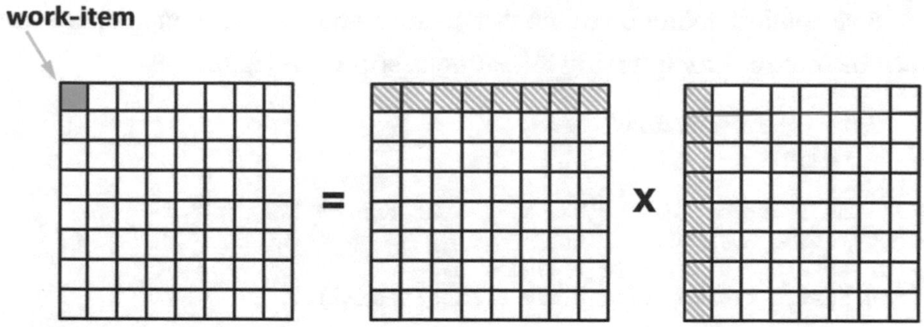

Figure 4-8. *Mapping matrix multiplication work to items in the execution range*

The diagram in Figure 4-8 shows how the work in our matrix multiplication kernel is mapped to individual items. Note that the number of items is derived from the size of the *output* range and that the same input values may be read by multiple items: each item computes a single value of the C matrix, by iterating sequentially over a (contiguous) row of the A matrix and a (noncontiguous) column of the B matrix.

Details of Basic Data-Parallel Kernels

The functionality of basic data-parallel kernels is exposed via three C++ classes: `range`, `id`, and `item`. We have already seen the `range` and `id` classes a few times in previous chapters, but we revisit them here with a different focus.

The `range` Class

A `range` represents a one-, two-, or three-dimensional range. The dimensionality of a `range` is a template argument and must therefore be known at compile time, but its size in each dimension is dynamic and is passed to the constructor at runtime. Instances of the `range` class are used to describe both the execution ranges of parallel constructs and the sizes of buffers.

A simplified definition of the range class, showing the constructors and various methods for querying its extent, is shown in Figure 4-9.

```
template <int Dimensions = 1>
class range {
 public:
  // Construct a range with one, two or three dimensions
  range(size_t dim0);
  range(size_t dim0, size_t dim1);
  range(size_t dim0, size_t dim1, size_t dim2);

  // Return the size of the range in a specific dimension
  size_t get(int dimension) const;
  size_t &operator[](int dimension);
  size_t operator[](int dimension) const;

  // Return the product of the size of each dimension
  size_t size() const;

  // Arithmetic operations on ranges are also supported
};
```

Figure 4-9. *Simplified definition of the `range` class*

The `id` Class

An `id` represents an index into a one-, two-, or three-dimensional range. The definition of `id` is similar in many respects to `range`: its dimensionality must also be known at compile time, and it may be used to index an individual instance of a kernel in a parallel construct or an offset into a buffer.

As shown by the simplified definition of the `id` class in Figure 4-10, an `id` is conceptually nothing more than a container of one, two, or three integers. The operations available to us are also very simple: we can query the component of an index in each dimension, and we can perform simple arithmetic to compute new indices.

Although we can construct an `id` to represent an arbitrary index, to obtain the `id` associated with a specific kernel instance, we must accept it (or an `item` containing it) as an argument to a kernel function. This `id` (or values returned by its member functions) must be forwarded to any function in which we want to query the index—there are not currently any free functions for querying the index at arbitrary points in a program, but this may be simplified in a future version of SYCL.

Each instance of a kernel accepting an `id` knows only the index in the range that it has been assigned to compute and knows nothing about the range itself. If we want our kernel instances to know about their own index *and* the range, we need to use the `item` class instead.

```
template <int Dimensions = 1>
class id {
 public:
  // Construct an id with one, two or three dimensions
  id(size_t dim0);
  id(size_t dim0, size_t dim1);
  id(size_t dim0, size_t dim1, size_t dim2);

  // Return the component of the id in a specific dimension
  size_t get(int dimension) const;
  size_t &operator[](int dimension);
  size_t operator[](int dimension) const;

  // Arithmetic operations on ids are also supported
};
```

Figure 4-10. *Simplified definition of the `id` class*

The `item` Class

An `item` represents an individual instance of a kernel function, encapsulating both the execution range of the kernel and the instance's index within that range (using a `range` and an `id`, respectively). Like `range` and `id`, its dimensionality must be known at compile time.

A simplified definition of the `item` class is given in Figure 4-11. The main difference between `item` and `id` is that `item` exposes additional functions to query properties of the execution range (e.g., its size) and a convenience function to compute a linearized index. As with `id`, the only way to obtain the `item` associated with a specific kernel instance is to accept it as an argument to a kernel function.

```
template <int Dimensions = 1, bool WithOffset = true>
class item {
 public:
  // Return the index of this item in the kernel's execution
  // range
  id<Dimensions> get_id() const;
  size_t get_id(int dimension) const;
  size_t operator[](int dimension) const;

  // Return the execution range of the kernel executed by
  // this item
  range<Dimensions> get_range() const;
  size_t get_range(int dimension) const;

  // Return the offset of this item (if WithOffset == true)
  id<Dimensions> get_offset() const;

  // Return the linear index of this item
  // e.g. id(0) * range(1) * range(2) + id(1) * range(2) +
  // id(2)
  size_t get_linear_id() const;
};
```

Figure 4-11. *Simplified definition of the* `item` *class*

Explicit ND-Range Kernels

The second form of parallel kernel replaces the flat execution range of basic data-parallel kernels with an execution range where items belong to groups. This form is most appropriate for cases where we would like to express some notion of locality within our kernels. Different behaviors are defined and guaranteed for different types of groups, giving us more insight into and/or control over how work is mapped to specific hardware platforms.

These explicit ND-range kernels are thus an example of a more *prescriptive* parallel construct—we *prescribe* a mapping of work to each type of group, and the implementation must obey that mapping. However, it is not completely prescriptive, as the groups themselves may execute in any order and an implementation retains some freedom over how each type of group is mapped to hardware resources. This combination of prescriptive and descriptive programming enables us to design and tune our kernels for locality without destroying their portability.

Like basic data-parallel kernels, ND-range kernels are written in a SPMD style where all work-items execute the same kernel "program" applied to multiple pieces of data. The key difference is that each program instance can query its position within the groups that contain it and can access additional functionality specific to each type of group (see Chapter 9).

Understanding Explicit ND-Range Parallel Kernels

The execution range of an ND-range kernel is divided into work-groups, sub-groups, and work-items. The ND-range represents the total execution range, which is divided into work-groups of uniform size (i.e., the work-group size must divide the ND-range size exactly in each dimension). Each work-group can be further divided by the implementation into sub-groups. Understanding the execution model defined for work-items and each type of group is an important part of writing correct and portable programs.

Figure 4-12 shows an example of an ND-range of size (8, 8, 8) divided into 8 work-groups of size (4, 4, 4). Each work-group contains 16 one-dimensional sub-groups of 4 work-items. Pay careful attention to the numbering of the dimensions: sub-groups are always one-dimensional, and so dimension 2 of the ND-range and work-group becomes dimension 0 of the sub-group.

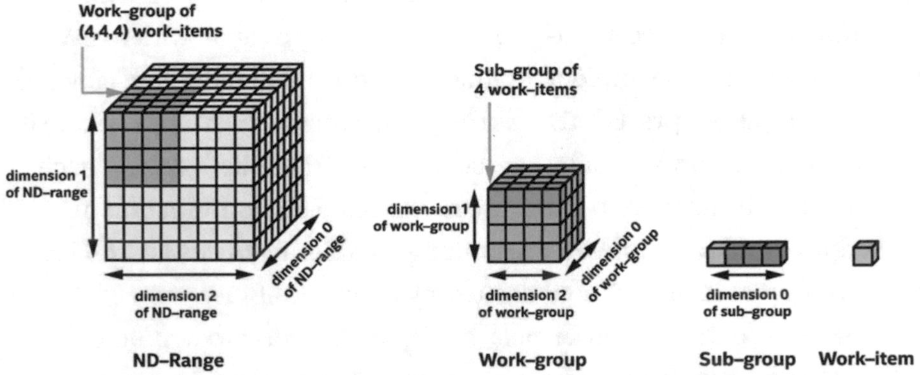

Figure 4-12. *Three-dimensional ND-range divided into work-groups, sub-groups, and work-items*

The exact mapping from each type of group to hardware resources is *implementation-defined*, and it is this flexibility that enables programs to execute on a wide variety of hardware. For example, work-items could be executed completely sequentially, executed in parallel by hardware threads and/or SIMD instructions, or even executed by a hardware pipeline specifically configured for a kernel.

In this chapter, we are focused only on the semantic guarantees of the ND-range execution model in terms of a generic target platform, and we will not cover its mapping to any one platform. See Chapters 15, 16, and 17 for details of the hardware mapping and performance recommendations for GPUs, CPUs, and FPGAs, respectively.

Work-Items

Work-items represent the individual instances of a kernel function. In the absence of other groupings, work-items can be executed in any order and cannot communicate or synchronize with each other except by way of atomic memory operations to global memory (see Chapter 19).

Work-Groups

The work-items in an ND-range are organized into work-groups. Work-groups can execute in any order, and work-items in different work-groups cannot communicate with each other except by way of atomic memory operations to global memory (see Chapter 19). However, the work-items within a work-group have some scheduling guarantees when certain constructs are used, and this locality provides some additional capabilities:

1. Work-items in a work-group have access to *work-group local memory*, which may be mapped to a dedicated fast memory on some devices (see Chapter 9).

2. Work-items in a work-group can synchronize using *work-group barriers* and guarantee memory consistency using *work-group memory fences* (see Chapter 9).

3. Work-items in a work-group have access to *group functions*, providing implementations of common communication routines (see Chapter 9) and *group algorithms*, providing implementations of common parallel patterns such as reductions and scans (see Chapter 14).

The number of work-items in a work-group is typically configured for each kernel at runtime, as the best grouping will depend upon both the amount of parallelism available (i.e., the size of the ND-range) and properties of the target device. We can determine the maximum number of work-items per work-group supported by a specific device using the query functions of the `device` class (see Chapter 12), and it is our responsibility to ensure that the work-group size requested for each kernel is valid.

There are some subtleties in the work-group execution model that are worth emphasizing.

First, although the work-items in a work-group are scheduled to a single compute unit, there need not be any relationship between the number of work-groups and the number of compute units. In fact, the number of work-groups in an ND-range can be many times larger than the number of work-groups that a given device can execute simultaneously! We may be tempted to try and write kernels that synchronize across work-groups by relying on very clever device-specific scheduling, but we strongly recommend against doing this—such kernels may appear to work today, but they are not guaranteed to work with future implementations and are highly likely to break when moved to a different device.

Second, although the work-items in a work-group are scheduled such that they can cooperate with one another, they are not required to provide any specific *forward progress guarantees*—executing the work-items within a work-group sequentially between barriers and collectives is a valid implementation. Communication and synchronization between work-items in the same work-group is only guaranteed to be safe when performed using the barrier and collective functions provided, and hand-coded synchronization routines may deadlock.

THINKING IN WORK-GROUPS

Work-groups are similar in many respects to the concept of a task in other programming models (e.g., Threading Building Blocks): tasks can execute in any order (controlled by a scheduler); it's possible (and even desirable) to oversubscribe a machine with tasks; and it's often not a good idea to try and implement a barrier across a group of tasks (as it may be very expensive or incompatible with the scheduler). If we're already familiar with a task-based programming model, we may find it useful to think of work-groups as though they are data-parallel tasks.

Sub-Groups

On many modern hardware platforms, subsets of the work-items in a work-group known as *sub-groups* are executed with additional scheduling guarantees. For example, the work-items in a sub-group could be executed simultaneously as a result of compiler vectorization, and/or the sub-groups themselves could be executed with strong forward progress guarantees because they are mapped to independent hardware threads.

When working with a single platform, it is tempting to bake assumptions about these execution models into our codes, but this makes them inherently unsafe and non-portable—they may break when moving between different compilers or even when moving between different generations of hardware from the same vendor!

Defining sub-groups as a core part of the language gives us a safe alternative to making assumptions that may later prove to be device-specific. Leveraging sub-group functionality also allows us to reason about the execution of work-items at a low level (i.e., close to hardware) and is key to achieving very high levels of performance across many platforms.

As with work-groups, the work-items within a sub-group can synchronize, guarantee memory consistency, or execute common parallel patterns via group functions and group algorithms. However, there is no equivalent of work-group local memory for sub-groups (i.e., there is no sub-group local memory). Instead, the work-items in a sub-group can exchange data directly—without explicit memory operations—using a subset of the group algorithms colloquially known as "*shuffle*" operations (Chapter 9).

WHY "SHUFFLE"?

The "shuffle" operations in languages like OpenCL, CUDA, and SPIR-V all include "shuffle" in their name (e.g., `sub_group_shuffle`, `__shfl`, and `OpGroupNonUniformShuffle`). SYCL adopts a different naming convention to avoid confusion with the `std::shuffle` function defined in C++ (which randomly reorders the contents of a range).

Some aspects of sub-groups are implementation-defined and outside of our control. However, a sub-group has a fixed (one-dimensional) size for a given combination of device, kernel, and ND-range, and we can query this size using the query functions of the `kernel` class (see Chapters 10 and 12). By default, the number of work-items per sub-group is also chosen by the implementation—we can override this behavior by requesting a particular sub-group size at compile time but must ensure that the sub-group size we request is compatible with the device.

Like work-groups, the work-items in a sub-group are not required to provide any specific forward progress guarantees—an implementation is free to execute each work-item in a sub-group sequentially and only switch between work-items when a sub-group collective function is encountered. However, on some devices, all sub-groups within a work-group are guaranteed to execute (make progress) eventually, which is a cornerstone of several producer–consumer patterns. This is currently implementation-defined behavior, and so we cannot rely on sub-groups to make progress if we want our kernels to remain portable. We expect a future version of SYCL to provide device queries describing the progress guarantees of sub-groups.

When writing kernels for a specific device, the mapping of work-items to sub-groups is known, and our codes can often take advantage of properties of this mapping to improve performance. However, a common mistake is to assume that because our code works on one device, it will work on all devices. Figures 4-13 and 4-14 show just two of the possibilities when mapping work-items in a multidimensional kernel with a range of {4, 4} to sub-groups, for a maximum sub-group size of 8. The mapping in Figure 4-13 produces two sub-groups of eight work-items, while the mapping in Figure 4-14 produces four sub-groups of four work-items!

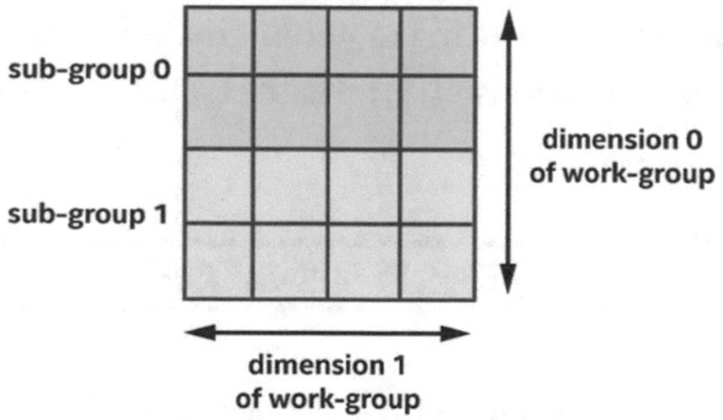

Figure 4-13. *One possible sub-group mapping, where the sub-group size is permitted to be larger than the extent of the highest-numbered (contiguous) dimension of the work-group, and so the sub-group appears to "wrap around"*

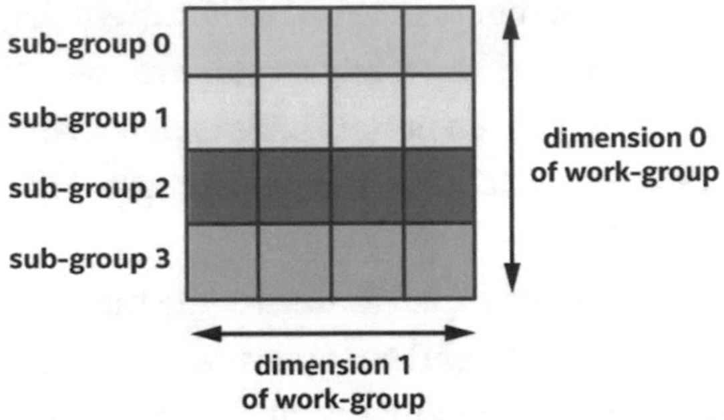

Figure 4-14. *Another possible sub-group mapping, where the sub-group size is not permitted to be larger than the extent of the highest-numbered (contiguous) dimension of the work-group*

SYCL does not currently provide a way to query how work-items are mapped to sub-groups nor a mechanism to request a specific mapping. The best ways to write portable code using sub-groups are using one-dimensional work-groups or using multidimensional work-groups where the highest-numbered dimension is divisible by the kernel's required sub-group size.

THINKING IN SUB-GROUPS

If we are coming from a programming model that requires us to think about explicit vectorization, it may be useful to think of each sub-group as a set of work-items packed into a SIMD register, where each work-item in the sub-group corresponds to a SIMD lane. When multiple sub-groups are in flight simultaneously and a device guarantees they will make forward progress, this mental model extends to treating each sub-group as though it were a separate stream of vector instructions executing in parallel.

Writing Explicit ND-Range Data-Parallel Kernels

```
range global{N, N};
range local{B, B};
h.parallel_for(nd_range{global, local},
               [=](nd_item<2> it) {
                 int j = it.get_global_id(0);
                 int i = it.get_global_id(1);

                 for (int k = 0; k < N; ++k) {
                   c[j][i] += a[j][k] * b[k][i];
                 }
               });
```

***Figure 4-15.** Expressing a naïve matrix multiplication kernel with ND-range `parallel_for`*

Figure 4-15 reimplements the matrix multiplication kernel that we saw previously using the ND-range parallel kernel syntax, and the diagram in Figure 4-16 shows how the work in this kernel is mapped to the work-items in each work-group. Grouping our work-items in this way ensures locality of access and hopefully improves cache hit rates: for example, the work-group in Figure 4-16 has a local range of (4, 4) and contains 16 work-items, but only accesses four times as much data as a single work-item—in other words, each value we load from memory can be reused four times.

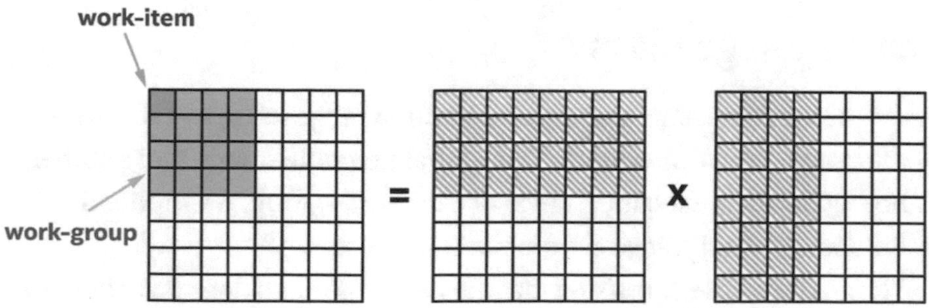

***Figure 4-16.** Mapping matrix multiplication to work-groups and work-items*

So far, our matrix multiplication example has relied on a hardware cache to optimize repeated accesses to the A and B matrices from work-items in the same work-group. Such hardware caches are commonplace on traditional CPU architectures and are becoming increasingly common on GPU architectures, but several architectures have explicitly managed "scratchpad" memories that can deliver higher performance (e.g., via lower latency). ND-range kernels can use local accessors to describe allocations that should be placed in work-group local memory, and an implementation is then free to map these allocations to special memory (where it exists). Usage of this work-group local memory will be covered in Chapter 9.

Details of Explicit ND-Range Data-Parallel Kernels

ND-range data-parallel kernels use different classes compared to basic data-parallel kernels: `range` is replaced by `nd_range`, and `item` is replaced by `nd_item`. There are also two new classes, representing the different types of groups to which a work-item may belong: functionality tied to work-groups is encapsulated in the `group` class, and functionality tied to sub-groups is encapsulated in the `sub_group` class.

The `nd_range` Class

An `nd_range` represents a grouped execution range using two instances of the `range` class: one denoting the global execution range and another denoting the local execution range of each work-group. A simplified definition of the `nd_range` class is given in Figure 4-17.

It may be a little surprising that the `nd_range` class does not mention sub-groups at all: the sub-group range is not specified during construction and cannot be queried. There are two reasons for this omission. First, sub-groups are a low-level implementation detail that can be ignored for many kernels. Second, there are several devices supporting exactly one valid sub-group size and specifying this size everywhere would be unnecessarily verbose. All functionality related to sub-groups is encapsulated in a dedicated class that will be discussed shortly.

```
template <int Dimensions = 1>
class nd_range {
 public:
  // Construct an nd_range from global and work-group local
  // ranges
  nd_range(range<Dimensions> global,
           range<Dimensions> local);

  // Return the global and work-group local ranges
  range<Dimensions> get_global_range() const;
  range<Dimensions> get_local_range() const;

  // Return the number of work-groups in the global range
  range<Dimensions> get_group_range() const;
};
```

Figure 4-17. *Simplified definition of the nd_range class*

The nd_item Class

An nd_item is the ND-range form of an item, again encapsulating the execution range of the kernel and the item's index within that range. Where nd_item differs from item is in how its position in the range is queried and represented, as shown by the simplified class definition in Figure 4-18. For example, we can query the item's index in the (global) ND-range using the get_global_id() function or the item's index in its (local) parent work-group using the get_local_id() function.

The nd_item class also provides functions for obtaining handles to classes describing the group and sub-group that an item belongs to. These classes provide an alternative interface for querying an item's index in an ND-range.

```
template <int Dimensions = 1>
class nd_item {
 public:
  // Return the index of this item in the kernel's execution
  // range
  id<Dimensions> get_global_id() const;
  size_t get_global_id(int dimension) const;
  size_t get_global_linear_id() const;

  // Return the execution range of the kernel executed by
  // this item
  range<Dimensions> get_global_range() const;
  size_t get_global_range(int dimension) const;

  // Return the index of this item within its parent
  // work-group
  id<Dimensions> get_local_id() const;
  size_t get_local_id(int dimension) const;
  size_t get_local_linear_id() const;

  // Return the execution range of this item's parent
  // work-group
  range<Dimensions> get_local_range() const;
  size_t get_local_range(int dimension) const;

  // Return a handle to the work-group
  // or sub-group containing this item
  group<Dimensions> get_group() const;
  sub_group get_sub_group() const;
};
```

Figure 4-18. *Simplified definition of the `nd_item` class*

The `group` Class

The `group` class encapsulates all functionality related to work-groups, and a simplified definition is shown in Figure 4-19.

```
template <int Dimensions = 1>
class group {
 public:
  // Return the index of this group in the kernel's
  // execution range
  id<Dimensions> get_id() const;
  size_t get_id(int dimension) const;
  size_t get_linear_id() const;

  // Return the number of groups in the kernel's execution
  // range
  range<Dimensions> get_group_range() const;
  size_t get_group_range(int dimension) const;

  // Return the number of work-items in this group
  range<Dimensions> get_local_range() const;
  size_t get_local_range(int dimension) const;
};
```

Figure 4-19. *Simplified definition of the group class*

Many of the functions that the group class provides each have equivalent functions in the nd_item class: for example, calling group.get_group_id() is equivalent to calling item.get_group_id(), and calling group.get_local_range() is equivalent to calling item.get_local_range(). If we are not using any group functions or algorithms, should we still use the group class? Wouldn't it be simpler to use the functions in nd_item directly, instead of creating an intermediate group object? There is a trade-off here: using group requires us to write slightly more code, but that code may be easier to read. For example, consider the code snippet in Figure 4-20: it is clear that body expects to be called by all work-items in the group, and it is clear that the range returned by get_local_range() in the body of the parallel_for is the range of the group. The same code could very easily be written using only nd_item, but it would likely be harder for readers to follow.

```
void body(group& g);

h.parallel_for(nd_range{global, local}, [=](nd_item<1> it) {
  group<1> g = it.get_group();
  range<1> r = g.get_local_range();
  ...
  body(g);
});
```

Figure 4-20. *Using the group class to improve readability*

Another powerful option enabled by the `group` class is the ability to write generic group functions that accept any type of group via a template argument. Although SYCL does not (yet) define an official Group "concept" (in the C++20 sense), the `group` and `sub_group` classes expose a common interface, allowing templated SYCL functions to be constrained using traits like `sycl::is_group_v`. Today, the primary advantages of this generic form of coding are the ability to support work-groups with an arbitrary number of dimensions, and the ability to allow the caller of a function to decide whether the function should divide work across the work-items in a work-group or the work-items in a sub-group. However, the SYCL group interface has been designed to be extensible, and we expect a larger number of classes representing different groupings of work-items to appear in future versions of SYCL.

The `sub_group` Class

The `sub_group` class encapsulates all functionality related to sub-groups, and a simplified definition is shown in Figure 4-21. Unlike with work-groups, the `sub_group` class is the only way to access sub-group functionality; none of its functions are duplicated in `nd_item`.

```
class sub_group {
 public:
  // Return the index of the sub-group
  id<1> get_group_id() const;

  // Return the number of sub-groups in this item's parent
  // work-group
  range<1> get_group_range() const;

  // Return the index of the work-item in this sub-group
  id<1> get_local_id() const;

  // Return the number of work-items in this sub-group
  range<1> get_local_range() const;

  // Return the maximum number of work-items in any
  // sub-group in this item's parent work-group
  range<1> get_max_local_range() const;
};
```

Figure 4-21. *Simplified definition of the* `sub_group` *class*

Note that there are separate functions for querying the number of work-items in the current sub-group and the maximum number of work-items in any sub-group within the work-group. Whether and how these differ depends on exactly how sub-groups are implemented for a specific device, but the intent is to reflect any differences between the sub-group size targeted by the compiler and the runtime sub-group size. For example, very small work-groups may contain fewer work-items than the compile-time sub-group size, or sub-groups of different sizes may be used to handle work-groups and dimensions that are not divisible by the sub-group size.

Mapping Computation to Work-Items

Most of the code examples so far have assumed that each instance of a kernel function corresponds to a single operation on a single piece of data. This is a straightforward way to write kernels, but such a one-to-one mapping is not dictated by SYCL or any of the kernel forms—we always have complete control over the assignment of data (and computation) to individual work-items and making this assignment parameterizable can be a good way to improve performance portability.

One-to-One Mapping

When we write kernels such that there is a one-to-one mapping of work to work-items, those kernels must always be launched with a `range` or `nd_range` with a size exactly matching the amount of work that needs to be done. This is the most obvious way to write kernels, and in many cases, it works very well—we can trust an implementation to map work-items to hardware efficiently.

However, when tuning for performance on a specific combination of system and implementation, it may be necessary to pay closer attention to low-level scheduling behaviors. The scheduling of work-groups to compute resources is implementation-defined and could potentially be *dynamic* (i.e., when a compute resource completes one work-group, the next work-group it executes may come from a shared queue). The impact of dynamic scheduling on performance is not fixed, and its significance depends upon factors including the execution time of each instance of the kernel function and whether the scheduling is implemented in software (e.g., on a CPU) or hardware (e.g., on a GPU).

Many-to-One Mapping

The alternative is to write kernels with a many-to-one mapping of work to work-items. The *meaning* of the range changes subtly in this case: the range no longer describes the amount of work to be done, but rather the number of workers to use. By changing the number of workers and the amount of work assigned to each worker, we can fine-tune work distribution to maximize performance.

Writing a kernel of this form requires two changes:

1. The kernel must accept a parameter describing the total amount of work.
2. The kernel must contain a loop assigning work to work-items.

A simple example of such a kernel is given in Figure 4-22. Note that the loop inside the kernel has a slightly unusual form—the starting index is the work-item's index in the global range, and the stride is the total number of work-items. This *round-robin* scheduling of data to work-items ensures that all N iterations of the loop will be executed by a work-item, but also that linear work-items access contiguous memory locations (to improve cache locality and vectorization behavior). Work can be similarly distributed across groups or the work-items in individual groups to further improve locality.

```
size_t N = ...;  // amount of work
size_t W = ...;  // number of workers
h.parallel_for(range{W}, [=](item<1> it) {
  for (int i = it.get_id()[0]; i < N;
       i += it.get_range()[0]) {
    output[i] = function(input[i]);
  }
});
```

Figure 4-22. *Kernel with separate data and execution ranges*

These work distribution patterns are common, and we expect that future versions of SYCL will introduce syntactic sugar to simplify the expression of work distribution in ND-range kernels.

Choosing a Kernel Form

Choosing between the different kernel forms is largely a matter of personal preference and heavily influenced by prior experience with other parallel programming models and languages.

The other main reason to choose a specific kernel form is that it is the only form to expose certain functionality required by a kernel. Unfortunately, it can be difficult to identify which functionality will be required before development begins—especially while we are still unfamiliar with the different kernel forms and their interaction with various classes.

We have constructed two guides based on our own experience to help us navigate this complex space. These guides should be considered initial suggestions and are definitely not intended to replace our own experimentation—the best way to choose between the different kernel forms will always be to spend some time writing in each of them, in order to learn which form is the best fit for our application and development style.

The first guide is the flowchart in Figure 4-23, which selects a kernel form based on

1. Whether we have previous experience with parallel programming

2. Whether we are writing a new code from scratch or are porting an existing parallel program written in a different language

3. Whether our kernel is embarrassingly parallel or reuses data between different instances of the kernel function

4. Whether we are writing a new kernel in SYCL to maximize performance, to improve the portability of our code, or because it provides a more productive means of expressing parallelism than lower-level languages

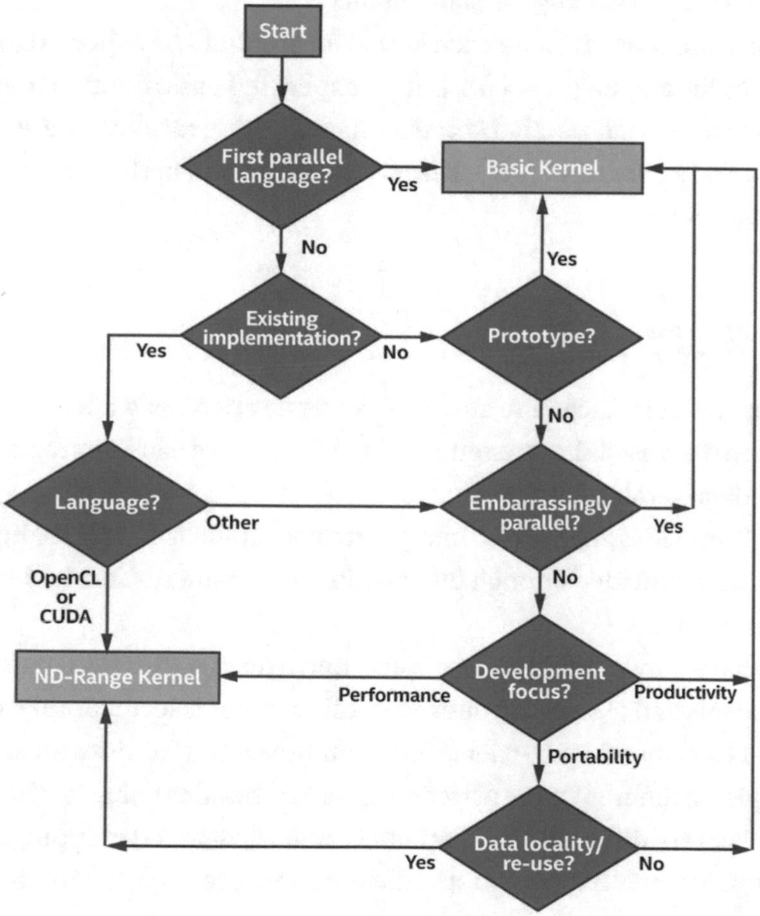

Figure 4-23. *Helping choose the right form for our kernel*

The second guide is the set of features exposed to each of the kernel forms. Work-groups, sub-groups, group barriers, group-local memory, group functions (e.g., broadcast), and group algorithms (e.g., scan, reduce) are only available to ND-range kernels, and so we should prefer ND-range kernels in situations where we are interested in expressing complex algorithms or fine-tuning for performance.

The features available to each kernel form should be expected to change as the language evolves, but we expect the basic trend to remain the same: basic data-parallel kernels will not expose locality-aware features and explicit ND-range kernels will expose all performance-enabling features.

Summary

This chapter introduced the basics of expressing parallelism in C++ with SYCL and discussed the strengths and weaknesses of each approach to writing data-parallel kernels.

SYCL provides support for many forms of parallelism, and we hope that we have provided enough information to prepare readers to dive in and start coding!

We have only scratched the surface, and a deeper dive into many of the concepts and classes introduced in this chapter is forthcoming: the usage of local memory, barriers, and communication routines are covered in Chapter 9; different ways of defining kernels besides using lambda expressions are discussed in Chapters 10 and 20; detailed mappings of the ND-range execution model to specific hardware are explored in Chapters 15, 16, and 17; and best practices for expressing common parallel patterns using SYCL are presented in Chapter 14.

CHAPTER 5

Error Handling

Error handling is a key capability of C++. This chapter discusses the unique error handling challenges when offloading work to a device (accelerator) and how these challenges are made fully manageable to us by SYCL.

Detecting and dealing with unexpected conditions and errors can be helpful during application development (think: the *other* programmer who works on the project who *does* make mistakes), but more importantly play a critical role in stable and safe production applications and libraries. We devote this chapter to describing the error handling mechanisms available in C++ with SYCL so that we can understand what our options are and how to architect applications if we care about detecting and managing errors.

This chapter overviews synchronous and asynchronous errors in SYCL, describes the behavior of an application if we do nothing in our code to handle errors, and dives into the SYCL-specific mechanisms that allow us to handle asynchronous errors.

Safety First

A core aspect of C++ error handling is that if we do nothing to handle an error that has been detected (thrown), then the application will terminate and indicate that something went wrong. This behavior allows us to write applications without focusing on error management and still be confident that errors will somehow be signaled to a developer or user. We're not suggesting that we should ignore error handling, of course! Production applications should be written with error management as a core part of

J. Reinders et al., *Data Parallel C++*, https://doi.org/10.1007/978-1-4842-9691-2_5

the architecture, but applications often start development without such a focus. C++ aims to make code which doesn't handle errors still able to observe many errors, even when they are not dealt with explicitly.

Since SYCL is data parallel C++, the same philosophy holds: if we do nothing in our code to manage errors and an error is detected, an abnormal termination of the program will occur to let us know that something bad happened. Production applications should of course consider error management as a core part of the software architecture, not only reporting but often also recovering from error conditions.

If we don't add any error management code and an error occurs, we will still see an abnormal program termination which is an indication to dig deeper.

Types of Errors

C++ provides a framework for notification and handling of errors through its exception mechanism. Heterogeneous programming requires an additional level of error management beyond this because some errors occur on a device or when trying to launch work on a device. These errors are typically decoupled in time from the host program's execution, and as such they don't integrate cleanly with regular C++ exception handling mechanisms. To solve this, there are additional mechanisms to make asynchronous errors as manageable and controllable as typical C++ exceptions.

Figure 5-1 shows two components of a typical application: (1) the host code that runs sequentially and submits work to the task graph for future execution and (2) the task graph which runs asynchronously from the host program and executes kernels or other actions on devices when the necessary dependences are met. The example shows a `parallel_for` as the operation that executes asynchronously as part of the task graph, but other operations are possible as well as discussed in Chapters 3, 4, and 8.

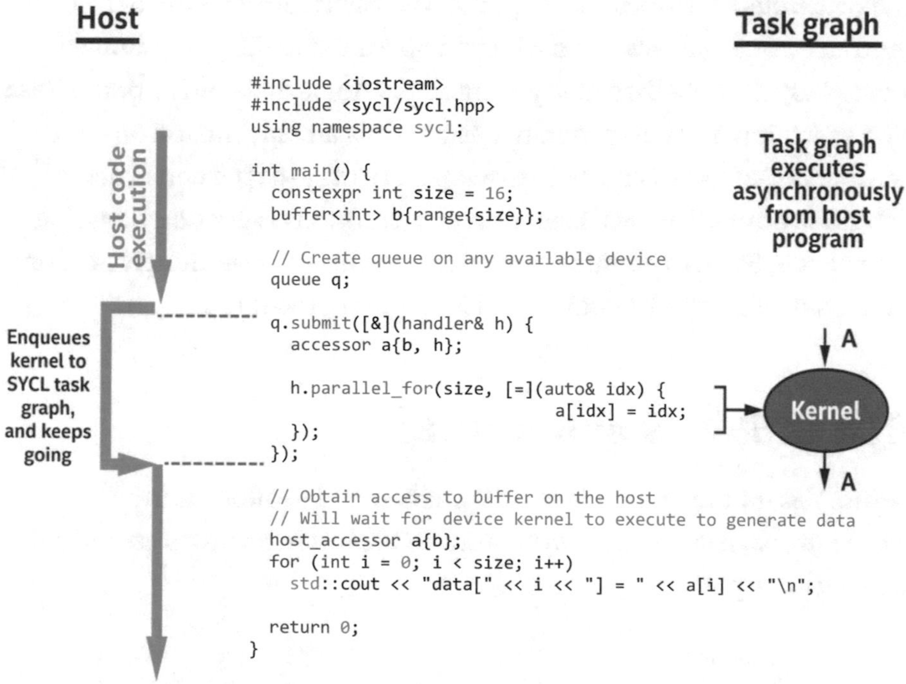

Figure 5-1. *Separation of host program and task graph executions*

The distinction between the left and right (host and task graph) sides of Figure 5-1 is the key to understanding the differences between *synchronous* and *asynchronous* errors.

Synchronous errors occur when an error condition can be detected as the host program executes an operation, such as an API call or object construction. They can be detected before an instruction on the left side of the figure completes, and the error can be thrown immediately by the operation that caused the error. We can wrap specific instructions on the left side of the diagram with a `try-catch` construct, expecting that errors occurring as a result of operations within the `try` will be detected before the try block ends (and therefore caught). The C++ exception mechanism is designed to handle exactly these types of errors.

Asynchronous errors occur as part of the right side of Figure 5-1, where an error is only detected when an operation in the task graph is executed. By the time that an asynchronous error is detected as part of task graph execution, the host program has typically already moved on with its execution, so there is no code to wrap with a `try-catch` construct to catch these errors. There is instead an asynchronous exception handling framework in SYCL to handle these errors that occur at seemingly random and uncontrolled times relative to host program execution.

Let's Create Some Errors!

As examples for the remainder of this chapter and to allow us to experiment, we'll create both synchronous and asynchronous errors in the following examples.

```
#include <sycl/sycl.hpp>
using namespace sycl;

int main() {
  buffer<int> b{range{16}};

  // ERROR: Create sub-buffer larger than size of parent
  // buffer. An exception is thrown from within the buffer
  // constructor.
  buffer<int> b2(b, id{8}, range{16});

  return 0;
}

Example Output:
terminate called after throwing an instance of 'sycl::_V1::invalid_object_error'
  what():  Requested sub-buffer size exceeds the size of the parent buffer -30
(PI_ERROR_INVALID_VALUE)
Aborted
```

Figure 5-2. *Creating a synchronous error*

Synchronous Error

In Figure 5-2, a sub-buffer is created from a buffer but with an illegal size (larger than the original buffer). The constructor of the sub-buffer detects this error and throws an exception before the constructor's execution completes. This is a synchronous error because it occurs as part of (synchronously with) the host program's execution. The error is detectable *before the constructor returns*, so the error may be handled immediately at its point of origin or detection in the host program.

Our code example doesn't do anything to catch and handle C++ exceptions, so the default C++ uncaught exception handler calls `std::terminate` for us, signaling that something went wrong.

Asynchronous Error

Generating an asynchronous error is a bit trickier because implementations work hard to detect and report errors synchronously whenever possible. Synchronous errors are easier to debug because they occur at a specific point of origin in the host program, so are preferred by implementations whenever possible. One way to generate an asynchronous error for our demonstration purpose is to throw an exception inside a host task, which executes asynchronously as part of the task graph. Figure 5-3 demonstrates such an exception. Asynchronous errors can occur and be reported in many situations, so note that this host task example shown in Figure 5-3 is only one possibility and in no way a requirement for asynchronous errors.

```
#include <sycl/sycl.hpp>
using namespace sycl;

// Our example asynchronous handler function
auto handle_async_error = [](exception_list elist) {
  for (auto &e : elist) {
    try {
      std::rethrow_exception(e);
    } catch (...) {
      std::cout << "Caught SYCL ASYNC exception!!\n";
    }
  }
};

void say_device(const queue &Q) {
  std::cout << "Device : "
            << Q.get_device().get_info<info::device::name>()
            << "\n";
}

class something_went_wrong {};  // Example exception type

int main() {
  queue q{cpu_selector_v, handle_async_error};
  say_device(q);

  q.submit([&](handler &h) {
     h.host_task([]() { throw(something_went_wrong{}); });
   }).wait();

  return 0;
}
```

```
Example output:
Device : Intel(R) Xeon(R) Gold 6128 CPU @ 3.40GHz
Caught SYCL ASYNC exception!!
```

Figure 5-3. *Creating an asynchronous error*

Application Error Handling Strategy

The C++ *exception* features are designed to cleanly separate the point in a program where an error is detected from the point where it may be handled, and this concept fits very well with both synchronous and asynchronous errors in SYCL. Through the `throw` and `catch` mechanisms, a hierarchy of handlers can be defined which can be important in production applications.

Building an application that can handle errors in a consistent and reliable way requires a strategy up front and a resulting software architecture built for error management. C++ provides flexible tools to implement many alternative strategies, but such architecture is beyond the scope of this chapter. There are many books and other references devoted to this topic, so we encourage looking to them for full coverage of C++ error management strategies.

This said, error detection and reporting doesn't always need to be production-scale. Errors in a program can be reliably detected and reported through minimal code if the goal is simply to detect errors during execution and to report them (but not necessarily to recover from them). The following sections cover first what happens if we ignore error handling and do nothing (the default behavior isn't all that bad!), followed by recommended error reporting that is simple to implement in basic applications.

Ignoring Error Handling

C++ and SYCL are designed to tell us that something went wrong even when we don't handle errors explicitly. The default result of unhandled synchronous or asynchronous errors is abnormal program termination which an operating system should tell us about. The following two examples mimic the behavior that will occur if we do not handle a synchronous and an asynchronous error, respectively.

Figure 5-4 shows the result of an unhandled C++ exception, which could be an unhandled SYCL synchronous error, for example. We can use this code to test what a particular operating system will report in such a case.

```
#include <iostream>

class something_went_wrong {};

int main() {
  std::cout << "Hello\n";

  throw(something_went_wrong{});
}

Example output:
Hello
terminate called after throwing an instance of 'something_went_wrong'
Aborted
```

Figure 5-4. *Unhandled exception in C++*

Figure 5-5 shows example output from `std::terminate` being called, which will be the result of an unhandled SYCL asynchronous error in our application. We can use this code to test what a particular operating system will report in such a case.

```
#include <iostream>

int main() {
  std::cout << "Hello\n";

  std::terminate();
}

Example output:
Hello
terminate called without an active exception
Aborted
```

Figure 5-5. *`std::terminate` is called when a SYCL asynchronous exception isn't handled*

Although we should probably handle errors in our programs, uncaught exceptions will eventually be caught and the program terminated, which is better than exceptions being silently lost!

Synchronous Error Handling

We keep this section very short because SYCL synchronous errors are just C++ exceptions. Most of the additional error mechanisms added in SYCL relate to asynchronous errors which we cover in the next section, but synchronous errors are important because implementations try to detect and report as many errors synchronously as possible, since they are easier to reason about and handle.

Synchronous errors defined by SYCL are of type `sycl::exception`, a class derived from `std::exception`, which allows us to catch the SYCL errors specifically though a `try-catch` structure such as what we see in Figure 5-6.

```
try {
  // Do some SYCL work
} catch (sycl::exception &e) {
  // Do something to output or handle the exception
  std::cout << "Caught sync SYCL exception: " << e.what()
            << "\n";
  return 1;
}
```

Figure 5-6. *Pattern to catch `sycl::exception` specifically*

On top of the C++ error handling mechanisms, SYCL adds a `sycl::exception` type for the exceptions thrown by the runtime. Everything else is standard C++ exception handling, so will be familiar to most developers.

A slightly more complete example is provided in Figure 5-7, where additional classes of exception are handled.

```
#include <sycl/sycl.hpp>
using namespace sycl;

int main() {
  try {
    buffer<int> b{range{16}};

    // ERROR: Create sub-buffer larger than size of parent
    // buffer. An exception is thrown from within the buffer
    // constructor.
    buffer<int> b2(b, id{8}, range{16});

  } catch (sycl::exception &e) {
    // Do something to output or handle the exception
    std::cout << "Caught synchronous SYCL exception: "
              << e.what() << "\n";
    return 1;
  } catch (std::exception &e) {
    std::cout << "Caught std exception: " << e.what()
              << "\n";
    return 2;
  } catch (...) {
    std::cout << "Caught unknown exception\n";
    return 3;
  }

  return 0;
}
```

```
Example output:
Caught synchronous SYCL exception: Requested sub-buffer
size exceedsthe size of the parent buffer -30
(PI_ERROR_INVALID_VALUE)
```

Figure 5-7. *Pattern to catch exceptions from a block of code*

Asynchronous Error Handling

Asynchronous errors are detected by the SYCL runtime (or an underlying backend), and the errors occur independently of execution of commands in the host program. The errors are stored in lists internal to the SYCL runtime and only released for processing at specific points that the programmer can control. There are two topics that we need to discuss to cover handling of asynchronous errors:

1. **What** the handler should do, when invoked on outstanding asynchronous errors to process
2. **When** the asynchronous handler is invoked

The Asynchronous Handler

The asynchronous handler is a function that the application defines, which is registered with SYCL contexts and/or queues. At the times defined by the next section, if there are any unprocessed asynchronous exceptions that are available to be handled, then the asynchronous handler is invoked by the SYCL runtime and passed a list of these exceptions.

The asynchronous handler is passed to a context or queue constructor as a `std::function` and can be defined in ways such as a regular function, lambda expression, or function object, depending on our preference. The handler must accept a `sycl::exception_list` argument, such as in the example handler shown in Figure 5-8.

```
// Our simple asynchronous handler function
auto handle_async_error = [](exception_list elist) {
  for (auto& e : elist) {
    try {
      std::rethrow_exception(e);
    } catch (sycl::exception& e) {
      std::cout << "ASYNC EXCEPTION!!\n";
      std::cout << e.what() << "\n";
    }
  }
};
```

Figure 5-8. *Example asynchronous handler implementation defined as a lambda*

In Figure 5-8, the `std::rethrow_exception` followed by catch of a specific exception type provides filtering of the type of exception, in this case to only `sycl::exception`. We can also use alternative filtering approaches in C++ or just choose to handle all exceptions regardless of the type.

The handler is associated with a queue or context (low-level detail covered more in Chapter 6) at construction time. For example, to register the handler defined in Figure 5-8 with a queue that we are creating, we could write

```
queue my_queue{ gpu_selector_v, handle_async_error };
```

Likewise, to register the handler defined in Figure 5-8 with a context that we are creating, we could write

```
context my_context{ handle_async_error };
```

Most applications do not need contexts to be explicitly created or managed (they are created behind the scenes for us automatically), so if an asynchronous handler is going to be used, most developers should associate such handlers with queues that are being constructed for specific devices (and not explicit contexts).

In defining asynchronous handlers, most developers should define them on queues unless already explicitly managing contexts for other reasons.

If an asynchronous handler is not defined for a queue or the queue's parent context and an asynchronous error occurs on that queue (or in the context) that must be processed, then the default asynchronous handler is invoked. The default handler operates as if it was coded as shown in Figure 5-9.

```
// Our simple asynchronous handler function
auto handle_async_error = [](exception_list elist) {
  for (auto& e : elist) {
    try {
      std::rethrow_exception(e);
    } catch (sycl::exception& e) {
      // Print information about the asynchronous exception
    } catch (...) {
      // Print information about non-sycl::exception
    }
  }

  // Terminate abnormally to make clear to user that
  // something unhandled happened
  std::terminate();
};
```

```
Example output:
Device : Intel(R) Xeon(R) Gold 6128 CPU @ 3.40GHz
terminate called without an active exception
Aborted
```

Figure 5-9. *Example of how the default asynchronous handler behaves*

The default handler should display some information to the user on any errors in the exception list and then will end the application through `std::terminate`, which should cause the operating system to report that termination was abnormal.

What we put within an asynchronous handler is up to us. It can range from logging of an error to application termination to recovery of the error condition so that an application can continue executing normally. The common case is to report any details of the error available by calling `sycl::exception::what()`, followed by termination of the application.

Although it's up to us to decide what an asynchronous handler does internally, a common mistake is to print an error message (that may be missed in the noise of other messages from the program), followed by completion of the handler function. Unless we have error management principles in place that allow us to recover a known program state and to be confident that it's safe to continue execution, we should consider terminating the application within our asynchronous handler function(s). This reduces the chance that incorrect results will appear from a program where an error was detected, but where the application was inadvertently allowed to continue with execution regardless. In many programs, abnormal termination is the preferred result once we have detected an asynchronous exception.

Consider terminating applications within an asynchronous handler, after outputting information about the error, if comprehensive error recovery and management mechanisms are not in place.

Invocation of the Handler

The asynchronous handler is called by the runtime at specific times. Errors aren't reported immediately as they occur because management of errors and safe application programming (particularly multithreaded) would become more difficult and expensive (e.g., additional synchronizations between host and device) if that was the case. The asynchronous handler is instead called at the following very specific times:

1. When the host program calls `queue::throw_asynchronous()` on a specific queue
2. When the host program calls `queue::wait_and_throw()` on a specific queue
3. When the host program calls `event::wait_and_throw()` on a specific event
4. When a queue is destroyed
5. When a `context` is destroyed

Methods 1–3 provide a mechanism for a host program to control when asynchronous exceptions are handled, so that thread safety and other details specific to an application can be managed. They effectively provide controlled points at which asynchronous exceptions enter the host program control flow and can be processed almost as if they were synchronous errors.

If a user doesn't explicitly call one of the methods 1–3, then asynchronous errors are commonly reported during program teardown when queues and contexts are destroyed. This is often enough to signal to a user that something went wrong and that program results shouldn't be trusted.

Relying on error detection during program teardown doesn't work in all cases, though. For example, if a program will only terminate when some algorithm convergence criteria are achieved and if those criteria are only achievable by successful execution of device kernels, then an asynchronous exception may signal that the algorithm will never converge and begin the teardown (where the error would be noticed). In these cases, and also in production applications where more complete error handling strategies are in place, it makes sense to invoke `throw_asynchronous()` or `wait_and_throw()` at regular and controlled points in the program (e.g., before checking whether algorithm convergence has occurred).

Errors on a Device

The error detection and handling mechanisms discussed in this chapter have been host-based. They are mechanisms through which the host program can detect and deal with something that may have gone wrong either in the host program or potentially during execution of kernels on devices. What we have not covered is how to signal, from within the device code that we write, that something has gone wrong. This omission is not a mistake, but quite intentional.

SYCL explicitly disallows C++ exception handling mechanisms (such as `throw`) within device code, because there are performance costs for some types of devices that we usually don't want to pay. If we detect that something has gone wrong within our device code, we should signal the error using existing non-exception-based techniques. For example, we could write to a buffer that logs errors or returns some invalid result from our numeric calculation that we define to mean that an error occurred. The right strategy in these cases is very application specific.

Summary

In this chapter, we introduced synchronous and asynchronous errors, covered the default behavior to expect if we do nothing to manage errors that might occur, and covered the mechanisms used to handle asynchronous errors at controlled points in our application. Error management strategies are a major topic in software engineering and a significant percentage of the code written in many applications. SYCL integrates with the C++ knowledge that we already have when it comes to error handling and provides flexible mechanisms to integrate with whatever our preferred error management strategy is.

CHAPTER 6

Unified Shared Memory

The next two chapters provide a deeper look into how to manage data. There are two different approaches that complement each other: Unified Shared Memory (USM) and buffers. USM exposes a different level of abstraction for memory than buffers—USM uses pointers, and buffers are a higher-level interface. This chapter focuses on USM. The next chapter will focus on buffers.

Unless we specifically know that we want to use buffers, USM is a good place to start. USM is a pointer-based model that allows memory to be read and written through regular C++ pointers.

Why Should We Use USM?

Since USM is based on C++ pointers, it is a natural place to start for existing pointer-based C++ codes. Existing functions that take pointers as parameters continue to work without modification. In the majority of cases, the only changes required are to replace existing calls to `malloc` or `new` with USM-specific allocation routines that we will discuss later in this chapter.

J. Reinders et al., *Data Parallel C++*, https://doi.org/10.1007/978-1-4842-9691-2_6

Allocation Types

While USM is based on C++ pointers, not all pointers are created equal. USM defines three different types of allocations, each with unique semantics. A device may not support all types (or even *any* type) of USM allocation. We will learn how to query what a device supports later. The three types of allocations and their characteristics are summarized in Figure 6-1.

Type	Description	Accessible on host?	Accessible on device?	Located on
device	Allocations in device memory	×	✓	device
host	Allocations in host memory	✓	✓	host
shared	Allocations shared between host and device	✓	✓	Can migrate between host and device

Figure 6-1. *USM allocation types*

Device Allocations

This first type of allocation is what we need in order to have a pointer into a device's attached memory, such as (G)DDR or HBM. Device allocations can be read from or written to by kernels running on a specific device, but they cannot be directly accessed from code executing on the host (and usually not by devices either). Trying to access a device allocation on the host can result in either incorrect data or a program crashing due to an error. We must copy data between host and device using the explicit USM `memcpy` mechanisms, which specify how much data must be copied between two places, that will be covered later in this chapter.

Host Allocations

This second type of allocation is easier to use than device allocations since we do not have to manually copy data between the host and the device. Host allocations are allocations in host memory that are accessible on both the host and the device. These allocations, while accessible on the device, cannot migrate to the device's attached memory. Instead, kernels may *remotely* read from or write to this memory, often over a slower bus such as PCI Express (or really not differently at all if it's a CPU device or integrated GPU device). This trade-off between convenience and performance is something that we must take into consideration. Despite the higher access costs that host allocations can incur, there are still valid reasons to use them. Examples include rarely accessed data, large data sets that cannot fit inside device-attached memory, or that a device may not support alternatives like shared allocations which are described next.

Shared Allocations

The final type of allocation combines attributes of both device and host allocations, combining the programmer convenience of host allocations with the greater performance afforded by device allocations. Like host allocations, shared allocations are accessible on both the host and device. The difference between them is that shared allocations are free to migrate between host memory and device-attached memory, automatically, without our intervention. If an allocation has migrated to the device, any kernel executing on that device accessing it will do so with greater performance than remotely accessing it from the host. However, shared allocations do not give us all the benefits without any drawbacks.

Automatic migration can be implemented in a variety of ways. No matter which way the runtime chooses to implement shared allocations, they usually pay a price of increased latency. With device allocations, we know exactly how much memory needs to be copied and can schedule the copy to begin as early as possible. The automatic migration mechanisms cannot see the future and, in some cases, do not begin moving data until a kernel tries to access it. The kernel must then wait, or block, until the data movement has completed before it can continue executing. In other cases, the runtime may not know exactly how much data the kernel will access and might conservatively move a larger amount of data than is required, also increasing latency for the kernel.

We should also note that while shared allocations *can* migrate, it does not necessarily mean that all implementations of SYCL *will* migrate them. We expect most implementations to implement shared allocations with migration, but some devices may prefer to implement them identically to host allocations. In such an implementation, the allocation is still visible on both host and device, but we may not see the performance gains that a migrating implementation could provide.

Allocating Memory

USM allows us to allocate memory in a variety of different ways that cater to different needs and preferences. However, before we go over all the methods in greater detail, we should discuss how USM allocations differ from regular C++ allocations.

What Do We Need to Know?

Regular C++ programs can allocate memory in multiple ways: `new`, `malloc`, or allocators. No matter which syntax we prefer, memory allocation is ultimately performed by the system allocator in the host operating system. When we allocate memory in C++, the only concerns are "How much memory do we need?" and "How much memory is available to allocate?" However, USM requires extra information before an allocation can be performed.

First, USM allocation needs to specify which type of allocation is desired: device, host, or shared. It is important to request the right type of allocation in order to obtain the desired behavior. Next, every USM allocation must specify a `context` object against which the allocation will be made. Most of the examples in the book instead pass a queue object (which then provides the context). The `context` object hasn't had a lot of discussion in this book up to this point, so it's worth saying a little about it here. A context represents a device or set of devices on which we can execute kernels. We can think of a context as a convenient place for the runtime to stash some state about what it's doing. Programmers are not likely to directly interact with contexts outside of passing them around in most SYCL programs. We do offer a few tips regarding contexts in Chapter 13.

USM allocations are not guaranteed to be usable across different contexts—it is important that all USM allocations, queues, and kernels share the same `context` object. Typically, we can obtain this context from the queue being used to submit work to a device.

Finally, `device` allocations (and some `shared` allocations) also require that we specify which device will provide the memory for the allocation. This is important since we do not want to oversubscribe the memory of our devices (unless the device is able to support this—we will say more about that later in the chapter when we discuss migration of data). USM allocation routines can be distinguished from their C++ analogues by the addition of these extra parameters.

Multiple Styles

Sometimes, trying to please everyone with a single option proves to be an impossible task, just as some people prefer coffee over tea, or `emacs` over `vi`. If we ask programmers what an allocation interface should look like, we will get several different answers back. USM embraces this diversity of choice and provides several different flavors of allocation interfaces. These different flavors are C-style, C++-style, and C++ allocator–style. We will now discuss each and point out their similarities and differences.

Allocations à la C

The first style of allocation functions (listed in Figure 6-2, later used in examples shown in Figures 6-6 and 6-7) is modeled after memory allocation in C: `malloc` functions that take a number of bytes to allocate and return a `void *` pointer. This style of function is type agnostic. We must specify the total number of bytes to allocate, which means if we want to allocate `N` objects of type `X`, one must ask for `N * sizeof(X)` total bytes. The returned pointer is of type `void *`, which means that we must then cast it to an appropriate pointer to type `X`. This style is very simple but can be verbose due to the size calculations and typecasting required.

We can further divide this style of allocation into two categories: named functions and single function. The distinction between these two flavors is how we specify the desired type of USM allocation. With the named functions (`malloc_device`, `malloc_host`, and `malloc_shared`), the type of USM allocation is encoded in the function name. The single function `malloc` requires the type of USM allocation to be specified as an additional parameter. Neither flavor is better than the other, and the choice of which to use is governed by our preference.

We cannot move on without briefly mentioning alignment. Each version of `malloc` also has an `aligned_alloc` counterpart. The `malloc` functions return memory aligned to the default behavior of our device. On success it will return a legal pointer with a valid alignment, but there may be cases where we would prefer to manually specify an alignment. In these cases, we should use one of the `aligned_alloc` variants that also require us to specify the desired alignment for the allocation. Legal alignments are powers of two. It's worth noting that on many devices, allocations are maximally aligned to correspond to features of the hardware, so while we may ask for allocations to be 4-, 8-, 16-, or 32-byte aligned, we might in practice see larger alignments that give us what we ask for and then some.

```
// Named Functions
void *malloc_device(size_t size, const device &dev,
                    const context &ctxt);
void *malloc_device(size_t size, const queue &q);
void *aligned_alloc_device(size_t alignment, size_t size,
                           const device &dev,
                           const context &ctxt);
void *aligned_alloc_device(size_t alignment, size_t size,
                           const queue &q);

void *malloc_host(size_t size, const context &ctxt);
void *malloc_host(size_t size, const queue &q);
void *aligned_alloc_host(size_t alignment, size_t size,
                         const context &ctxt);
void *aligned_alloc_host(size_t alignment, size_t size,
                         const queue &q);

void *malloc_shared(size_t size, const device &dev,
                    const context &ctxt);
void *malloc_shared(size_t size, const queue &q);
void *aligned_alloc_shared(size_t alignment, size_t size,
                           const device &dev,
                           const context &ctxt);
void *aligned_alloc_shared(size_t alignment, size_t size,
                           const queue &q);

// Single Function
void *malloc(size_t size, const device &dev,
             const context &ctxt, usm::alloc kind);
void *malloc(size_t size, const queue &q, usm::alloc kind);
void *aligned_alloc(size_t alignment, size_t size,
                    const device &dev, const context &ctxt,
                    usm::alloc kind);
void *aligned_alloc(size_t alignment, size_t size,
                    const queue &q, usm::alloc kind);
```

Figure 6-2. *C-style USM allocation functions*

Allocations à la C++

The next flavor of USM allocation functions (listed in Figure 6-3) is very similar to the first but with more of a C++ look and feel. We once again have both named and single function versions of the allocation routines as well as our default and user-specified alignment versions. The difference is that now our functions are C++ templated functions that allocate `Count` objects of type `T` and return a pointer of type `T *`. Taking advantage of modern C++ simplifies things, since we no longer need to manually calculate the total size of the allocation in bytes or cast the returned pointer to the appropriate type. This also tends to yield a more compact and less error-prone expression in code. However, we should note that unlike "new" in C++, malloc-style interfaces do not invoke constructors for the objects being allocated—we are simply allocating enough bytes to fit that type.

This flavor of allocation is a good place to start for new codes written with USM in mind. The previous C-style is a good starting point for existing C++ codes that already make heavy use of C or C++ `malloc`, to which we will add the use of USM.

```
// Named Functions
template <typename T>
T *malloc_device(size_t Count, const device &Dev,
                 const context &Ctxt);
template <typename T>
T *malloc_device(size_t Count, const queue &Q);
template <typename T>
T *aligned_alloc_device(size_t Alignment, size_t Count,
                        const device &Dev,
                        const context &Ctxt);
template <typename T>
T *aligned_alloc_device(size_t Alignment, size_t Count,
                        const queue &Q);

template <typename T>
T *malloc_host(size_t Count, const context &Ctxt);
template <typename T>
T *malloc_host(size_t Count, const queue &Q);
template <typename T>
T *aligned_alloc_host(size_t Alignment, size_t Count,
                      const context &Ctxt);
template <typename T>
T *aligned_alloc_host(size_t Alignment, size_t Count,
                      const queue &Q);

template <typename T>
T *malloc_shared(size_t Count, const device &Dev,
                 const context &Ctxt);
template <typename T>
T *malloc_shared(size_t Count, const queue &Q);
template <typename T>
T *aligned_alloc_shared(size_t Alignment, size_t Count,
                        const device &Dev,
                        const context &Ctxt);
template <typename T>
T *aligned_alloc_shared(size_t Alignment, size_t Count,
                        const queue &Q);

// Single Function
template <typename T>
T *malloc(size_t Count, const device &Dev,
          const context &Ctxt, usm::alloc Kind);
template <typename T>
T *malloc(size_t Count, const queue &Q, usm::alloc Kind);
template <typename T>
T *aligned_alloc(size_t Alignment, size_t Count,
                 const device &Dev, const context &Ctxt,
                 usm::alloc Kind);
template <typename T>
T *aligned_alloc(size_t Alignment, size_t Count,
                 const queue &Q, usm::alloc Kind);
```

Figure 6-3. *C++-style USM allocation functions*

C++ Allocators

The final flavor of USM allocation (Figure 6-4) embraces modern C++ even more than the previous flavor. This flavor is based on the C++ allocator interface, which defines objects that are used to perform memory allocations either directly or indirectly inside a container such as `std::vector`. This allocator flavor is most useful if our code makes heavy use of container objects that can hide the details of memory allocation and deallocation from the user, simplifying code and reducing the opportunity for bugs.

```
template <typename T, usm::alloc AllocKind,
          size_t Alignment = 0>
class usm_allocator {
 public:
  using value_type = T;
  using propagate_on_container_copy_assignment =
      std::true_type;
  using propagate_on_container_move_assignment =
      std::true_type;
  using propagate_on_container_swap = std::true_type;

 public:
  template <typename U>
  struct rebind {
    typedef usm_allocator<U, AllocKind, Alignment> other;
  };

  usm_allocator() = delete;
  usm_allocator(const context& syclContext,
                const device& syclDevice,
                const property_list& propList = {});
  usm_allocator(const queue& syclQueue,
                const property_list& propList = {});
  usm_allocator(const usm_allocator& other);
  usm_allocator(usm_allocator&&) noexcept;
  usm_allocator& operator=(const usm_allocator&);
  usm_allocator& operator=(usm_allocator&&);

  template <class U>
  usm_allocator(usm_allocator<U, AllocKind,
                              Alignment> const&) noexcept;

  /// Allocate memory
  T* allocate(size_t count);

  /// Deallocate memory
  void deallocate(T* Ptr, size_t count);

  /// Equality Comparison
  ///
  /// Allocators only compare equal if they are of the same
  /// USM kind, alignment, context, and device
  template <class U, usm::alloc AllocKindU,
            size_t AlignmentU>
  friend bool operator==(
      const usm_allocator<T, AllocKind, Alignment>&,
      const usm_allocator<U, AllocKindU, AlignmentU>&);

  /// Inequality Comparison
  /// Allocators only compare unequal if they are not of the
  /// same USM kind, alignment, context, or device
  template <class U, usm::alloc AllocKindU,
            size_t AlignmentU>
  friend bool operator!=(
      const usm_allocator<T, AllocKind, Alignment>&,
      const usm_allocator<U, AllocKindU, AlignmentU>&);
};
```

Figure 6-4. *C++ allocator–style USM allocation functions*

Deallocating Memory

Whatever a program allocates must eventually be deallocated. USM defines a `free` method to deallocate memory allocated by one of the `malloc` or `aligned_malloc` functions. This `free` method also takes the context in which the memory was allocated as an extra parameter. The queue can also be substituted for the context. If memory was allocated with a C++ allocator object, it should also be deallocated using that object.

```
#include <sycl/sycl.hpp>
using namespace sycl;
constexpr int N = 42;

int main() {
  queue q;

  // Allocate N floats

  // C-style
  float *f1 = static_cast<float *>(malloc_shared(
      N * sizeof(float), q.get_device(), q.get_context()));

  // C++-style
  float *f2 = malloc_shared<float>(N, q);

  // C++-allocator-style
  usm_allocator<float, usm::alloc::shared> alloc(q);
  float *f3 = alloc.allocate(N);

  // Free our allocations
  free(f1, q.get_context());
  free(f2, q);
  alloc.deallocate(f3, N);

  return 0;
}
```

Figure 6-5. *Three styles for allocation*

Allocation Example

In Figure 6-5, we show how to perform the same allocation using the three styles just described. In this example, we allocate `N` single-precision floating-point numbers as shared allocations. The first allocation `f1` uses the C-style `void *` returning malloc routines. For this allocation, we explicitly pass the device and context that we obtain from the queue. We must also cast the result back to a `float *`. The second allocation `f2` does the same thing but using the C++-style templated malloc. Since we pass the type of our elements, `float`, to the allocation routine, we only need to specify how many floats we want to allocate, and we do not need to cast the result. We also use the form that takes the queue instead of the device and context, yielding a very simple and compact statement. The third allocation `f3` uses the USM C++ allocator class. We instantiate an allocator object of the proper type and then perform the allocation using that object. Finally, we show how to properly deallocate each allocation.

Data Management

Now that we understand how to allocate memory using USM, we will discuss how data is managed. We can look at this in two pieces: data initialization and data movement.

Initialization

Data initialization concerns filling our memory with values before we perform computations on it. One example of a common initialization pattern is to fill an allocation with zeroes before it is used. If we were to do this using USM allocations, we could do it in a variety of ways. First, we could write a kernel to do this. If our data set is particularly large or the initialization requires complex calculations, this is a reasonable way to go since the initialization can be performed in parallel (and it makes the initialized data ready to go on the device). Second, we could implement this as a loop in host code over all the elements of an allocation that sets each to zero. However, there is potentially a problem with this approach. A loop would work fine for host and shared allocations since these are accessible on the host. However, since device allocations are *not* accessible on the host, a loop in host code would not be able to write to them. This brings us to the third option.

The `memset` function is designed to efficiently implement this initialization pattern. USM provides a version of `memset` that is a member function of both the `handler` and `queue` classes. It takes three arguments: the pointer representing the base address of the memory we want to set, a byte value representing the byte pattern to set, and the number of bytes to set to that pattern. Unlike a loop on the host, `memset` happens in parallel and also works with `device` allocations.

While `memset` is a useful operation, the fact that it only allows us to specify a byte pattern to fill into an allocation is rather limiting. USM also provides a `fill` method (as a member of the `handler` and `queue` classes) that lets us fill memory with an arbitrary pattern. The fill method is a function templated on the type of the pattern we want to write into the allocation. Template it with an `int`, and we can fill an allocation with the 32-bit integer number "`42`". Similar to `memset`, `fill` takes three arguments: the pointer to the base address of the allocation to fill, the value to fill, and the number of times we want to write that value into the allocation.

Data Movement

Data movement is probably the most important aspect of USM to understand. If the right data is not in the right place at the right time, our program will produce incorrect results. USM defines two strategies that we can use to manage data: explicit and implicit. The choice of which strategy we want to use is related to the types of USM allocations our hardware supports or that we want to use.

Explicit

The first strategy USM offers is explicit data movement (Figure 6-6). Here, we must explicitly copy data between the host and device. We can do this by invoking the `memcpy` method, found on both the `handler` and `queue` classes. The `memcpy` method takes three arguments: a pointer to the destination memory, a pointer to the source memory, and the number of bytes to copy between host and device. We do not need to specify in which direction the copy is meant to happen—this is implicit in the source and destination pointers.

The most common usage of explicit data movement is copying to or from `device` allocations in USM since they are not accessible on the host. Having to insert explicit copying of data does require effort on our part. Additionally, it can be a source of bugs: copies could be accidentally omitted, an incorrect amount of data could be copied, or the source or destination pointer could be incorrect.

However, explicit data movement does not only come with disadvantages. It gives us large advantage: total control over data movement. Control over both how much data is copied and when the data gets copied is very important for achieving the best performance in some applications. Ideally, we can overlap computation with data movement whenever possible, ensuring that the hardware runs with high utilization.

The other types of USM allocations, `host` and `shared`, are both accessible on host and device and do not need to be explicitly copied to the device. This leads us to the other strategy for data movement in USM.

```
#include <array>
#include <sycl/sycl.hpp>
using namespace sycl;
constexpr int N = 42;

int main() {
  queue q;

  std::array<int, N> host_array;
  int* device_array = malloc_device<int>(N, q);
  for (int i = 0; i < N; i++) host_array[i] = N;

  q.submit([&](handler& h) {
    // copy host_array to device_array
    h.memcpy(device_array, &host_array[0], N * sizeof(int));
  });
  q.wait();  // needed for now (we learn a better way later)

  q.submit([&](handler& h) {
    h.parallel_for(N, [=](id<1> i) { device_array[i]++; });
  });
  q.wait();  // needed for now (we learn a better way later)

  q.submit([&](handler& h) {
    // copy device_array back to host_array
    h.memcpy(&host_array[0], device_array, N * sizeof(int));
  });
  q.wait();  // needed for now (we learn a better way later)

  free(device_array, q);
  return 0;
}
```

Figure 6-6. *USM explicit data movement example*

Implicit

The second strategy that USM provides is implicit data movement (example usage shown in Figure 6-7). In this strategy, data movement happens *implicitly*, that is, without requiring input from us. With implicit data movement, we do not need to insert calls to `memcpy` since we can directly access the data through the USM pointers wherever we want to use it. Instead, it becomes the job of the system to ensure that the data will be available in the correct location when it is being used.

With host allocations, one could argue whether they really cause data movement. Since, by definition, they always remain pointers to host memory, the memory represented by a given host pointer cannot be stored on the device. However, data movement does occur as host allocations are accessed on the device. Instead of the memory being migrated to the device, the values we read or write are transferred over the appropriate interface to or from the kernel. This can be useful for streaming kernels where the data does not need to remain resident on the device.

Implicit data movement mostly concerns USM shared allocations. This type of allocation is accessible on both host and device and, more importantly, can migrate between host and device. The key point is that this migration happens automatically, or implicitly, simply by accessing the data in a different location. Next, we will discuss several things to think about when it comes to data migration for shared allocations.

```
#include <sycl/sycl.hpp>
using namespace sycl;
constexpr int N = 42;

int main() {
  queue q;

  int* host_array = malloc_host<int>(N, q);
  int* shared_array = malloc_shared<int>(N, q);
  for (int i = 0; i < N; i++) host_array[i] = i;

  q.submit([&](handler& h) {
    h.parallel_for(N, [=](id<1> i) {
      // access shared_array and host_array on device
      shared_array[i] = host_array[i] + 1;
    });
  });
  q.wait();

  free(shared_array, q);
  free(host_array, q);
  return 0;
}
```

Figure 6-7. *USM implicit data movement example*

Migration

With explicit data movement, we control how much data movement occurs. With implicit data movement, the system handles this for us, but it might not do it as efficiently. The SYCL runtime is not an oracle—it cannot predict what data an application will access before it does it. Additionally, pointer analysis remains a very difficult problem for compilers, which may not be able to accurately analyze and identify every allocation that might be used inside a kernel. Consequently, implementations of the mechanisms for implicit data movement may make different decisions based on the capabilities of the device that supports USM, which affects both how shared allocations can be used and how they perform.

If a device is very capable, it might be able to migrate memory on demand. In this case, data movement would occur after the host or device attempts to access an allocation that is not currently in the desired location. On-demand data greatly simplifies programming as it provides the desired semantic that a USM shared pointer can be accessed anywhere and just work. If a device cannot support on-demand migration (Chapter 12 explains how to query a device for capabilities), it might still be able to guarantee the same semantics with extra *restrictions* on how shared pointers can be used.

The restricted form of USM shared allocations governs when and where shared pointers may be accessed and how large shared allocations can be. If a device cannot migrate memory on demand, that means the runtime must be conservative and assume that a kernel might access any allocation in its device-attached memory. This brings a couple of consequences.

First, it means that the host and device should not try to access a shared allocation at the same time. Applications should instead alternate access in phases. The host can access an allocation, then a kernel can compute using that data, and finally the host can read the results. Without this restriction, the host is free to access different parts of an allocation than a kernel is currently touching. Such concurrent access typically happens at the granularity of a device memory page. The host could access one page, while the device accesses another. Atomically accessing the same piece of data will be covered in Chapter 19. Programmers may query whether a device is limited by this restriction, and we will learn more about the device query mechanism later.

The next consequence of this restricted form of shared allocations is that allocations are limited by the total amount of memory attached to a device. If a device cannot migrate memory on demand, it cannot migrate data to the host to make room to bring in different data. If a device does support on-demand migration, it is possible to *oversubscribe* its attached memory, allowing a kernel to compute on more data than the device's memory could normally contain, although this flexibility may come with a performance penalty due to extra data movement.

Fine-Grained Control

When a device supports on-demand migration of shared allocations, data movement occurs after memory is accessed in a location where it is not currently resident. However, a kernel can stall while waiting for the data movement to complete. The next statement it executes may even cause more data movement to occur and introduce additional latency to the kernel execution.

SYCL gives us a way to modify the performance of the automatic migration mechanisms. It does this by defining two functions: `prefetch` and `mem_advise`. Figure 6-8 shows a simple utilization of each. These functions let us give hints to the runtime about how kernels will access data so that the runtime can choose to start moving data *before* a kernel tries to access it. Note that this example uses the queue shortcut methods that directly invoke `parallel_for` on the `queue` object instead of inside a lambda passed to the `submit` method (a command group).

```
#include <sycl/sycl.hpp>
using namespace sycl;

// Appropriate values depend on your HW
constexpr int BLOCK_SIZE = 42;
constexpr int NUM_BLOCKS = 2500;
constexpr int N = NUM_BLOCKS * BLOCK_SIZE;

int main() {
  queue q;
  int *data = malloc_shared<int>(N, q);
  int *read_only_data = malloc_shared<int>(BLOCK_SIZE, q);

  for (int i = 0; i < N; i++) {
    data[i] = -i;
  }

  // Never updated after initialization
  for (int i = 0; i < BLOCK_SIZE; i++) {
    read_only_data[i] = i;
  }

  // Mark this data as "read only" so the runtime can copy
  // it to the device instead of migrating it from the host.
  // Real values will be documented by your backend.
  int HW_SPECIFIC_ADVICE_RO = 0;
  q.mem_advise(read_only_data, BLOCK_SIZE,
               HW_SPECIFIC_ADVICE_RO);
  event e = q.prefetch(data, BLOCK_SIZE * sizeof(int));

  for (int b = 0; b < NUM_BLOCKS; b++) {
    q.parallel_for(range{BLOCK_SIZE}, e, [=](id<1> i) {
      data[b * BLOCK_SIZE + i] += read_only_data[i];
    });
    if ((b + 1) < NUM_BLOCKS) {
      // Prefetch next block
      e = q.prefetch(data + (b + 1) * BLOCK_SIZE,
                     BLOCK_SIZE * sizeof(int));
    }
  }
  q.wait();

  free(data, q);
  free(read_only_data, q);
  return 0;
}
```

Figure 6-8. *Fine-grained control via `prefetch` and `mem_advise`*

The simplest way for us to do this is by invoking `prefetch`. This function is invoked as a member function of the `handler` or `queue` class and takes a base pointer and number of bytes. This lets us inform the runtime that certain data is about to be used on a device so that it can eagerly start migrating it. Ideally, we would issue these prefetch hints early enough such that by the time the kernel touches the data, it is already resident on the device, eliminating the latency we previously described.

The other function provided by SYCL is `mem_advise`. This function allows us to provide device-specific hints about how memory will be used in kernels. An example of such possible *advice* that we could specify is that the data will only be read in a kernel, not written. In that case, the system could realize it could copy, or duplicate, the data on the device, so that the host's version does not need to be updated after the kernel is complete. However, the *advice* passed to `mem_advise` is specific to a particular device, so be sure to check the documentation for hardware before using this function.

Queries

Finally, not all devices support every feature of USM. We should not assume that all USM features are available if we want our programs to be portable across different devices. USM defines several things that we can query. These queries can be separated into two categories: pointer queries and device capability queries. Figure 6-9 shows a simple utilization of each.

The pointer queries in USM answer two questions. The first question is "What type of USM allocation does this pointer point to?" The `get_pointer_type` function takes a pointer and SYCL context and returns a result of type `usm::alloc`, which can have four possible values: *host, device, shared,* or *unknown*. The second question is "What device was this USM pointer allocated against?" We can pass a pointer and a context to the function `get_pointer_device` and get back a device object. This is mostly used with device or shared USM allocations since it does not make much sense with host allocations. The SYCL specification states that when used with host allocations, the first device in the context is returned—this is not for any particular reason other than to avoid throwing an exception, which would seem a bit odd for code that may be templated on USM allocation type.

The second type of query provided by USM concerns the capabilities of a device. USM has its own list of device aspects that can be queried by calling `has` on a device object. These queries can be used to test which types of USM allocations are supported by a device. Additionally, we can query if shared allocations may be concurrently accessed by the host and device. The full list of queries is shown in Figure 6-10. In Chapter 12, we will look at the query mechanism in more detail.

```
#include <sycl/sycl.hpp>
using namespace sycl;
namespace dinfo = info::device;
constexpr int N = 42;

template <typename T>
void foo(T data, id<1> i) {
  data[i] = N;
}

int main() {
  queue q;
  auto dev = q.get_device();
  auto ctxt = q.get_context();
  bool usm_shared = dev.has(aspect::usm_shared_allocations);
  bool usm_device = dev.has(aspect::usm_device_allocations);
  bool use_USM = usm_shared || usm_device;

  if (use_USM) {
    int *data;
    if (usm_shared) {
      data = malloc_shared<int>(N, q);
    } else /* use device allocations */ {
      data = malloc_device<int>(N, q);
    }
    std::cout << "Using USM with "
              << ((get_pointer_type(data, ctxt) ==
                   usm::alloc::shared)
                      ? "shared"
                      : "device")
              << " allocations on "
              << get_pointer_device(data, ctxt)
                     .get_info<dinfo::name>()
              << "\n";
    q.parallel_for(N, [=](id<1> i) { foo(data, i); });
    q.wait();
    free(data, q);
  } else /* use buffers */ {
    buffer<int, 1> data{range{N}};
    q.submit([&](handler &h) {
      accessor a(data, h);
      h.parallel_for(N, [=](id<1> i) { foo(a, i); });
    });
    q.wait();
  }
  return 0;
}
```

Figure 6-9. *Queries on USM pointers and devices*

Aspect	Description
aspect::usm_device_allocations	This device supports device allocations
aspect::usm_host_allocations	This device supports host allocations
aspect::usm_atomic_host_allocations	This device supports host allocations that may be modified atomically by the device
aspect::shared_allocations	This device supports shared allocations
aspect::atomic_shared_allocations	This device supports shared allocations and the host and device may concurrently access and atomically modify shared allocations
aspect::usm_system_allocations	This device supports using allocations made with the system allocator on the device

Figure 6-10. *USM device aspects*

One More Thing

There is one more form of USM that we haven't covered. The forms of USM we have described in this chapter all require the use of special allocation functions. While not a huge burden, this represents a change from traditional C++ code that uses the system allocator in the form of `malloc` or the `new` operator. While some devices today, such as CPUs, may not need this requirement, most accelerator devices still need it. Thus, we have described how to use the USM allocation functions in the name of greater portability. However, we believe that we will soon see more accelerator designs that support use of the system allocator. Such devices will greatly simplify programs by freeing the programmer from worrying about allocating the right type of USM memory or copying the correct data at the appropriate time. In some sense, one can view eventual system allocator support as the final evolution of USM—it would provide the benefits of shared USM allocations without requiring the use of special allocation functions.

Summary

In this chapter, we've described Unified Shared Memory, a pointer-based strategy for data management. We covered the three types of allocations that USM defines. We discussed all the different ways that we can allocate and deallocate memory with USM and how data movement can be either explicitly controlled by us (the programmers) for device allocations or implicitly controlled by the system for host or shared allocations. Finally, we discussed how to query the different USM capabilities that a device supports and how to query information about USM pointers in a program.

Since we have not discussed synchronization in this book in detail yet, there is more on USM in later chapters when we discuss scheduling, communications, and synchronization. Specifically, we cover these additional considerations for USM in Chapters 8, 9, and 19.

In the next chapter, we will cover the second strategy for data management: *buffers*.

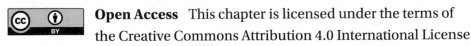

CHAPTER 7

Buffers

In this chapter, we will learn about the buffer abstraction. We learned about Unified Shared Memory (USM), the pointer-based strategy for data management, in the previous chapter. USM forces us to think about where memory lives and what should be accessible where. The buffer abstraction is a higher-level model that hides this from the programmer. Buffers simply represent data, and it becomes the job of the runtime to manage how the data is stored and moved in memory.

This chapter presents an alternative approach to managing our data. The choice between buffers and USM often comes down to personal preference and the style of existing code, and applications are free to mix and match the two styles in representation of different data within the application.

USM simply exposes different abstractions for memory. USM has pointers, and buffers are a higher-level abstraction. The abstraction level of buffers allows the data contained within to be used on any device within the application, where the runtime manages whatever is needed to make that data available. The pointer-based model of USM is probably a better fit for applications that use pointer-based data structures such as linked lists, trees, or others. Buffers can also be trickier to retrofit into existing codes that already use pointers. However, buffers are guaranteed to work on every device in the system, while some devices may not support specific (or any) modes of USM. Choices are good, so let's dive into buffers.

J. Reinders et al., *Data Parallel C++*, https://doi.org/10.1007/978-1-4842-9691-2_7

We will look more closely at how buffers are created and used. A discussion of *buffers* would not be complete without also discussing the *accessor*. While buffers abstract how we represent and store data in a program, we do not directly access the data using the buffer. Instead, we use accessor objects that inform the runtime how we intend to use the data we are accessing, and accessors are tightly coupled to the powerful data dependence mechanisms within task graphs. After we cover all the things we can do with buffers, we will also explore how to create and use accessors in our programs.

Buffers

A buffer is a high-level abstraction for data. Buffers are not necessarily tied to a single location or virtual memory address. Indeed, the runtime is free to use many different locations in memory (even across different devices) to represent a buffer, but the runtime must be sure to always give us a consistent view of the data. A buffer is accessible on the host and on any device.

```
template <typename T, int Dimensions, AllocatorT allocator>
class buffer;
```

Figure 7-1. *Buffer class definition*

The `buffer` class is a template class with three template arguments, as shown in Figure 7-1. The first template argument is the type of the object that the buffer will contain. This type must be *device copyable,* which extends the notion of *trivially copyable* as defined by C++. Types that are trivially copyable are safe to copy byte by byte without using any special copy or move constructors. Device copyable types extend this notion recursively to certain C++ types like `std::pair` or `std::tuple`. The next template argument is an integer describing the dimensionality of the buffer. The final template argument is optional, and the default value is usually what is used. This argument specifies a C++-style allocator class that is used to perform any memory allocations on the host that are needed for the buffer. First, we will examine the many ways that buffer objects can be created.

Buffer Creation

In the following figures, we show several ways in which buffer objects can be created. Let's walk through the example and look at each instance.

```
// Create a buffer of 2x5 ints using the default allocator
buffer<int, 2, buffer_allocator<int>> b1{range<2>{2, 5}};

// Create a buffer of 2x5 ints using the default allocator
// and CTAD for range
buffer<int, 2> b2{range{2, 5}};

// Create a buffer of 20 floats using a
// default-constructed std::allocator
buffer<float, 1, std::allocator<float>> b3{range{20}};

// Create a buffer of 20 floats using a passed-in
// allocator
std::allocator<float> myFloatAlloc;
buffer<float, 1, std::allocator<float>> b4{range(20),
                                           myFloatAlloc};
```

Figure 7-2. *Creating buffers, Part 1*

The first buffer we create in Figure 7-2, `b1`, is a two-dimensional buffer of ten integers. We explicitly pass all template arguments, even explicitly passing the default value of `buffer_allocator<T>` as the allocator type. Since `buffer_allocator` is also a templated type, we must explicitly specialize it just as we do the buffer by specifying `buffer_allocator<int>`. However, using modern C++, we can express this much more compactly. Buffer `b2` is also a two-dimensional buffer of ten integers using the default allocator. Here we make use of C++17's class template argument deduction (CTAD) to automatically infer template arguments. CTAD is an all-or-none tool—it must either infer every template argument for a class or infer none of them. In this case, we use the fact that we are initializing b2 with a range that takes two arguments to infer that it is a two-dimensional range. The allocator template argument has a default value, so we do not need to explicitly list it when creating the buffer.

With buffer b3, we create a buffer of 20 floats and use a default-constructed std::allocator to allocate any necessary memory on the host. When using a custom allocator type with a buffer, we often want to pass an actual allocator object to the buffer to use instead of the default-constructed one. Buffer b4 shows how to do this, taking the allocator object after the range in the call to its constructor.

For the first four buffers in our example, we let the buffer allocate any memory it needs and we do not initialize that data with any values at the time of their creation. It is a common pattern to use buffers to effectively wrap existing C++ allocations, which may already have been initialized with data. We can do this by passing a source of initial values to the buffer constructor. Doing so allows us to do several things, which we will see with the next example.

```
// Create a buffer of 4 doubles and initialize it from a
// host pointer
double myDoubles[4] = {1.1, 2.2, 3.3, 4.4};
buffer b5{myDoubles, range{4}};

// Create a buffer of 5 doubles and initialize it from a
// host pointer to const double
const double myConstDbls[5] = {1.0, 2.0, 3.0, 4.0, 5.0};
buffer b6{myConstDbls, range{5}};

// Create a buffer from a shared pointer to int
auto sharedPtr = std::make_shared<int>(42);
buffer b7{sharedPtr, range{1}};
```

Figure 7-3. *Creating buffers, Part 2*

In Figure 7-3, buffer `b5` creates a one-dimensional buffer of four doubles. We pass the host pointer to the C array `myDoubles` to the buffer constructor in addition to the range that specifies the size of the buffer. Here we can make full use of CTAD to infer all the template arguments of our buffer. The host pointer we pass points to doubles, which gives us the data type of our buffer. The number of dimensions is automatically inferred from the one-dimensional range, which itself is inferred because it is created with only one number. Finally, the default allocator is used, so we do not have to specify that.

Passing a host pointer has a few ramifications of which we should be aware. By passing a pointer to host memory, we are promising the runtime that we will not try to access the host memory during the lifetime of the buffer. This is not (and cannot be) enforced by a SYCL implementation—it is our responsibility to ensure that we do not break this contract. One reason that we should not try to access this memory while the buffer is alive is that the buffer may choose to use different memory on the host to represent the buffer content, often for optimization reasons. If it does so, the values will be copied into this new memory from the host pointer. If subsequent kernels modify the buffer, the original host pointer will not reflect the updated values until certain specified synchronization points. We will talk more about when data gets written back to a host pointer later in this chapter.

Buffer `b6` is very similar to buffer `b5` with one major difference. This time, we are initializing the buffer with a pointer to const double. This means that we can only read values through the host pointer and not write them. However, the type for our buffer in this example is still `double`, not `const double` since the deduction guides do not take `const`-ness into consideration. This means that the buffer may be written to by a kernel, but we must use a different mechanism to update the host after the buffer has outlived its use (covered later in this chapter).

Buffers can also be initialized using C++ shared pointer objects. This is useful if our application already uses shared pointers, as this method of initialization will properly count the reference and ensure that the memory is not deallocated. Buffer b7 creates a buffer containing a single integer and initializes it using a shared pointer.

```
// Create a buffer of ints from an input iterator
std::vector<int> myVec;
buffer b8{myVec.begin(), myVec.end()};
buffer b9{myVec};

// Create a buffer of 2x5 ints and 2 non-overlapping
// sub-buffers of 5 ints.
buffer<int, 2> b10{range{2, 5}};
buffer b11{b10, id{0, 0}, range{1, 5}};
buffer b12{b10, id{1, 0}, range{1, 5}};
```

Figure 7-4. *Creating buffers, Part 3*

Containers are commonly used in modern C++ applications, with examples including `std::array`, `std::vector`, `std::list`, or `std::map`. We can initialize one-dimensional buffers using containers in two different ways. The first way, as shown in Figure 7-4 by buffer `b8`, uses input iterators. Instead of a host pointer, we pass two iterators to the buffer constructor, one representing the beginning of the data and another representing the end. The size of the buffer is computed as the number of elements returned by incrementing the start iterator until it equals the end iterator. This is useful for any data type that implements the C++ `InputIterator` interface. If the container object that provides the initial values for a buffer is also contiguous, then we can use an even simpler form to create the buffer. Buffer `b9` creates a buffer from a vector simply by passing the vector to the constructor. The size of the buffer is determined by the size of the container being used to initialize it, and the type for the buffer data comes from the type of the container data. Creating buffers using this approach is common and recommended from containers such as `std::vector` and `std::array`.

The final example of buffer creation illustrates another feature of the buffer class. It is possible to create a *sub*-buffer, which is a view of a buffer from another buffer. A sub-buffer requires three things: a reference to a parent buffer, a base index, and the range of the sub-buffer. A sub-buffer cannot be created from a sub-buffer. Multiple sub-buffers can be created from the same buffer, and they are free to overlap. Buffer `b10` is created exactly like buffer `b2`, a two-dimensional buffer of integers with five integers per row. Next, we create two sub-buffers from buffer `b10`, sub-buffers `b11` and `b12`. Sub-buffer `b11` starts at index `(0,0)` and contains every element in the first row. Similarly, sub-buffer `b12` starts at index `(1,0)` and contains every element in the second row. This yields two disjoint sub-buffers. Since the sub-buffers do not overlap, different kernels could operate on the different sub-buffers concurrently, but we will talk more about scheduling execution graphs and dependences in the next chapter.

```
queue q;
int my_ints[42];

// Create a buffer of 42 ints
buffer<int> b{range(42)};

// Create a buffer of 42 ints, initialize with a host
// pointer, and add the use_host_pointer property
buffer b1{my_ints,
          range(42),
          {property::buffer::use_host_ptr{}}};

// Create a buffer of 42 ints, initialize with a host
// pointer, and add the use_mutex property
std::mutex myMutex;
buffer b2{my_ints,
          range(42),
          {property::buffer::use_mutex{myMutex}}};
// Retrieve a pointer to the mutex used by this buffer
auto mutexPtr =
    b2.get_property<property::buffer::use_mutex>()
        .get_mutex_ptr();
// Lock the mutex until we exit scope
std::lock_guard<std::mutex> guard{*mutexPtr};

// Create a context-bound buffer of 42 ints, initialized
// from a host pointer
buffer b3{
    my_ints,
    range(42),
    {property::buffer::context_bound{q.get_context()}}};
```

***Figure 7-5.** Buffer properties*

Buffer Properties

Buffers can also be created with special properties that alter their behavior. In Figure 7-5, we will walk through an example of the three different optional buffer properties and discuss how they might be used. Note that these properties are relatively uncommon in most codes.

use_host_ptr

The first property that may be optionally specified during buffer creation is use_host_ptr. When present, this property requires the buffer to not allocate any memory on the host, and any allocator passed or specified on buffer construction is effectively ignored. Instead, the buffer must use the memory pointed to by a host pointer that is passed to the constructor. Note that this does not require the device to use the same memory to hold the buffer's data. A device is free to cache the contents of a buffer in its attached memory. Also note that this property may only be used when a host pointer is passed to the constructor. This option can be useful when the program wants full control over all host memory allocations—for example, it allows programmers to try to minimize the memory footprint of an application.

In our example in Figure 7-5, we create a buffer b as we saw in our previous examples. We next create buffer b1 and initialize it with a pointer to myInts. We also pass the property use_host_ptr, which means that buffer b1 will only use the memory pointed to by myInts and not allocate any additional temporary storage on the host.

use_mutex

The next property, use_mutex, concerns fine-grained sharing of memory between buffers and host code. Buffer b2 is created using this property. The property takes a reference to a mutex object that can later be queried from the buffer as we see in the example. This property also requires a host pointer be passed to the constructor, and it lets the runtime determine when it is safe to access updated values in host code through the provided host pointer. We cannot lock the mutex until the runtime guarantees that the host pointer sees the latest value of the buffer. While this could be combined with the use_host_ptr property, it is not required. use_mutex is a mechanism that allows host code to access data within a buffer while the buffer is still alive and without using the host accessor mechanism (described later). In general, the host accessor mechanism should be preferred unless we have a specific reason to use a mutex, particularly because there are no guarantees on how long it will take before the mutex will be successfully locked and the data ready for use by host code.

context_bound

The final property is shown in the creation of buffer `b3` in our example. Here, our buffer of 42 integers is created with the `context_bound` property. The property takes a reference to a context object. Normally, a buffer is free to be used on any device or context. However, if this property is used, it locks the buffer to the specified context. Attempting to use the buffer on another context will result in a runtime error. This could be useful for debugging programs by identifying cases where a kernel might be submitted to the wrong queue, for instance. In practice, we do not expect to see this property used in many programs, and the ability for buffers to be accessed on any device in any context is one of the most powerful properties of the buffer abstraction (which this property undoes).

What Can We Do with a Buffer?

Many things can be done with buffer objects. We can query characteristics of a buffer, determine if and where any data is written back to host memory after the buffer is destroyed, or reinterpret a buffer as one with different characteristics. One thing that cannot be done, however, is to directly access the data that a buffer represents. Instead, we must create accessor objects to access the data, and we will learn all about this later in the chapter.

Examples of things that can be queried about a buffer include its range, the total number of data elements it represents, and the number of bytes required to store its elements. We can also query which allocator object is being used by the buffer and whether the buffer is a sub-buffer or not.

Updating host memory when a buffer is destroyed is an important aspect to consider when using buffers. Depending on how a buffer is created, host memory may or may not be updated with the results of a computation after buffer destruction. If a buffer is created and initialized from a host pointer to non-`const` data, that same pointer is updated with the latest data when the buffer is destroyed. However, there is also a way to update host memory regardless of how a buffer was created. The `set_final_data` method is a template method of `buffer` that can accept either a raw pointer, a C++ `OutputIterator`, or a `std::weak_ptr`. When the buffer is destroyed, data contained by the buffer will be written to the host using the supplied location. Note that if the buffer was created and initialized from a host pointer to non-`const` data, it's as if `set_final_data` was called with that pointer. Technically, a raw pointer is a special case of an `OutputIterator`. If the parameter passed to `set_final_data` is a `std::weak_ptr`, the data is not written to the host if the pointer has expired or has already been deleted. Whether or not writeback occurs can also be controlled by the `set_write_back` method.

Accessors

Data represented by a buffer cannot be directly accessed through the buffer object. Instead, we must create accessor objects that allow us to safely access a buffer's data. Accessors inform the runtime where and how we want to access data, allowing the runtime to ensure that the right data is in the right place at the right time. This is a very powerful concept, especially when combined with the task graph that schedules kernels for execution based in part on data dependences.

Accessor objects are instantiated from the templated `accessor` class. This class has five template parameters. The first parameter is the type of the data being accessed. This should be the same as the type of data being stored by the corresponding buffer. Similarly, the second parameter describes the dimensionality of the data and buffer and defaults to a value of one.

Mode	Description
`read`	Read-only access
`write`	Write-only access preserving previous contents
`read_write`	Read and write access

***Figure 7-6.** Access modes*

The next three template parameters are unique to accessors. The first of these is the *access mode*. The access mode describes how we intend to use an accessor in a program. The possible modes are listed in Figure 7-6. We will learn how these modes are used to order the execution of kernels and perform data movement in Chapter 8. The access mode parameter does have a default value if none is specified or automatically inferred. If we do not specify otherwise, accessors will default to `read_write` access mode for non-`const` data types and `read` for `const` data types. These defaults are always correct but providing more accurate information may improve a runtime's ability to perform optimizations. When starting application development, it is safe and concise to simply not specify an access mode, and we can then refine the access modes based on profiling of performance-critical regions of the application.

Target	Description
device	Access a buffer via device global memory
host_task	Access a buffer from a host task

***Figure 7-7.** Access targets*

The next template parameter is the *access target*. Buffers are an abstraction of data and do not describe where and how data is stored. The access target describes where we are accessing data. The two possible access targets are listed in Figure 7-7.

When using C++ with SYCL, there are only two targets: `device` and `host_task`. The default template value is `device`, and this means that we intend to access a buffer's data on a device. This is reasonable as accessors are most commonly used in operations on a device such as kernels or data transfers. The other access target is `host_task`, which is used when a host task needs to access a buffer's data.

Devices may have different types of memories available. In particular, many devices have some sort of fast local memory that is shared across multiple work-items in a work-group. Prior versions of SYCL had special access targets for local memory, but SYCL 2020 handles it in a different way. We will learn how to use work-group local memory in Chapter 9. Prior versions of SYCL also had a special access target for the host (outside of host tasks, which are new to SYCL 2020). This has been replaced with the new `host_accessor` class, which provides access to a buffer's data in host code. However, the access will remain valid for the lifetime of the `host_accessor`. Given that a buffer is locked to the host while a `host_accessor` is valid, one should take special care to limit the scope of `host_accessor` objects.

The final template parameter governs whether an accessor is a *placeholder* accessor or not. This is not a parameter that a programmer is likely to ever directly set and is usually deduced by which constructor call is used to create the accessor. A placeholder accessor is one that is declared outside of a command group but meant to be used to access data on a device inside a kernel. We will see what differentiates a placeholder accessor from one that is not once we look at examples of accessor creation.

While accessors can be extracted from a buffer object using its `get_access` method, it's simpler to directly create (construct) them. This is the style we will use in upcoming examples since it is very simple to understand and is compact.

Accessor Creation

Figure 7-8 shows an example program with everything that we need to get started with accessors. In this example, we have three buffers, `A`, `B`, and `C`. The first parallel task we submit to the queue creates accessors to each buffer and defines a kernel that uses these accessors to initialize the buffers with some values. Each accessor is constructed with a reference to the buffer it will access as well as the handler object defined by the command group we're submitting to the queue. This effectively binds the accessor to the kernel we're submitting as part of the command group. Regular accessors are device accessors since they, by default, target global buffers stored in device memory. This is the most common use case.

```
#include <cassert>
#include <sycl/sycl.hpp>
using namespace sycl;
constexpr int N = 42;

int main() {
  queue q;
  // Create 3 buffers of 42 ints
  buffer<int> a_buf{range{N}};
  buffer<int> b_buf{range{N}};
  buffer<int> c_buf{range{N}};
  accessor pc{c_buf};

  q.submit([&](handler &h) {
    accessor a{a_buf, h};
    accessor b{b_buf, h};
    accessor c{c_buf, h};
    h.parallel_for(N, [=](id<1> i) {
      a[i] = 1;
      b[i] = 40;
      c[i] = 0;
    });
  });
  q.submit([&](handler &h) {
    accessor a{a_buf, h};
    accessor b{b_buf, h};
    accessor c{c_buf, h};
    h.parallel_for(N,
                   [=](id<1> i) { c[i] += a[i] + b[i]; });
  });
  q.submit([&](handler &h) {
    h.require(pc);
    h.parallel_for(N, [=](id<1> i) { pc[i]++; });
  });

  host_accessor result{c_buf};
  for (int i = 0; i < N; i++) {
    assert(result[i] == N);
  }
  return 0;
}
```

Figure 7-8. *Simple accessor creation*

The second task we submit also defines three accessors to the buffers. We then use those accessors in the second kernel to add the elements of buffers A and B into buffer C. Since this second task operates on the same data as the first one, the runtime will execute this task after the first one is complete. We will learn about this in detail in the next chapter.

The third task shows how we can use a placeholder accessor. The accessor pC is declared at the beginning of the example in Figure 7-8 after we create our buffers. Note that the constructor is not passed a handler object since we don't have one to pass. This lets us create a reusable accessor object ahead of time. However, in order to use this accessor inside a kernel, we need to bind it to a command group during submission. We do this using the handler object's `require` method. Once we have bound our placeholder accessor to a command group, we can then use it inside a kernel as we would any other accessor.

Finally, we create a `host_accessor` object in order to read the results of our computations back on the host. Note that this is a different type than we used inside our kernels. Note that the host accessor `result` in this example also does not take a handler object since we once again do not have one to pass. The special type for host accessors also lets us disambiguate them from placeholders. An important aspect of host accessors is that the constructor only completes when the data is available for use on the host, which means that construction of a host accessor can appear to take a long time. The constructor must wait for any kernels to finish executing that produce the data to be copied as well as for the copy itself to finish. Once the host accessor construction is complete, it is safe to use the data that it accesses directly on the host, and we are guaranteed that the latest version of the data is available to us on the host.

While this example is perfectly correct, we don't say anything about how we intend to use our accessors when we create them. Instead, we use the default access mode, which is `read_write`, for the non-`const` `int` data in our buffers. This is potentially overconservative and may create unnecessary dependences between operations or superfluous data movement. A runtime may be able to do a better job if it has more information about how we plan to use the accessors we create. However, before we go through an example where we do this, we should first introduce one more tool—the deduction tag.

Deduction tags are a compact way to express the desired combination of access mode and target for an accessor. Deduction tags, when used, are passed as a parameter to an accessor's constructor. The possible tags are shown in Figure 7-9. When an accessor is constructed with a tag parameter, C++ CTAD can then properly deduce the desired access mode and target, providing an easy way to override the default values for those template parameters. We could also manually specify the desired template parameters, but tags provide a simpler, more compact way to get the same result without spelling out fully templated accessors.

Tag value	`access_mode::`	`target::`
`read_only`	read	device
`read_write`	read_write	device
`write_only`	write	device
`read_only_host_task`	read	host_task
`read_write_host_task`	read_write	host_task
`write_only_host_task`	write	host_task

Figure 7-9. *Deduction tags*

Let's take our previous example and rewrite it to add deduction tags. This new and improved example is shown in Figure 7-10.

```
#include <cassert>
#include <sycl/sycl.hpp>
using namespace sycl;
constexpr int N = 42;

int main() {
  queue q;

  // Create 3 buffers of 42 ints
  buffer<int> buf_a{range{N}};
  buffer<int> buf_b{range{N}};
  buffer<int> buf_c{range{N}};

  accessor pc{buf_c};

  q.submit([&](handler &h) {
    accessor a{buf_a, h, write_only, no_init};
    accessor b{buf_b, h, write_only, no_init};
    accessor c{buf_c, h, write_only, no_init};
    h.parallel_for(N, [=](id<1> i) {
      a[i] = 1;
      b[i] = 40;
      c[i] = 0;
    });
  });
  q.submit([&](handler &h) {
    accessor a{buf_a, h, read_only};
    accessor b{buf_b, h, read_only};
    accessor c{buf_c, h, read_write};
    h.parallel_for(N,
                   [=](id<1> i) { c[i] += a[i] + b[i]; });
  });
  q.submit([&](handler &h) {
    h.require(pc);
    h.parallel_for(N, [=](id<1> i) { pc[i]++; });
  });

  host_accessor result{buf_c, read_only};

  for (int i = 0; i < N; i++) {
    assert(result[i] == N);
  }
  return 0;
}
```

Figure 7-10. *Accessor creation with specified usage*

We begin by declaring our buffers as we did in Figure 7-8. We also create our placeholder accessor that we'll use later. Let's now look at the first task we submit to the queue. Previously, we created our accessors by passing a reference to a buffer and the handler object for the command group. Now, we add two extra parameters to our constructor calls. The first new parameter is a deduction tag. Since this kernel is writing the initial values for our buffers, we use the `write_only` deduction tag. This lets the runtime know that this kernel is producing new data and will not read from the buffer.

The second new parameter is an optional accessor property, similar to the optional properties for buffers that we saw earlier in the chapter. The property we pass, `no_init`, lets the runtime know that the previous contents of the buffer can be discarded. This is useful because it can let the runtime eliminate unnecessary data movement. In this example, since the first task is writing the initial values for our buffers, it's unnecessary for the runtime to copy the uninitialized host memory to the device before the kernel executes. The `no_init` property is useful for this example, but it should not be used for read-modify-write cases or kernels where only some values in a buffer may be updated.

The second task we submit to our queue is identical to before, but now we add deduction tags to our accessors. Here, we add the tags `read_only` to accessors `aA` and `aB` to let the runtime know that we will only read the values of buffers `A` and `B` through these accessors. The third accessor, `aC`, gets the `read_write` deduction tag since we accumulate the sum of the elements of `A` and `B` into `C`. We explicitly use the tag in the example to be consistent, but this is unnecessary since the default access mode is `read_write`.

The default usage is retained in the third task where we use our placeholder accessor. This remains unchanged from the simplified example we saw in Figure 7-8. Our final accessor, the host accessor `result`, now receives a deduction tag when we create it. Since we only read the final values on the host, we pass the `read_only` tag to the constructor. If we rewrote the program in such a way that the host accessor was destroyed, launching another kernel that operated on buffer `C` would not require it to be written back to the device since the `read_only` tag lets the runtime know that it will not be modified by the host.

What Can We Do with an Accessor?

Many things can be done with an accessor object. However, the most important thing we can do is spelled out in the accessor's name—access data. This is usually done through one of the accessor's `[]` operators. We use the `[]` operator in our examples in Figures 7-8 and 7-10. This operator takes either an `id` object that can properly index multidimensional data or a single `size_t`. The second case can be used when an accessor has more than one dimension. In that case, it returns an object that is then meant to be indexed again with `[]` until we arrive at a scalar value, and this would be of the form `a[i][j]` in a two-dimensional case. Remember that the ordering of accessor dimensions follows the convention of C++ where the rightmost dimension is the unit-stride dimension (iterates "fastest").

An accessor can also return a pointer to the underlying data. This pointer can be accessed directly following normal C++ rules. Note that there can be additional complexity involved with respect to the address space of this pointer.

Many things can also be queried from an accessor object. Examples include the number of elements accessible through the accessor, the size in bytes of the region of the buffer it covers, or the range of data accessible.

Accessors provide a similar interface to C++ containers and may be used in many situations where containers may be passed. The container interface supported by accessors includes the `data` method, which is equivalent to `get_pointer`, and several flavors of forward and backward iterators.

Summary

In this chapter, we have learned about buffers and accessors. Buffers are an abstraction of data that hides the underlying details of memory management from the programmer. They do this in order to provide a simpler, higher-level abstraction. We went through several examples that showed us the different ways to construct buffers as well as the different optional properties that can be specified to alter their behavior. We learned how to initialize a buffer with data from host memory as well as how to write data back to host memory when we are done with a buffer.

Since we cannot access buffers directly, we learned how to access the data in a buffer by using accessor objects. We learned the difference between device accessors and host accessors. We discussed the different access modes and targets and how they inform the runtime how and where an accessor will be used by the program. We showed the simplest way to use accessors using the default access modes and targets, and we learned how to distinguish between a placeholder accessor and one that is not. We then saw how to further optimize the example program by giving the runtime more information about our accessor usage by adding deduction tags to our accessor declarations. Finally, we covered many of the different ways that accessors can be used in a program.

In the next chapter, we will learn in greater detail how the runtime can use the information we give it through accessors to schedule the execution of different kernels. We will also see how this information informs the runtime about when and how the data in buffers needs to be copied between the host and a device. We will learn how we can explicitly control data movement involving buffers—and USM allocations too.

CHAPTER 8

Scheduling Kernels and Data Movement

We need to discuss our role as the conductor for our parallel programs. The proper orchestration of a parallel program is a thing of beauty—code running full speed without waiting for data, because we have arranged for all data to arrive and depart at the proper times—code carefully constructed to keep the hardware maximally busy. It is the thing that dreams are made of!

Life in the fast lanes—not just one lane!—demands that we take our work as the conductor seriously. In order to do that, we can think of our job in terms of task graphs.

Therefore, in this chapter, we will cover task graphs, the mechanism that is used to run complex sequences of kernels correctly and efficiently. There are two things that need sequencing in an application: kernel executions and data movement. Task graphs are the mechanism that we use to achieve proper sequencing.

First, we will quickly review how we can use dependences to order tasks from Chapter 3. Next, we will cover how the SYCL runtime builds graphs. We will discuss the basic building block of SYCL graphs, the command group. We will then illustrate the different ways we can build graphs of common patterns. We will also discuss how data movement, both explicit and implicit, is represented in graphs. Finally, we will discuss the various ways to synchronize our graphs with the host.

J. Reinders et al., *Data Parallel C++*, https://doi.org/10.1007/978-1-4842-9691-2_8

What Is Graph Scheduling?

In Chapter 3, we discussed data management and ordering the uses of data. That chapter described the key abstraction behind graphs in SYCL: dependences. Dependences between kernels are fundamentally based on what data a kernel accesses. A kernel needs to be certain that it reads the correct data before it can compute its output.

We described the three types of data dependences that are important for ensuring correct execution. The first, Read-after-Write (RAW), occurs when one task needs to read data produced by a different task. This type of dependence describes the flow of data between two kernels. The second type of dependence happens when one task needs to update data after another task has read it. We call that type of dependence a Write-after-Read (WAR) dependence. The final type of data dependence occurs when two tasks try to write the same data. This is known as a Write-after-Write (WAW) dependence.

Data dependences are the building blocks we will use to build graphs. This set of dependences is all we need to express both simple linear chains of kernels and large, complex graphs with hundreds of kernels with elaborate dependences. No matter which types of graph a computation needs, SYCL graphs ensure that a program will execute correctly based on the expressed dependences. However, it is up to the programmer to make sure that a graph correctly expresses all the dependences in a program.

How Graphs Work in SYCL

A command group can contain three different things: an action, its dependences, and miscellaneous host code. Of these three things, the one that is always required is the action, since without it the command group really doesn't do anything. Most command groups will also express dependences, but there are cases where they may not. One such example is the first action submitted in a program. It does not depend on anything to begin execution; therefore, we would not specify any dependence. The other thing that can appear inside a command group is arbitrary C++ code that executes on the host. This is perfectly legal and can be useful to help specify the action or its dependences, and this code is executed while the command group is created (not later, when the action is performed based on dependences having been met).

Command groups are typically expressed as a C++ lambda expression passed to the submit method. Command groups can also be expressed through shortcut methods on queue objects that take a kernel and set of event-based dependences.

Command Group Actions

There are two types of actions that may be performed by a command group: kernel executions and explicit memory operations. A command group may only perform a single action. As we've seen in earlier chapters, kernels are defined through calls to a `parallel_for` or `single_task` method and express computations that we want to perform on our devices. Operations for explicit data movement are the second type of action. Examples from USM include `memcpy`, `memset`, and `fill` operations. Examples from buffers include `copy`, `fill`, and `update_host`.

How Command Groups Declare Dependences

The other main component of a command group is the set of dependences that must be satisfied before the action defined by the group can execute. SYCL allows these dependences to be specified in several ways.

If a program uses in-order SYCL queues, the in-order semantics of the queue specify implicit dependences between successively enqueued command groups. One task cannot execute until the previously submitted task has completed.

Event-based dependences are another way to specify what must be complete before a command group may execute. These event-based dependences may be specified in two styles. The first way is used when a command group is specified as a lambda passed to a queue's `submit` method. In this case, the programmer invokes the `depends_on` method of the command group handler object, passing either an event or vector of events as parameter. The other way is used when a command group is created from the shortcut methods defined on the queue object. When the programmer directly invokes `parallel_for` or `single_task` on a queue, an event or vector of events may be passed as an extra parameter.

The last way that dependences may be specified is through the creation of accessor objects. Accessors specify how they will be used to read or write data in a buffer object, letting the runtime use this information to determine the data dependences that exist between different kernels. As we reviewed in the beginning of this chapter, examples of data dependences include one kernel reading data that another produces, two kernels writing the same data, or one kernel modifying data after another kernel reads it.

Examples

Now we will illustrate everything we've just learned with several examples. We will present how one might express two different dependence patterns in several ways. The two patterns we will illustrate are linear dependence chains where one task executes after another and a "Y" pattern where two independent tasks must execute before successive tasks.

Graphs for these dependence patterns can be seen in Figures 8-1 and 8-2. Figure 8-1 depicts a linear dependence chain. The first node represents the initialization of data, while the second node presents the reduction operation that will accumulate the data into a single result. Figure 8-2 depicts a "Y" pattern where we independently initialize two different pieces of data. After the data is initialized, an addition kernel will sum the two vectors together. Finally, the last node in the graph accumulates the result into a single value.

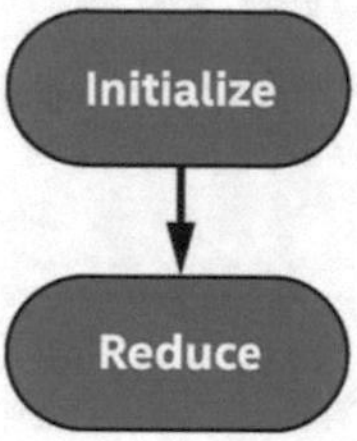

Figure 8-1. *Linear dependence chain graph*

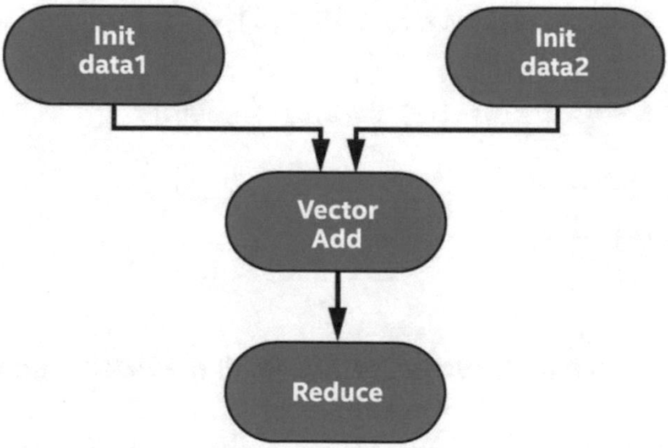

Figure 8-2. *"Y" pattern dependence graph*

For each pattern, we will show three different implementations. The first implementation will use in-order queues. The second will use event-based dependences. The last implementation will use buffers and accessors to express data dependences between command groups.

Figure 8-3 shows how to express a linear dependence chain using in-order queues. This example is very simple because the semantics of in-order queues already guarantee a sequential order of execution between command groups. The first kernel we submit initializes the elements of an array to 1. The next kernel then takes those elements and sums them together into the first element. Since our queue is in order, we do not need to do anything else to express that the second kernel should not execute until the first kernel has completed. Finally, we wait for the queue to finish executing all its tasks, and we check that we obtained the expected result.

```
#include <sycl/sycl.hpp>
using namespace sycl;
constexpr int N = 42;

int main() {
  queue q{property::queue::in_order()};

  int *data = malloc_shared<int>(N, q);

  q.parallel_for(N, [=](id<1> i) { data[i] = 1; });

  q.single_task([=]() {
    for (int i = 1; i < N; i++) data[0] += data[i];
  });
  q.wait();

  assert(data[0] == N);
  return 0;
}
```

Figure 8-3. *Linear dependence chain with in-order queues*

Figure 8-4 shows the same example using an out-of-order queue and event-based dependences. Here, we capture the event returned by the first call to `parallel_for`. The second kernel is then able to specify a dependence on that event and the kernel execution it represents by passing it as a parameter to `depends_on`. We will see in Figure 8-6 how we could shorten the expression of the second kernel using one of the shortcut methods for defining kernels.

```
#include <sycl/sycl.hpp>
using namespace sycl;
constexpr int N = 42;

int main() {
  queue q;

  int *data = malloc_shared<int>(N, q);

  auto e = q.parallel_for(N, [=](id<1> i) { data[i] = 1; });

  q.submit([&](handler &h) {
    h.depends_on(e);
    h.single_task([=]() {
      for (int i = 1; i < N; i++) data[0] += data[i];
    });
  });
  q.wait();

  assert(data[0] == N);
  return 0;
}
```

Figure 8-4. *Linear dependence chain with events*

Figure 8-5 rewrites our linear dependence chain example using buffers and accessors instead of USM pointers. Here we once again use an out-of-order queue but use data dependences specified through accessors instead of event-based dependences to order the execution of the command groups. The second kernel reads the data produced by the first kernel, and the runtime can see this because we declare accessors based on the same underlying buffer object. Unlike the previous examples, we do not wait for the queue to finish executing all its tasks. Instead, we construct a host accessor that defines a data dependence between the output of the second kernel and our assertion that we computed the correct answer on the host. Note that while a host accessor gives us an up-to-date view of data on the host, it does not guarantee that the original host memory has been updated if any was specified when the buffer was created. We can't safely access the original host memory unless the buffer is first destroyed or unless we use a more advanced mechanism like the mutex mechanism described in Chapter 7.

```
#include <sycl/sycl.hpp>
using namespace sycl;
constexpr int N = 42;

int main() {
  queue q;

  buffer<int> data{range{N}};

  q.submit([&](handler &h) {
    accessor a{data, h};
    h.parallel_for(N, [=](id<1> i) { a[i] = 1; });
  });

  q.submit([&](handler &h) {
    accessor a{data, h};
    h.single_task([=]() {
      for (int i = 1; i < N; i++) a[0] += a[i];
    });
  });

  host_accessor h_a{data};
  assert(h_a[0] == N);
  return 0;
}
```

Figure 8-5. *Linear dependence chain with buffers and accessors*

Figure 8-6 shows how to express a "Y" pattern using in-order queues. In this example, we declare two arrays, `data1` and `data2`. We then define two kernels that will each initialize one of the arrays. These kernels do not depend on each other, but because the queue is in order, the kernels must execute one after the other. Note that it would be perfectly legal to swap the order of these two kernels in this example. After the second kernel has executed, the third kernel adds the elements of the second array to those of the first array. The final kernel sums up the elements of the first array to compute the same result we did in our examples for linear dependence chains. This summation kernel depends on the previous kernel, but this linear chain is also captured by the in-order queue. Finally, we wait for all kernels to complete and validate that we successfully computed our magic number.

```
#include <sycl/sycl.hpp>
using namespace sycl;
constexpr int N = 42;

int main() {
  queue q{property::queue::in_order()};

  int *data1 = malloc_shared<int>(N, q);
  int *data2 = malloc_shared<int>(N, q);

  q.parallel_for(N, [=](id<1> i) { data1[i] = 1; });

  q.parallel_for(N, [=](id<1> i) { data2[i] = 2; });

  q.parallel_for(N, [=](id<1> i) { data1[i] += data2[i]; });

  q.single_task([=]() {
    for (int i = 1; i < N; i++) data1[0] += data1[i];

    data1[0] /= 3;
  });
  q.wait();

  assert(data1[0] == N);
  return 0;
}
```

Figure 8-6. *"Y" pattern with in-order queues*

Figure 8-7 shows our "Y" pattern example with out-of-order queues instead of in-order queues. Since the dependences are no longer implicit due to the order of the queue, we must explicitly specify the dependences between command groups using events. As in Figure 8-6, we begin by defining two independent kernels that have no initial dependences. We represent these kernels by two events, e1 and e2. When we define our third kernel, we must specify that it depends on the first two kernels.

We do this by saying that it depends on events e1 and e2 to complete before it may execute. However, in this example, we use a shortcut form to specify these dependences instead of the handler's depends_on method. Here, we pass the events as an extra parameter to parallel_for. Since we want to pass multiple events at once, we use the form that accepts a std::vector of events, but luckily modern C++ simplifies this for us by automatically converting the expression {e1, e2} into the appropriate vector.

```
#include <sycl/sycl.hpp>
using namespace sycl;
constexpr int N = 42;

int main() {
  queue q;

  int *data1 = malloc_shared<int>(N, q);
  int *data2 = malloc_shared<int>(N, q);

  auto e1 =
      q.parallel_for(N, [=](id<1> i) { data1[i] = 1; });

  auto e2 =
      q.parallel_for(N, [=](id<1> i) { data2[i] = 2; });

  auto e3 = q.parallel_for(
      range{N}, {e1, e2},
      [=](id<1> i) { data1[i] += data2[i]; });

  q.single_task(e3, [=]() {
    for (int i = 1; i < N; i++) data1[0] += data1[i];

    data1[0] /= 3;
  });
  q.wait();

  assert(data1[0] == N);
  return 0;
}
```

Figure 8-7. *"Y" pattern with events*

In our final example, seen in Figure 8-8, we again replace USM pointers and events with buffers and accessors. This example represents the two arrays `data1` and `data2` as buffer objects. Our kernels no longer use the shortcut methods for defining kernels since we must associate accessors with a command group handler. Once again, the third kernel must capture the dependence on the first two kernels. Here this is accomplished by declaring accessors for our buffers. Since we have previously declared accessors for these buffers, the runtime is able to properly order the execution of these kernels. Additionally, we also provide extra information to the runtime here when we declare accessor `b`. We add the access tag `read_only` to let the runtime know that we're only going to read this data, not produce new values. As we saw in our buffer and accessor example for linear dependence chains, our final kernel orders itself by updating the values produced in the third kernel. We retrieve the final value of our computation by declaring a host accessor that will wait for the final kernel to finish executing before moving the data back to the host where we can read it and assert we computed the correct result.

```
#include <sycl/sycl.hpp>
using namespace sycl;
constexpr int N = 42;

int main() {
  queue q;

  buffer<int> data1{range{N}};
  buffer<int> data2{range{N}};

  q.submit([&](handler &h) {
    accessor a{data1, h};
    h.parallel_for(N, [=](id<1> i) { a[i] = 1; });
  });

  q.submit([&](handler &h) {
    accessor b{data2, h};
    h.parallel_for(N, [=](id<1> i) { b[i] = 2; });
  });

  q.submit([&](handler &h) {
    accessor a{data1, h};
    accessor b{data2, h, read_only};
    h.parallel_for(N, [=](id<1> i) { a[i] += b[i]; });
  });

  q.submit([&](handler &h) {
    accessor a{data1, h};
    h.single_task([=]() {
      for (int i = 1; i < N; i++) a[0] += a[i];

      a[0] /= 3;
    });
  });

  host_accessor h_a{data1};
  assert(h_a[0] == N);
  return 0;
}
```

Figure 8-8. *"Y" pattern with accessors*

When Are the Parts of a Command Group Executed?

Since task graphs are asynchronous, it makes sense to wonder when exactly command groups are executed. By now, it should be clear that kernels may be executed as soon as their dependences have been satisfied, but what happens with the host portion of a command group?

When a command group is submitted to a queue, it is executed immediately on the host (before the `submit` call returns). This host portion of the command group is executed only once. Any kernel or explicit data operation defined in the command group is enqueued for execution on the device.

Data Movement

Data movement is another very important aspect of graphs in SYCL that is essential for understanding application performance. However, it can often be accidentally overlooked if data movement happens implicitly in a program, either using buffers and accessors or using USM shared allocations. Next, we will examine the different ways that data movement can affect graph execution in SYCL.

Explicit Data Movement

Explicit data movement has the advantage that it appears *explicitly* in a graph, making it obvious to programmers what goes on within execution of a graph. We will separate explicit data operations into those for USM and those for buffers.

As we learned in Chapter 6, explicit data movement in USM occurs when we need to copy data between device allocations and the host. This is done with the `memcpy` method, found in both the queue and handler classes. Submitting the action or command group returns an event that can be used to order the copy with other command groups.

Explicit data movement with buffers occurs by invoking either the `copy` or `update_host` method of the command group handler object. The `copy` method can be used to manually exchange data between host memory and an accessor object on a device. This can be done for a variety of reasons. A simple example is checkpointing a long-running sequence of computations. With the copy method, data can be written from the device to arbitrary host memory in a one-way fashion. If this were done using buffers, most cases (i.e., those where the buffer was not created with `use_host_ptr`) would require the data to first be copied to the host and then from the buffer's memory to the desired host memory.

The `update_host` method is a very specialized form of `copy`. If a buffer was created around a host pointer, this method will copy the data represented by the accessor back to the original host memory. This can be useful if a program manually synchronizes host data with a buffer that was created with the special `use_mutex` property. However, this use case is not likely to occur in most programs.

Implicit Data Movement

Implicit data movement can have hidden consequences for command groups and task graphs in SYCL. With implicit data movement, data is copied between host and device either by the SYCL runtime or by some combination of hardware and software. In either case, copying occurs without explicit input from the user. Let's again look separately at the USM and buffer cases.

With USM, implicit data movement occurs with `host` and `shared` allocations. As we learned in Chapter 6, `host` allocations do not really move data so much as access it remotely, and `shared` allocations may migrate between host and device. Since this migration happens automatically, there is really nothing to think about with USM implicit data movement and command groups. However, there are some nuances with `shared` allocations worth keeping in mind.

The `prefetch` operation works in a similar fashion to `memcpy` in order to let the runtime begin migrating shared allocations before a kernel attempts to use them. However, unlike `memcpy` where data must be copied in order to ensure correct results, prefetches are often treated as *hints* to the runtime to increase performance, and prefetches do not invalidate pointer values in memory (as a copy would when copying to a new address range). The program will still execute correctly if a prefetch has not completed before a kernel begins executing, and so many codes may choose to make command groups in a graph not depend on prefetch operations since they are not a functional requirement.

Buffers also carry some nuance. When using buffers, command groups must construct accessors for buffers that specify how the data will be used. These data dependences express the ordering between different command groups and allow us to construct task graphs. However, command groups with buffers sometimes fill another purpose: they specify the requirements on data movement.

Accessors specify that a kernel will read or write to a buffer. The corollary from this is that the data must also be available on the device, and if it is not, the runtime must move it there before the kernel may begin executing. Consequently, the SYCL runtime must keep track of where the current version of a buffer resides so that data movement operations can be scheduled. Accessor creation effectively creates an extra, hidden node in the graph. If data movement is necessary, the runtime must perform it first. Only then may the kernel being submitted execute.

Let us take another look at Figure 8-8. In this example, our first two kernels will require buffers `data1` and `data2` to be copied to the device; the runtime implicitly creates extra graph nodes to perform the data movement. When the third kernel's command group is submitted, it is likely that these buffers will still be on the device, so the runtime will not need to perform any extra data movement. The fourth kernel's data is also likely to not require any extra data movement, but the creation of the host accessor requires the runtime to schedule a movement of buffer `data1` back to the host before the accessor is available for use.

Synchronizing with the Host

The last topic we will discuss is how to synchronize graph execution with the host. We have already touched on this throughout the chapter, but we will now examine all the different ways a program can do this.

The first method for host synchronization is one we've used in many of our previous examples: waiting on a queue. Queue objects have two methods, `wait` and `wait_and_throw`, that block host execution until every command group that was submitted to the queue has completed. This is a very simple method that handles many common cases. However, it is worth pointing out that this method is very coarse-grained. If finer-grained synchronization is desired (to possibly improve performance, for example), one of the other approaches we will discuss may be better suit an application's needs.

The next method for host synchronization is to synchronize on events. This gives more flexibility over synchronizing on a queue since it lets an application only synchronize on specific actions or command groups. This is done by either invoking the `wait` method on an event or invoking the static method `wait` on the event class, which can accept a vector of events.

We have seen the next method used in Figures 8-5 and 8-8: host accessors. Host accessors perform two functions. First, they make data available for access on the host, as their name implies. Second, they synchronize the device and the host by defining a new dependence between the currently accessing graph and the host. This ensures that the data that gets copied back to the host has the correct value of the computation the graph was performing. However, we once again note that if the buffer was constructed from existing host memory, this original memory is not guaranteed to contain the updated values.

Note that host accessors are blocking. Execution on the host may not proceed past the creation of the host accessor until the data is available. Likewise, a buffer cannot be used on a device while a host accessor exists and keeps its data available. A common pattern is to create host accessors inside additional C++ scopes in order to free the data once the host accessor is no longer needed. This is an example of the next method for host synchronization.

Certain objects in SYCL have special behaviors when they are destroyed, and their destructors are invoked. We just learned how host accessors can make data remain on the host until they are destroyed. Buffers and images also have special behavior when they are destroyed or leave scope. When a buffer is destroyed, it waits for all command groups that use that buffer to finish execution. Once a buffer is no longer being used by any kernel or memory operation, the runtime may have to copy data back to the host. This copy occurs either if the buffer was initialized with a host pointer or if a host pointer was passed to the method `set_final_data`. The runtime will then copy back the data for that buffer and update the host pointer before the object is destroyed.

The final option for synchronizing with the host involves an uncommon feature first described in Chapter 7. Recall that the constructors for buffer objects optionally take a property list. One of the valid properties that may be passed when creating a buffer is `use_mutex`. When a buffer is created in this fashion, it adds the requirement that the memory owned by the buffer can be shared with the host application. Access to this memory is governed by the mutex used to initialize the buffer. The host is able to obtain the lock on the mutex when it is safe to access the memory shared with the buffer. If the lock cannot be obtained, the user may need to enqueue memory movement operations to synchronize the data with the host. This use is very specialized and unlikely to be found in the majority of DPC++ applications.

Summary

In this chapter, we have learned about graphs and how they are built, scheduled, and executed in SYCL. We went into detail on what command groups are and what function they serve. We discussed the three things that can be within a command group: dependences, an action, and miscellaneous host code. We reviewed how to specify dependences between tasks using events as well as through data dependences described by accessors. We learned that the single action in a command group may be either a kernel or an explicit memory operation, and we then looked at several examples that showed the different ways we can construct common execution graph patterns. Next, we reviewed how data movement is an important part of SYCL graphs, and we learned how it can appear either explicitly or implicitly in a graph. Finally, we looked at all the ways to synchronize the execution of a graph with the host.

Understanding the program flow can enable us to understand the sort of debug information that can be printed if we have runtime failures to debug. Chapter 13 has a table in the section "Debugging Runtime Failures" that will make a little more sense given the knowledge we have gained by this point in the book. However, this book does not attempt to discuss these advanced compiler dumps in detail.

Hopefully this has left you feeling like a graph expert who can construct graphs that range in complexity from linear chains to enormous graphs with hundreds of nodes and complex data and task dependences! In the next chapter, we'll begin to dive into low-level details that are useful for improving the performance of an application on a specific device.

CHAPTER 9

Communication and Synchronization

In Chapter 4, we discussed ways to express parallelism, using basic data-parallel kernels or explicit ND-range kernels. We discussed how basic data-parallel kernels apply the same operation to every piece of data independently. We also discussed how explicit ND-range kernels divide the execution range into work-groups of work-items.

In this chapter, we will revisit the question of how to break up a problem into bite-sized chunks in our continuing quest to *Think Parallel*. This chapter provides more detail regarding explicit ND-range kernels and describes how groupings of work-items may be used to improve the performance of some types of algorithms. We will describe how groups of work-items provide additional guarantees for how parallel work is executed, and we will introduce language features that support groupings of work-items. Many of these ideas and concepts will be important when optimizing programs for specific devices in Chapters 15, 16, and 17 and to describe common parallel patterns in Chapter 14.

Work-Groups and Work-Items

Recall from Chapter 4 that explicit ND-range kernels organize work-items into work-groups and that all work-items in the same work-group have

J. Reinders et al., *Data Parallel C++*, https://doi.org/10.1007/978-1-4842-9691-2_9

additional scheduling guarantees. This property is important, because it means that the work-items in a work-group can cooperate to solve a problem.

Figure 9-1 shows an ND-range divided into work-groups, where each work-group is represented by a different color. The work-items in each work-group can safely communicate with other work-items that share the same color.

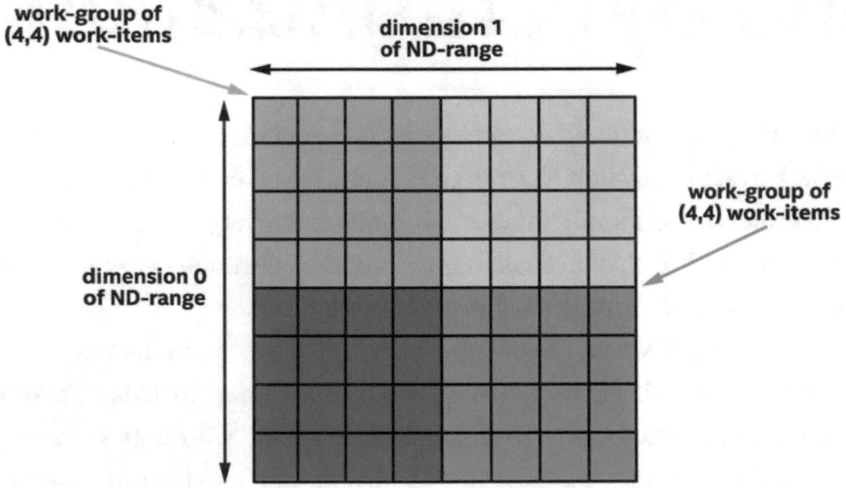

***Figure 9-1.** Two-dimensional ND-range of size (8, 8) divided into four work-groups of size (4,4)*

There are no guarantees that work-items in different work-groups will be executing at the same time, and so a work-item with one color cannot reliably communicate with a work-item with a different color. A kernel may deadlock if one work-item attempts to communicate with another work-item that is not currently executing. Since we want our kernels to complete execution, we must ensure that when one work-item communicates with another work-item, they are in the same work-group.

Building Blocks for Efficient Communication

This section describes building blocks that support efficient communication between work-items in a group. Some are fundamental building blocks that enable construction of custom algorithms, whereas others are higher level and describe common operations used by many kernels.

Synchronization via Barriers

The most fundamental building block for communication is the *barrier* function. The barrier function serves two key purposes:

First, the barrier function synchronizes execution of work-items in a group. By synchronizing execution, one work-item can ensure that another work-item in the same group has completed an operation before using the result of that operation. Alternatively, one work-item is given time to complete its operation before another work-item uses the result of the operation.

Second, the barrier function synchronizes how each work-item views the state of memory. This type of synchronization operation is known as enforcing *memory consistency* or *fencing* memory (more details in Chapter 19). Memory consistency is at least as important as synchronizing execution since it ensures that the results of memory operations performed before the barrier are visible to other work-items after the barrier. Without memory consistency, an operation in one work-item is like a tree falling in a forest, where the sound may or may not be heard by other work-items!

Figure 9-2 shows four work-items in a group that synchronize at a barrier function. Even though the execution time for each work-item may differ, no work-items can execute past the barrier until all work-items execute the barrier. After executing the barrier function, all work-items have a consistent view of memory.

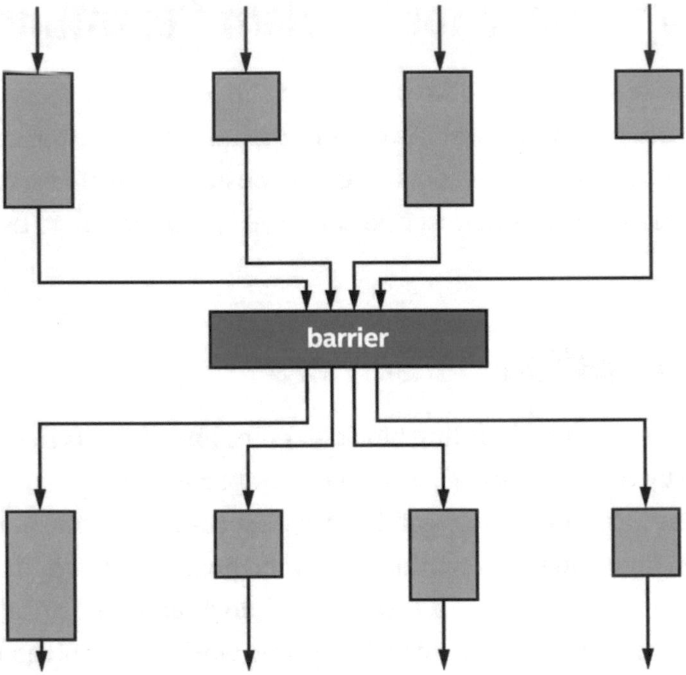

Figure 9-2. *Four work-items in a group synchronize at a barrier function*

WHY ISN'T MEMORY CONSISTENT BY DEFAULT?

For many programmers, the idea of memory consistency—and that different work-items can have different views of memory—can feel very strange. Wouldn't it be easier if all memory was consistent for all work-items by default? The short answer is that it would, but it would also be very expensive to implement. By allowing work-items to have inconsistent views of memory and only requiring memory consistency at defined points during program execution, accelerator hardware may be cheaper, may perform better, or both.

Because barrier functions synchronize execution, it is critically important that either all work-items in the group execute the barrier or no work-items in the group execute the barrier. If some work-items in the group branch around any barrier function, the other work-items in the group may wait at the barrier forever—or at least until the user gives up and terminates the program!

COLLECTIVE FUNCTIONS

When a function is required to be executed by all work-items in a group, it may be called a *collective function*, since the operation is performed by the group and not by individual work-items in the group. Barrier functions are not the only collective functions available in SYCL. Other collective functions are described later in this chapter.

Work-Group Local Memory

The work-group barrier function is sufficient to coordinate communication among work-items in a work-group, but the communication itself must occur through memory. Communication may occur through USM or buffers, but this can be inconvenient and inefficient: it requires a dedicated allocation for communication and requires partitioning the allocation among work-groups.

To simplify kernel development and accelerate communication between work-items in a work-group, SYCL defines a special *local memory* space specifically for communication between work-items in a work-group.

In Figure 9-3, two work-groups are shown. Both work-groups may access USM and buffers in the *global memory* space. Each work-group may access variables in its own *local memory* space but cannot access variables in another work-group's local memory.

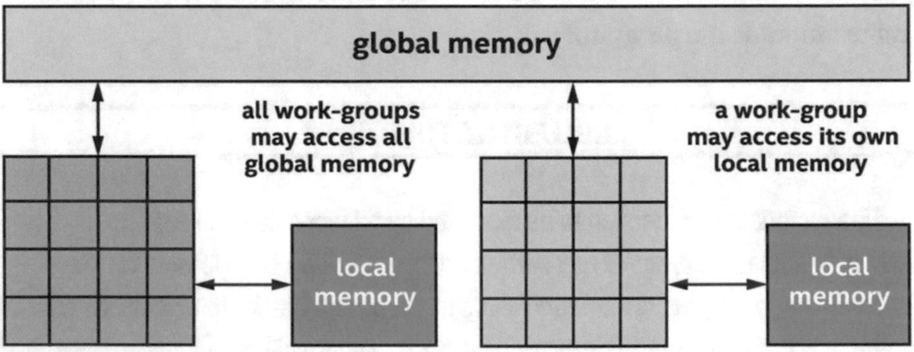

Figure 9-3. *Each work-group may access all global memory, but only its own local memory*

When a work-group begins, the contents of its local memory are uninitialized, and local memory does not persist after a work-group finishes executing. Because of these properties, local memory may only be used for temporary storage while a work-group is executing.

For some devices, such as for many CPU devices, local memory is a software abstraction and is implemented using the same memory subsystems as global memory. On these devices, using local memory is primarily a convenience mechanism for communication. Some compilers may use the memory space information for compiler optimizations, but otherwise using local memory for communication will not fundamentally perform better than communication via global memory on these devices.

For other devices, such as many GPU devices, there are dedicated resources for local memory. On these devices, communicating via local memory will perform better than communicating via global memory.

Communication between work-items in a work-group can be more convenient and faster when using local memory!

We can use the device query `info::device::local_mem_type` to determine whether an accelerator has dedicated resources for local memory or whether local memory is implemented as a software abstraction of global memory. Please refer to Chapter 12 for more information about querying properties of a device and to Chapters 15, 16, and 17 for more information about how local memory is typically implemented for CPUs, GPUs, and FPGAs.

Using Work-Group Barriers and Local Memory

Now that we have identified the basic building blocks for efficient communication between work-items, we can describe how to express work-group barriers and local memory in kernels. Remember that communication between work-items requires a notion of work-item grouping, so these concepts can only be expressed for ND-range kernels and are not included in the execution model for basic data-parallel kernels.

This chapter will build upon the naïve matrix multiplication kernel examples introduced in Chapter 4 by introducing communication between the work-items in the work-groups executing the matrix multiplication. On many devices—but not necessarily all!—communicating through local memory will improve the performance of the matrix multiplication kernel.

A NOTE ABOUT MATRIX MULTIPLICATION

In this book, matrix multiplication kernels are used to demonstrate how changes in a kernel affect performance. Although matrix multiplication performance may be improved on many devices using the techniques described in this chapter, matrix multiplication is such an important and common operation that many vendors have implemented highly tuned versions of matrix multiplication. Vendors invest significant time and effort implementing and validating functions for specific devices and in some cases may use functionality or techniques that are difficult or impossible to use in standard parallel kernels.

USE VENDOR-PROVIDED LIBRARIES!

When a vendor provides a library implementation of a function, it is almost always beneficial to use it rather than reimplementing the function as a parallel kernel! For matrix multiplication, one can look to oneMKL as part of Intel's toolkits for solutions appropriate for C++ with SYCL programmers.

Figure 9-4 shows the naïve matrix multiplication kernel we will be starting from, similar to the matrix multiplication kernel from Chapter 4. For this kernel, and for all of the matrix multiplication kernels in this chapter, `T` is a template type indicating the type of data stored in the matrix, such as a 32-bit `float` or a 64-bit `double`.

```
h.parallel_for(range{M, N}, [=](id<2> id) {
  int m = id[0];
  int n = id[1];

  // Template type T is the type of data stored
  // in the matrix
  T sum = 0;
  for (int k = 0; k < K; k++) {
    sum += matrixA[m][k] * matrixB[k][n];
  }

  matrixC[m][n] = sum;
});
```

Figure 9-4. *The naïve matrix multiplication kernel from Chapter 4*

In Chapter 4, we observed that the matrix multiplication algorithm has a high degree of reuse, and that grouping work-items may improve locality of access and therefore may also improve cache hit rates. In this chapter, instead of relying on *implicit* cache behavior to improve performance, our modified matrix multiplication kernels will instead use local memory as an *explicit cache*, to guarantee locality of access.

For many algorithms, it is helpful to think of local memory as an explicit cache.

Figure 9-5 is a modified diagram from Chapter 4 showing a work-group consisting of a single row, which makes the algorithm using local memory easier to understand. Observe that for elements in a row of the result matrix, every result element is computed using a unique column of data from one of the input matrices, shown in blue and orange. Because there is no data sharing for this input matrix, it is not an ideal candidate for local memory. Observe, though, that every result element in the row accesses the exact same data in the other input matrix, shown in green. Because this data is reused, it is an excellent candidate to benefit from work-group local memory.

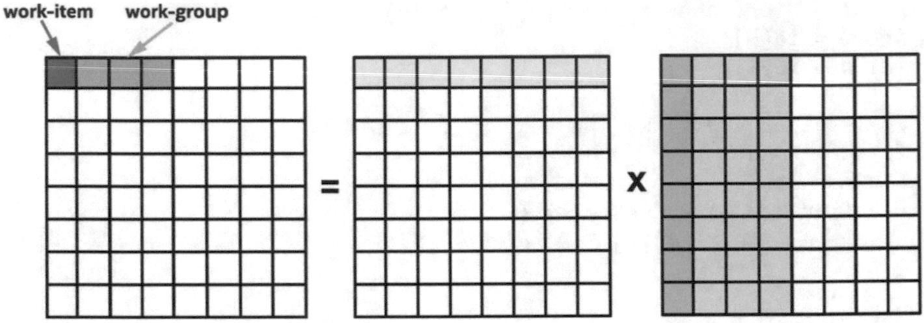

***Figure 9-5.** Mapping of matrix multiplication to work-groups and work-items*

Because we want to multiply matrices that are potentially very large and because work-group local memory may be a limited resource, our modified kernels will process subsections of each matrix, which we will refer to as a matrix *tile*. For each tile, our modified kernel will load data for the tile into local memory, synchronize the work-items in the group, and then load the data from local memory rather than global memory. The data that is accessed for the first tile is shown in Figure 9-6.

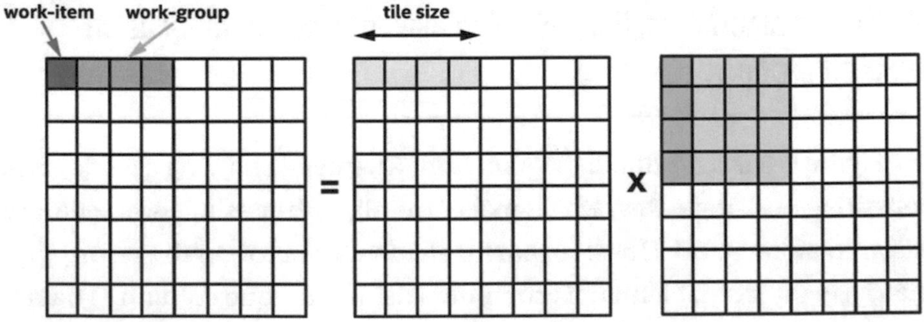

***Figure 9-6.** Processing the first tile: the green input data (left of X) is reused and is read from local memory, the blue and orange input data (right of X) is read from global memory*

In our kernels, we have chosen the tile size to be equivalent to the work-group size. This is not required, but because it simplifies transfers into or out of local memory, it is common and convenient to choose a tile size that is a multiple of the work-group size.

Work-Group Barriers and Local Memory in ND-Range Kernels

This section describes how work-group barriers and local memory are expressed in ND-range kernels. For ND-range kernels, the representation is explicit: a kernel declares and operates on a local accessor representing an allocation in the local address space and calls a barrier function to synchronize the work-items in a work-group.

Local Accessors

To declare local memory for use in an ND-range kernel, use a *local accessor*. Like other accessor objects, a local accessor is constructed within a command group handler, but unlike the accessor objects discussed in Chapters 3 and 7, a local accessor is not created from a buffer object. Instead, a local accessor is created by specifying a type and a range describing the number of elements of that type. Like other accessors, local accessors may be one-dimensional, two-dimensional, or three-dimensional. Figure 9-7 demonstrates how to declare local accessors and use them in a kernel.

```
/ This is a typical global accessor.
accessor dataAcc{dataBuf, h};

// This is a 1D local accessor consisting of 16 ints:
auto localIntAcc = local_accessor<int, 1>(16, h);

// This is a 2D local accessor consisting of 4 x 4
// floats:
auto localFloatAcc =
    local_accessor<float, 2>({4, 4}, h);

h.parallel_for(
    nd_range<1>{{size}, {16}}, [=](nd_item<1> item) {
      auto index = item.get_global_id();
      auto local_index = item.get_local_id();

      // Within a kernel, a local accessor may be read
      // from and written to like any other accessor.
      localIntAcc[local_index] = dataAcc[index] + 1;
      dataAcc[index] = localIntAcc[local_index];
    });
```

Figure 9-7. *Declaring and using local accessors*

Remember that local memory is uninitialized when each work-group begins and does not persist after each work-group completes. This means that a local accessor must always be `read_write`, since otherwise a kernel would have no way to assign the contents of local memory or view the results of an assignment. Local accessors may optionally be atomic though, in which case accesses to local memory via the accessor are performed atomically. Atomic accesses are discussed in more detail in Chapter 19.

Synchronization Functions

To synchronize the work-items in an ND-range kernel work-group, call the `group_barrier` function with a group representing the work-group. Because the group representing the work-group may only be queried from an `nd_item` and cannot be queried from an `item`, work-group barriers are only available to ND-range kernels and are not available to basic data-parallel kernels.

The `group_barrier` function accepts one additional optional argument to describe the *scope* of any memory consistency operations that are performed by the barrier. When no additional arguments are passed to the `group_barrier` function, the barrier function will determine the default scope based on the passed-in group. The default scope is usually correct and therefore an explicit scope is rarely required, but the memory scope can be broadened if necessary for some algorithms.

Please note that the explicit scope only affects the memory operations that are performed by the barrier, and that the set of work-items that synchronize execution at the barrier is determined entirely by the group object passed to the barrier. We cannot synchronize more or fewer work-items by passing a different memory scope to the barrier, but we can synchronize a different set of work-items by passing a different group object to the barrier.

A Full ND-Range Kernel Example

Now that we know how to declare a local memory accessor and synchronize accesses to it using a barrier function, we can implement an ND-range kernel version of matrix multiplication that coordinates communication among work-items in the work-group to reduce traffic to global memory. The complete example is shown in Figure 9-8.

```
// Traditional accessors, representing matrices in
// global memory:
accessor matrixA{bufA, h};
accessor matrixB{bufB, h};
accessor matrixC{bufC, h};

// Local accessor, for one matrix tile:
constexpr int tile_size = 16;

// Template type T is the type of data stored in the matrix
auto tileA = local_accessor<T, 1>(tile_size, h);

h.parallel_for(
    nd_range<2>{{M, N}, {1, tile_size}},
    [=](nd_item<2> item) {
      // Indices in the global index space:
      int m = item.get_global_id()[0];
      int n = item.get_global_id()[1];

      // Index in the local index space:
      int i = item.get_local_id()[1];

      T sum = 0;
      for (int kk = 0; kk < K; kk += tile_size) {
        // Load the matrix tile from matrix A, and
        // synchronize to ensure all work-items have a
        // consistent view of the matrix tile in local
        // memory.
        tileA[i] = matrixA[m][kk + i];
        group_barrier(item.get_group());

        // Perform computation using the local memory
        // tile, and matrix B in global memory.
        for (int k = 0; k < tile_size; k++) {
          sum += tileA[k] * matrixB[kk + k][n];
        }

        // After computation, synchronize again, to
        // ensure all reads from the local memory tile
        // are complete.
        group_barrier(item.get_group());
      }

      // Write the final result to global memory.
      matrixC[m][n] = sum;
    });
```

***Figure 9-8.** Expressing a tiled matrix multiplication kernel with an ND-range `parallel_for` and work-group local memory*

The main loop in this kernel can be thought of as two distinct phases: in the first phase, the work-items in the work-group collaborate to load shared data from the A matrix into work-group local memory; and in the second, the work-items perform their own computations using the shared data. To ensure that all work-items have completed the first phase before moving onto the second phase, the two phases are separated by a call to `group_barrier` to synchronize all work-items in the work-group and to provide a memory fence. This pattern is a common one, and the use of work-group local memory in a kernel almost always necessitates the use of work-group barriers.

Note that there must also be a call to `group_barrier` to synchronize execution between the computation phase for the current tile and the loading phase for the next matrix tile. Without this synchronization operation, part of the current matrix tile may be overwritten by one work-item in the work-group before another work-item is finished computing with it. In general, any time that one work-item is reading or writing data in local memory that was read or written by another work-item, synchronization is required. In Figure 9-8, the synchronization is done at the end of the loop, but it would be equally correct to synchronize at the beginning of each loop iteration instead.

Sub-Groups

So far in this chapter, work-items have communicated with other work-items in the work-group by exchanging data through work-group local memory and by synchronizing using the `group_barrier` function on a work-group.

In Chapter 4, we discussed another grouping of work-items. A sub-group is an implementation-defined subset of work-items in a work-group that execute together on the same hardware resources or with additional scheduling guarantees. Because the implementation decides how to group work-items into sub-groups, the work-items in a sub-group may be able to communicate or synchronize more efficiently than the work-items in an arbitrary work-group.

This section describes the building blocks for communication among work-items in a sub-group. Sub-groups also require a notion of work-item grouping, so sub-groups also require ND-range kernels and are not included in the execution model for basic data-parallel kernels.

Synchronization via Sub-Group Barriers

Just like how the work-items in a work-group may synchronize using a work-group barrier, the work-items in a sub-group may synchronize using a sub-group barrier. To perform a sub-group barrier, call the same `group_barrier` function, but pass a group object representing the sub-group rather than the work-group, as shown in Figure 9-9. Like for work-group objects, a group object representing the sub-group can be queried from the `nd_item` class for ND-range kernels but cannot be queried from a basic data-parallel `item`.

```
h.parallel_for(
    nd_range{{size}, {16}}, [=](nd_item<1> item) {
      auto sg = item.get_sub_group();
      group_barrier(sg);
      // ...
      auto index = item.get_global_id();
      data_acc[index] = data_acc[index] + 1;
    });
```

Figure 9-9. *Querying and using the `sub_group` class*

Also like the work-group barrier, the sub-group barrier may accept optional arguments to broaden the scope of any memory operations associated with the sub-group barrier, but this is uncommon and in most cases we can simply use the default memory scope.

Exchanging Data Within a Sub-Group

Unlike work-groups, sub-groups do not have a dedicated memory space for exchanging data. Instead, work-items in the sub-group may exchange data through work-group local memory, through global memory, or more commonly by using sub-group *collective functions*.

As described previously, a *collective function* is a function that describes an operation performed by a group of work-items, not an individual work-item. Because a barrier synchronization function is an operation performed by a group of work-items, it is one example of a collective function.

Other collective functions express common communication patterns. We will describe the semantics for many collective functions in detail later in this chapter, but for now, we focus on the `group_broadcast` collective function that we will use to implement matrix multiplication using sub-groups.

The `group_broadcast` collective function takes a value from one work-item in the group and communicates it to all other work-items in the group. An example is shown in Figure 9-10. Notice that the semantics of the broadcast function require that the `local_id` identifying the value in the group to communicate must be the same for all work-items in the group, ensuring that the result of the broadcast function is also the same for all work-items in the group.

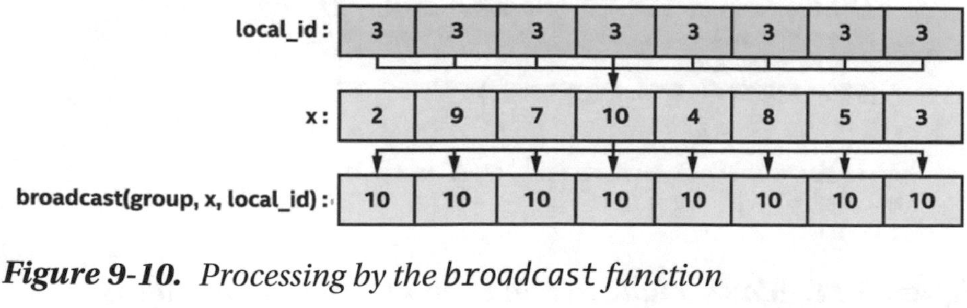

Figure 9-10. *Processing by the* `broadcast` *function*

If we look at the innermost loop of our local memory matrix multiplication kernel, shown in Figure 9-11, we can see that the access to the matrix tile is a broadcast operation, since each work-item in the group reads the same value out of the matrix tile.

```
h.parallel_for(
    nd_range<2>{{M, N}, {1, tile_size}},
    [=](nd_item<2> item) {
      // Indices in the global index space:
      int m = item.get_global_id()[0];
      int n = item.get_global_id()[1];

      // Index in the local index space:
      int i = item.get_local_id()[1];

      // Template type T is the type of data stored in
      // the matrix
      T sum = 0;
      for (int kk = 0; kk < K; kk += tile_size) {
        // Load the matrix tile from matrix A, and
        // synchronize to ensure all work-items have a
        // consistent view of the matrix tile in local
        // memory.
        tileA[i] = matrixA[m][kk + i];
        group_barrier(item.get_group());

        // Perform computation using the local memory
        // tile, and matrix B in global memory.
        for (int k = 0; k < tile_size; k++) {
          // Because the value of k is the same for
          // all work-items in the group, these reads
          // from tileA are broadcast operations.
          sum += tileA[k] * matrixB[kk + k][n];
        }

        // After computation, synchronize again, to
        // ensure all reads from the local memory tile
        // are complete.
        group_barrier(item.get_group());
      }

      // Write the final result to global memory.
      matrixC[m][n] = sum;
    });
```

***Figure 9-11.** Matrix multiplication kernel includes a broadcast operation*

We will use the `group_broadcast` function with a sub-group object to implement a matrix multiplication kernel that does not require work-group local memory or barriers. On many devices, sub-group broadcasts are faster than work-group broadcasts using work-group local memory and barriers.

A Full Sub-Group ND-Range Kernel Example

Figure 9-12 is a complete example that implements matrix multiplication using sub-groups. Notice that this kernel requires no work-group local memory or explicit synchronization and instead uses a sub-group broadcast collective function to communicate the contents of the matrix tile among the work-items in the sub-group.

```
// Note: This example assumes that the sub-group size
// is greater than or equal to the tile size!
constexpr int tile_size = 4;
h.parallel_for(
    nd_range<2>{{M, N}, {1, tile_size}},
    [=](nd_item<2> item) {
      auto sg = item.get_sub_group();

      // Indices in the global index space:
      int m = item.get_global_id()[0];
      int n = item.get_global_id()[1];

      // Index in the local index space:
      int i = item.get_local_id()[1];

      // Template type T is the type of data stored
      // in the matrix
      T sum = 0;
      for (int kk = 0; kk < K; kk += tile_size) {
        // Load the matrix tile from matrix A.
        T tileA = matrixA[m][kk + i];

        // Perform computation by broadcasting from
        // the matrix tile and loading from matrix B
        // in global memory.  The loop variable k
        // describes which work-item in the sub-group
        // to broadcast data from.
        for (int k = 0; k < tile_size; k++) {
          sum += group_broadcast(sg, tileA, k) *
                 matrixB[kk + k][n];
        }
      }

      // Write the final result to global memory.
      matrixC[m][n] = sum;
    });
```

***Figure 9-12.** Tiled matrix multiplication kernel expressed with ND-range `parallel_for` and sub-group collective functions*

Group Functions and Group Algorithms

In the "Sub-Groups" section of this chapter, we described collective functions and how collective functions express common communication patterns. We specifically discussed the broadcast collective function, which is used to communicate a value from one work-item in a group to the other work-items in the group. This section describes additional collective functions.

Although the collective functions described in this section can be implemented directly in our programs using features such as atomics, work-group local memory, and barriers, many devices include dedicated hardware to accelerate collective functions. Even when a device does not include specialized hardware, vendor-provided implementations of collective functions are likely tuned for the device they are running on, so calling a built-in collective function will usually perform better than a general-purpose implementation that we might write.

Use collective functions for common communication patterns to simplify code and increase performance!

Broadcast

The `group_broadcast` function enables one work-item in a group to share the value of a variable with all other work-items in the group. A diagram showing how the broadcast function works can be found in Figure 9-10. The `group_broadcast` function is supported for both work-groups and sub-groups.

Votes

The any_of_group, all_of_group, and none_of_group functions (henceforth referred to as "vote" functions) enable work-items to compare the result of a Boolean condition across their group: any_of_group returns true if the condition is true for at least one work-item in the group, all_of_group returns true if the condition is true for all work-items in the group, and none_of_group returns true if the condition is false for all of the work-items in the group. A comparison of these two functions for an example input is shown in Figure 9-13.

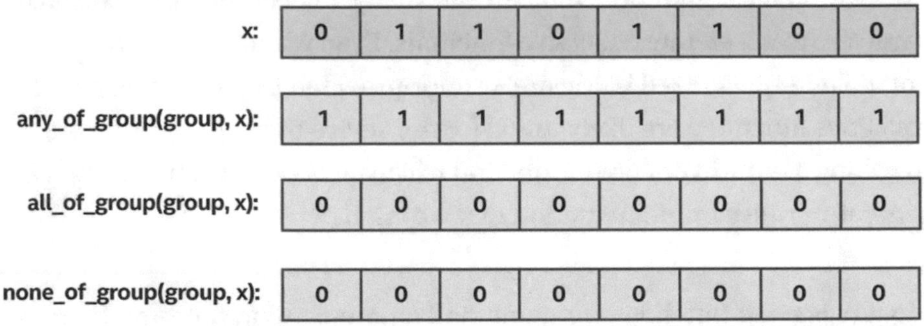

Figure 9-13. *Comparison of the any_of_group, all_of_group, and none_of_group functions*

SYCL 2020 also supports another variant of these functions where the work-items in a group cooperate to evaluate a range of data like the standard C++ all_of, any_of, and none_of algorithms. These functions are named joint_any_of, joint_all_of, and joint_none_of to differentiate from the variants where each work-item in the group holds the data to compare directly.

The vote functions are useful for some iterative algorithms to determine when a solution has converged for all work-items in the group, for example. The vote functions are supported for work-groups and sub-groups.

Shuffles

One of the most useful features of sub-groups is the ability to communicate directly between individual work-items without explicit memory operations. In many cases, such as the sub-group matrix multiplication kernel, these *shuffle* operations enable us to both remove work-group local memory usage from our kernels and avoid unnecessary repeated accesses to global memory. There are several flavors of these shuffle functions available.

The most general of the shuffle functions is called `select_from_group`, and as shown in Figure 9-14, it allows for arbitrary communication between any pair of work-items in the sub-group. This generality may come at a performance cost, however, and we strongly encourage making use of the more specialized shuffle functions wherever possible.

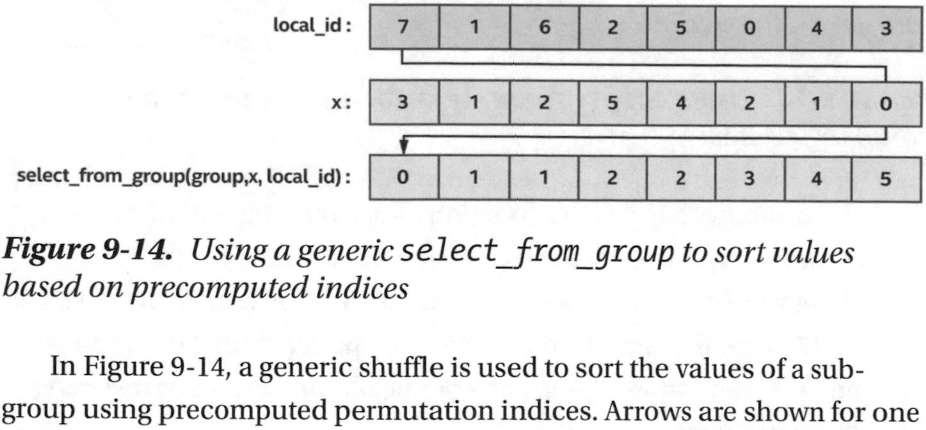

***Figure 9-14.** Using a generic `select_from_group` to sort values based on precomputed indices*

In Figure 9-14, a generic shuffle is used to sort the values of a sub-group using precomputed permutation indices. Arrows are shown for one work-item in the sub-group, where the result of the shuffle is the value of `x` for the work-item with `local_id` equal to 7.

Note that the sub-group `group_broadcast` function can be thought of as a specialized version of the general-purpose `select_from_group` function, where the shuffle index is the same for all work-items in the sub-group. When the shuffle index is known to be the same for all work-items in the sub-group, using `group_broadcast` instead of `select_from_group` provides the compiler additional information and may increase performance on some implementations.

The `shift_group_right` and `shift_group_left` functions effectively *shift* the contents of a sub-group by a fixed number of elements in a given direction, as shown in Figure 9-15. Note that the values returned to the last five work-items in the sub-group are undefined and are shown as blank in Figure 9-15. Shifting can be useful for parallelizing loops with loop-carried dependences or when implementing common algorithms such as exclusive or inclusive scans.

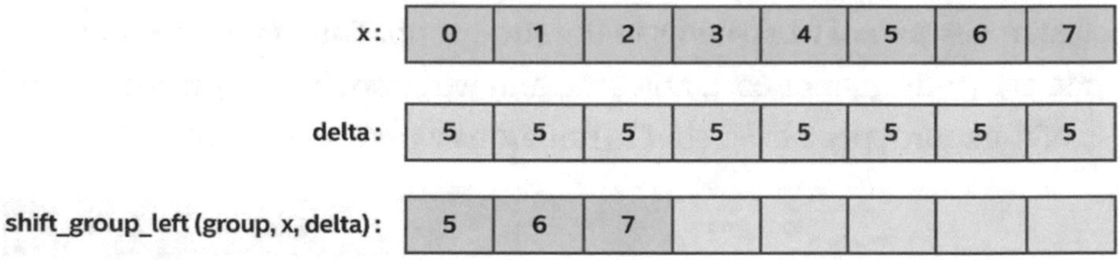

Figure 9-15. *Using `shift_group_left` to shift x values of a sub-group by five items*

The `permute_group_by_xor` function swaps the values of two work-items, specified by the result of an XOR operation applied to the work-item's sub-group local id and a fixed constant. As shown in Figure 9-16 and Figure 9-17, several common communication patterns can be expressed using an XOR, such as swapping pairs of neighboring values or reversing the sub-group values.

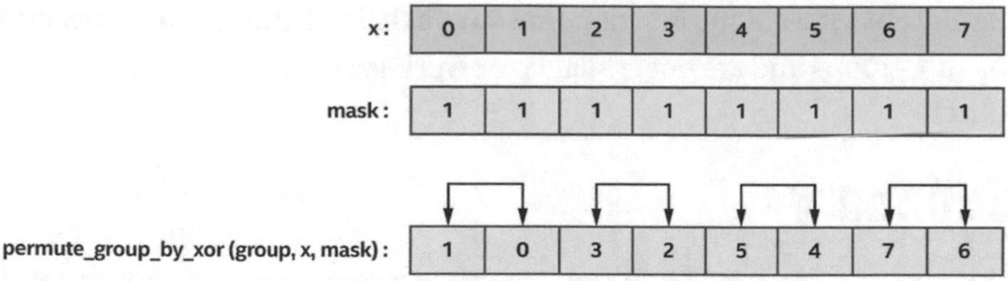

***Figure 9-16.** Swapping neighboring pairs of `x` using a `permute_group_by_xor`*

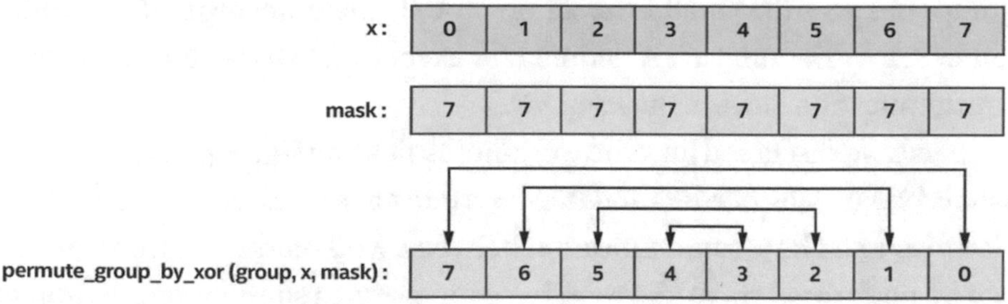

***Figure 9-17.** Reversing the values of `x` using a `permute_group_by_xor`*

> **SUB-GROUP OPTIMIZATIONS USING BROADCAST, VOTE, AND COLLECTIVES**
>
> The behavior of broadcast, vote, and other collective functions applied to sub-groups is identical to when they are applied to work-groups, but they deserve additional attention because they may enable aggressive optimizations in certain compilers. For example, a compiler may be able to reduce register usage for variables that are broadcast to all work-items in a sub-group, or may be able to reason about control flow divergence based on usage of the `any_of_group` and `all_of_group` functions.

Because the shuffle functions are so specialized, they are only available for sub-groups and are not available for work-groups.

Summary

This chapter discussed how work-items in a group may communicate and cooperate to improve the performance of some types of kernels.

We first discussed how ND-range kernels support grouping work-items into work-groups. We discussed how grouping work-items into work-groups changes the parallel execution model, guaranteeing that the work-items in a work-group are scheduled for execution in a way that enables communication and synchronization.

Next, we discussed how the work-items in a work-group may synchronize using barriers and how barriers are expressed in kernels. We also discussed how communication between work-items in a work-group can be performed via work-group local memory, to simplify kernels and to improve performance, and we discussed how work-group local memory is represented using local accessors.

We discussed how work-groups in ND-range kernels may be further divided into sub-groupings of work-items, where the sub-groups of work-items may support additional communication patterns or scheduling guarantees.

For both work-groups and sub-groups, we discussed how common communication patterns may be expressed and accelerated through the use of collective functions.

The concepts in this chapter are an important foundation for understanding the common parallel patterns described in Chapter 14 and for understanding how to optimize for specific devices in Chapters 15, 16, and 17.

CHAPTER 10

Defining Kernels

Thus far in this book, our code examples have represented kernels using C++ lambda expressions. Lambda expressions are a concise and convenient way to represent a kernel right where it is used, but they are not the only way to represent a kernel in SYCL. In this chapter, we will explore various ways to define kernels in detail, helping us to choose a kernel form that is most natural for our C++ coding needs.

This chapter explains and compares three ways to represent a kernel:

- Lambda expressions.
- Named function objects (functors).
- Via interoperability with kernels created via other languages or APIs. This topic is covered briefly in this chapter, and in more detail in Chapter 20.

This chapter closes with a discussion of how to explicitly manipulate kernels in a kernel bundle to query kernel properties and to control when and how kernels are compiled.

Why Three Ways to Represent a Kernel?

Before we dive into the details, let's start with a summary of why there are three ways to define a kernel and the advantages and disadvantages of each method. A useful summary is given in Figure 10-1.

J. Reinders et al., *Data Parallel C++*, https://doi.org/10.1007/978-1-4842-9691-2_10

Bear in mind that a kernel is used to express a unit of computation and that many instances of a kernel will usually execute in parallel on an accelerator. SYCL supports multiple ways to express a kernel to integrate naturally and seamlessly into codebases with different coding styles, while also executing efficiently on a wide diversity of accelerator types.

Kernel Representation	Description
Lambda Expression	Pros: • Lambda expressions are a concise way to represent a kernel right where it is used. • Lambda expressions are a familiar way to represent kernel-like operations in modern C++ codebases. • Lambda capture rules automatically pass data to kernels. Cons: • Kernels represented as lambda expressions cannot be templated, and do not assemble as a library (like regular functions) without extra work. • The lambda syntax may be unfamiliar to some C++ codebases.
Named Function Object (Functor)	Pros: • Functors can be templated, reused, and shipped as a part of a library, just like any other C++ class. • Functors provide more control over the data that gets passed into a kernel. Cons: • Kernels represented as functors require more code than kernels represented as lambda expressions. • Kernel arguments must be explicitly passed to functors and are not captured automatically.
Interoperability with Other Languages or APIs	Pros: • Enables re-use of previously written kernels or libraries. • Enables large application codebases to incrementally add support for SYCL. • Kernel languages from other APIs may support features that have not been added or are difficult to express with SYCL. Cons: • Interoperability is an optional feature that may not be supported by all SYCL implementations or by all SYCL devices in an implementation. • Kernels written in other APIs are not compiled by the SYCL device compiler, which may limit compile-time syntax checking, type checking for kernel arguments, and optimization opportunities. • Kernels written in other APIs may not support the latest C++ features.

Figure 10-1. *Three ways to represent a kernel*

Kernels as Lambda Expressions

C++ lambda expressions, also referred to as *anonymous function objects, unnamed function objects, closures,* or simply *lambdas,* are a convenient way to express a kernel right where it is used. This section describes how to represent a kernel as a C++ lambda expression. This expands on the introductory refresher on C++ lambda expressions, in Chapter 1, which included some basic coding samples with output.

C++ lambda expressions are very powerful and have an expressive syntax, but only a specific subset of the full C++ lambda expression syntax is required (and supported) when expressing a kernel in SYCL.

```
h.parallel_for(
    size,
    // This is the start of a kernel lambda expression:
    [=](id<1> i) { data_acc[i] = data_acc[i] + 1; }
    // This is the end of the kernel lambda expression.
);
```

Figure 10-2. *Simple kernel defined using a lambda expression*

Elements of a Kernel Lambda Expression

Figure 10-2 shows a simple kernel written as a typical lambda expression—the code examples so far in this book have used this syntax.

The illustration in Figure 10-3 shows elements of a lambda expression that may be used with kernels, but many of these elements are not typical. In most cases, the lambda defaults are sufficient, so a typical kernel lambda expression looks more like the lambda expression in Figure 10-2 than the more complicated lambda expression in Figure 10-3.

```
q.submit([&](handler& h) {
  accessor data_acc{data_buf, h};
  h.parallel_for(
      nd_range{{size}, {8}},
       1     2     4  5                          6              7
      [=](id<1> i) noexcept [[sycl::reqd_work_group_size(8)]]  ->void  {
          data_acc[i] = data_acc[i] + 1;       3
        });
});
```

Figure 10-3. *More elements of a kernel lambda expression, including optional elements*

1. The first part of a lambda expression describes the lambda *captures*. *Capturing* a variable from a surrounding scope enables it to be used within the lambda expression, without explicitly passing it to the lambda expression as a parameter.

   C++ lambda expressions support capturing a variable by copying it or by creating a reference to it, but for kernel lambda expressions, variables may only be captured by copy. General practice is to simply use the default capture mode [=], which implicitly captures all variables by value, although it is possible to explicitly name each captured variable in a comma-separated capture-list as well. Any variable used within a kernel that is not captured by value will cause a compile-time error. Note that global variables are not captured by a lambda expression, as per the C++ standard.

2. The second part of a lambda expression describes parameters that are passed to the lambda expression, just like parameters that are passed to named functions.

For kernel lambda expressions, the parameter depends on how the kernel was invoked and identifies the index of the work-item in the parallel execution space. Please refer to Chapter 4 for more details about the various parallel execution spaces and how to identify the index of a work-item in each execution space.

3. The last part of the lambda expression defines the function body. For a kernel lambda expression, the function body describes the operations that should be performed at each index in the parallel execution space.

There are other parts of a lambda expression, but they are either optional, infrequently used, or unsupported by SYCL 2020:

4. No *specifiers* (such as `mutable`) are defined by SYCL 2020, so none are shown in the example code.

5. The *exception specification* is supported, but must be `noexcept` if provided, since exceptions are not supported for kernels.

6. Lambda *attributes* are supported and may be used to control how the kernel is compiled. For example, the `reqd_work_group_size` attribute can be used to require a specific work-group size for a kernel, and the `device_has` attribute can be used to require specific device aspects for a kernel. Chapter 12 contains more information on kernel specialization using `attributes` and `aspects`.

7. The *return type* may be specified but must be `void` if provided, since non-`void` return types are not supported for kernels.

LAMBDA CAPTURES: IMPLICIT OR EXPLICIT?

Some C++ style guides recommend against implicit (or default) captures for lambda expressions due to possible dangling pointer issues, especially when lambda expressions cross scope boundaries. The same issues may occur when lambdas are used to represent kernels, since kernel lambdas execute asynchronously on the device, separately from host code.

Because implicit captures are useful and concise, it is common practice for SYCL kernels and a convention we use in this book, but it is ultimately our decision whether to prefer the brevity of implicit captures or the clarity of explicit captures.

Identifying Kernel Lambda Expressions

There is one more element that must be provided in some cases when a kernel is written as a lambda expression: because lambda expressions are *anonymous,* at times SYCL requires an explicit kernel name template parameter to uniquely identify a kernel written as a lambda expression.

```
// In this example, "class Add" names the kernel
// lambda expression.
h.parallel_for<class Add>(size, [=](id<1> i) {
  data_acc[i] = data_acc[i] + 1;
});
```

Figure 10-4. *Identifying kernel lambda expressions*

Naming a kernel lambda expression is a way for a host code compiler to identify which kernel to invoke when the kernel was compiled by a separate device code compiler. Naming a kernel lambda also enables runtime introspection of a compiled kernel or building a kernel by name, as shown in Figure 10-9.

To support more concise code when the kernel name template parameter is not required, the kernel name template parameter is optional for most SYCL 2020 compilers. When no kernel name template parameter is required, our code can be more compact, as shown in Figure 10-5.

```
h.parallel_for(size, [=](id<1> i) {
  data_acc[i] = data_acc[i] + 1;
});
```

Figure 10-5. *Using unnamed kernel lambda expressions*

Because the kernel name template parameter for lambda expressions is not required in most cases, we can usually start with an unnamed lambda and only add a kernel name in specific cases when the kernel name template parameter is required.

When the kernel name template parameter is not required, using unnamed kernel lambdas is preferred to reduce verbosity.

Kernels as Named Function Objects

Named function objects, also known as *functors*, are an established pattern in C++ that allows operating on an arbitrary collection of data while maintaining a well-defined interface. When used to represent a kernel, the member variables of a named function object define the state that the kernel may operate on, and the overloaded function call `operator()` is invoked for each work-item in the parallel execution space.

Named function objects require more code than lambda expressions to express a kernel, but the extra verbosity provides more control and additional capabilities. It may be easier to analyze and optimize kernels expressed as named function objects, for example, since any buffers and data values used by the kernel must be explicitly passed to the kernel, rather than captured automatically by a lambda expression.

Kernels expressed as named function objects may also be easier to debug, easier to reuse, and they may be shipped as part of a separate header file or library.

Finally, because named function objects are just like any other C++ class, kernels expressed as named function objects may be templated. C++20 added templated lambda expressions, but templated lambda expressions are not supported for kernels in SYCL 2020, which is based on C++17.

Elements of a Kernel Named Function Object

The code in Figure 10-6 demonstrates typical usage of a kernel represented as a named function object. In this example, the parameters to the kernel are passed to the class constructor, and the kernel itself is in the overloaded function call `operator()`.

```
class Add {
 public:
  Add(accessor<int> acc) : data_acc(acc) {}
  void operator()(id<1> i) const {
    data_acc[i] = data_acc[i] + 1;
  }

 private:
  accessor<int> data_acc;
};

int main() {
  constexpr size_t size = 16;
  std::array<int, size> data;

  for (int i = 0; i < size; i++) {
    data[i] = i;
  }

  {
    buffer data_buf{data};

    queue q;
    std::cout
        << "Running on device: "
        << q.get_device().get_info<info::device::name>()
        << "\n";

    q.submit([&](handler& h) {
      accessor data_acc{data_buf, h};
      h.parallel_for(size, Add(data_acc));
    });
  }
  // ...
```

Figure 10-6. *Kernel as a named function object*

When a kernel is expressed as a named function object, the named function object type must follow SYCL 2020 rules to be *device copyable*. Informally, this means that the named function objects may be safely copied byte by byte, enabling the member variables of the named function object to be passed to and accessed by kernel code executing on a device. Any C++ type that is trivially copyable is implicitly device copyable.

The argument to the overloaded function call `operator()` depends on how the kernel is launched, just like for kernels expressed as lambda expressions.

The code in Figure 10-7 shows how to use optional kernel attributes, like the `reqd_work_group_size` attribute, on kernels defined as named function objects. There are two valid positions for the optional kernel attribute when a kernel is defined as a named function object. This is different than a kernel written as a lambda expression, where only one position for the optional kernel attribute is valid.

```
class AddWithAttribute {
 public:
  AddWithAttribute(accessor<int> acc) : data_acc(acc) {}
  [[sycl::reqd_work_group_size(8)]] void operator()(
      id<1> i) const {
    data_acc[i] = data_acc[i] + 1;
  }

 private:
  accessor<int> data_acc;
};

class MulWithAttribute {
 public:
  MulWithAttribute(accessor<int> acc) : data_acc(acc) {}
  void operator()
      [[sycl::reqd_work_group_size(8)]] (id<1> i) const {
    data_acc[i] = data_acc[i] * 2;
  }

 private:
  accessor<int> data_acc;
};
```

***Figure 10-7.** Using optional attributes with a named function object*

Because all function objects are named, the host code compiler can use the function object type to identify the kernel code produced by the device code compiler even if the function object is templated. No additional kernel name template parameter is needed to name a kernel function object.

Kernels in Kernel Bundles

One final topic we should be aware of related to SYCL kernels concerns SYCL *kernel objects* and SYCL *kernel bundles*. Knowledge of kernel objects and kernel bundles is not required for typical application development but is useful in some cases to tune application performance. Knowledge of kernel objects and kernel bundles can also help to understand how kernels are organized and managed by a SYCL implementation.

A SYCL kernel bundle is a container for SYCL kernels or SYCL functions used by an application. The number of kernel bundles in an application depends on the specific SYCL compiler. Some applications may have just one kernel bundle, even if they have multiple kernels, while other applications may have more than one kernel bundle, even if they just have a few kernels.

A SYCL kernel bundle and the kernels or functions it contains can be in one of three states:

- **An *input* state**: Kernel bundles in this state are typically in some sort of intermediate representation and must be just-in-time (JIT) compiled before they can execute on a device.
- **An *object* state**: Kernel bundles in this state are usually compiled but not linked, like object files created by host application compilers.
- **An *executable* state**: Kernel bundles in this state are fully compiled to device code and are ready to be executed on the device. Kernel bundles that are ahead-of-time (AOT) compiled when the host application is compiled will initially be in this state.

While not required by the specification, many SYCL compilers compile kernels to an intermediate representation initially, for portability to the largest number of SYCL devices. This means that usually the application kernel bundles are in the input state initially. Then, many SYCL runtime libraries compile the kernel bundles from the input state to the executable state "lazily," on an as-needed basis.

This is usually a good policy because it enables fast application startup and does not compile kernels unnecessarily if they are never executed. The disadvantage of this policy, though, is that the first use of a kernel takes longer than subsequent uses, since it includes both the time needed to compile the kernel and the usual time needed to submit and execute the kernel. For complex kernels, the time to compile the kernel can be significant, making it desirable to shift compilation to a different point during application execution, such as when the application is loading, or to a separate background thread.

To provide more control over when and how a kernel is compiled, we can explicitly request a kernel bundle to be compiled before submitting a kernel to a queue. The precompiled kernel bundle can be used when the kernel is submitted to a queue for execution. Figure 10-8 shows how to compile all the kernels used by an application before any of the kernels are submitted to a queue, and how to use the precompiled kernel bundle.

```
auto kb = get_kernel_bundle<bundle_state::executable>(
    q.get_context());

std::cout
    << "All kernel compilation should be done now.\n";

q.submit([&](handler& h) {
  // Use the pre-compiled kernel from the kernel bundle.
  h.use_kernel_bundle(kb);

  accessor data_acc{data_buf, h};
  h.parallel_for(range{size}, [=](id<1> i) {
    data_acc[i] = data_acc[i] + 1;
  });
});
```

Figure 10-8. *Compiling kernels explicitly using kernel bundles*

This example requests a kernel bundle in an executable state for all the devices in the SYCL context associated with the SYCL queue, which will cause any kernels in the application to be just-in-time compiled if they are not already in the executable state. In this specific example, the kernel is very short and should not take long to compile, but if there were many kernels, or if they were more complicated, this step could take a significant amount of time. Of course, if all kernels were ahead-of-time compiled, or if all kernels had already been just-in-time compiled, this operation would effectively be free because all kernels would already be in the executable state.

If we want even more control over when and how our kernels are compiled, we can request a kernel bundle for a specific device, or even specific kernels in our program. This allows us to selectively compile some of the kernels in our program immediately, while leaving other kernels to be compiled later or on an as-needed basis. Figure 10-9 shows how to compile only the kernel identified by the `class Add` kernel name and only for the SYCL device associated with the SYCL queue, rather than all kernels in the program and all devices in the SYCL context.

```
auto kid = get_kernel_id<class Add>();
auto kb = get_kernel_bundle<bundle_state::executable>(
    q.get_context(), {q.get_device()}, {kid});

std::cout << "Kernel compilation should be done now.\n";

q.submit([&](handler& h) {
  // Use the pre-compiled kernel from the kernel bundle.
  h.use_kernel_bundle(kb);

  accessor data_acc{data_buf, h};
  h.parallel_for<class Add>(range{size}, [=](id<1> i) {
    data_acc[i] = data_acc[i] + 1;
  });
});
```

Figure 10-9. *Compiling kernels explicitly and selectively using kernel bundles*

This is a rare case where we needed to name our kernel lambda expression; otherwise, we would have no way to identify the kernel to compile.

Use kernel bundles to compile kernels predictably in an application!

Kernels in kernel bundles can also be used to query information about a compiled kernel, say to determine the maximum work-group size for a kernel for a specific device. In some cases, these types of kernel queries may be needed to choose valid values to use for a kernel and a specific device. In other cases, kernel queries can provide hints, allowing our application to dynamically adapt and choose optimal values for a kernel and a specific device.

The basic mechanism to identify a kernel, get a kernel object from a compiled kernel bundle, and use the kernel object to perform device-specific queries is shown in Figure 10-10. A more complete list of available kernel queries is described in Chapter 12.

```
auto kid = get_kernel_id<class Add>();
auto kb = get_kernel_bundle<bundle_state::executable>(
    q.get_context(), {q.get_device()}, {kid});
auto kernel = kb.get_kernel(kid);

std::cout
    << "The maximum work-group size for the kernel and "
       "this device is: "
    << kernel.get_info<info::kernel_device_specific::
                           work_group_size>(
           q.get_device())
    << "\n";

std::cout
    << "The preferred work-group size multiple for the "
       "kernel and this device is: "
    << kernel.get_info<
           info::kernel_device_specific::
               preferred_work_group_size_multiple>(
           q.get_device())
    << "\n";

Example Output:
Running on device: NVIDIA GeForce RTX 3060
The maximum work-group size for the kernel and this device is: 1024
The preferred work-group size multiple for the kernel and this device is: 32

Example Output:
Running on device: Intel(R) Data Center GPU Max 1100
The maximum work-group size for the kernel and this device is: 1024
The preferred work-group size multiple for the kernel and this device is: 16

Example Output:
Running on device: Intel(R) UHD Graphics 770
The maximum work-group size for the kernel and this device is: 512
The preferred work-group size multiple for the kernel and this device is: 64
```

Figure 10-10. *Querying kernels in kernel bundles*

This is another rare case where we need to name our kernel lambda expression; otherwise, we would have no way to identify the kernel to query.

Interoperability with Other APIs

When a SYCL implementation is built on top of another API, the implementation may be able to interoperate with kernels defined using mechanisms of the underlying API. This allows an application to integrate SYCL easily and incrementally into existing codebases that are already using the underlying API. This topic is covered in detail in Chapter 20. For the purposes of this chapter, we can simply recognize that interoperability with kernels or kernel bundles created via other source languages or APIs provides a third way to represent a kernel.

Summary

In this chapter, we explored different ways to define kernels. We described how to seamlessly integrate SYCL into existing C++ codebases by representing kernels as C++ lambda expressions or named function objects. For new codebases, we also discussed the pros and cons of the different kernel representations to help choose the best way to define kernels based on the needs of our application or library.

We described how kernels are typically compiled in a SYCL application and how to directly manipulate kernels in kernel bundles to control the compilation process. Even though this level of control will not be required for most applications, it is a useful technique to be aware of when we are tuning our applications.

CHAPTER 11

Vectors and Math Arrays

Vectors are collections of data. Vectors can be useful because parallelism in our computers comes from collections of computer hardware, and data is often processed in related groupings (e.g., the color channels in an RGB pixel). The concept is so important that we spend a chapter discussing the different SYCL vector types and how to utilize them. Note that we will not dive into *vectorization* of scalar operations in this chapter since that varies based on device type and implementations. Vectorization of scalar operations is covered in Chapter 16.

This chapter seeks to address the following questions:

- What are vector types?
- What is the difference between the SYCL math array (`marray`) and vector (`vec`) types?
- When and how should I use `marray` and `vec`?

We discuss `marray` and `vec` using working code examples and highlight the most important aspects of exploiting these types.

J. Reinders et al., *Data Parallel C++*, https://doi.org/10.1007/978-1-4842-9691-2_11

The Ambiguity of Vector Types

Vectors are a surprisingly controversial topic when we talk with parallel programming experts. In the authors' experience, this is because different people define and think about vectors in different ways.

There are two broad ways to think about what this chapter calls vector types:

1. **As a convenience type**, which groups data that we might want to refer to and operate on as a group, for example, the RGB or YUV color channels of a pixel. We could define a pixel class or struct and define math operators like + on it, but convenience types do this for us out of the box. Convenience types can be found in many shader languages used to program GPUs, so this way of thinking is common among many GPU developers.

2. As a mechanism to describe how code **maps to a SIMD (single instruction, multiple data) instruction set** in hardware. For example, in some languages and implementations, operations on a `float8` could map to an eight-lane SIMD instruction in hardware. SIMD vector types are used in many languages as a high-level alternative to CPU-specific intrinsics, so this way of thinking is already common among many CPU developers.

Although these two interpretations of vector types are very different, they unintentionally became combined and muddled together as SYCL and other languages became applicable to both CPUs and GPUs. The `vec` class (which existed in SYCL 1.2.1, and still exists in SYCL 2020) is compatible with either interpretation, whereas the `marray` class (which was introduced in SYCL 2020) is explicitly described as a convenience type unrelated to SIMD vector hardware instructions.

CHANGES ARE ON THE HORIZON: SIMD TYPES

SYCL 2020 does not yet include a vector type explicitly tied to the second interpretation (SIMD mappings). However, there are already extensions that allow us to write explicit vector code that maps directly to SIMD instructions in the hardware, designed for expert programmers who want to tune code for a specific architecture and take control from the compiler vectorizers. We should also expect another vector type to eventually appear in SYCL to cover the second interpretation, likely aligned with the proposed C++ **`std::simd`** templates. This new class would make it very clear when code is written in an explicit vector style, to reduce confusion. Both the existing extensions and a future **`std::simd`**-like type in SYCL are niche features that we expect will be used by few developers.

With **`marray`** and a dedicated SIMD class, our intent as programmers will be clear from the code that we write. This will be less error prone, less confusing, and may even reduce the number of heated discussions between expert developers when the question arises: "What is a vector?"

Our Mental Model for SYCL Vector Types

Throughout this book, we talk about how work-items can be grouped together to expose powerful communication and synchronization primitives, such as sub-group barriers and shuffles. For these operations to be efficient on vector hardware, there is an assumption that different work-items in a sub-group combine and map to SIMD instructions. Said another way, multiple work-items are grouped together by the compiler, at which point they can map to SIMD instructions in the hardware. Remember from Chapter 4 that this is a basic premise of SPMD (single program, multiple data) programming models that operate on top of vector hardware, where a single work-item constitutes a *lane* of what *might* be a SIMD instruction in hardware, instead of a work-item defining the *entire* operation that will be a SIMD instruction in the hardware. You can think of the compiler as always vectorizing across work-items when mapping to SIMD instructions in hardware, when programming in a SPMD style.

For developers coming from languages that don't have vector types, or from GPU shading languages, we can think of SYCL vector types as being local to a work-item, in that if there is an addition of two four-element vectors that addition might take four instructions in the hardware (it would be scalarized from the perspective of the work-item). Each element of the vectors would be added by a different instruction/clock cycle in the hardware. This is consistent with our interpretation of vector types as a convenience—we can add two vectors in a single operation in our source code, as opposed to performing four scalar operations in our source.

For developers coming from a CPU background, we should know that implicit vectorization for SIMD hardware occurs by default in many compilers, independent of vector type usage. The compiler may perform this implicit vectorization across work-items, extract the vector operations from well-formed loops, or honor vector types when mapping to vector instructions—see Chapter 16 for more information.

The rest of this chapter focuses on teaching vectors using the convenience interpretation of vector types (for both `marray` and `vec`), and that is the one that we should keep in our minds when programming in SYCL.

OTHER IMPLEMENTATIONS POSSIBLE!

Different compilers and implementations of SYCL can in theory make different decisions on how vector data types in code map to SIMD vector hardware instructions. We should read a vendor's documentation and optimization guides to understand how to write code that will map to efficient SIMD instructions, though the thinking and programming patterns that are described in this chapter are applicable to most (ideally all) SYCL implementations.

Math Array (marray)

The SYCL math array type (`marray`), see Figure 11-1, is a new addition in SYCL 2020 which has been defined to disambiguate different interpretations of how vector types should behave. `marray` explicitly represents the first interpretation of vector types introduced in the previous section of this chapter—a convenience type unrelated to vector hardware instructions. By removing "vector" from the name and by including "array" instead, it becomes easier to remember and reason about how the type will be logically implemented on hardware.

Type Alias	`marray` **Equivalent**
mcharN	marray<int8_t, N>
mucharN	marray<uint8_t, N>
mshortN	marray<int16_t, N>
mushortN	marray<uint16_t, N>
mintN	marray<int32_t, N>
muintN	marray<uint32_t, N>
mlongN	marray<int64_t, N>
mulongN	marray<uint64_t, N>
mhalfN	marray<half, N>
mfloatN	marray<float, N>
mdoubleN	marray<double N>
mboolN	marray<bool, N>

Figure 11-1. *Type aliases for math arrays*

The `marray` class is templated on its element type and number of elements. The number of elements parameter, `NumElements`, is a positive integer—when `NumElements` is 1, an `marray` is implicitly convertible to an equivalent scalar type. The element type parameter, `DataT`, must be a numeric type as defined by C++.

`Marray` is an array container, like `std::array`, with additional support for mathematical operators (e.g., +, +=) and SYCL mathematical functions (e.g., `sin`, `cos`) on arrays. It is designed to provide efficient and optimized array operations for parallel computation on SYCL devices.

For convenience, SYCL provides type aliases for math arrays. For these type aliases, the number of elements `N` must be 2, 3, 4, 8, or 16.

Figure 11-2 shows a simple example how to apply the `cos` function to every element in an `marray` consisting of four floats. This example highlights the convenience of using `marray` to express operations that apply to all elements of a collection of data assigned to each work-item.

```
queue q;
marray<float, 4> input{1.0004f, 1e-4f, 1.4f, 14.0f};
marray<float, 4> res[M];
for (int i = 0; i < M; i++)
  res[i] = {-(i + 1), -(i + 1), -(i + 1), -(i + 1)};
{
  buffer in_buf(&input, range{1});
  buffer re_buf(res, range{M});

  q.submit([&](handler &cgh) {
    accessor re_acc{re_buf, cgh, read_write};
    accessor in_acc{in_buf, cgh, read_only};

    cgh.parallel_for(range<1>(M), [=](id<1> idx) {
      int i = idx[0];
      re_acc[i] = cos(in_acc[0]);
    });
  });
}
```

Figure 11-2. *A simple example using `marray`*

By executing this kernel over a large range of data `M`, we can achieve good parallelism on many different types of devices, including those that are much wider than the four elements of the `marray`, without prescribing how our code maps to a SIMD instruction set operating on vector types.

Vector (vec)

The SYCL vector type (vec) existed in SYCL 1.2.1 and is still included in SYCL 2020. As mentioned previously, vec is compatible with either interpretation of a vector type. In practice, vec is typically interpreted as a convenience type, and our recommendation is therefore to use `marray` instead to improve code readability and reduce ambiguity. However, there are three exceptions to this recommendation, which we will cover in this section: vector loads and stores, interoperability with backend-native vector types, and operations known as "swizzles".

Like marray, the vec class is templated on its number of elements and element type. However, unlike marray, the NumElements parameter must be either 1, 2, 3, 4, 8, or 16, and any other value will produce a compilation failure. This is a good example of the confusion around vector types impacting vec's design: limiting the size of a vector to small powers of 2 makes sense for SIMD instruction sets but appears arbitrary from the perspective of a programmer looking for a convenience type. The element type parameter, DataT, can be any of the basic scalar types supported in device code.

Also, like marray, vec exposes shorthand type aliases for 2, 3, 4, 8, and 16 elements. Whereas marray aliases are prefixed with an "m", vec aliases are not, for example, uint4 is an alias to vec<uint32_t, 4> and float16 is an alias to vec<float, 16>. It is important we pay close attention to the presence or absence of this "m" when working with vector types, to ensure we know which class we are dealing with.

Loads and Stores

The vec class provides member functions for loading and storing the elements of a vector. These operations act on contiguous memory locations storing objects of the same type as the channels of the vector.

The load and store functions are shown in Figure 11-3. The load member function reads values of type DataT from memory at the address of the multi_ptr, offset by NumElements * offset elements of DataT, and writes those values to the channels of the vec. The store member function reads the channels of a vec and writes those values to memory at the address of the multi_ptr, offset by NumElements * offset elements of DataT.

Note that the parameter is a multi_ptr, rather than an accessor or raw pointer. The data type of the multi_ptr is DataT, that is, the data type of the components of the vec class specialization. This requires that the pointer passed to either load or store must match the component type of the vec instance itself.

```
template <access::address_space AddressSpace, access::decorated IsDecorated>
  void load(size_t offset, multi_ptr<DataT, AddressSpace, IsDecorated> ptr);

template <access::address_space addressSpace, access::decorated IsDecorated>
  void store(size_t offset, multi_ptr<DataT, AddressSpace, IsDecorated> ptr) const;
```

Figure 11-3. *vec load and store functions*

A simple example of using the load and store functions is shown in Figure 11-4.

```
std::array<float, size> fpData;
for (int i = 0; i < size; i++) {
  fpData[i] = 8.0f;
}

buffer fpBuf(fpData);

queue q;
q.submit([&](handler& h) {
  accessor acc{fpBuf, h};

  h.parallel_for(workers, [=](id<1> idx) {
    float16 inpf16;
    inpf16.load(idx, acc.get_multi_ptr<access::decorated::no>());
    float16 result = inpf16 * 2.0f;
    result.store(idx, acc.get_multi_ptr<access::decorated::no>());
  });
});
```

Figure 11-4. *Use of load and store member functions*

The SYCL vector `load` and `store` functions provide abstractions for expressing vector operations, but the underlying hardware architecture and compiler optimizations will determine any actual performance benefits. We recommend analyzing performance using profiling tools and experimenting with different strategies to find the best utilization of vector load and store operations for specific use cases.

Even though we should not expect vector load and store operations to map to SIMD instructions, using vector `load` and `store` functions can still help to improve memory bandwidth utilization. Operating on vector types effectively is a hint to the compiler that each work-item is accessing a contiguous block of memory, and certain devices may be able to leverage this information to load or store multiple elements at once, thereby improving efficiency.

Interoperability with Backend-Native Vector Types

The SYCL vec class template may also provide interoperability with a backend's native vector type (if one exists). The backend-native vector type is defined by the member type `vector_t` and is available only in device code. The vec class can be constructed from an instance of `vector_t` and can be implicitly converted to an instance of `vector_t`.

Most of us will never need to use `vector_t`, as its use cases are very limited; it exists only to allow interoperability with backend-native functions called from *within* a kernel function (e.g., calling a function written in OpenCL C from within a SYCL kernel).

Swizzle Operations

In graphics applications, *swizzling* means rearranging the data elements of a vector. For example, if a vector a contains the elements `{1, 2, 3, 4}`, and knowing that the components of a four-element vector can be referred to as `{x, y, z, w}`, we could write `b = a.wxyz()`, and the values in the vector b would be `{4, 1, 2, 3}`. This syntax is common in applications for code compactness and where there is efficient hardware for such operations.

The vec class allows swizzles to be performed in one of two ways, as shown in Figure 11-5.

```
template <int... swizzleindexes>
__swizzled_vec__ swizzle() const;
__swizzled_vec__ XYZW_ACCESS() const;
__swizzled_vec__ RGBA_ACCESS() const;
__swizzled_vec__ INDEX_ACCESS() const;

#ifdef SYCL_SIMPLE_SWIZZLES
// Available only when numElements <= 4
// XYZW_SWIZZLE is all permutations with repetition of:
// x, y, z, w, subject to numElements
__swizzled_vec__ XYZW_SWIZZLE() const;

// Available only when numElements == 4
// RGBA_SWIZZLE is all permutations with repetition of: r,
// g, b, a.
__swizzled_vec__ RGBA_SWIZZLE() const;
#endif
```

Figure 11-5. *vec swizzle member functions*

The swizzle member function template allows us to perform swizzle operations by calling the template member function `swizzle`. This member function takes a variadic number of integer template arguments, where each argument represents the swizzle index for the corresponding element in the vector. The swizzle indices must be integers between `0` and `NumElements-1`, where `NumElements` represents the number of elements in the original SYCL vector (e.g., `vec.swizzle<2, 1, 0, 3>()` for a vector of four elements). The return type of the `swizzle` member function is always an instance of `__swizzled_vec__`, which is an implementation-defined temporary class representing the swizzled vector. Note that the swizzle operation is not performed immediately when calling `swizzle`. Instead, the swizzle operation is performed when the returned `__swizzled_vec__` instance is used within an expression.

The set of simple swizzle member functions, described in the SYCL specification as `XYZW_SWIZZLE` and `RGBA_SWIZZLE`, are provided as an alternative way to perform swizzle operations. These member functions are only available for vectors with up to four elements, and only if the `SYCL_SIMPLE_SWIZZLES` macro is defined before any SYCL header files.

The simple swizzle member functions allow us to refer to the elements of a vector using the names `{x, y, z, w}` or `{r, g, b, a}` and to perform swizzle operations by calling member functions using these element names directly.

For example, simple swizzles enable the XYZW swizzle syntax `a.wxyz()` used previously. The same operation can be performed equivalently using RGBA swizzles by writing `a.argb()`. Using simple swizzles can produce more compact code and code that is a closer match to other languages, especially graphics shading languages. Simple swizzles can also better express programmer intent when a vector contains XYZW position data or RGBA color data. The return type of the simple swizzle member functions is also `__swizzled_vec__`. Like the swizzle member function template, the actual swizzle operation is performed when the returned `__swizzled_vec__` instance is used within an expression.

```
constexpr int size = 16;

std::array<float4, size> input;
for (int i = 0; i < size; i++) {
  input[i] = float4(8.0f, 6.0f, 2.0f, i);
}

buffer b(input);

queue q;
q.submit([&](handler& h) {
  accessor a{b, h};

  //  We can access the individual elements of a vector by
  //  using the functions x(), y(), z(), w() and so on.
  //
  //  "Swizzles" can be used by calling a vector member
  //  equivalent to the swizzle order that we need, for
  //  example zyx() or any combination of the elements.
  //  The swizzle need not be the same size as the
  //  original vector.
  h.parallel_for(size, [=](id<1> idx) {
    auto e = a[idx];
    float w = e.w();
    float4 sw = e.xyzw();
    sw = e.xyzw() * sw.wzyx();
    sw = sw + w;
    a[idx] = sw.xyzw();
  });
});
```

***Figure 11-6.** Example of using the `__swizzled_vec__` class*

Figure 11-6 demonstrates the usage of simple swizzles and the `__swizzled_vec__` class. Although the `__swizzled_vec__` does not appear directly in our code, it is used within expressions such as `b.xyzw() * sw.wzyx()`: the return type of `b.xyzw()` and `sw.wzyx()` is instances of `__swizzled_vec__`, and the multiplication is not evaluated until the result is assigned back to the `float4` variable `sw`.

How Vector Types Execute

As described throughout this chapter, there are two different interpretations of vector types and how they might map to hardware. Until this point, we have deliberately only discussed these mappings at a high level. In this section, we will take a deeper look into exactly how different interpretations of the vector types may map to low-level hardware features such as SIMD registers, demonstrating that both interpretations can make efficient use of vector hardware.

Vectors as Convenience Types

There are three primary points that we'd like to make around how vectors map from convenience types (e.g., `marray` and usually `vec`) to hardware implementations:

1. To leverage the portability and expressiveness of the SPMD programming model, we should think of multiple work-items being combined to create vector hardware instructions. More specifically, we should *not* think of vector hardware instructions being created from a single work-item in isolation.

2. As a consequence of (1), we should think of operations (e.g., addition) on a vector as executing per-channel or per-element in time, from the perspective of one work-item. Using vectors in our source code is *usually* unrelated to taking advantage of underlying vector hardware instructions.

3. Compilers are required to obey the memory layout requirements of vectors and math arrays if we write code in certain ways, such as by passing the address of a vector to a function, which can cause surprising performance impacts. Understanding this can make it easier to write code which compilers can aggressively optimize.

We will start by further describing the first two points, because a clear mental model can make it much easier to write code.

As described in Chapters 4 and 9, a work-item is the leaf node of the parallelism hierarchy and represents an individual instance of a kernel function. Work-items can be executed in any order and cannot communicate or synchronize with each other except through atomic memory operations to local or global memory, or through group collective functions (e.g., `select_from_group`, `group_barrier`).

Instances of convenience types are local to a single work-item and can therefore be thought of as equivalent to a private array of `NumElements` per work-item. For example, the storage of a `float4 y4` declaration can be considered equivalent to `float y4[4]`. Consider the example shown in Figure 11-7.

```
h.parallel_for(8, [=](id<1> i) {
  float x = a[i];
  float4 y4 = b[i];
  a[i] = x + sycl::length(y4);
});
```

Figure 11-7. *Vector execution example*

For the scalar variable `x`, the result of kernel execution with multiple work-items on hardware that has SIMD instructions (e.g., CPUs, GPUs) might use a vector register and SIMD instructions, but the vectorization is across work-items and unrelated to any vector type in our code. Each work-item, with its own scalar `x`, could form a different lane in an implicit

SIMD hardware instruction that the compiler generates, as shown in Figure 11-8. The scalar data in a work-item can be thought of as being implicitly vectorized (combined into SIMD hardware instructions) across work-items that happen to execute at the same time, in some implementations and on some hardware, but the work-item code that we write does not encode this in any way—this is the core of the SPMD style of programming.

Work-item ID	w0	w1	w2	w3	w4	w5	w6	w7
SIMD hardware instruction lanes	x[w0]	x[w1]	x[w2]	x[w3]	x[w4]	x[w5]	x[w6]	x[w7]

Figure 11-8. *Possible expansion from scalar variable* x *to eight-wide hardware vector instruction*

Exposing potential parallelism in a hardware-agnostic way ensures that our applications can scale up (or down) to fit the capabilities of different platforms, including those with vector hardware instructions. Striking the right balance between work-item and other forms of parallelism during application development is a challenge that we must all engage with, and is covered in more detail in Chapters 15, 16, and 17.

With the implicit vector expansion from scalar variable x to a vector hardware instruction by the compiler as shown in Figure 11-8, the compiler creates a SIMD operation in hardware from a scalar operation that occurs in multiple work-items.

Returning to the code example in Figure 11-7, for the vector variable y4, the result of kernel execution for multiple work-items (e.g., eight work-items) does not process the four-element vector by using vector operations in hardware. Instead, each work-item independently sees its own vector (float4 in this case), and the operations on elements of that vector may occur across multiple clock cycles/instructions. This is shown in Figure 11-9. We can think of the vectors as having been scalarized by the compiler from the perspective of a work-item.

Scalarized ops	Exec cycle	Work-item ID							
		w0	w1	w2	w3	w4	w5	w6	w7
y4.x	N	y4[w0].x	y4[w1].x	y4[w2].x	y4[w3].x	y4[w4].x	y4[w5].x	y4[w6].x	y4[w7].x
y4.y	N+1	y4[w0].y	y4[w1].y	y4[w2].y	y4[w3].y	y4[w4].y	y4[w5].y	y4[w6].y	y4[w7].y
y4.z	N+2	y4[w0].z	y4[w1].z	y4[w2].z	y4[w3].z	y4[w4].z	y4[w5].z	y4[w6].z	y4[w7].z
y4.w	N+3	y4[w0].w	y4[w1].w	y4[w2].w	y4[w3].w	y4[w4].w	y4[w5].w	y4[w6].w	y4[w7].w

Figure 11-9. *Vector hardware instructions access strided memory locations across SIMD lanes*

Figure 11-9 also demonstrates the third key point for this section, that the convenience interpretation of vectors can have memory access implications that are important to understand. In the preceding code example, each work-item sees the original (consecutive) data layout of y4, which provides an intuitive model to reason about and tune.

From a performance perspective, the downside of this work-item-centric vector data layout is that if a compiler vectorizes across work-items to create vector hardware instructions, the lanes of the vector hardware instruction do not access consecutive memory locations. Depending on the vector data size and the capabilities of a specific device; a compiler may need to generate, gather, or scatter memory instructions; as shown in Figure 11-10. This is required because the vectors are contiguous in memory, and neighboring work-items are operating on different vectors in parallel. See Chapters 15 and 16 for more discussion of how vector types may impact execution on specific devices, and be sure to check vendor documentation, compiler optimization reports, and use runtime profiling to understand the efficiency of specific scenarios.

```
q.submit([&](sycl::handler &h) { // assume sub group size is 8
  // ...
  h.parallel_for(range<1>(8), [=](id<1> i) {
    // ...
    float4 y4 = b[i];  // i=0, 1, 2, ...
    // ...
    float x = dowork(&y4);  // the "dowork" expects y4,
                            // i.e., vec_y[8][4] layout
  });
```

Figure 11-10. *Vector code example with address escaping*

When the compiler can prove that the address of y4 does not escape from the current kernel work-item, or if all callee functions are inlined, then the compiler may perform aggressive optimizations that may improve performance. For example, the compiler can legally transpose the storage of y4 if it is not observable, enabling consecutive memory accesses that avoid the need for gather or scatter instructions. Compiler optimization reports can provide information how our source code has been transformed into vector hardware instructions and can provide hints on how to tweak our code for increased performance.

As a general guideline, we should use convenience vectors (e.g., marray) whenever they make logical sense, because code using these types is much easier to write and maintain. Only when we see performance hotspots in our application should we investigate whether a source code vector operation has been lowered into suboptimal hardware implementation.

Vectors as SIMD Types

Although we have emphasized in this chapter that marray and vec are *not* SIMD types, for completeness we include here a brief discussion of how SIMD types *may* map to vector hardware. This discussion is not coupled to vectors within our SYCL source code but provides background that will be useful as we progress to the later chapters of this book that describe specific device types (GPU, CPU, FPGA), and may help to prepare us for the possible introduction of SIMD types in future versions of SYCL.

SYCL devices may contain SIMD instruction hardware that operates on multiple data values contained in one vector register or a register file. On devices that provide SIMD hardware, we can consider a vector addition operation, for example, on an eight-element vector, as shown in Figure 11-11.

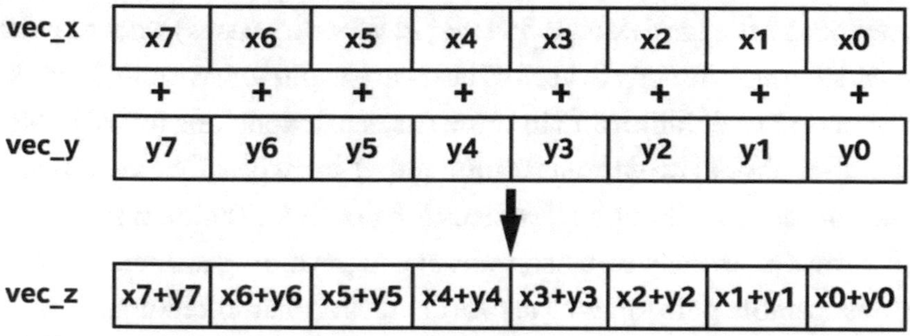

***Figure 11-11.** SIMD addition with eight-way data parallelism*

The vector addition in this example could execute in a single instruction using vector hardware, adding the vector registers `vec_x` and `vec_y` in parallel with that SIMD instruction.

This mapping of SIMD types to vector hardware is very straightforward and predictable, and likely to be performed the same way by any compiler. These properties make SIMD types very attractive for low-level performance tuning on SIMD hardware but come with a cost—the code is less portable and becomes sensitive to details of the specific architecture. The SPMD programming model evolved to combat these costs.

That developers expect SIMD types to have predictable hardware mapping properties is precisely why it is critical to cleanly separate the two interpretations of vectors via two distinct language features: if a developer uses a convenience type expecting it to behave as a SIMD type, they will likely be working *against* compiler optimizations and will likely see lower performance than hoped or expected.

Summary

There are multiple interpretations of the term *vector* within programming languages, and understanding the interpretation that a particular language or compiler has been built around is important when writing performant and scalable code. SYCL has been built around the idea that vector types in source code are convenience types local to a work-item and that implicit vectorization by the compiler across work-items map to SIMD instructions in the hardware. When we (in very rare cases) want to write code which maps directly to vector hardware explicitly, we should look to vendor documentation and in some cases to extensions to SYCL. Most applications should be written assuming that kernels will be vectorized across work-items—doing so leverages the powerful abstraction of SPMD, which provides an easy-to-reason-about programming model, and that provides scalable performance across devices and architectures.

This chapter described the `marray` interface, which offers convenience out of the box when we have groupings of similarly typed data that we want to operate on (e.g., a pixel with multiple color channels). In addition, we discussed the legacy `vec` class, which may be convenient for expressing certain patterns (with swizzles) or optimizations (with loads/stores and backend interoperability).

CHAPTER 12

Device Information and Kernel Specialization

In this chapter, we look at the advanced concept of making our program more flexible and therefore more portable. This is done by looking at mechanisms to match the capabilities of any system (and accelerators) our application might be executed upon, with a selection of kernels and code that we have written. This is an advanced topic because we can always simply "use the default accelerator" and run the kernels we write on that regardless of what it is. We have learned that this will work even on systems which may have no accelerator because SYCL guarantees there is always a device available that will run a kernel even if it is the CPU that is also running our host application.

When we move beyond "use the default accelerator" and general-purpose kernels, we find mechanisms are available to choose which device(s) to use, and mechanisms to create more specialized kernels. We discuss both capabilities in this chapter. Together, these two capabilities allow us to construct applications that are highly adaptable to the system on which they are executed.

J. Reinders et al., *Data Parallel C++*, https://doi.org/10.1007/978-1-4842-9691-2_12

Fortunately, the creators of the SYCL specification thought about these needs and gave us interfaces to let us solve this problem. The SYCL specification defines a `device` class that encapsulates a device on which kernels may be executed. We first cover the ability to query the device class, so that our program can adapt to the device characteristics and capabilities. We may occasionally choose to write different algorithms for different devices. Later in this chapter, we learn that we can apply `aspects` to a kernel to specialize a kernel and let a compiler take advantage of that. Such specialization helps make a kernel more tailored to a certain class of devices while likely rendering it unsuitable for other devices. Combining these concepts allows us to adapt our program as much, or as little, as we wish. This ensures we can decide how much investment to make in squeezing out performance while starting with broad portability.

Is There a GPU Present?

Many of us will start with having logic to figure out "Is there a GPU present?" to inform the choices our program will make as it executes. That is the start of what this chapter covers. As we will see, there is much more information available to help us make our programs robust and performant.

Parameterizing a program can help with correctness, functional portability, performance portability, and future proofing.

This chapter dives into the most important queries and how to use them effectively in our programs. Implementations doubtlessly offer more detailed properties that we can query. To learn all possible queries, we would need to review the latest SYCL specification, the documentation for our particular compiler, and documentation for any runtimes/drivers we may encounter.

Device-specific properties are queryable using `get_info` functions, including access to device-specific *kernel* and *work-group* properties.

Refining Kernel Code to Be More Prescriptive

It is useful to consider that our coding, kernel by kernel, will fall broadly into one of these three categories:

- **Generic kernel code**: Run anywhere, not tuned to a specific class of device.
- **Device type–specific kernel code**: Run on a type of device (e.g., GPU, CPU, FPGA), not tuned to specific *models* of a device type. This is particularly useful because many device types share common features, so it is safe to make some assumptions that would not apply to fully general code written for all devices.
- **Tuned device-specific kernel code**: Run on a type of device, with tuning that reacts to specific parameters of a device—this covers a broad range of possibilities from a small amount of tuning to very detailed optimization work.

It is our job as programmers to determine when different patterns are needed for different device types. We dedicate Chapters 14, 15, 16, and 17 to illuminating this important thinking.

It is most common to start by focusing on getting things working with a functionally correct implementation of a generic kernel. Chapter 2 specifically talks about what methods are easiest to debug when getting started with a kernel implementation. Once we have a kernel working, we may evolve it to target the capabilities of a specific device type or device model.

Chapter 14 offers a framework of thinking to consider parallelism first, before we dive into device considerations. It is our choice of pattern (a.k.a. algorithm) that dictates our code, and it is our job as programmers to determine when different patterns are needed for different devices. Chapters 15 (GPU), 16 (CPU), and 17 (FPGA) dive more deeply into the qualities that distinguish these device types and motivate a choice in pattern to use. It is these qualities that motivate us to consider writing distinct versions of kernels when the best approach (pattern choice) varies on different device types.

When we have a kernel written for a specific type of device (e.g., a specific CPU, GPU, FPGA, etc.), it is logical to adapt it to specific vendors or even models of such devices. Good coding style is to parameterize code based on features (e.g., item size support found from a device query).

We should write code to query parameters that describe the actual capabilities of a device instead of its marketing information; it is bad programming practice to query the model number of a device and react to that—such code is less portable because it is not future-proof.

It is common to write a different kernel for each device type that we want to support (a GPU version of a kernel and an FPGA version of a kernel and maybe a generic version of a kernel). When we get more specific, to support a specific device vendor or even device model, we may benefit when we can parameterize a kernel rather than duplicate it. We are free to do either, as we see fit. Code cluttered with too many parameter adjustments may be hard to read or excessively burdened at runtime. It is common however that parameters can fit neatly into a single version of a kernel.

Parameterizing makes the most sense when the algorithm is broadly the same but has been tuned for the capabilities of a specific device. Writing a different kernel is much cleaner when using a completely different approach, pattern, or algorithm.

How to Enumerate Devices and Capabilities

Chapter 2 enumerates and explains five methods for choosing a device on which to execute. Essentially, Method#1 was the least prescriptive *run it somewhere*, and we evolve to the most prescriptive Method#5, which considered executing on a fairly precise model of a device from a family of devices. The enumerated methods in between gave a mix of flexibility and prescriptiveness. Figure 12-1, Figure 12-2, and Figure 12-4 help to illustrate how we can select a device.

Figure 12-1 shows that even if we allow the implementation to select a default device for us (Method#1 in Chapter 2), we can still query for information about the selected device.

Figure 12-2 shows how we can try to set up a queue using a specific device (in this case, a GPU), but fall back explicitly on the default device if no GPU is available. This gives us some control of our device choice by biasing us to get a GPU whenever one is available. We know that at least one device is always guaranteed to exist so our kernels can always run in a properly configured system. When there is no GPU, many systems will default to a CPU device but there is no guarantee. Likewise, if we ask for a CPU device explicitly, there is no guarantee there is such a device (but we are guaranteed that *some* device *will* exist).

It is not recommended that we use the solution shown in Figure 12-2. In addition to appearing a little scary and error prone, Figure 12-2 does not give us control over which GPU is selected if there are choices of GPUs at runtime. Despite being both instructive and functional, there is a better way. It is recommended that we write custom device selectors as shown in the next code example (Figure 12-4).

```
queue q;

std::cout << "By default, we are running on "
          << q.get_device().get_info<info::device::name>()
          << "\n";

Example Outputs (one line per run - depends on system):
By default, we are running on NVIDIA GeForce RTX 3060
By default, we are running on AMD Radeon RX 5700 XT
By default, we are running on Intel(R) UHD Graphics 770
By default, we are running on Intel(R) Xeon(R) Gold 6336Y CPU @ 2.40GHz
By default, we are running on Intel(R) Data Center GPU Max 1100
```

Figure 12-1. *Device we have been assigned by default*

Queries about devices rely on installed software (special user-level drivers), to respond regarding a device. SYCL relies on this, just as an operating system needs drivers to access hardware—it is not sufficient that the hardware simply be installed in a machine.

```
auto GPU_is_available = false;

try {
  device testForGPU(gpu_selector_v);
  GPU_is_available = true;
} catch (exception const& ex) {
  std::cout << "Caught this SYCL exception: " << ex.what()
            << std::endl;
}

auto q = GPU_is_available ? queue(gpu_selector_v)
                          : queue(default_selector_v);

std::cout
    << "After checking for a GPU, we are running on:\n "
    << q.get_device().get_info<info::device::name>()
    << "\n";

Four Example Outputs (using four different
  systems, each with a GPU):
After checking for a GPU, we are running on:
 AMD Radeon RX 5700 XT
After checking for a GPU, we are running on:
 Intel(R) Data Center GPU Max 1100
After checking for a GPU, we are running on:
 NVIDIA GeForce RTX 3060
After checking for a GPU, we are running on:
 Intel(R) UHD Graphics 770

Example Output (using a system without GPU):
Caught this SYCL exception: No device of
requested type 'info::device_type::gpu' available.
...(PI_ERROR_DEVICE_NOT_FOUND)
After checking for a GPU, we are running on:
 AMD Ryzen 5 3600 6-Core Processor
```

***Figure 12-2.** Using try-catch to select a GPU device if possible, use the default device if not*

Aspects

The SYCL standard has a small list of device *aspects* that can be used to understand the capabilities of a device, to control which devices we choose to use, and to control which kernels we submit to a device. At the end of this chapter, we will discuss "kernel specialization" and kernel templating. For now, we will enumerate the aspects and how to use them in device queries and selection. Figure 12-3 lists aspects that are defined by the SYCL standard to be available for use in every C++ program using SYCL. Aspects are Boolean—a device either has or does not have an aspect. The first four (cpu/gpu/accelerator/custom) are mutually exclusive since device types are defined as an enum by SYCL 2020. Features including `aspect::fp16`, `aspect::fp64`, and `aspect::atomic64` are "optional features" so they may not be supported by all devices—testing for these can be especially important for a robust application.

Standard `aspect` (all booleans)	**The device...**
`aspect::cpu`	executes code on a CPU
`aspect::gpu`	executes code on a GPU
`aspect::accelerator`	executes code on an accelerator
`aspect::custom`	executes fixed functions only, no support for programmable kernels
`aspect::emulated`	executes code in an emulator, not for performance – typically used for debug, profiling, etc.
`aspect::host_debuggable`	can fully support standard debugging
`aspect::fp16`	supports the `sycl::half` data type
`aspect::fp64`	supports the `double` data type
`aspect::atomic64`	supports 64-bit atomic operations
`aspect::image`	supports images, a topic not covered in this book (we emphasize the more general and portable `buffer` instead)
`aspect::online_compiler` `aspect::online_linker`	supports online compilation and/or linking of device code. Such devices may support the build(), compile(), and link() functions, all very advanced topics not covered in this book
`aspect::queue_profiling`	supports queue profiling, an advanced topic discussed a bit, along with other practical tips, in Chapter 13

`aspect::usm_device_allocations`
`aspect::usm_host_allocations`
`aspect::usm_atomic_host_allocations`
`aspect::usm_shared_allocations`
`aspect::usm_atomic_shared_allocations`
	supports the corresponding USM capability

`aspect::usm_system_allocations`	supports sharing data allocated by the system allocators, not just the SYCL USM allocation calls; such usage will impact portability and may impact performance

Figure 12-3. *Aspects defined by the SYCL standard (implementations can add more)*

Custom Device Selector

Figure 12-4 uses a custom device selector. Custom device selectors were first discussed in Chapter 2 as Method#5 for choosing where our code runs (Figure 2-16). The custom device selector evaluates each device available to the application. A particular device is selected based on receiving the highest score (or no device if the highest score is -1). In this example, we will have a little fun with our selector:

- Reject non-GPUs (return -1).
- Favor GPUs with a vendor name including the word "ACME" (return 24 if Martian, 824 otherwise).
- Any other non-Martian GPU is a good one (return 799).
- Martian GPUs, which are not ACME, are rejected (return -1).

The next section, "Being Curious: `get_info<>`," dives into the rich information that `get_devices()`, `get_platforms()`, and `get_info<>` offer. Those interfaces open up any type of logic we might want to utilize to pick our devices, including the simple vendor name checks shown in Figure 2-16 and Figure 12-4.

```
#include <iostream>
#include <sycl/sycl.hpp>
using namespace sycl;

int my_selector(const device& dev) {
  int score = -1;

  // We prefer non-Martian GPUs, especially ACME GPUs
  if (dev.is_gpu()) {
    if (dev.get_info<info::device::vendor>().find("ACME") !=
        std::string::npos)
      score += 25;

    if (dev.get_info<info::device::vendor>().find(
            "Martian") == std::string::npos)
      score += 800;
  }

  // If there is no GPU on the system all devices will be
  // given a negative score and the selector will not select
  // a device. This will cause an exception.
  return score;
}

int main() {
  try {
    auto q = queue{my_selector};
    std::cout
        << "After checking for a GPU, we are running on:\n "
        << q.get_device().get_info<info::device::name>()
        << "\n";
  } catch (exception const& ex) {
    std::cout << "Custom device selector did not select a "
                 "device.\n";
    std::cout << "Caught this SYCL exception: " << ex.what()
              << std::endl;
  }

  return 0;
}
Four Example Outputs (using four different
  systems, each with a GPU):
After checking for a GPU, we are running on:
 Intel(R) Gen9 HD Graphics NEO.
After checking for a GPU, we are running on:
 NVIDIA GeForce RTX 3060
After checking for a GPU, we are running on:
 Intel(R) Data Center GPU Max 1100
After checking for a GPU, we are running on:
 AMD Radeon RX 5700 XT

Example Output (using a system without GPU):
After checking for a GPU, we are running on:
Custom device selector did not select a device.
Caught this SYCL exception: No device of requested
type available. ...(PI_ERROR_DEVICE_NOT_FOUND)
```

***Figure 12-4.** Custom device selector—our preferred solution*

Being Curious: get_info<>

In order for our program to "know" what devices are available at runtime, we can have our program query available devices from the device class, and then we can learn more details using get_info<> to inquire about a specific device. We provide a simple program, called *curious* (see Figure 12-5), that uses these interfaces to dump out information for us to look at directly. This can be especially useful for doing a sanity check when developing or debugging a program that uses these interfaces. Failure of this program to work as expected can often tell us that the software drivers we need are not installed correctly. Figure 12-6 shows a sample output from this program, with the high-level information about the devices that are present.

You may want to see if your system supports a utility such as sycl-ls, before you write your own "list all available SYCL devices" program.

```
// Loop through available platforms
for (auto const& this_platform :
     platform::get_platforms()) {
  std::cout
      << "Found platform: "
      << this_platform.get_info<info::platform::name>()
      << "\n";

  // Loop through available devices in this platform
  for (auto const& this_device :
       this_platform.get_devices()) {
    std::cout
        << " Device: "
        << this_device.get_info<info::device::name>()
        << "\n";
  }
  std::cout << "\n";
}
```

Figure 12-5. *Simple use of device query mechanisms: curious.cpp*

```
% clang++ -fsycl fig_12_5_curious.cpp -o curious

% ./curious
Found platform: NVIDIA CUDA BACKEND
 Device: NVIDIA GeForce RTX 3060

Found platform: AMD HIP BACKEND
 Device: AMD Radeon RX 5700 XT

Found platform: Intel(R) OpenCL
 Device: Intel(R) Xeon(R) E-2176G CPU @ 3.70GHz

Found platform: Intel(R) OpenCL HD Graphics
 Device: Intel(R) UHD Graphics P630 [0x3e96]

Found platform: Intel(R) Level-Zero
 Device: Intel(R) UHD Graphics P630 [0x3e96]

Found platform: Intel(R) FPGA Emulation Platform for OpenCL(TM)
 Device: Intel(R) FPGA Emulation Device
```

Figure 12-6. *Example output from curious.cpp*

Being More Curious: Detailed Enumeration Code

We offer a program, which we have named verycurious.cpp (Figure 12-7), to illustrate some of the detailed information available using `get_info`. Again, we find ourselves writing code like this to help when developing or debugging a program.

Now that we have shown how to access the information, we will discuss the information fields that prove the most important to query and act upon in applications.

```
template <typename queryT, typename T>
void do_query(const T& obj_to_query,
              const std::string& name, int indent = 4) {
  std::cout << std::string(indent, ' ') << name << " is '"
            << obj_to_query.template get_info<queryT>()
            << "'\n";
}

int main() {
  // Loop through the available platforms
  for (auto const& this_platform :
       platform::get_platforms()) {
    std::cout << "Found Platform:\n";
    do_query<info::platform::name>(this_platform,
                                   "info::platform::name");
    // query information like these (more in program than
    // shown here in this figure - see book github)

    // Loop through the devices available in this plaform
    for (auto& dev : this_platform.get_devices()) {
      std::cout << "  Device: "
                << dev.get_info<info::device::name>()
                << "\n";
      // is_cpu() == has(aspect::cpu)
      std::cout << "    is_cpu(): "
                << (dev.is_cpu() ? "Yes" : "No") << "\n";
      // is_cpu() == has(aspect::gpu)
      std::cout << "    is_gpu(): "
                << (dev.is_gpu() ? "Yes" : "No") << "\n";
      std::cout << "    has(fp16): "
                << (dev.has(aspect::fp16) ? "Yes" : "No")
                << "\n";
      // many more queries shown in fig_12_7_very_curious.cpp
      // see book github for source code
    }
    std::cout << "\n";
  }
  return 0;
}
```

Figure 12-7. *More detailed use of device query mechanisms: verycurious.cpp (subset shown)*

Very Curious: `get_info` plus `has()`

The `has()` interface allows a program to test directly for a feature using aspects listed in Figure 12-3. Simple usage is shown in Figure 12-7—with more in the full verycurious.cpp source code in the book GitHub. The verycurious.cpp program is helpful for seeing the details about devices on your system.

Device Information Descriptors

Our "curious" and "verycurious" program examples, used earlier in this chapter, utilize popular SYCL device class member functions (i.e., `is_cpu`, `is_gpu`, `is_accelerator`, `get_info`, `has`). These member functions are documented in the SYCL specification in a table titled "Member functions of the SYCL device class."

The "curious" program examples also queried for information using the `get_info` member function. There is a set of queries that must be supported by all SYCL devices. The complete list of such items is described in the SYCL specification in a table titled "Device information descriptors."

Device-Specific Kernel Information Descriptors

Like platforms and devices, we can query information about our kernels using a `get_info` function. Such information (e.g., supported work-group sizes, preferred work-group size, the amount of private memory required per work-item) may be device-specific, and so the `get_info` member function of the `kernel` class accepts a `device` as an argument.

The Specifics: Those of "Correctness"

We will divide the specifics into information about necessary conditions (correctness) and information useful for tuning but not necessary for correctness.

In this first correctness category, we will enumerate conditions that should be met in order for kernels to launch properly. Failure to abide by these device limitations will lead to program failures. Figure 12-8 shows how we can fetch a few of these parameters in a way that the values are available for use in host code and in kernel code (via lambda capture). We can modify our code to utilize this information; for instance, it could guide our code on buffer sizing or work-group sizing.

```
queue q;
device dev = q.get_device();

std::cout << "We are running on:\n"
          << dev.get_info<info::device::name>() << "\n";

// Query results like the following can be used to
// calculate how large your kernel invocations can be.
auto maxWG =
    dev.get_info<info::device::max_work_group_size>();
auto maxGmem =
    dev.get_info<info::device::global_mem_size>();
auto maxLmem =
    dev.get_info<info::device::local_mem_size>();

std::cout << "Max WG size is " << maxWG
          << "\nGlobal memory size is " << maxGmem
          << "\nLocal memory size is " << maxLmem << "\n";
```

Figure 12-8. *Fetching parameters that can be used to shape a kernel*

Submitting a kernel that violates a required condition (e.g., `sub_group_sizes`) will generate a runtime error.

Device Queries

device_type: cpu, gpu, accelerator, custom,[1] automatic, all. These are most often tested by is_cpu, is_gpu(), and so on (see Figure 12-7):

`max_work_item_sizes`: The maximum number of work-items that are permitted in each dimension of the work-group of the `nd_range`. The minimum value is `(1, 1, 1)`.

`max_work_group_size`: The maximum number of work-items that are permitted in a work-group executing a kernel on a single compute unit. The minimum value is 1.

`global_mem_size`: The size of global memory in bytes.

`local_mem_size`: The size of local memory in bytes. The minimum size is 32 K.

`max_compute_units`: Indicative of the amount of parallelism available on a device—implementation-defined, interpret with care!

`sub_group_sizes`: Returns the set of sub-group sizes supported by the device.

Note that many more characteristics are encoded as aspects (see Figure 12-3), such as USM capabilities.

[1] Custom devices are not discussed in this book (do not confuse "custom device" with a "custom device selector"). If we find ourselves programming a device that identifies itself using the *custom* type, we will need to study the documentation for that device to learn more. Put less gently: custom devices are uncommon and weird so we are not going to talk about them—we've purposefully ignored limits they may impose on some of the features we discuss.

WE STRONGLY ADVISE AVOIDING MAX_COMPUTE_UNITS IN PROGRAM LOGIC

We have found that querying the maximum number of compute units should be avoided, in part because the definition isn't crisp enough to be useful in code tuning. Instead of using `max_compute_units`, most programs should express their parallelism and let the runtime map it onto available parallelism. Relying on `max_compute_units` for correctness only makes sense when augmented with implementation- and device-specific information. Experts might do that, but most developers do not and do not need to do so! Let the runtime do its job in this case!

Kernel Queries

The mechanisms discussed in Chapter 10, under "Kernels in Kernel Bundles," are needed to perform these kernel queries:

`work_group_size`: Returns the maximum work-group size that can be used to execute a kernel on a specific device

`compile_work_group_size`: Returns the work-group size specified by a kernel if applicable; otherwise returns (0, 0, 0)

`compile_sub_group_size`: Returns the sub-group size specified by a kernel if applicable; otherwise returns 0

`compile_num_sub_groups`: Returns the number of sub-groups specified by a kernel if applicable; otherwise returns 0 `max_sub_group_size`: Returns the maximum sub-group size for a kernel launched with the specified work-group size

`max_num_sub_groups`: Returns the maximum number of sub-groups for a kernel

The Specifics: Those of "Tuning/Optimization"

There are a few additional parameters that can be considered as fine-tuning parameters for our kernels. These can be ignored without jeopardizing the correctness of a program. These allow our kernels to really utilize the particulars of the hardware for performance.

Paying attention to the results of these queries can help when tuning for a cache (if it exists).

Device Queries

`global_mem_cache_line_size`: Size of global memory cache line in bytes.

`global_mem_cache_size`: Size of global memory cache in bytes.

`local_mem_type`: The type of local memory supported. This can be `info::local_mem_type::local` implying dedicated local memory storage such as SRAM or `info::local_mem_type::global`. The latter type means that local memory is just implemented as an abstraction on top of global memory with potentially no performance gains.

Kernel Queries

`preferred_work_group_size`: The preferred work-group size for executing a kernel on a specific device.

`preferred_work_group_size_multiple`: Work-group size should be a multiple of this value (`preferred_work_group_size_multiple`) for executing a kernel on a particular device for best performance. The value must not be greater than `work_group_size`.

Runtime vs. Compile-Time Properties

Implementations may offer compile-time constants/macros, or other functionality, but they are not standard and therefore we do not encourage their use nor do we discuss them in this book. The queries described in this chapter are performed through runtime APIs (`get_info`) so the results are not known until runtime. In the next section, we discuss how attributes may be used to control how the kernel is compiled. Other than attributes, the SYCL standard promotes only the use of runtime information with one fairly esoteric exception. SYCL does offer two traits that the application can use to query aspects at compilation time. These traits are there specifically to help avoid instantiating a templated kernel for device features that are not supported by any device. This is a very advanced, and seldom used, feature we do not elaborate upon in this book. The SYCL standard has an example toward the end of the "Device aspects" section that shows the use of `any_device_has_v<aspect>` and `all_devices_have_v<aspect>` for this purpose. The standard also defines "specialization constants," which we do not discuss in this book because they are typically used in very advanced targeted development, such as in libraries. An experimental compile-time property extension is discussed in the Epilogue under "Compile-Time Properties."

Kernel Specialization

We can specialize our kernels by having different kernels for different uses and select the appropriate kernel based on aspects (see Figure 12-3) of the device we are targeting. Of course, we can write specialized kernels explicitly and use C++ templating to help. We can inform the compiler that we want our kernel to use specific feature by using SYCL attributes (Figure 12-9) and aspects (Figure 12-3).

For example, the `reqd_work_group_size` attribute (Figure 12-9) can be used to require a specific work-group size for a kernel, and the `device_has` attribute can be used to require specific device aspects for a kernel.

Using attributes helps in two ways:

1. A kernel will throw an exception if it is submitted to a device that does not have one of the listed aspects.

2. The compiler will issue a diagnostic if the kernel (or any of the functions it calls) uses an optional feature (e.g., fp16) that is associated with an aspect that is not listed in the attribute.

The first helps prevent an application from proceeding if it will likely fail, and the second helps catch errors at compile time. For these reasons, using attributes can be helpful.

Figure 12-10 provides an example for illustration that uses run time logic to choose between two code sequences and uses attributes to specialize one of the kernels.

Standard `attribute`	**Specifies**
`device_has(aspect, ...)`	This attribute is the only attribute that can be used to decorate a non-kernel function, in addition to the ability (of all attributes) to decorate a kernel function. Requires: that the kernel is only launched with devices meeting the specified aspect(s) from Figure 12-3).

`reqd_work_group_size(dim0)`
`reqd_work_group_size(dim0, dim1)`
`reqd_work_group_size(dim0, dim1, dim2)`
	Requires: that the kernel *must* be launched with the specified workgroup size.

`work_group_size_hint(dim0)`
`work_group_size_hint(dim0, dim1)`
`work_group_size_hint(dim0, dim1, dim2)`
	Hints: that the kernel *will most likely* be launched with the specified workgroup size.

`reqd_sub_group_size(dim)`	Requires: that the kernel must be compiled and executed with the specified sub-group size.

***Figure 12-9.** Attributes defined by the SYCL standard (and not deprecated)*

```
#include <iostream>
#include <sycl/sycl.hpp>
using namespace sycl;

int main() {
  queue q;

  constexpr int size = 16;
  std::array<double, size> data;

  // Using "sycl::device_has()" as an attribute does not
  // affect the device we select. Therefore, our host code
  // should check the device's aspects before submitting a
  // kernel which does require that attribute.
  if (q.get_device().has(aspect::fp64)) {
    buffer B{data};
    q.submit([&](handler& h) {
      accessor A{B, h};
      // the attributes here say that the kernel is allowed
      // to require fp64 support any attribute(s) from
      // Figure 12-3 could be specified note that namespace
      // stmt above (for C++) does not affect attributes (a
      // C++ quirk) so sycl:: is needed here
      h.parallel_for(
          size, [=](auto& idx)
                    [[sycl::device_has(aspect::fp64)]] {
                      A[idx] = idx * 2.0;
                    });
    });
    std::cout << "doubles were used\n";
  } else {
    // here we use an alternate method (not needing double
    // math support on the device) to help our code be
    // flexible and hence more portable
    std::array<float, size> fdata;
    {
      buffer B{fdata};
      q.submit([&](handler& h) {
        accessor A{B, h};
        h.parallel_for(
            size, [=](auto& idx) { A[idx] = idx * 2.0f; });
      });
    }

    for (int i = 0; i < size; i++) data[i] = fdata[i];

    std::cout << "no doubles used\n";
  }
  for (int i = 0; i < size; i++)
    std::cout << "data[" << i << "] = " << data[i] << "\n";
  return 0;
}
```

Figure 12-10. *Specialization of kernel explicitly with the help of attributes*

Summary

The most portable programs will query the devices that are available in a system and adjust their behavior based on runtime information. This chapter opens the door to the rich set of information that is available to allow such tailoring of our code to adjust to the hardware that is present at runtime. We also discussed various ways to specialize kernels so they can be more closely adapted to a particular device type when we decide the investment is worthwhile. These give us the tools to balance portability and performance as necessary to meet our needs, all within the bounds of using C++ with SYCL.

Our programs can be made more functionally portable, more performance portable, and more future-proof by parameterizing our application to adjust to the characteristics of the hardware. We can also test that the hardware present falls within the bounds of any assumptions we have made in the design of our program and either warns or aborts when hardware is found that lies outside the bounds of our assumptions.

CHAPTER 13

Practical Tips

This chapter is home to a number of pieces of useful information, practical tips, advice, and techniques that have proven useful when programming C++ with SYCL. None of these topics are covered exhaustively, so the intent is to raise awareness and encourage learning more as needed.

Getting the Code Samples and a Compiler

Chapter 1 covers how to get a SYCL compiler (e.g., oneapi.com/implementations or github.com/intel/llvm) and where to get the code samples used in this book (github.com/Apress/data-parallel-CPP). This is mentioned again to emphasize how useful it can be to try the examples (including making modifications!) to gain hands-on experience. Join those who know what the code in Figure 1-1 actually prints out!

Online Resources

Key online resources include

- Extensive resources at sycl.tech/
- The official SYCL home at khronos.org/sycl/ with great resources listed at khronos.org/sycl/resources

J. Reinders et al., *Data Parallel C++*, https://doi.org/10.1007/978-1-4842-9691-2_13

- Resources to help migrate from CUDA to C++ with SYCL at tinyurl.com/cuda2sycl
- Migration tool GitHub home github.com/oneapi-src/SYCLomatic

Platform Model

A C++ compiler with SYCL support is designed to act and feel like any other C++ compiler we have ever used. It is worth understanding the inner workings, at a high level, that enable a compiler with SYCL support to produce code for a host (e.g., CPU) *and* devices.

The platform model (Figure 13-1) used by SYCL specifies a host that coordinates and controls the compute work that is performed on the devices. Chapter 2 describes how to assign work to devices, and Chapter 4 dives into how to program devices. Chapter 12 describes using the platform model at various levels of specificity.

As we discussed in Chapter 2, there *should always be* a device to run on in a system *using a properly configured SYCL runtime and compatible hardware*. This allows device code to be written assuming that at least one device *will be* available. The choice of the devices on which to run device code is under program control—it is entirely our choice as programmers if, and how, we want to execute code on specific devices (device selection options are discussed in Chapter 12).

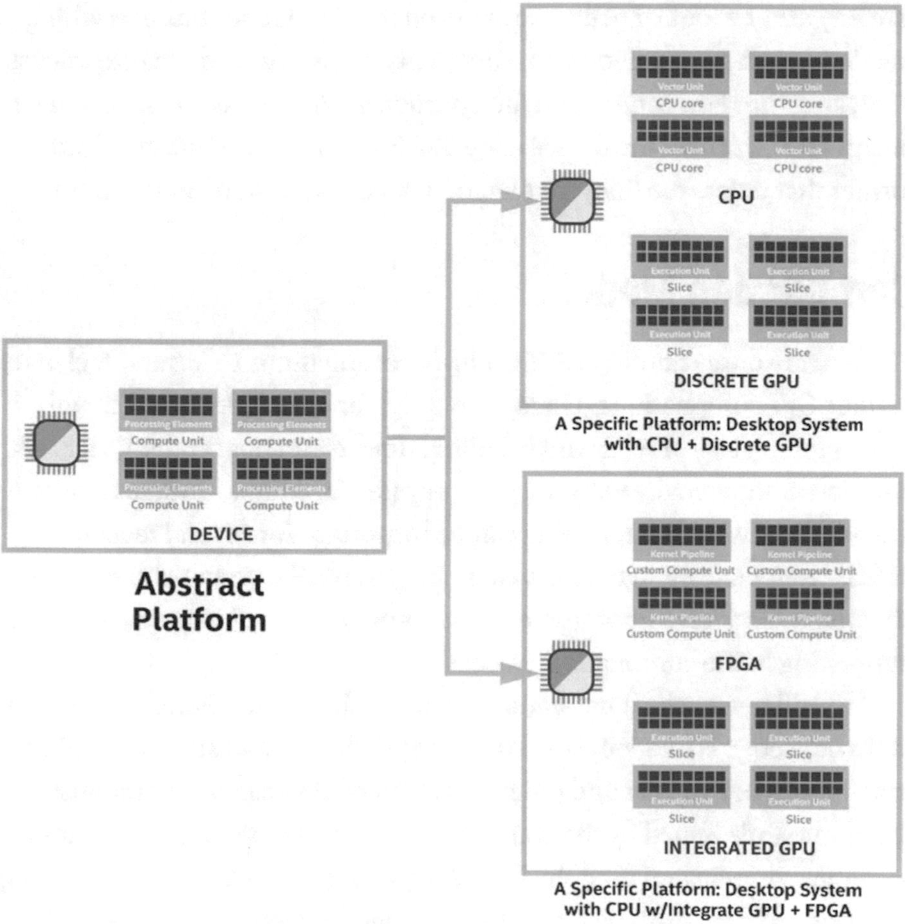

Figure 13-1. *Platform model: can be used abstractly or with specificity*

Multiarchitecture Binaries

Since our goal is to have a single-source code to support a heterogeneous machine, it is only natural to want a single executable file to be the result.

A multiarchitecture binary (a.k.a. a *fat binary*) is a single binary file that has been expanded to include all the compiled and intermediate code needed for our heterogeneous machine. A multiarchitecture binary acts like any other `a.out` or `a.exe` we are used to—but it contains everything needed for a heterogeneous machine. This helps to automate the process of picking the right code to run for a particular device. As we discuss next, one possible form of the device code in a fat binary is an intermediate format that defers the final creation of device instructions until runtime.

Compilation Model

The single-source nature of SYCL allows compilations to act and feel like regular C++ compilations. There is no need for us to invoke additional passes for devices or deal with bundling device and host code. That is all handled automatically for us by the compiler. Of course, understanding the details of what is happening can be important for several reasons. This is useful knowledge if we want to target specific architectures more effectively, and it is important to understand if we need to debug a failure happening in the compilation process.

We will review the compilation model so that we are educated for when that knowledge is needed. Since the compilation model supports code that executes on both a host and potentially several devices simultaneously, the commands issued by the compiler, linker, and other supporting tools are more complicated than the C++ compilations we are used to (targeting only one architecture). Welcome to the heterogeneous world!

This heterogeneous complexity is intentionally hidden from us by the compiler and "just works."

The compiler can generate target-specific executable code similar to traditional C++ compilers (*ahead-of-time* (AOT) compilation, sometimes referred to as offline kernel compilation), or it can generate an intermediate representation that can be *just-in-time* (JIT) compiled to a specific target at runtime.

Compilation can be "ahead-of-time" (AOT) or "just-in-time" (JIT).

The compiler can only compile ahead of time if the device target is known ahead of time (at the time when we compile our program). Using JIT compilation will give more portability for our compiled program but requires the compiler and the runtime to perform additional work while our application is running.

For most devices, including GPUs, the most common practice is to rely on JIT compilation. Some devices (e.g., FPGAs) may have exceptionally slow compilation processes and therefore the practice is to use AOT compilation.

Use JIT unless you know there is a need (e.g., FPGA) or benefit to using AOT code.

By default, when we compile our code for most devices, the output for device code is stored in an intermediate form. At runtime, the device driver on the system will *just-in-time* compile the intermediate form into code to run on the device(s) to match what is available on the system.

Unlike AOT code, the goal of JIT code is to be able to be compiled at runtime to use whatever device is on a system. This may include devices that did not exist when the program was originally compiled to JIT code.

We can ask the compiler to compile ahead-of-time for specific devices or classes of devices. This has the advantage of saving runtime, but it has the disadvantage of added compile time and fatter binaries! Code that is compiled ahead-of-time is not as portable as just-in-time because it cannot be adapted to match the available hardware at runtime. We can include both in our binary to get the benefits of both AOT and JIT.

To maximize portability, even when including some AOT code, we like to have JIT code in our binary too.

Compiling for a specific device ahead-of-time also helps us to check at build time that our program should work on that device. With just-in-time compilation, it is possible that a program will fail to compile at runtime (which can be caught using the mechanisms in Chapter 5). There are a few debugging tips for this in the upcoming "Debugging" section of this chapter, and Chapter 5 details how these errors can be caught at runtime to avoid requiring that our applications abort.

Figure 13-2 illustrates a compilation process from source code to fat binary (executable). Whatever combinations we choose are combined into a fat binary. The fat binary is employed by the runtime when the application executes (and it is the binary that we execute on the host!). At times, we may want to compile device code for a particular device in a separate compile. We would want the results of such a separate compilation to eventually be combined into our fat binary. This can be very useful for FPGA development when full compile (doing a full synthesis place-and-route) times can be very long and is in fact a requirement for FPGA development to avoid requiring the synthesis tools to be installed on a runtime system. Figure 13-3 shows the flow of the bundling/unbundling activity supported for such needs. We always have the option to compile everything at once, but during development, the option to break up compilation can be very useful.

Every C++ compiler supporting SYCL has a compilation model with the same goal, but the exact implementation details will vary. The specific diagrams shown here are courtesy of the DPC++ compiler toolchain implementors.

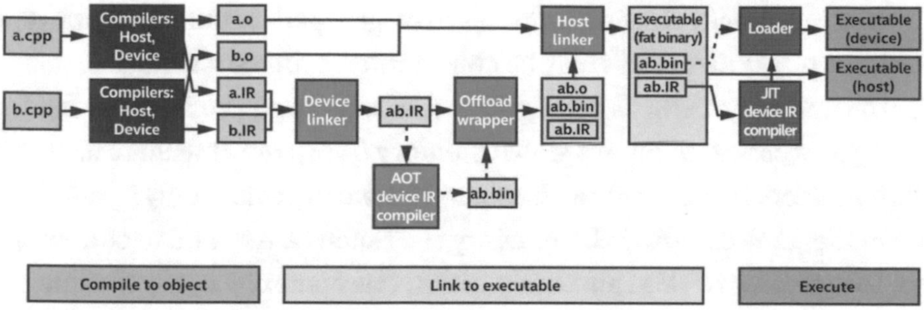

Figure 13-2. *Compilation process: ahead-of-time and just-in-time options*

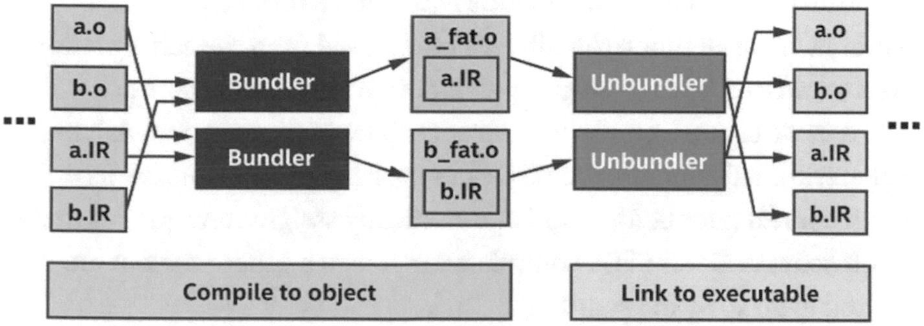

Figure 13-3. *Compilation process: offload bundler/unbundler*

Contexts: Important Things to Know

As mentioned in Chapter 6, a context represents a device or set of devices on which we can execute kernels. We can think of a context as a convenient place for the runtime to stash some state about what it is doing. Programmers are not likely to directly interact with contexts outside of passing them around in most SYCL programs.

Devices can be subdivided into sub-devices. This can be useful for partitioning a problem. Since sub-devices are treated exactly as devices (same C++ type), everything we say about grouping devices applies to sub-devices also.

SYCL abstractly considers devices to be grouped together in platforms. Within a platform, devices may be able to interact in ways including sharing memory. Devices belonging to the same context must have the ability to access each other's global memory using some mechanism. SYCL USM memory (Chapter 6) can be shared between devices only if they are in the same context. USM memory allocations are bound to contexts, not to devices, so a USM allocation within one context is not accessible to other contexts. Therefore, USM allocations are limited to use within a single context—possibly a subset of the device.

Contexts do not abstract what hardware cannot support. For instance, we cannot create a context to include two GPUs which cannot share memory with each other. Not all devices exposed from the same platform are required to be able to be grouped together in the same context.

When we create a queue, we can specify which context we wish to place it within. By default, the DPC++ compiler project implements a default context per platform and automatically assigns new queues to the default context. Other SYCL compilers are free to do the same but are not required to do so by the standard.

Contexts are expensive to create—having less makes our applications more efficient.

Having all devices from a given platform always be placed in the same context has two advantages: (1) since a context is expensive to create, our application is more efficient; and (2) the maximum sharing supported by the hardware is allowed (e.g., USM).

Adding SYCL to Existing C++ Programs

Adding the appropriate exploitation of parallelism to an existing C++ program is the first step to using SYCL. If a C++ application is already exploiting parallel execution, that may be a bonus, or it may be a headache. That is because the way we divide the work of an application into parallel execution greatly affects what we can do with it. When programmers talk about refactoring a program parallelism, they are referring to rearranging the flow of execution and data within a program to get it ready to exploit parallelism. This is a complex topic that we will only touch briefly upon. There is no *one-size-fits-all* answer on how to prepare an application for parallelism, but there are some tips worth noting.

When adding parallelism to a C++ application, an easy approach to consider is to find an isolated point in the program where the opportunity for parallelism is the greatest. We can start our modification there and then continue to add parallelism in other areas as needed. A complicating factor is that refactoring (i.e., rearranging the program flow and redesigning data structures) may improve the opportunity for parallelism.

Once we find an isolated point in the program where the opportunity for parallelism is the greatest, we will need to consider how to use SYCL at that point in the program. That is what the rest of the book teaches.

At a high level, the key steps for introducing parallelism consist of the following:

1. Safety with concurrency (commonly called thread safety in conventional CPU programming): Adjusting the usage of all shared mutable data (data that can change and may be acted upon concurrently) to prevent data races. See Chapter 19.

2. Introducing concurrency and/or parallelism.

3. Tuning for parallelism (best scaling, optimizing for throughput or latency).

It is important to consider step #1 first. Many applications have already been refactored for concurrency, but many have not. With SYCL as the sole source of parallelism, we focus on safety for the data being used within kernels and possibly shared with the host. If we have other techniques in our program (OpenMP, MPI, TBB, etc.) that introduce parallelism, that is an additional concern on top of our SYCL programming. It is important to note that it is okay to use multiple techniques inside a single program—SYCL does not need to be the only source of parallelism within a program. This book does not cover the advanced topic of mixing with other parallelism techniques.

Considerations When Using Multiple Compilers

C++ compilers that support SYCL also support linking with object code (libraries, object files, etc.) from other C++ compilers. In general, any issues that arise from using multiple compilers are the same as for any C++ compiler, requiring consideration of name mangling, targeting the same standard libraries, aligning calling conventions, etc. These are the same issues we must deal with when mixing and matching compilers for other languages such as Fortran or C.

In addition, applications must use the SYCL runtime that comes with the compiler used to build programs. It is not safe to mix and match SYCL compilers and SYCL runtimes—different runtimes may have different implementations and data layouts for important SYCL objects.

SYCL *interoperability* with non-SYCL source languages refers to the ability of SYCL to work with kernel functions or device functions that are written in other programming languages, such as OpenCL, C, or CUDA, or to consume code in an intermediate representation precompiled by another compiler. Refer to Chapter 20 for more information about interoperability with non-SYCL source languages.

Finally, the same compiler toolchain that was used for compiling SYCL device code is also required to do the linking phase of our compilation. Using a linker from a different compiler toolchain to do the linking will not result in a functional program as compilers that are not SYCL-aware will not know how to properly integrate host and device code.

Debugging

This section conveys some modest debugging advice, to ease the challenges unique to debugging a parallel program, especially one targeting a heterogeneous machine.

We should never forget that we have the option to debug our applications while they are running on a CPU device. This debugging tip is described as Method#2 in Chapter 2. Because the architectures of devices often include fewer debugging hooks than general-purpose CPUs, tools can often probe code on a CPU more precisely. An important difference when running *everything* on a CPU is that many errors relating to synchronization will disappear, including moving memory back and forth between the host and devices. While we eventually need to debug all such errors, this can allow incremental debugging so we can resolve some bugs before others. Experience will show that running on the device we are targeting as often as possible is important, as is leveraging portability to the CPU (and other devices) as part of the debugging process—running multiple devices will help expose issues and can help isolate whether a bug we encounter is device-specific.

Debugging tip Running on a CPU is a powerful debugging tool.

Parallel programming errors, specifically data races and deadlocks, are generally easier for tools to detect and eliminate when running all code on the host. Much to our chagrin, we will most often see program failures from such parallel programming errors when running on a combination of host and devices. When such issues strike, it is very useful to remember that pulling back to CPU-only is a powerful debugging tool. Thankfully, SYCL is carefully designed to keep this option available to us and easy to access.

Debugging tip If a program is deadlocking, check that the host accessors are being destroyed properly and that work-items in kernels are obeying the synchronization rules from the SYCL specification.

The following compiler options are a good idea when we start debugging:

- `-g`: Put debug information in the output
- `-ferror-limit=1`: Maintain sanity when using C++ with template libraries such as those heavily used by SYCL

- `-Werror -Wall -Wpedantic`: Have the compiler enforce good coding to help avoid producing incorrect code to debug at runtime

We really do not need to get bogged down fixing pedantic warnings just to use C++ with SYCL, so choosing to not use `-Wpedantic` is understandable.

When we leave our code to be compiled just-in-time during runtime, there is code we can inspect. This is *highly dependent* on the layers used by our compiler, so looking at the compiler documentation for suggestions is a good idea.

Debugging Deadlock and Other Synchronization Issues

Parallel programming relies on the proper coordination between our work that happens in parallel. Data usage needs to be gated by when the data is ready for use—such data dependencies need to be encoded in the logic of our program for proper behavior.

Debugging dependency issues, especially with USM, can be a challenge when an error in our synchronization/dependency logic occurs. We may see a program hang (never complete) or generate erroneous information intermittently. In such cases, we may see behavior such as "it fails until I run it in the debugger—then it works perfectly!" Such intermittent failures often stem from dependencies which are not properly synchronized via waits, locks, explicit dependencies between queue submission, etc.

Useful debugging techniques include

- Switching from out-of-order to in-order queues
- Sprinkle `queue.wait()` calls around

Using either, or both, of these while debugging can help to identify where dependency information may be missing. If such change makes program failures change or disappear, it is a strong hint that we have an issue to correct in our synchronization/dependency logic. Once fixed, we remove these temporary debugging measures.

Debugging Kernel Code

While debugging kernel code, start by running on a CPU device (as advised in Chapter 2). The code for device selectors in Chapter 2 can easily be modified to accept runtime options, or compiler-time options, to redirect work to the host device when we are debugging.

When debugging kernel code, SYCL defines a C++-style `stream` that can be used within a kernel (Figure 13-4). The DPC++ compiler also offers an experimental implementation of a C-style `printf` that has useful capabilities, with some restrictions.

```
q.submit([&](handler &h) {
  stream out(1024, 256, h);
  h.parallel_for(range{8}, [=](id<1> idx) {
    out << "Testing my sycl stream (this is work-item ID:"
        << idx << ")\n";
  });
});
```

Figure 13-4. *`sycl::stream`*

When debugging kernel code, experience encourages that we put breakpoints before `parallel_for` or inside `parallel_for`, but not actually on the `parallel_for`. A breakpoint placed on a `parallel_for` can trigger a breakpoint multiple times even after performing the next operation. This C++ debugging advice applies to many template expansions like those in SYCL, where a breakpoint on the template call will translate into a complicated set of breakpoints when it is expanded by the compiler. There may be ways that implementations can ease this, but the key point here is that we can avoid some confusion on all implementations by not setting the breakpoint precisely on the `parallel_for` itself.

Debugging Runtime Failures

When a runtime error occurs while compiling just-in-time, we are either dealing with a case where we used a feature explicitly that the available hardware cannot support (e.g., fp16 or simd8), a compiler/runtime bug, or we have accidentally programmed nonsense that was not detected until it tripped up the runtime and created difficult-to-understand runtime error messages. In all three cases, it can be a bit intimidating to dive into these bugs. Thankfully, even a cursory look may allow us to get a better idea of what caused a particular issue. It might yield some additional knowledge that will guide us to avoid the issue, or it may just help us submit a short bug report to the compiler team. Either way, knowing that some tools exist to help can be important.

Output from our program that indicates a runtime failure may look like these examples:

```
terminate called after throwing an instance of 'sycl::_
V1::runtime_error'
  what():  Native API failed. Native API returns: ...
```

or

```
terminate called after throwing an instance of 'sycl::_
V1::compile_program_error'
  what():  The program was built for 1 devices
...
```

```
error: Kernel compiled with required subgroup size 8, which is
unsupported on this platform
in kernel: 'typeinfo name for main::'lambda'(sycl::_V1::nd_
item<2>)'
error: backend compiler failed build.
 -11 (PI_ERROR_BUILD_PROGRAM_FAILURE)
```

Seeing such exceptions here lets us know that our host program could have been constructed to catch this error. The first shows a bit of a catch-all error for accessing any API that is not supported natively (in this case it was using a host side memory allocation not supported on the platform); the second is easier to realize that SIMD8 was specified for a device that did not support it (in this case it supported SIMD16 instead). Runtime compiler failures do not need to abort our application; we could catch them, or code to avoid them, or both. Chapter 5 dives into this topic.

When we see a runtime failure and have any difficulty debugging it quickly, it is worth simply trying a rebuild using ahead-of-time compilations. If the device we are targeting has an ahead-of-time compilation option, this can be an easy thing to try that may yield easier-to-understand diagnostics. If our errors can be seen at compile time instead of JIT or runtime, often much more useful information will be found in the error messages from the compiler instead of the small amount of error information we usually see from a JIT or the runtime.

Figure 13-5 lists two of the flags and additional environment variables (supported on Windows and Linux) supported by compilers or runtimes to aid in advanced debugging. These are DPC++ compiler–specific advanced debug options that exist to inspect and control the compilation model. They are not discussed or utilized in this book; they are explained in detail online with the GitHub project at intel.github.io/llvm-docs/EnvironmentVariables.html and tinyurl.com/IGCoptions.

Environment variables	Value	description
ONEAPI_DEVICE_SELECTOR	See online documentation for examples of the numerous options in the documents at intel.github.io.	Can be used to limit the choice of devices available when a SYCL-using application is run. Useful for limiting devices to a certain type (like GPUs or accelerators) or backends (like Level Zero or OpenCL).
SYCL_PI_TRACE	1 (basic), 2 (advanced), -1 (all)	Runtime: Value of 1 enables tracing of Runtime Plugin Interface (PI) for plugin and device discovery; Value of 2 enables tracing of all PI calls. Value of -1 unleashes all levels of tracing.
SYCL_PRINT_EXECUTION_GRAPH	always (or ask to dump only select files by specifying: before_addCG, after_addCG, before_addCopyBack, after_addCopyBack, before_addHostAcc, or after_addHostAcc)	Runtime: create text files (with DOT extension) tracing the execution graph. Relatively easy to browse traces of what is happening during runtime.
IGC_ShaderDumpEnable	0 or 1	Linux only. Runtime: ask the Intel Graphics Compiler (JIT) to dump some information.
IGC_ShaderDumpEnableAll	0 or 1	Linux only. Runtime: ask the Intel Graphics Compiler (JIT) to dump *lots* of information.

Figure 13-5. *DPC++ compiler advanced debug options*

These options are not described more within this book, but they are mentioned here to open up this avenue of advanced debugging as needed. These options *may* give us insight into how to work around an issue or bug. It is possible that our source code is inadvertently triggering an issue that can be resolved by correcting the source code. Otherwise, the use of these options is for very advanced debugging of the compiler itself. Therefore, they are associated more with compiler developers than with users of the compiler. Some advanced users find these options useful; therefore, they are mentioned here and never again in this book. To dig deeper, see DPC++ compiler GitHub project intel.github.io/llvm-docs/EnvironmentVariables.html.

Debugging tip When other options are exhausted and we need to debug a runtime issue, we look for dump tools that might give us hints toward the cause.

Queue Profiling and Resulting Timing Capabilities

Many devices support *queue profiling* (`device::has(aspect::queue_profiling)`—for more on aspects in general, see Chapter 12. A simple and powerful interface makes it easy to access detailed timing information on queue submission, actual start of execution on the device, completion on the device, and completion of the command. This profiling will be more precise about the device timings than using host timing mechanisms (e.g., `chrono`) because they will generally not include host to/from device data transfer times. See the examples shown in Figure 13-6 and Figure 13-7 with sample outputs shown in Figure 13-8. The samples outputs shown in Figure 13-8 illustrate what is possible with this technique but have not been optimized and should not be used as representations of the merits of any particular system choice in any manner.

The `aspect::queue_profiling` aspect indicates that the device supports queue profiling via `property::queue::enable_profiling`. For such devices, we can specify `property::queue::enable_profiling` when constructing a queue—a property list is an optional final parameter to the queue constructor. Doing so activates the SYCL runtime captures of profiling information for the command groups that are submitted to that queue. The captured information is then made available via the SYCL event class `get_profiling_info` member function. If the queue's associated device does not have `aspect::queue_profiling`, this will cause the constructor to throw a synchronous exception with the `errc::feature_not_supported` error code.

An event can be queried for profiling information using the `get_profiling_info` member function of the event class, specifying one of the profiling info parameters enumerated in `info::event_profiling`. The possible values for each info paramcter and any restrictions are defined in the specification of the SYCL backend associated with the event. All info parameters in `info::event_profiling` are specified in SYCL specification's table entitled "Profiling information descriptors for the SYCL event class," and the synopsis for `info::event_profiling` is described in an Appendix of the specification under "Event information descriptors."

Each profiling descriptor returns a timestamp that represents the number of nanoseconds that have elapsed since some implementation-defined time base. All events that share the same backend are guaranteed to share the same time base; therefore, the difference between two timestamps from the same backend yields the number of nanoseconds that have elapsed between those events.

As a final note, we do caution that enabling event profiling does increase overhead, so the best practice is to enable it during development or tuning and then to disable for production.

Tip Due to slight overhead, enable queue profiling only during development or tuning—disable for production.

```
#include <iostream>
#include <sycl/sycl.hpp>
using namespace sycl;

// Array type and data size for this example.
constexpr size_t array_size = (1 << 16);
typedef std::array<int, array_size> IntArray;
// Define VectorAdd (see Figure 13-7)

void InitializeArray(IntArray &a) {
  for (size_t i = 0; i < a.size(); i++) a[i] = i;
}

int main() {
  IntArray a, b, sum;
  InitializeArray(a);
  InitializeArray(b);

  queue q(property::queue::enable_profiling{});

  std::cout << "Vector size: " << a.size()
            << "\nRunning on device: "
            << q.get_device().get_info<info::device::name>()
            << "\n";

  VectorAdd(q, a, b, sum);

  return 0;
}
```

Figure 13-6. *Setting up to use queue profiling*

```
void VectorAdd(queue &q, const IntArray &a,
               const IntArray &b, IntArray &sum) {
  range<1> num_items{a.size()};
  buffer a_buf(a), b_buf(b);
  buffer sum_buf(sum.data(), num_items);
  auto t1 =
      std::chrono::steady_clock::now();  // Start timing

  event e = q.submit([&](handler &h) {
    auto a_acc = a_buf.get_access<access::mode::read>(h);
    auto b_acc = b_buf.get_access<access::mode::read>(h);
    auto sum_acc =
        sum_buf.get_access<access::mode::write>(h);

    h.parallel_for(num_items, [=](id<1> i) {
      sum_acc[i] = a_acc[i] + b_acc[i];
    });
  });
  q.wait();

  double timeA =
      (e.template get_profiling_info<
           info::event_profiling::command_end>() -
       e.template get_profiling_info<
           info::event_profiling::command_start>());

  auto t2 =
      std::chrono::steady_clock::now();  // Stop timing

  double timeB = (std::chrono::duration_cast<
                      std::chrono::microseconds>(t2 - t1)
                      .count());

  std::cout
      << "profiling: Vector add completed on device in "
      << timeA << " nanoseconds\n";
  std::cout << "chrono: Vector add completed on device in "
            << timeB * 1000 << " nanoseconds\n";
  std::cout << "chrono more than profiling by "
            << (timeB * 1000 - timeA) << " nanoseconds\n";
}
```

Figure 13-7. *Using queue profiling*

```
Vector size: 65536
Running on device: Intel(R) UHD Graphics P630 [0x3e96]
profiling: Vector add completed on device in 57602 nanoseconds
chrono: Vector add completed on device in 2.85489e+08 nanoseconds
chrono more than profiling by 2.85431e+08 nanoseconds

Vector size: 65536
Running on device: NVIDIA GeForce RTX 3060
profiling: Vector add completed on device in 17410 nanoseconds
chrono: Vector add completed on device in 3.6071e+07 nanoseconds
chrono more than profiling by 3.60536e+07 nanoseconds

Vector size: 65536
Running on device: Intel(R) Data Center GPU Max 1100
profiling: Vector add completed on device in 9440 nanoseconds
chrono: Vector add completed on device in 5.6976e+07 nanoseconds
chrono more than profiling by 5.69666e+07 nanoseconds
```

Figure 13-8. *Three sample outputs from queue profiling example*

Tracing and Profiling Tools Interfaces

Tracing and profiling tools can help us understand our runtime behaviors in our application, and often shed light on opportunities to improve our algorithms. Insights are often portable, in that they can be generalized to a wide class of devices, so we recommend using whatever tracing and profiling tools you find most valuable on whatever platform you prefer. Of course, fine-tuning any platform can require being on the exact platform in question. For maximally portable applications, we encourage first looking for opportunities to tune with an eye toward making any adjustments as portable as possible.

When our SYCL programs are running on top of an OpenCL runtime and using the OpenCL backend, we can run our programs with the OpenCL Intercept Layer: github.com/intel/opencl-intercept-layer. This is a tool that can inspect, log, and modify OpenCL commands that an application (or higher-level runtime) is generating. It supports a lot of controls, but good ones to set initially are `ErrorLogging`, `BuildLogging`, and maybe `CallLogging` (though it generates a lot of output). Useful dumps are possible with `DumpProgramSPIRV`. The OpenCL Intercept Layer is a separate utility and is not part of any specific OpenCL implementation, so it works with many SYCL compilers.

There are a number of additional excellent tools for collecting performance data that are popular for SYCL developers. They are open source (github.com/intel/pti-gpu) along with samples to help to get us started.

Two of the most popular tools are as follows:

- onetrace: Host and device tracing tool for OpenCL and Level Zero backends with support of DPC++ (both for CPU and GPU) and OpenMP GPU offload
- oneprof: GPU HW metrics collection tool for OpenCL and Level Zero backends with support of DPC++ and OpenMP* GPU offload

Both tools use information from instrumented runtimes, so they apply to GPUs and CPUs. SYCL, ISPC, and OpenMP support in compilers that use these runtimes can all benefit from these tools. Consult the websites for the tools to explore their applicability for your usage. In general, we can find a platform that is supported and use the tools to learn useful information about your program even if every platform we target is not supported. Much of what we learn about a program is useful everywhere.

Initializing Data and Accessing Kernel Outputs

In this section, we dive into a topic that causes confusion for new users of SYCL and that leads to the most common (in our experience) first bugs that we encounter as new SYCL developers.

Put simply, when we create a buffer from a host memory allocation (e.g., array or vector), we can't access the host allocation directly until the buffer has been destroyed. The buffer owns any host allocation passed to it at construction time, for the buffer's entire lifetime. There are rarely used mechanisms that *do* let us access the host allocation while a buffer is still alive (e.g., buffer mutex), but those advanced features don't help with the early bugs described here.

EVERYONE MAKES THIS ERROR—KNOWING THAT CAN HELP US DEBUG IT QUICKLY RATHER THAN PUZZLE OVER IT A LONG TIME!!!

If we construct a buffer from a host memory allocation, we must not directly access the host allocation until the buffer has been destroyed! While it is alive, the buffer owns the allocation. Understand buffer scope—and rules inside the scope!

A common bug appears when the host program accesses a host allocation while a buffer still owns that allocation. All bets are off once this happens because we don't know what the buffer is using the allocation for. Don't be surprised if the data is incorrect—the kernels that we're trying to read the output from may not have even started running yet! As described in Chapters 3 and 8, SYCL is built around an asynchronous task graph mechanism. Before we try to use output data from task graph operations, we need to be sure that we have reached synchronization points in the code where the graph has executed and made data available to the host. Both buffer destruction and creation of host accessors are operations that cause this synchronization.

Figure 13-9 shows a common pattern of code that we often write, where we cause a buffer to be destroyed by closing the block scope within which it was defined. By causing the buffer to go out of scope and be destroyed, we can then safely read kernel results through the original host allocation that was passed to the buffer constructor.

```
constexpr size_t N = 1024;

// Set up queue on any available device
queue q;

// Create host containers to initialize on the host
std::vector<int> in_vec(N), out_vec(N);

// Initialize input and output vectors
for (int i = 0; i < N; i++) in_vec[i] = i;
std::fill(out_vec.begin(), out_vec.end(), 0);

// Nuance: Create new scope so that we can easily cause
// buffers to go out of scope and be destroyed
{
  // Create buffers using host allocations (vector in this
  // case)
  buffer in_buf{in_vec}, out_buf{out_vec};

  // Submit the kernel to the queue
  q.submit([&](handler& h) {
    accessor in{in_buf, h};
    accessor out{out_buf, h};

    h.parallel_for(
        range{N}, [=](id<1> idx) { out[idx] = in[idx]; });
  });

  // Close the scope that buffer is alive within!  Causes
  // buffer destruction which will wait until the kernels
  // writing to buffers have completed, and will copy the
  // data from written buffers back to host allocations
  // (our std::vectors in this case).  After the buffer
  // destructor runs, caused by this closing of scope,
  // then it is safe to access the original in_vec and
  // out_vec again!
}

// Check that all outputs match expected value
// WARNING: The buffer destructor must have run for us to
// safely use in_vec and out_vec again in our host code.
// While the buffer is alive it owns those allocations,
// and they are not safe for us to use!  At the least they
// will contain values that are not up to date.  This code
// is safe and correct because the closing of scope above
// has caused the buffer to be destroyed before this point
// where we use the vectors again.
for (int i = 0; i < N; i++)
  std::cout << "out_vec[" << i << "]=" << out_vec[i]
            << "\n";
```

Figure 13-9. *Common pattern: buffer creation from a host allocation*

There are two common reasons to associate a buffer with existing host memory like Figure 13-9:

1. To simplify initialization of data in a buffer. We can just construct the buffer from host memory that we (or another part of the application) have already initialized.

2. To reduce the characters typed because closing scope with a '}' is slightly more concise (though more error prone) than creating a `host_accessor` to the buffer.

If we use a host allocation to dump or verify the output values from a kernel, we need to put the buffer allocation into a block scope (or other scopes) so that we can control when it is destructed. We must then make sure that the buffer is destroyed before we access the host allocation to obtain the kernel output. Figure 13-9 shows this done correctly, while Figure 13-10 shows a common bug where the output is accessed while the buffer is still alive.

Advanced users may prefer to use buffer destruction to return result data from kernels into a host memory allocation. But for most users, and especially new developers, it is recommended to use scoped host accessors.

```
constexpr size_t N = 1024;

// Set up queue on any available device
queue q;

// Create host containers to initialize on the host
std::vector<int> in_vec(N), out_vec(N);

// Initialize input and output vectors
for (int i = 0; i < N; i++) in_vec[i] = i;
std::fill(out_vec.begin(), out_vec.end(), 0);

// Create buffers using host allocations (vector in this
// case)
buffer in_buf{in_vec}, out_buf{out_vec};

// Submit the kernel to the queue
q.submit([&](handler& h) {
  accessor in{in_buf, h};
  accessor out{out_buf, h};

  h.parallel_for(range{N},
                 [=](id<1> idx) { out[idx] = in[idx]; });
});

// BUG!!! We're using the host allocation out_vec, but the
// buffer out_buf is still alive and owns that allocation!
// We will probably see the initialiation value (zeros)
// printed out, since the kernel probably hasn't even run
// yet, and the buffer has no reason to have copied any
// output back to the host even if the kernel has run.
for (int i = 0; i < N; i++)
  std::cout << "out_vec[" << i << "]=" << out_vec[i]
            << "\n";
```

***Figure 13-10.** Common bug: reading data directly from host allocation during buffer lifetime*

To avoid these bugs, we recommend using host accessors instead of buffer scoping when getting started using C++ with SYCL. Host accessors provide access to a buffer from the host, and once their constructor has finished running, we are guaranteed that any previous writes (e.g., from kernels submitted before the host_accessor was created) to the buffer have executed and are visible. This book uses a mixture of both styles (i.e., host accessors and host allocations passed to the buffer constructor) to provide familiarity with both. Using host accessors tends to be less error prone when getting started. Figure 13-11 shows how a host accessor can be used to read output from a kernel, without destroying the buffer first.

```
constexpr size_t N = 1024;

// Set up queue on any available device
queue q;

// Create host containers to initialize on the host
std::vector<int> in_vec(N), out_vec(N);

// Initialize input and output vectors
for (int i = 0; i < N; i++) in_vec[i] = i;
std::fill(out_vec.begin(), out_vec.end(), 0);

// Create buffers using host allocations (vector in this
// case)
buffer in_buf{in_vec}, out_buf{out_vec};

// Submit the kernel to the queue
q.submit([&](handler& h) {
  accessor in{in_buf, h};
  accessor out{out_buf, h};

  h.parallel_for(range{N},
                 [=](id<1> idx) { out[idx] = in[idx]; });
});

// Check that all outputs match expected value
// Use host accessor!  Buffer is still in scope / alive
host_accessor A{out_buf};

for (int i = 0; i < N; i++)
  std::cout << "A[" << i << "]=" << A[i] << "\n";
```

Figure 13-11. *Recommendation: Use a host accessor to read kernel results*

Host accessors can be used whenever a buffer is alive, such as at both ends of a typical buffer lifetime—for initialization of the buffer content and for reading of results from our kernels. Figure 13-12 shows an example of this pattern.

```
constexpr size_t N = 1024;

// Set up queue on any available device
queue q;

// Create buffers of size N
buffer<int> in_buf{N}, out_buf{N};

// Use host accessors to initialize the data
{  // CRITICAL: Begin scope for host_accessor lifetime!
  host_accessor in_acc{in_buf}, out_acc{out_buf};
  for (int i = 0; i < N; i++) {
    in_acc[i] = i;
    out_acc[i] = 0;
  }
}  // CRITICAL: Close scope to make host accessors go out
   // of scope!

// Submit the kernel to the queue
q.submit([&](handler& h) {
  accessor in{in_buf, h};
  accessor out{out_buf, h};

  h.parallel_for(range{N},
                 [=](id<1> idx) { out[idx] = in[idx]; });
});

// Check that all outputs match expected value
// Use host accessor!  Buffer is still in scope / alive
host_accessor A{out_buf};

for (int i = 0; i < N; i++)
  std::cout << "A[" << i << "]=" << A[i] << "\n";
```

Figure 13-12. *Recommendation: Use host accessors for buffer initialization and reading of results*

One final detail to mention is that host accessors sometime cause an opposite bug in applications, because they also have a lifetime. While a `host_accessor` to a buffer is alive, the runtime will not allow that buffer to be used by any devices! The runtime does not analyze our host programs to determine when they *might* access a host accessor, so the only way for it to know that the host program has finished accessing a buffer is for the `host_accessor` destructor to run. As shown in Figure 13-13, this can cause applications to appear to hang if our host program is waiting for some kernels to run (e.g., `queue::wait()` or acquiring another host accessor) and if the SYCL runtime is waiting for our earlier host accessor(s) to be destroyed before it can run kernels that use a buffer.

When using host accessors, be sure that they are destroyed when no longer needed to unlock use of the buffer by kernels or other host accessors.

```
constexpr size_t N = 1024;

// Set up queue on any available device
queue q;

// Create buffers using host allocations (vector in this
// case)
buffer<int> in_buf{N}, out_buf{N};

// Use host accessors to initialize the data
host_accessor in_acc{in_buf}, out_acc{out_buf};
for (int i = 0; i < N; i++) {
  in_acc[i] = i;
  out_acc[i] = 0;
}

// BUG: Host accessors in_acc and out_acc are still alive!
// Later q.submits will never start on a device, because
// the runtime doesn't know that we've finished accessing
// the buffers via the host accessors.  The device kernels
// can't launch until the host finishes updating the
// buffers, since the host gained access first (before the
// queue submissions). This program will appear to hang!
// Use a debugger in that case.

// Submit the kernel to the queue
q.submit([&](handler& h) {
  accessor in{in_buf, h};
  accessor out{out_buf, h};

  h.parallel_for(range{N},
                 [=](id<1> idx) { out[idx] = in[idx]; });
});

std::cout << "This program will deadlock here!!!  Our "
             "host_accessors used\n"
          << " for data initialization are still in "
             "scope, so the runtime won't\n"
          << " allow our kernel to start executing on "
             "the device (the host could\n"
          << " still be initializing the data that is "
             "used by the kernel). The next line\n"
          << " of code is acquiring a host accessor for "
             "the output, which will wait for\n"
          << " the kernel to run first.  Since in_acc "
             "and out_acc have not been\n"
          << " destructed, the kernel is not safe for "
             "the runtime to run, and we deadlock.\n";

// Check that all outputs match expected value
// Use host accessor!  Buffer is still in scope / alive
host_accessor A{out_buf};

for (int i = 0; i < N; i++)
  std::cout << "A[" << i << "]=" << A[i] << "\n";
```

***Figure 13-13.** Deadlock (bug—it hangs!) from improper use of `host_accessors`*

Multiple Translation Units

When we want to call functions inside a kernel that are defined in a different translation unit, those functions need to be labeled with SYCL_EXTERNAL. Without this decoration, the compiler will only compile a function for use outside of device code (making it illegal to call that external function from within device code).

There are a few restrictions on SYCL_EXTERNAL functions that do not apply if we define the function within the same translation unit:

- SYCL_EXTERNAL can only be used on functions.
- SYCL_EXTERNAL functions cannot use raw pointers as parameter or return types. Explicit pointer classes must be used instead.
- SYCL_EXTERNAL functions cannot call a parallel_for_work_item method.
- SYCL_EXTERNAL functions cannot be called from within a parallel_for_work_group scope.

If we try to compile a kernel that is calling a function that is not inside the same translation unit and is not declared with SYCL_EXTERNAL, then we can expect a compile error similar to

```
error: SYCL kernel cannot call an undefined function without
SYCL_EXTERNAL attribute
```

If the function itself is compiled without a SYCL_EXTERNAL attribute, we can expect to see either a link or runtime failure such as

```
terminate called after throwing an instance of '...compile_
program_error'...
error: undefined reference to ...
```

SYCL does not require compilers to support SYCL_EXTERNAL; it is an *optional* feature in general. DPC++ supports SYCL_EXTERNAL.

Performance Implication of Multiple Translation Units

An implication of the compilation model (see earlier in this chapter) is that if we scatter our device code into multiple translation units, that may trigger more invocations of just-in-time compilation than if our device code is colocated. This is highly implementation-dependent and is subject to changes over time as implementations mature.

Such effects on performance are minor enough to ignore through most of our development work, but when we get to fine-tuning to maximize code performance, there are two things we can consider to mitigate these effects: (1) group device code together in the same translation unit, and (2) use ahead-of-time compilation to avoid just-in-time compilation effects entirely. Since both of these require some effort on our part, we only do this when we have finished our development and are trying to squeeze every ounce of performance out of our application. When we do resort to this detailed tuning, it is worth testing changes to observe their effect on the exact SYCL implementation that we are using.

When Anonymous Lambdas Need Names

SYCL allows for assigning names to lambdas in case tools need it and for debugging purposes (e.g., to enable displays in terms of user-defined names). Naming lambdas is optional per the SYCL 2020 specification. Throughout most of this book, anonymous lambdas are used for kernels because names are not needed when using C++ with SYCL (except for passing of compile options as described with lambda naming discussion in Chapter 10).

When we have an advanced need to mix SYCL tools from multiple vendors in a codebase, the tooling may require that we name lambdas. This is done by adding a `<class uniquename>` to the SYCL action construct in which the lambda is used (e.g., `parallel_for`). This naming allows tools from multiple vendors to interact in a defined way within a single compilation and can also help by displaying kernel names that we define within debug tools and layers.

We also need to name kernels if we want to use kernel queries. The SYCL standards committee was unable to find a solution to requiring this in the SYCL 2020 standard. For instance, querying a kernel's `preferred_work_group_size_multiple` requires us to call the `get_info()` member function of the `kernel` class, which requires an instance of the `kernel` class, which ultimately requires that we know the name (and `kernel_id`) of the kernel in order to extract a handle to it from the relevant `kernel_bundle`.

Summary

Popular culture today often refers to tips as *life hacks*. Unfortunately, programming culture often assigns a negative connotation to *hack*, so the authors refrained from naming this chapter "SYCL Hacks." Undoubtedly, this chapter has just touched the surface of what practical tips can be given for using C++ with SYCL. More tips can be shared by all of us as we learn together how to make the most out of C++ with SYCL.

CHAPTER 14

Common Parallel Patterns

When we are at our best as programmers, we recognize patterns in our work and apply techniques that are time-tested to be the best solution. Parallel programming is no different, and it would be a serious mistake not to study the patterns that have proven to be useful in this space. Consider the MapReduce frameworks adopted for Big Data applications; their success stems largely from being based on two simple yet effective parallel patterns—*map* and *reduce*.

There are a number of common patterns in parallel programming that crop up time and again, independent of the programming language that we're using. These patterns are versatile and can be employed at any level of parallelism (e.g., sub-groups, work-groups, full devices) and on any device (e.g., CPUs, GPUs, FPGAs). However, certain properties of the patterns (such as their scalability) may affect their suitability for different devices. In some cases, adapting an application to a new device may simply require choosing appropriate parameters or fine-tuning an implementation of a pattern; in others, we may be able to improve performance by selecting a different pattern entirely.

Developing an understanding of how, when, and where to use these common parallel patterns is a key part of improving our proficiency in SYCL (and parallel programming in general). For those with existing

J. Reinders et al., *Data Parallel C++*, https://doi.org/10.1007/978-1-4842-9691-2_14

parallel programming experience, seeing how these patterns are expressed in SYCL can be a quick way to spin up and gain familiarity with the capabilities of the language.

This chapter aims to provide answers to the following questions:

- What are some common patterns that we should understand?
- How do the patterns relate to the capabilities of different devices?
- Which patterns are already provided as SYCL functions and libraries?
- How would the patterns be implemented using direct programming?

Understanding the Patterns

The patterns discussed here are a subset of the parallel patterns described in the book *Structured Parallel Programming* by McCool et al. We do not cover the patterns related to *types* of parallelism (e.g., fork-join, branch-and-bound) but focus on some of the algorithmic patterns most useful for writing data-parallel kernels.

We wholeheartedly believe that understanding this subset of parallel patterns is critical to becoming an effective SYCL programmer. The table in Figure 14-1 presents a high-level overview of the different patterns, including their primary use cases, their key attributes, and how their attributes impact their affinity for different hardware devices.

Pattern	Useful For	Key Attributes	Device Affinity
Map	Simple parallel kernels	No data dependences and high scalability	All
Stencil	Structured data dependences	Data dependences and data re-use	Depends on stencil size
Reduction	Combining partial results	Data dependences	All
Scan Pack/Unpack	Filtering and restructuring data	Limited scalability	Depends on problem size

Figure 14-1. *Parallel patterns and their affinity for different device types*

Map

The map pattern is the simplest parallel pattern of all and will be immediately familiar to readers with experience in functional programming languages. As shown in Figure 14-2, each input element of a range is independently *mapped* to an output by applying some function. Many data-parallel operations can be expressed as instances of the map pattern (e.g., vector addition).

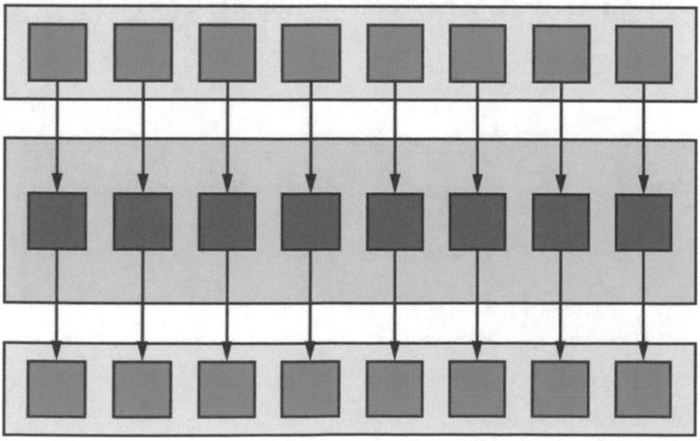

Figure 14-2. *Map pattern*

Since every application of the function is completely independent, expressions of map are often very simple, relying on the compiler and/or runtime to do most of the hard work. We should expect kernels written to the map pattern to be suitable for any device and for the performance of those kernels to scale very well with the amount of available hardware parallelism.

However, we should think carefully before deciding to rewrite entire applications as a series of map kernels! Such a development approach is highly productive and guarantees that an application will be portable to a wide variety of device types but encourages us to ignore optimizations that may significantly improve performance (e.g., improving data reuse, fusing kernels).

Stencil

The stencil pattern is closely related to the map pattern. As shown in Figure 14-3, a function is applied to an input and a set of neighboring inputs described by a *stencil* to produce a single output. Stencil patterns appear frequently in many domains, including scientific/engineering applications (e.g., finite difference codes) and computer vision/machine learning applications (e.g., image convolutions).

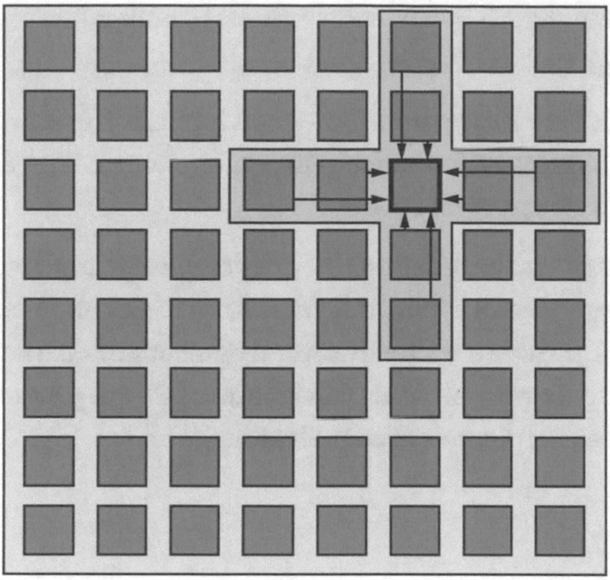

Figure 14-3. *Stencil pattern*

When the stencil pattern is executed out-of-place (i.e., writing the outputs to a separate storage location), the function can be applied to every input independently. Scheduling stencils in the real world is often more complicated than this: computing neighboring outputs requires the same data, and loading that data from memory multiple times will degrade performance; and we may wish to apply the stencil in-place (i.e., overwriting the original input values) in order to decrease an application's memory footprint.

The suitability of a stencil kernel for different devices is therefore highly dependent on properties of the stencil and the input problem. Generally speaking,

- Small stencils can benefit from the scratchpad storage of GPUs.

- Large stencils can benefit from the (comparatively) large caches of CPUs.
- Small stencils operating on small inputs can achieve significant performance gains via implementation as systolic arrays on FPGAs.

Since stencils are easy to describe but complex to implement efficiently, many stencil applications make use of a domain-specific language (DSL). There are already several embedded DSLs leveraging the template meta-programming capabilities of C++ to generate high-performance stencil kernels at compile time.

Reduction

A reduction is a common parallel pattern which *combines* partial results using an operator that is typically *associative* and *commutative* (e.g., addition). The most ubiquitous examples of reductions are computing a sum (e.g., while computing a dot product) or computing the minimum/maximum value (e.g., using maximum velocity to set time-step size).

Figure 14-4 shows the reduction pattern implemented by way of a tree reduction, which is a popular implementation requiring $\log_2(N)$ combination operations for a range of N input elements. Although tree reductions are common, other implementations are possible—in general, we should not assume that a reduction combines values in a specific order.

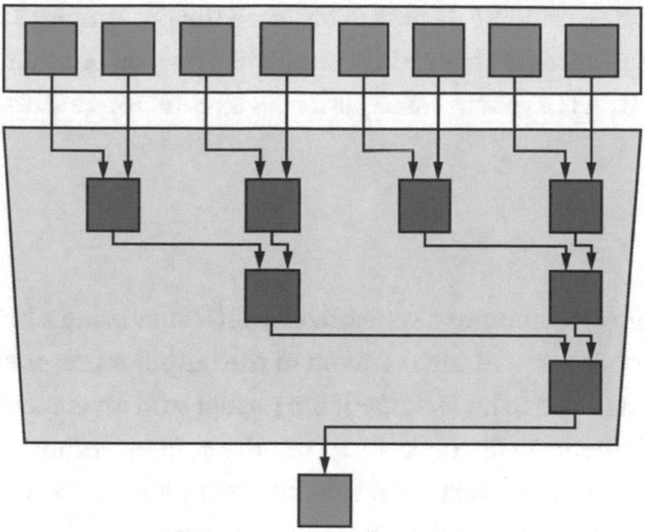

Figure 14-4. *Reduction pattern*

Kernels are rarely embarrassingly parallel in real life, and even when they are, they are often paired with reductions (as in MapReduce frameworks) to summarize their results. This makes reductions one of the most important parallel patterns to understand and one that we *must* be able to execute efficiently on any device.

Tuning a reduction for different devices is a delicate balancing act between the time spent computing partial results and the time spent combining them; using too little parallelism increases computation time, whereas using too much parallelism increases combination time.

It may be tempting to improve overall system utilization by using different devices to perform the computation and combination steps, but such tuning efforts must pay careful attention to the cost of moving data between devices. In practice, we find that performing reductions directly on data as it is produced and on the same device is often the best approach. Using multiple devices to improve the performance of reduction patterns therefore relies not on task parallelism but on another level of data parallelism (i.e., each device performs a reduction on part of the input data).

Scan

The scan pattern computes a generalized prefix sum using a binary associative operator, and each element of the output represents a partial result. A scan is said to be *inclusive* if the partial sum for element *i* is the sum of all elements in the range [0, *i*] (i.e., the sum *including* *i*). A scan is said to be *exclusive* if the partial sum for element *i* is the sum of all elements in the range [0, *i*) (i.e., the sum *excluding* *i*).

At first glance, a scan appears to be an inherently serial operation—the value of each output depends on the value of the previous output! While it is true that scan has less opportunities for parallelism than other patterns (and may therefore be less scalable), Figure 14-5 shows that it is possible to implement a parallel scan using multiple sweeps over the same data.

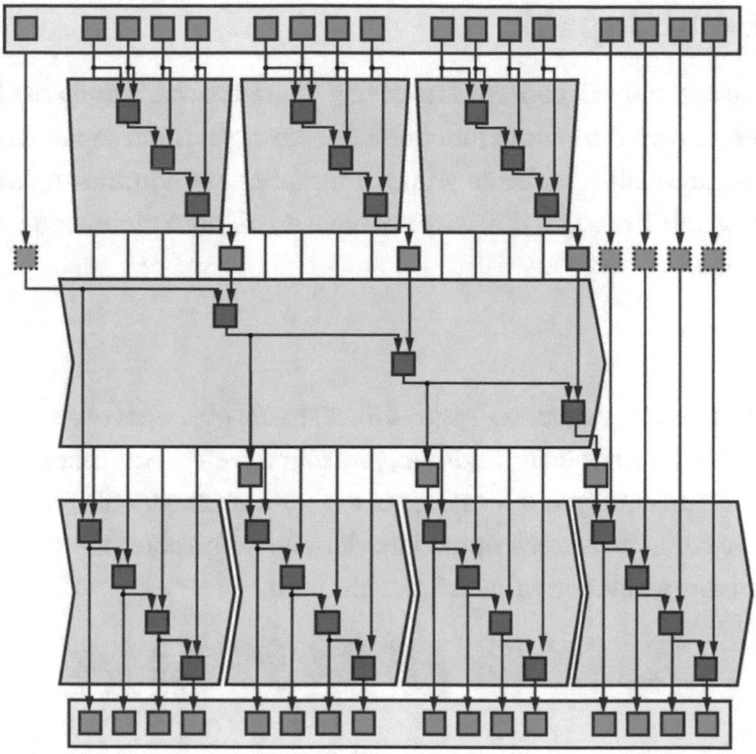

Figure 14-5. *Scan pattern*

Because the opportunities for parallelism within a scan operation are limited, the best device on which to execute a scan is highly dependent on problem size: smaller problems are a better fit for a CPU, since only larger problems will contain enough data parallelism to saturate a GPU. Problem size is less of a concern for FPGAs and other spatial architectures since scans naturally lend themselves to pipeline parallelism. As in the case of a reduction, it is usually a good idea to execute the scan operation on the same device that produced the data—considering where and how scan operations fit into an application during optimization will typically produce better results than focusing on optimizing the scan operations in isolation.

Pack and Unpack

The pack and unpack patterns are closely related to scans and are often implemented on top of scan functionality. We cover them separately here because they enable performant implementations of common operations (e.g., appending to a list) that may not have an obvious connection to prefix sums.

Pack

The pack pattern, shown in Figure 14-6, discards elements of an input range based on a Boolean condition, *packing* the elements that are not discarded into contiguous locations of the output range. This Boolean condition could be a precomputed mask or could be computed online by applying some function to each input element.

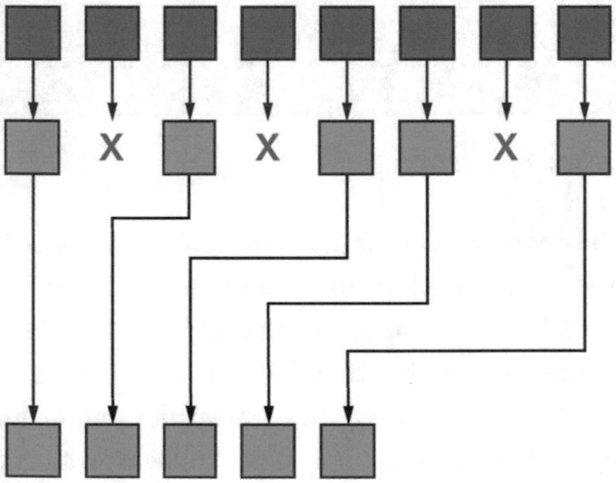

Figure 14-6. *Pack pattern*

Like with scan, there is an inherently serial nature to the pack operation. Given an input element to pack/copy, computing its location in the output range requires information about how many prior elements were also packed/copied into the output. This information is equivalent to an exclusive scan over the Boolean condition driving the pack.

Unpack

As shown in Figure 14-7 (and as its name suggests), the unpack pattern is the opposite of the pack pattern. Contiguous elements of an input range are *unpacked* into noncontiguous elements of an output range, leaving other elements untouched. The most obvious use case for this pattern is to unpack data that was previously packed, but it can also be used to fill in "gaps" in data resulting from some previous computation.

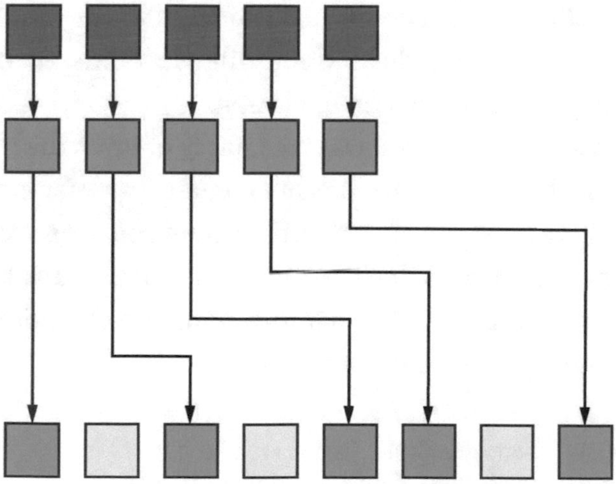

Figure 14-7. *Unpack pattern*

Using Built-In Functions and Libraries

Many of these patterns can be expressed directly using built-in functionality of SYCL or vendor-provided libraries written in SYCL. Leveraging these functions and libraries is the best way to balance performance, portability, and productivity in real large-scale software engineering projects.

The SYCL Reduction Library

Rather than require that each of us maintain our own library of portable and highly performant reduction kernels, SYCL provides a convenient abstraction for describing variables with reduction semantics. This abstraction simplifies the expression of reduction kernels and makes the fact that a reduction is being performed explicit, allowing implementations to select between different reduction algorithms for different combinations of device, data type, and reduction operation.

The kernel in Figure 14-8 shows an example of using the reduction library. Note that the kernel body doesn't contain any reference to reductions—all we must specify is that the kernel contains a reduction which combines instances of the `sum` variable using the `plus` functor. This provides enough information for an implementation to automatically generate an optimized reduction sequence.

```
h.parallel_for(
    range<1>{N}, reduction(sum, plus<>()),
    [=](id<1> i, auto& sum) { sum += data[i]; });
```

Figure 14-8. *Reduction expressed as a data-parallel kernel using the reduction library*

The result of a reduction is not guaranteed to be written back to the original variable until the kernel has completed. Apart from this restriction, accessing the result of a reduction behaves identically to accessing any other variable in SYCL: accessing a reduction result stored in a buffer requires the creation of an appropriate device or host accessor, and accessing a reduction result stored in a USM allocation may require explicit synchronization and/or memory movement.

One important way in which the SYCL reduction library differs from reduction abstractions found in other languages is that it restricts our access to the reduction variable during kernel execution—we cannot inspect the intermediate values of a reduction variable, and we are forbidden from updating the reduction variable using anything other than the specified combination function. These restrictions prevent us from making mistakes that would be hard to debug (e.g., adding to a reduction variable while trying to compute the maximum) and ensure that reductions can be implemented efficiently on a wide variety of different devices.

The `reduction` Class

The `reduction` class is the interface we use to describe the reductions present in a kernel. The only way to construct a reduction object is to use one of the functions shown in Figure 14-9. Note that there are three families of `reduction` function (for buffers, USM pointers and spans), each with two overloads (with and without an identity variable).

```
template <typename BufferT, typename BinaryOperation>
unspecified reduction(BufferT variable, handler& h,
                      BinaryOperation combiner,
                      const property_list& properties = {});

template <typename BufferT, typename BinaryOperation>
unspecified reduction(BufferT variable, handler& h,
                      const BufferT::value_type& identity,
                      BinaryOperation combiner,
                      const property_list& properties = {});

template <typename T, typename BinaryOperation>
unspecified reduction(T* variable, BinaryOperation combiner,
                      const property_list& properties = {});

template <typename T, typename BinaryOperation>
unspecified reduction(T* variable, const T& identity,
                      BinaryOperation combiner,
                      const property_list& properties = {});

template <typename T, typename Extent,
          typename BinaryOperation>
unspecified reduction(span<T, Extent> variables,
                      BinaryOperation combiner,
                      const property_list& properties = {});

template <typename T, typename Extent,
          typename BinaryOperation>
unspecified reduction(span<T, Extent> variables,
                      const T& identity,
                      BinaryOperation combiner,
                      const property_list& properties = {});
```

Figure 14-9. *Function prototypes of the* `reduction` *function*

If a reduction is initialized using a `buffer` or a USM pointer, the reduction is a *scalar* reduction, operating on the first object in an array. If a reduction is initialized using a `span`, the reduction is an *array* reduction. Each component of an array reduction is independent—we can think of an array reduction operating on an array of size *N* as equivalent to *N* scalar reductions with the same data type and operator.

The simplest overloads of the function allow us to specify the reduction variable and the operator used to combine the contributions from each work-item. The second set of overloads allow us to provide an optional *identity* value associated with the reduction operator—this is an optimization for user-defined reductions, which we will revisit later.

Note that the return type of the `reduction` function is unspecified, and the `reduction` class itself is completely implementation-defined. Although this may appear slightly unusual for a C++ class, it permits an implementation to use different classes (or a single class with any number of template arguments) to represent different reduction algorithms. Future versions of SYCL may decide to revisit this design in order to enable us to explicitly request specific reduction algorithms in specific execution contexts (most likely, via the `property_list` argument).

The `reducer` Class

An instance of the `reducer` class encapsulates a reduction variable, exposing a limited interface ensuring that we cannot update the reduction variable in any way that an implementation could consider to be unsafe. A simplified definition of the `reducer` class is shown in Figure 14-10. Like the `reduction` class, the precise definition of the `reducer` class is implementation-defined—a reducer's type will depend on how the reduction is being performed, and it is important to know this at compile time in order to maximize performance. However, the functions and operators that allow us to update the reduction variable are well defined and are guaranteed to be supported by any SYCL implementation.

```
template <typename T, typename BinaryOperation,
          /* implementation-defined */>
class reducer {
  // Combine partial result with reducer's value
  void combine(const T& partial);
};

// Other operators are available for standard binary
// operations
template <typename T>
auto& operator+=(reducer<T, plus::<T>>&, const T&);
```

Figure 14-10. *Simplified definition of the* `reducer` *class*

Specifically, every reducer provides a `combine()` function which combines the partial result (from a single work-item) with the value of the reduction variable. How this combine function behaves is implementation-defined but is not something that we need to worry about when writing a kernel. A reducer is also required to make other operators available depending on the reduction operator; for example, the += operator is defined for `plus` reductions. These additional operators are provided only as a programmer convenience and to improve readability; where they are available, these operators have identical behavior to calling `combine()` directly.

When working with array reductions, the reducer provides an additional subscript operator (i.e., `operator[]`), allowing access to individual elements of the array. Rather than returning a reference directly to an element of the array, this operator returns *another* reducer object, which exposes the same `combine()` function and shorthand operators as the reducers associated with a scalar reduction. Figure 14-11 shows a simple example of a kernel using an array reduction to compute a histogram, where the subscript operator is used to access only the histogram bin that is updated by the work-item.

```
h.parallel_for(
    range{N},
    reduction(span<int, 16>(histogram, 16), plus<>()),
    [=](id<1> i, auto& histogram) {
      histogram[i % B]++;
    });
```

***Figure 14-11.** An example kernel using an array reduction to compute a histogram*

User-Defined Reductions

Several common reduction algorithms (e.g., a tree reduction) do not see each work-item directly update a single shared variable, but instead accumulate some partial result in a private variable that will be combined at some point in the future. Such private variables introduce a problem: how should the implementation initialize them? Initializing variables to the first contribution from each work-item has potential performance ramifications, since additional logic is required to detect and handle uninitialized variables. Initializing variables to the identity of the reduction operator instead avoids the performance penalty but is only possible when the identity is known.

SYCL implementations can only automatically determine the correct identity value to use when a reduction is operating on simple arithmetic types and the reduction operator is one of several standard function objects (e.g., `plus`). For user-defined reductions (i.e., those operating on user-defined types and/or using user-defined function objects), we may be able to improve performance by specifying the identity value directly.

Support for user-defined reductions is limited to trivially copyable types and combination functions with no side effects, but this is enough to enable many real-life use cases. For example, the code in Figure 14-12 demonstrates the usage of a user-defined reduction to compute both the minimum element in a vector and its location.

```
template <typename T, typename I>
using minloc = minimum<std::pair<T, I>>;

int main() {
  constexpr size_t N = 16;

  queue q;
  float* data = malloc_shared<float>(N, q);
  std::pair<float, int>* res =
      malloc_shared<std::pair<float, int>>(1, q);
  std::generate(data, data + N, std::mt19937{});

  std::pair<float, int> identity = {
      std::numeric_limits<float>::max(),
      std::numeric_limits<int>::min()};
  *res = identity;

  auto red =
      sycl::reduction(res, identity, minloc<float, int>());

  q.submit([&](handler& h) {
     h.parallel_for(
         range<1>{N}, red, [=](id<1> i, auto& res) {
           std::pair<float, int> partial = {data[i], i};
           res.combine(partial);
         });
   }).wait();

  std::cout << "minimum value = " << res->first << " at "
            << res->second << "\n";
  ...
```

Figure 14-12. *Using a user-defined reduction to find the location of the minimum value*

Group Algorithms

Support for parallel patterns in SYCL device code is provided by a separate library of group algorithms. These functions exploit the parallelism of a specific group of work-items (i.e., a work-group or a sub-group) to implement common parallel algorithms at limited scope and can be used as building blocks to construct other more complex algorithms.

The syntax of the group algorithms in SYCL is based on that of the algorithm library in C++, and any restrictions from the C++ algorithms apply. However, there is a critical difference: whereas the STL's algorithms are called from sequential (host) code and indicate an opportunity for a library to employ parallelism, SYCL's group algorithms are designed to be called *within* (device) code that is already executing in parallel. To ensure that this difference cannot be overlooked, the group algorithms have slightly different syntax and semantics to their C++ counterparts.

SYCL distinguishes between two different kinds of parallel algorithm. If an algorithm is performed collaboratively by all work-items in a group but otherwise behaves identically to an algorithm from the STL, the algorithm is named with a "joint" prefix (because the members of the group "join" together to perform the algorithm). Such algorithms read their inputs from memory and write their results to memory and can only operate on data in memory locations visible to all work-items in a given group. If an algorithm instead operates over an implicit range reflecting the group itself, with inputs and outputs stored in work-item private memory, the algorithm name is modified to include the word "group" (because the algorithm is performed directly on data owned to the group).

The code examples in Figure 14-13 demonstrate these two different kinds of algorithm, comparing the behavior of `std::reduce` to the behaviors of `sycl::joint_reduce` and `sycl::reduce_over_group`.

```
// std::reduce
// Each work-item reduces over a given input range
q.parallel_for(number_of_reductions, [=](size_t i) {
   output1[i] = std::reduce(
       input + i * elements_per_reduction,
       input + (i + 1) * elements_per_reduction);
 }).wait();

// sycl::joint_reduce
// Each work-group reduces over a given input range
// The elements are automatically distributed over
// work-items in the group
q.parallel_for(nd_range<1>{number_of_reductions *
                               elements_per_reduction,
                           elements_per_reduction},
              [=](nd_item<1> it) {
                auto g = it.get_group();
                int sum = joint_reduce(
                    g,
                    input + g.get_group_id() *
                                elements_per_reduction,
                    input + (g.get_group_id() + 1) *
                                elements_per_reduction,
                    plus<>());
                if (g.leader()) {
                  output2[g.get_group_id()] = sum;
                }
              })
    .wait();

// sycl::reduce_over_group
// Each work-group reduces over data held in work-item
// private memory. Each work-item is responsible for
// loading and contributing one value
q.parallel_for(
     nd_range<1>{
         number_of_reductions * elements_per_reduction,
         elements_per_reduction},
     [=](nd_item<1> it) {
       auto g = it.get_group();
       int x = input[g.get_group_id() *
                         elements_per_reduction +
                     g.get_local_id()];
       int sum = reduce_over_group(g, x, plus<>());
       if (g.leader()) {
         output3[g.get_group_id()] = sum;
       }
     })
    .wait();
```

Figure 14-13. *A comparison of* `std::reduce`*,* `sycl::joint_reduce`*, and* `sycl::reduce_over_group`

Note that in both cases, the first argument to each group algorithm accepts a `group` or `sub_group` object in place of an execution policy, to describe the set of work-items that should be used to perform the algorithm. Since algorithms are performed collaboratively by all the work-items in the specified group, they must also be treated similarly to a group barrier—all work-items in the group must encounter the same algorithm in converged control flow (i.e., all work-items in the group must similarly encounter or not encounter the algorithm call), and the arguments provided by all work-items must be such that all work-items agree on the operation being performed. For example, `sycl::joint_reduce` requires all arguments to be the same for all work-items, to ensure that all work-items in the group operate on the same data and use the same operator to accumulate results.

The table in Figure 14-14 shows how the parallel algorithms available in the STL relate to the group algorithms, and whether there are any restrictions on the type of group that can be used. Note that in some cases, a group algorithm can only be used with sub-groups; these cases correspond to the "shuffle" operations introduced in earlier chapters.

C++ Algorithm	SYCL "Joint" Algorithm	SYCL "Group" Algorithm	Group Types
std::any_of	sycl::joint_any_of	sycl::any_of_group	All
std::all_of	sycl::joint_all_of	sycl::all_of_group	All
std::none_of	sycl::joint_none_of	sycl::none_of_group	All
std::shift_left	N/A	sycl::shift_group_left	sub_group
std::shift_right	N/A	sycl::shift_group_right	sub_group
N/A	N/A	sycl::permute_group_by_xor	sub_group
N/A	N/A	sycl::select_from_group	sub_group
std::reduce	sycl::joint_reduce	sycl::reduce_over_group	All
std::exclusive_scan	sycl::joint_exclusive_scan	sycl::exclusive_scan_over_group	All
std::inclusive_scan	sycl::joint_inclusive_scan	sycl::inclusive_scan_over_group	All

Figure 14-14. *Mapping between C++ algorithms and SYCL group algorithms*

At the time of writing, the group algorithms are limited to supporting only primitive data types and a set of built-in operators recognized by SYCL (i.e., `plus`, `multiplies`, `bit_and`, `bit_or`, `bit_xor`, `logical_and`, `logical_or`, `minimum`, and `maximum`). This is enough to cover most common use cases, but future versions of SYCL are expected to extend collective support to user-defined types and operators.

Direct Programming

Although we recommend leveraging libraries wherever possible, we can learn a lot by looking at how each pattern *could* be implemented using "native" SYCL kernels.

The kernels in the remainder of this chapter should not be expected to reach the same level of performance as highly tuned libraries but are useful in developing a greater understanding of the capabilities of SYCL—and may even serve as a starting point for prototyping new library functionality.

USE VENDOR-PROVIDED LIBRARIES!

When a vendor provides a library implementation of a function, it is almost always beneficial to use it rather than reimplementing the function as a kernel!

Map

Owing to its simplicity, the map pattern can be implemented directly as a basic parallel kernel. The code shown in Figure 14-15 shows such an implementation, using the map pattern to compute the square root of each input element in a range.

```
// Compute the square root of each input value
q.parallel_for(N, [=](id<1> i) {
   output[i] = sqrt(input[i]);
 }).wait();
```

Figure 14-15. *Implementing the map pattern in a data-parallel kernel*

Stencil

Implementing a stencil directly as a multidimensional basic data-parallel kernel with multidimensional buffers, as shown in Figure 14-16, is straightforward and easy to understand.

```
q.submit([&](handler& h) {
  accessor input{input_buf, h};
  accessor output{output_buf, h};

  // Compute the average of each cell and its immediate
  // neighbors
  h.parallel_for(stencil_range, [=](id<2> idx) {
    int i = idx[0] + 1;
    int j = idx[1] + 1;

    float self = input[i][j];
    float north = input[i - 1][j];
    float east = input[i][j + 1];
    float south = input[i + 1][j];
    float west = input[i][j - 1];
    output[i][j] =
        (self + north + east + south + west) / 5.0f;
  });
});
```

Figure 14-16. *Implementing the stencil pattern in a data-parallel kernel*

However, this expression of the stencil pattern is very naïve and should not be expected to perform very well. As mentioned earlier in the chapter, it is well known that leveraging locality (via spatial or temporal blocking) is required to avoid repeated reads of the same data from memory. A simple example of spatial blocking, using work-group local memory, is shown in Figure 14-17.

```
q.submit([&](handler& h) {
  accessor input{input_buf, h};
  accessor output{output_buf, h};

  constexpr size_t B = 4;
  range<2> local_range(B, B);
  range<2> tile_size =
      local_range +
      range<2>(2, 2);  // Includes boundary cells
  auto tile = local_accessor<float, 2>(tile_size, h);

  // Compute the average of each cell and its immediate
  // neighbors
  h.parallel_for(
      nd_range<2>(stencil_range, local_range),
      [=](nd_item<2> it) {
        // Load this tile into work-group local memory
        id<2> lid = it.get_local_id();
        range<2> lrange = it.get_local_range();
        for (int ti = lid[0]; ti < B + 2;
             ti += lrange[0]) {
          int gi = ti + B * it.get_group(0);
          for (int tj = lid[1]; tj < B + 2;
               tj += lrange[1]) {
            int gj = tj + B * it.get_group(1);
            tile[ti][tj] = input[gi][gj];
          }
        }
        group_barrier(it.get_group());

        // Compute the stencil using values from local
        // memory
        int gi = it.get_global_id(0) + 1;
        int gj = it.get_global_id(1) + 1;

        int ti = it.get_local_id(0) + 1;
        int tj = it.get_local_id(1) + 1;

        float self = tile[ti][tj];
        float north = tile[ti - 1][tj];
        float east = tile[ti][tj + 1];
        float south = tile[ti + 1][tj];
        float west = tile[ti][tj - 1];
        output[gi][gj] =
            (self + north + east + south + west) / 5.0f;
      });
});
```

***Figure 14-17.** Implementing the stencil pattern in an ND-range kernel, using work-group local memory*

Selecting the best optimizations for a given stencil requires compile-time introspection of block size, the neighborhood, and the stencil function itself, requiring a much more sophisticated approach than discussed here.

Reduction

It is possible to implement reduction kernels in SYCL by leveraging language features that provide synchronization and communication capabilities between work-items (e.g., atomic operations, work-group and sub-group functions, sub-group "shuffles"). The kernels in Figure 14-18 and Figure 14-19 show two possible reduction implementations: a naïve reduction using a basic `parallel_for` and an atomic operation for every work-item, and a slightly smarter reduction that exploits locality using an ND-range `parallel_for` and a work-group `reduce` function, respectively. We revisit these atomic operations in more detail in Chapter 19.

```
q.parallel_for(N, [=](id<1> i) {
   atomic_ref<int, memory_order::relaxed,
              memory_scope::system,
              access::address_space::global_space>(
       *sum) += data[i];
 }).wait();
```

***Figure 14-18.** Implementing a naïve reduction expressed as a data-parallel kernel*

```
q.parallel_for(nd_range<1>{N, B}, [=](nd_item<1> it) {
   int i = it.get_global_id(0);
   auto grp = it.get_group();
   int group_sum =
       reduce_over_group(grp, data[i], plus<>());
   if (grp.leader()) {
     atomic_ref<int, memory_order::relaxed,
                memory_scope::system,
                access::address_space::global_space>(
         *sum) += group_sum;
   }
 }).wait();
```

Figure 14-19. *Implementing a naïve reduction expressed as an ND-range kernel*

There are numerous other ways to write reduction kernels, and different devices will likely prefer different implementations, owing to differences in hardware support for atomic operations, work-group local memory size, global memory size, the availability of fast device-wide barriers, or even the availability of dedicated reduction instructions. On some architectures, it may even be faster (or necessary!) to perform a tree reduction using $\log_2(N)$ separate kernel calls.

We strongly recommend that manual implementations of reductions should only be considered for cases that are not supported by the SYCL reduction library or when fine-tuning a kernel for the capabilities of a specific device—and even then, only after being 100% sure that SYCL's built-in reductions are underperforming!

Scan

As we saw earlier in this chapter, implementing a parallel scan requires multiple sweeps over the data, with synchronization occurring between each sweep. Since SYCL does not provide a mechanism for synchronizing all work-items in an ND-range, a direct implementation of a device-wide scan must use multiple kernels that communicate partial results through global memory.

The code, shown in Figures 14-20, 14-21, and 14-22, demonstrates an inclusive scan implemented using several kernels. The first kernel distributes the input values across work-groups, computing work-group local scans in work-group local memory (note that we could have used the work-group `inclusive_scan` function instead). The second kernel computes a local scan using a single work-group, this time over the final value from each block. The third kernel combines these intermediate results to finalize the prefix sum. These three kernels correspond to the three layers of the diagram in Figure 14-5.

```
// Phase 1: Compute local scans over input blocks
q.submit([&](handler& h) {
  auto local = local_accessor<int32_t, 1>(L, h);
  h.parallel_for(nd_range<1>(N, L), [=](nd_item<1> it) {
    int i = it.get_global_id(0);
    int li = it.get_local_id(0);

    // Copy input to local memory
    local[li] = input[i];
    group_barrier(it.get_group());

    // Perform inclusive scan in local memory
    for (int32_t d = 0; d <= log2((float)L) - 1; ++d) {
      uint32_t stride = (1 << d);
      int32_t update =
          (li >= stride) ? local[li - stride] : 0;
      group_barrier(it.get_group());
      local[li] += update;
      group_barrier(it.get_group());
    }

    // Write the result for each item to the output
    // buffer Write the last result from this block to
    // the temporary buffer
    output[i] = local[li];
    if (li == it.get_local_range()[0] - 1) {
      tmp[it.get_group(0)] = local[li];
    }
  });
}).wait();
```

Figure 14-20. *Phase 1 for implementing a global inclusive scan in an ND-range kernel: computing across each work-group*

```
// Phase 2: Compute scan over partial results
q.submit([&](handler& h) {
   auto local = local_accessor<int32_t, 1>(G, h);
   h.parallel_for(nd_range<1>(G, G), [=](nd_item<1> it) {
     int i = it.get_global_id(0);
     int li = it.get_local_id(0);

     // Copy input to local memory
     local[li] = tmp[i];
     group_barrier(it.get_group());

     // Perform inclusive scan in local memory
     for (int32_t d = 0; d <= log2((float)G) - 1; ++d) {
       uint32_t stride = (1 << d);
       int32_t update =
           (li >= stride) ? local[li - stride] : 0;
       group_barrier(it.get_group());
       local[li] += update;
       group_barrier(it.get_group());
     }

     // Overwrite result from each work-item in the
     // temporary buffer
     tmp[i] = local[li];
   });
 }).wait();
```

Figure 14-21. *Phase 2 for implementing a global inclusive scan in an ND-range kernel: scanning across the results of each work-group*

```
// Phase 3: Update local scans using partial results
q.parallel_for(nd_range<1>(N, L), [=](nd_item<1> it) {
   int g = it.get_group(0);
   if (g > 0) {
     int i = it.get_global_id(0);
     output[i] += tmp[g - 1];
   }
 }).wait();
```

Figure 14-22. *Phase 3 (final) for implementing a global inclusive scan in an ND-range kernel*

Figure 14-20 and Figure 14-21 are very similar; the only differences are the size of the range and how the input and output values are handled. A real-life implementation of this pattern could use a single function taking different arguments to implement these two phases, and they are only presented as distinct code here for pedagogical reasons.

Pack and Unpack

Pack and unpack are also known as gather and scatter operations. These operations handle differences in how data is arranged in memory and how we wish to present it to the compute resources.

Pack

Since pack depends on an exclusive scan, implementing a pack that applies to all elements of an ND-range must also take place via global memory and over the course of several kernel enqueues. However, there is a common use case for pack that does not require the operation to be applied over all elements of an ND-range—namely, applying a pack only across items in a specific work-group or sub-group.

The snippet in Figure 14-23 shows how to implement a group pack operation on top of an exclusive scan.

```
uint32_t index =
    exclusive_scan(g, (uint32_t)predicate, plus<>());
if (predicate) dst[index] = value;
```

Figure 14-23. *Implementing a group pack operation on top of an exclusive scan*

The code in Figure 14-24 demonstrates how such a pack operation could be used in a kernel to build a list of elements which require some additional postprocessing (in a future kernel). The example shown is based on a real kernel from molecular dynamics simulations: the work-items in the sub-group assigned to particle *i* cooperate to identify all other particles within a fixed distance of *i*, and only the particles in this "neighbor list" will be used to calculate the force acting on each particle.

```
range<2> global(N, 8);
range<2> local(1, 8);
q.parallel_for(nd_range<2>(global, local), [=](nd_item<2>
                                                  it) {
   int i = it.get_global_id(0);
   sub_group sg = it.get_sub_group();
   int sglid = sg.get_local_id()[0];
   int sgrange = sg.get_local_range()[0];

   uint32_t k = 0;
   for (int j = sglid; j < N; j += sgrange) {
     // Compute distance between i and neighbor j
     float r = distance(position[i], position[j]);

     // Pack neighbors that require
     // post-processing into a list
     uint32_t pack = (i != j) and (r <= CUTOFF);
     uint32_t offset =
         exclusive_scan_over_group(sg, pack, plus<>());
     if (pack) {
       neighbors[i * MAX_K + k + offset] = j;
     }

     // Keep track of how many neighbors have been
     // packed so far
     k += reduce_over_group(sg, pack, plus<>());
   }
   num_neighbors[i] =
       reduce_over_group(sg, k, maximum<>());
 }).wait();
```

Figure 14-24. *Using a sub-group pack operation to build a list of elements needing additional postprocessing*

Note that the pack pattern never reorders elements—the elements that are packed into the output array appear in the same order as they did in the input. This property of pack is important and enables us to use pack functionality to implement other more abstract parallel algorithms (such as `std::copy_if` and `std::stable_partition`). However, there are other parallel algorithms that can be implemented on top of pack functionality where maintaining order is not required (such as `std::partition`).

Unpack

As with pack, we can implement unpack using scan. Figure 14-25 shows how to implement a sub-group unpack operation on top of an exclusive scan.

```
uint32_t index =
    exclusive_scan(sg, (uint32_t)predicate, plus<>());
return (predicate) ? new_value[index] : original_value;
```

Figure 14-25. *Implementing a sub-group unpack operation on top of an exclusive scan*

The code in Figure 14-26 demonstrates how such a sub-group unpack operation could be used to improve load balancing in a kernel with divergent control flow (in this case, computing the Mandelbrot set). Each work-item is assigned a separate pixel to compute and iterates until convergence or a maximum number of iterations is reached. An unpack operation is then used to replace completed pixels with new pixels.

```
// Keep iterating as long as one work-item has work to do
while (any_of_group(sg, i < Nx)) {
  uint32_t converged = next_iteration(
      params, i, j, count, cr, ci, zr, zi, mandelbrot);
  if (any_of_group(sg, converged)) {
    // Replace pixels that have converged using an
    // unpack. Pixels that haven't converged are not
    // replaced.
    uint32_t index = exclusive_scan_over_group(
        sg, converged, plus<>());
    i = (converged) ? iq + index : i;
    iq += reduce_over_group(sg, converged, plus<>());

    // Reset the iterator variables for the new i
    if (converged) {
      reset(params, i, j, count, cr, ci, zr, zi);
    }
  }
}
```

Figure 14-26. *Using a sub-group unpack operation to improve load balancing for kernels with divergent control flow*

The degree to which an approach like this improves efficiency (and decreases execution time) is highly application- and input-dependent, since checking for completion and executing the unpack operation both introduce some overhead! Successfully using this pattern in realistic applications will therefore require some fine-tuning based on the amount of divergence present and the computation being performed (e.g., introducing a heuristic to execute the unpack operation only if the number of active work-items falls below some threshold).

Summary

This chapter has demonstrated how to implement some of the most common parallel patterns using SYCL features, including built-in functions and libraries.

The SYCL ecosystem is still developing, and we expect to uncover new best practices for these patterns as developers gain more experience with the language and from the development of production-grade applications and libraries.

For More Information

- *Structured Parallel Programming: Patterns for Efficient Computation* by Michael McCool, Arch Robison, and James Reinders, © 2012, published by Morgan Kaufmann, ISBN 978-0-124-15993-8.
- Algorithms library, C++ Reference, `https://en.cppreference.com/w/cpp/algorithm`.

CHAPTER 15

Programming for GPUs

Over the last few decades, graphics processing units (GPUs) have evolved from specialized hardware devices capable of drawing images on a screen to general-purpose devices capable of executing complex parallel kernels. Nowadays, nearly every computer includes a GPU alongside a traditional CPU, and many programs may be accelerated by offloading part of a parallel algorithm from the CPU to the GPU.

In this chapter, we will describe how a typical GPU works, how GPU software and hardware execute a SYCL application, and tips and techniques to keep in mind when we are writing and optimizing parallel kernels for a GPU.

Performance Caveats

As with any processor type, GPUs differ from vendor to vendor or even from product generation to product generation; therefore, best practices for one device may not be best practices for a different device. The advice in this chapter is likely to benefit many GPUs, both now and in the future, but…

J. Reinders et al., *Data Parallel C++*, https://doi.org/10.1007/978-1-4842-9691-2_15

To achieve optimal performance for a particular GPU, always consult the GPU vendor's documentation!

Links to documentation from many GPU vendors are provided at the end of this chapter.

How GPUs Work

This section describes how typical GPUs work and how GPUs differ from other accelerator types.

GPU Building Blocks

Figure 15-1 shows a very simplified GPU consisting of three high-level building blocks:

1. **Execution resources**: A GPU's execution resources are the processors that perform computational work. Different GPU vendors use different names for their execution resources, but all modern GPUs consist of multiple programmable processors. The processors may be *heterogeneous* and specialized for particular tasks, like transforming vertices and shading pixels, or they may be *homogeneous* and interchangeable. Processors for most modern GPUs are *homogeneous* and interchangeable.

2. **Fixed functions**: GPU fixed functions are hardware units that are less programmable than the execution resources and are specialized for a single task. When a GPU is used for graphics, many parts of the

graphics pipeline such as rasterization or ray tracing are performed using fixed functions to improve power efficiency and performance. When a GPU is used for data-parallel computation, fixed functions may be used for tasks such as workload scheduling, texture sampling, and dependence tracking.

3. **Caches and memory**: Like other processor types, GPUs frequently have caches to store data accessed by the execution resources. GPU caches may be *implicit*, in which case they require no action from the programmer, or may be *explicit* scratchpad memories, in which case a programmer must purposefully move data into a cache before using it. Many GPUs also have a large pool of memory to provide fast access to data used by the execution resources.

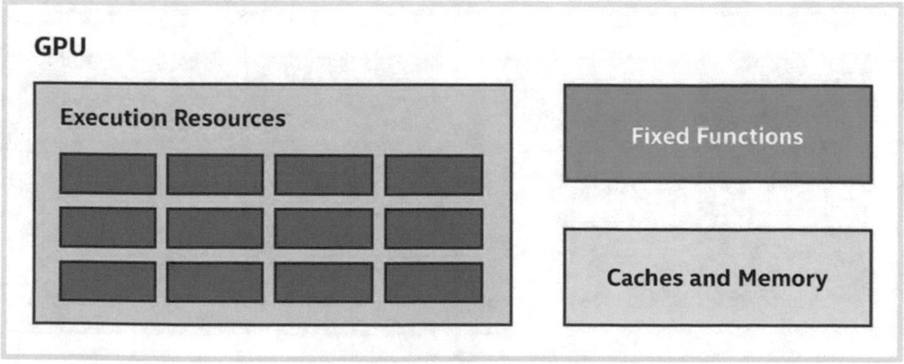

***Figure 15-1.** Typical GPU building blocks—not to scale!*

Simpler Processors (but More of Them)

Traditionally, when performing graphics operations, GPUs process large batches of data. For example, a typical game frame or rendering workload involves thousands of vertices that produce millions of pixels per frame. To maintain interactive frame rates, these large batches of data must be processed as quickly as possible.

A typical GPU design trade-off is to eliminate features from the processors forming the execution resources that accelerate single-threaded performance and to use these savings to build additional processors, as shown in Figure 15-2. For example, GPU processors may not include sophisticated out-of-order execution capabilities or branch prediction logic used by other types of processors. Due to these trade-offs, a single data element may be processed on a GPU slower than it would on another processor, but the larger number of processors enables GPUs to process many data elements quickly and efficiently.

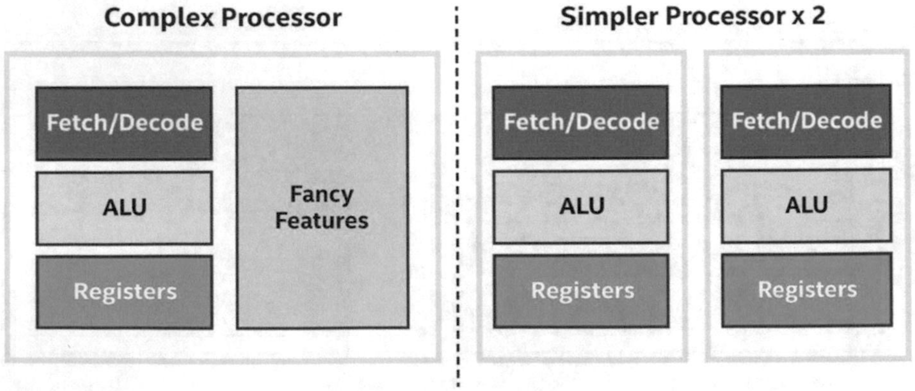

Figure 15-2. *GPU processors are simpler, but there are more of them*

To take advantage of this trade-off when executing kernels, it is important to give the GPU a sufficiently large range of data elements to process. To demonstrate the importance of offloading a large range of data, consider the matrix multiplication kernel we have been developing and modifying throughout this book.

A REMINDER ABOUT MATRIX MULTIPLICATION

In this book, matrix multiplication kernels are used to demonstrate how changes in a kernel or the way it is dispatched affects performance. Although matrix multiplication performance is significantly improved using the techniques described in this chapter, matrix multiplication is such an important and common operation that many hardware (GPU, CPU, FPGA, DSP, etc.) vendors have implemented highly tuned versions of many routines including matrix multiplication. Such vendors invest significant time and effort implementing and validating functions for specific devices and in some cases may use functionality or techniques that are difficult or impossible to use in standard kernels.

USE VENDOR-PROVIDED LIBRARIES!

When a vendor provides a library implementation of a function, it is almost always beneficial to use it rather than reimplementing the function as a kernel! The oneMKL project (part of oneAPI) proposes interfaces that will call Intel's MKL for Intel, cuBLAS for NVIDIA, and hipBLAS for AMD. If such interfaces are available, they might make things easier. Otherwise, we need to do our own work to make sure we are using the best libraries for the hardware we are targeting.

A matrix multiplication kernel may be trivially executed on a GPU by submitting it into a queue as a single task. The body of this matrix multiplication kernel looks exactly like a function that executes on the host CPU and is shown in Figure 15-3.

```
h.single_task([=]() {
  for (int m = 0; m < M; m++) {
    for (int n = 0; n < N; n++) {
      T sum = 0;
      for (int k = 0; k < K; k++) {
        sum +=
            matrixA[m * K + k] * matrixB[k * N + n];
      }
      matrixC[m * N + n] = sum;
    }
  }
});
```

Figure 15-3. *A single-task matrix multiplication looks a lot like CPU host code*

If we try to execute this kernel on a CPU, it will probably perform okay—not great, since it is not expected to utilize any parallel capabilities of the CPU, but potentially good enough for small matrix sizes. As shown in Figure 15-4, if we try to execute this kernel on a GPU, however, it will likely perform very poorly, because the single task will only utilize a single GPU processor.

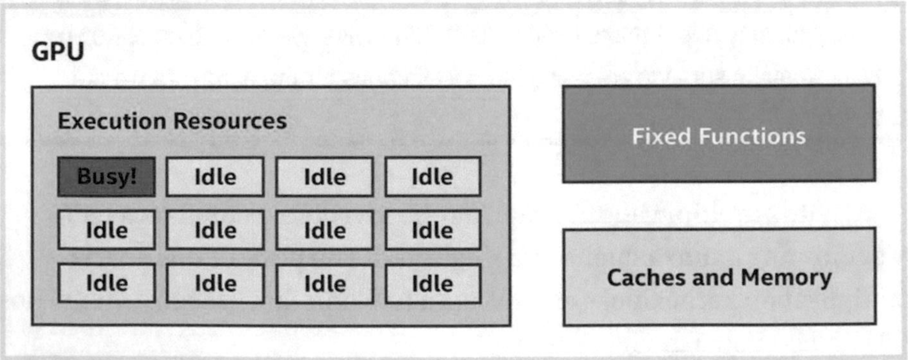

Figure 15-4. *A single-task kernel on a GPU leaves many execution resources idle*

Expressing Parallelism

To improve the performance of this kernel for both CPUs and GPUs, we can instead submit a range of data elements to process in parallel, by converting one of the loops to a parallel_for. For the matrix multiplication kernel, we can choose to submit a range of data elements representing either of the two outermost loops. In Figure 15-5, we've chosen to process rows of the result matrix in parallel.

```
h.parallel_for(range{M}, [=](id<1> idx) {
  int m = idx[0];

  for (int n = 0; n < N; n++) {
    T sum = 0;
    for (int k = 0; k < K; k++) {
      sum += matrixA[m * K + k] * matrixB[k * N + n];
    }
    matrixC[m * N + n] = sum;
  }
});
```

Figure 15-5. *Somewhat-parallel matrix multiplication*

CHOOSING HOW TO PARALLELIZE

Choosing which dimension to parallelize is one very important way to tune an application for both GPUs and other device types. Subsequent sections in this chapter will describe some of the reasons why parallelizing in one dimension may perform better than parallelizing in a different dimension.

Even though the somewhat-parallel kernel is very similar to the single-task kernel, it should run better on a CPU and much better on a GPU. As shown in Figure 15-6, the parallel_for enables work-items representing rows of the result matrix to be processed on multiple processor resources in parallel, so all execution resources stay busy.

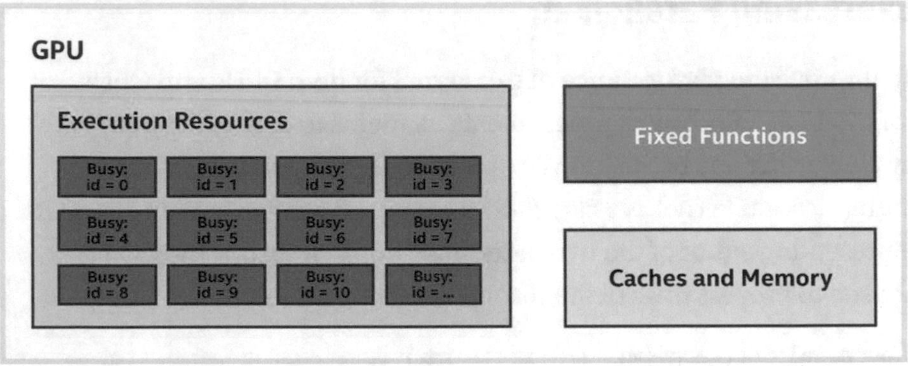

Figure 15-6. *Somewhat-parallel kernel keeps more processor resources busy*

Note that the exact way that the rows are partitioned and assigned to different processor resources is not specified, giving an implementation flexibility to choose how best to execute the kernel on a device. For example, instead of executing individual rows on a processor, an implementation may choose to execute consecutive rows on the same processor to gain locality benefits.

Expressing More Parallelism

We can parallelize the matrix multiplication kernel even more by choosing to process both outer loops in parallel. Because `parallel_for` can express parallel loops over up to three dimensions, this is straightforward, as shown in Figure 15-7. In Figure 15-7, note that both the range passed to `parallel_for` and the item representing the index in the parallel execution space are now two-dimensional.

```
h.parallel_for(range{M, N}, [=](id<2> idx) {
  int m = idx[0];
  int n = idx[1];

  T sum = 0;
  for (int k = 0; k < K; k++) {
    sum += matrixA[m * K + k] * matrixB[k * N + n];
  }

  matrixC[m * N + n] = sum;
});
```

***Figure 15-7.** Even more parallel matrix multiplication*

Exposing additional parallelism will likely improve the performance of the matrix multiplication kernel when run on a GPU. This is likely to be true even when the number of matrix rows exceeds the number of GPU processors. The next few sections describe possible reasons why this may be the case.

Simplified Control Logic (SIMD Instructions)

Many GPU processors optimize control logic by leveraging the fact that most data elements tend to take the same control flow path through a kernel. For example, in the matrix multiplication kernel, each data element executes the innermost loop the same number of times since the loop bounds are invariant.

When data elements take the same control flow path through a kernel, a processor may reduce the costs of managing an instruction stream by sharing control logic among multiple data elements and executing them as a group. One way to do this is to implement a *single instruction, multiple data,* or *SIMD,* instruction set, where multiple data elements are processed simultaneously by a single instruction.

THREADS VS. INSTRUCTION STREAMS

In many parallel programming contexts and GPU literature, the term "thread" is used to mean an "instruction stream." In these contexts, a "thread" is different than a traditional operating system thread and is typically much more lightweight. This isn't always the case, though, and in some cases, a "thread" is used to describe something completely different.

Since the term "thread" is overloaded and easily misunderstood, even among different GPU vendors, this chapter uses the term "instruction stream" instead.

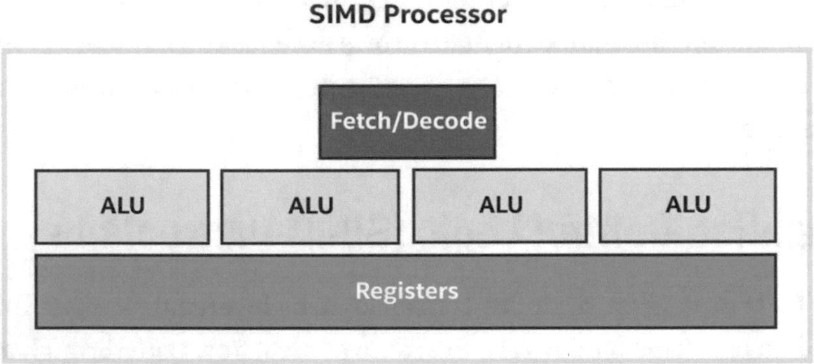

Figure 15-8. *Four-wide SIMD processor: the four ALUs share fetch/decode logic*

The number of data elements that are processed simultaneously by a single instruction is sometimes referred to as the *SIMD width* of the instruction or the processor executing the instruction. In Figure 15-8, the four ALUs share the same control logic, so this may be described as a four-wide SIMD processor.

GPU processors are not the only processors that implement SIMD instruction sets. Other processor types also implement SIMD instruction sets to improve efficiency when processing large sets of data. The main difference between GPU processors and other processor types is that GPU processors rely on executing multiple data elements in parallel to achieve good performance and that GPU processors may support wider SIMD widths than other processor types. For example, it is not uncommon for GPU processors to support SIMD widths of 16, 32, or more data elements.

PROGRAMMING MODELS: SPMD AND SIMD

Although GPU processors implement SIMD instruction sets with varying widths, this is usually an implementation detail and is transparent to the application executing data-parallel kernels on the GPU processor. This is because many GPU compilers and runtime APIs implement a single program, multiple data, or SPMD, programming model, where the GPU compiler and runtime API determine the most efficient group of data elements to process with a SIMD instruction stream, rather than expressing the SIMD instructions explicitly. The "Sub-Groups" section of Chapter 9 explores cases where the grouping of data elements is visible to applications.

In Figure 15-9, we have widened each of our execution resources to support four-wide SIMD, allowing us to process four times as many matrix rows in parallel.

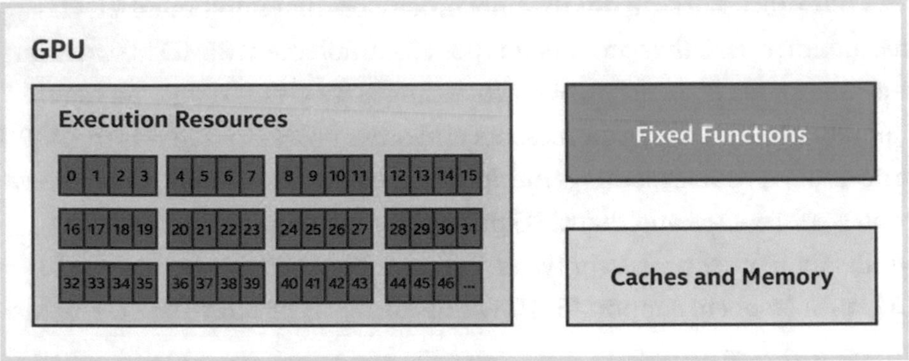

Figure 15-9. *Executing a somewhat-parallel kernel on SIMD processors*

The use of SIMD instructions that process multiple data elements in parallel is one of the ways that the performance of the parallel matrix multiplication kernels in Figures 15-5 and 15-7 is able to scale beyond the number of processors alone. The use of SIMD instructions also provides natural locality benefits in many cases, including matrix multiplication, by executing consecutive data elements on the same processor.

Kernels benefit from parallelism across processors and parallelism within processors!

Predication and Masking

Sharing an instruction stream among multiple data elements works well so long as all data elements take the same path through conditional code in a kernel. When data elements take different paths through conditional code, control flow is said to *diverge*. When control flow diverges in a SIMD instruction stream, usually both control flow paths are executed, with some channels masked off or *predicated*. This ensures correct behavior, but the correctness comes at a performance cost since channels that are masked do not perform useful work.

To show how predication and masking works, consider the kernel in Figure 15-10, which multiplies each data element with an "odd" index by two and increments each data element with an "even" index by one.

```
h.parallel_for(array_size, [=](id<1> i) {
  auto condition = i[0] & 1;
  if (condition) {
    dataAcc[i] = dataAcc[i] * 2;  // odd
  } else {
    dataAcc[i] = dataAcc[i] + 1;  // even
  }
});
```

Figure 15-10. *Kernel with divergent control flow*

Let's say that we execute this kernel on the four-wide SIMD processor shown in Figure 15-8, and that we execute the first four data elements in one SIMD instruction stream, the next four data elements in a different SIMD instruction stream, and so on. Figure 15-11 shows one of the ways channels may be masked and execution may be predicated to correctly execute this kernel with divergent control flow.

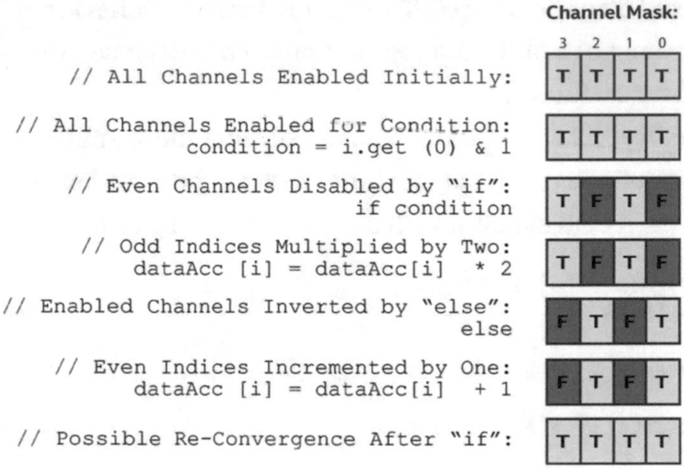
Channel Mask:
3 2 1 0
// All Channels Enabled Initially:
T T T T
// All Channels Enabled for Condition:
condition = i.get (0) & 1
T T T T
// Even Channels Disabled by "if":
if condition
T F T F
// Odd Indices Multiplied by Two:
dataAcc [i] = dataAcc[i] * 2
T F T F
// Enabled Channels Inverted by "else":
else
F T F T
// Even Indices Incremented by One:
dataAcc [i] = dataAcc[i] + 1
F T F T
// Possible Re-Convergence After "if":
T T T T

Figure 15-11. *Possible channel masks for a divergent kernel*

SIMD Efficiency

SIMD efficiency measures how well a SIMD instruction stream performs compared to equivalent scalar instruction streams. In Figure 15-11, since control flow partitioned the channels into two equal groups, each instruction in the divergent control flow executes with half efficiency. In a worst-case scenario, for highly divergent kernels, efficiency may be reduced by a factor of the processor's SIMD width.

All processors that implement a SIMD instruction set will suffer from divergence penalties that affect SIMD efficiency, but because GPU processors typically support wider SIMD widths than other processor types, restructuring an algorithm to minimize divergent control flow and maximize converged execution may be especially beneficial when optimizing a kernel for a GPU. This is not always possible, but as an example, choosing to parallelize along a dimension with more converged execution may perform better than parallelizing along a different dimension with highly divergent execution.

SIMD Efficiency and Groups of Items

All kernels in this chapter so far have been basic data-parallel kernels that do not specify any grouping of items in the execution range, which gives an implementation freedom to choose the best grouping for a device. For example, a device with a wider SIMD width may prefer a larger grouping, but a device with a narrower SIMD width may be fine with smaller groupings.

When a kernel is an ND-range kernel with explicit groupings of work-items, care should be taken to choose an ND-range work-group size that maximizes SIMD efficiency. When a work-group size is not evenly divisible by a processor's SIMD width, part of the work-group may execute with channels disabled for the entire duration of the kernel. The device-specific kernel query for the `preferred_work_group_size_multiple` can be used to choose an efficient work-group size. Please refer to Chapter 12 for more information on how to query properties of a device.

Choosing a work-group size consisting of a single work-item will likely perform very poorly since many GPUs will implement a single-work-item work-group by masking off all SIMD channels except for one. For example, the kernel in Figure 15-12 will likely perform much worse than the very similar kernel in Figure 15-5, even though the only significant difference between the two is a change from a basic data-parallel kernel to an inefficient single-work-item ND-range kernel (`nd_range<1>{M, 1}`).

```
h.parallel_for(
    nd_range<1>{M, 1}, [=](nd_item<1> idx) {
      int m = idx.get_global_id(0);

      for (int n = 0; n < N; n++) {
        T sum = 0;
        for (int k = 0; k < K; k++) {
          sum += matrixA[m * K + k] * matrixB[k * N + n];
        }
        matrixC[m * N + n] = sum;
      }
    });
```

Figure 15-12. *Inefficient single-item, somewhat-parallel matrix multiplication*

Switching Work to Hide Latency

Many GPUs use one more technique to simplify control logic, maximize execution resources, and improve performance: instead of executing a single instruction stream on a processor, many GPUs allow multiple instruction streams to be resident on a processor simultaneously.

Having multiple instruction streams resident on a processor is beneficial because it gives each processor a choice of work to execute. If one instruction stream is performing a long-latency operation, such as a read from memory, the processor can switch to a different instruction stream that is ready to run instead of waiting for the operation to complete. With enough instruction streams, by the time that the processor switches back to the original instruction stream, the long-latency operation may have completed without requiring the processor to wait at all.

Figure 15-13 shows how a processor uses multiple simultaneous instruction streams to hide latency and improve performance. Even though the first instruction stream took a little longer to execute with multiple streams, by switching to other instruction streams, the processor was able to find work that was ready to execute and never needed to idly wait for the long operation to complete.

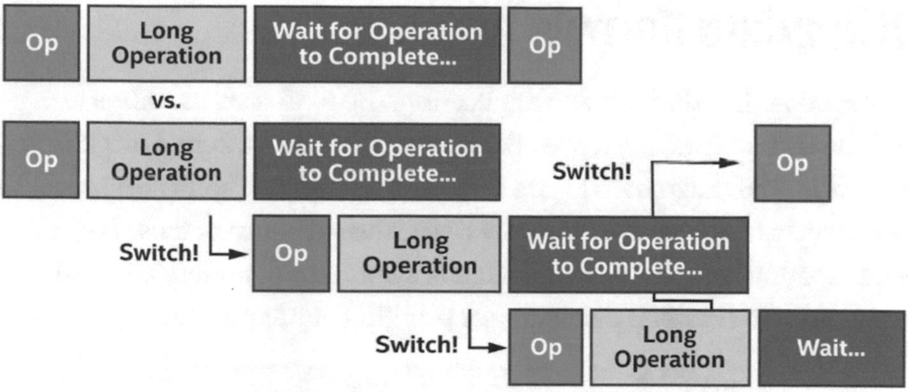

***Figure 15-13.** Switching instruction streams to hide latency*

GPU profiling tools may describe the number of instruction streams that a GPU processor is currently executing vs. the theoretical total number of instruction streams using a term such as *occupancy*.

Low occupancy does not necessarily imply low performance, since it is possible that a small number of instruction streams will keep a processor busy. Likewise, high occupancy does not necessarily imply high performance, since a GPU processor may still need to wait if all instruction streams perform inefficient, long-latency operations. All else being equal though, increasing occupancy maximizes a GPU processor's ability to hide latency and will usually improve performance. Increasing occupancy is another reason why performance may improve with the even more parallel kernel in Figure 15-7.

This technique of switching between multiple instruction streams to hide latency is especially well suited for GPUs and data-parallel processing. Recall from Figure 15-2 that GPU processors are frequently simpler than other processor types and hence lack complex latency-hiding features. This makes GPU processors more susceptible to latency issues, but because data-parallel programming involves processing a lot of data, GPU processors usually have plenty of instruction streams to execute!

Offloading Kernels to GPUs

This section describes how an application, the SYCL runtime library, and the GPU software driver work together to offload a kernel on GPU hardware. The diagram in Figure 15-14 shows a typical software stack with these layers of abstraction. In many cases, the existence of these layers is transparent to an application, but it is important to understand and account for them when debugging or profiling our application.

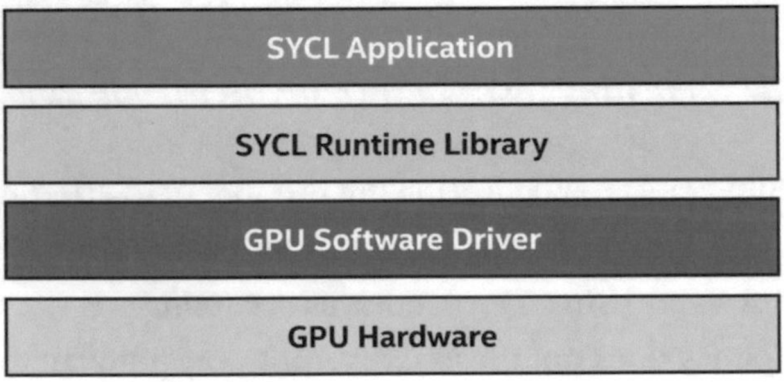

Figure 15-14. *Offloading parallel kernels to GPUs (simplified)*

SYCL Runtime Library

The SYCL runtime library is the primary software library that SYCL applications interface with. The runtime library is responsible for implementing classes such as `queues`, `buffers`, and `accessors` and the member functions of these classes. Parts of the runtime library may be in header files and hence directly compiled into the application executable. Other parts of the runtime library are implemented as library functions, which are linked with the application executable as part of the application build process. The runtime library is usually not device-specific, and the same runtime library may orchestrate offload to CPUs, GPUs, FPGAs, or other devices.

GPU Software Drivers

Although it is theoretically possible that a SYCL runtime library could offload directly to a GPU, in practice, most SYCL runtime libraries interface with a GPU software driver to submit work to a GPU.

A GPU software driver is typically an implementation of an API, such as OpenCL, Level Zero, or CUDA. Most of a GPU software driver is implemented in a user-mode driver library that the SYCL runtime calls into, and the user-mode driver may call into the operating system or a kernel-mode driver to perform system-level tasks such as allocating memory or submitting work to the device. The user-mode driver may also invoke other user-mode libraries; for example, the GPU driver may invoke a GPU compiler to just-in-time compile a kernel from an intermediate representation to GPU ISA (Instruction Set Architecture). These software modules and the interactions between them are shown in Figure 15-15.

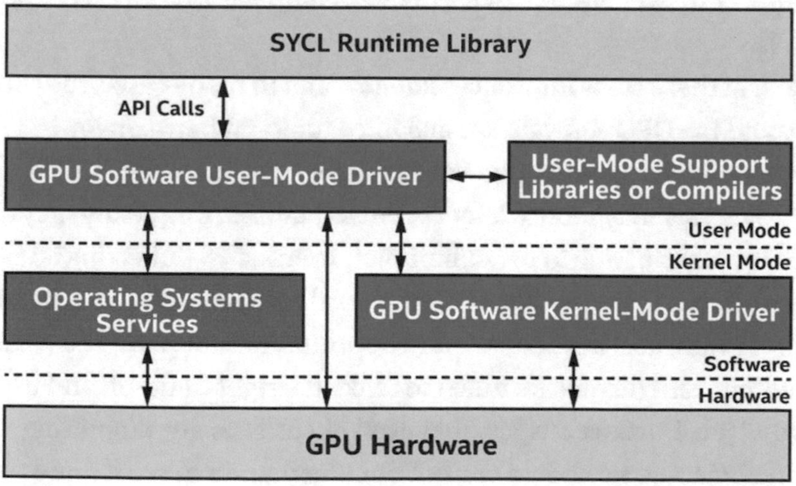

Figure 15-15. *Typical GPU software driver modules*

GPU Hardware

When the runtime library or the GPU software user-mode driver is explicitly requested to submit work, or when the GPU software heuristically determines that work should begin, it will typically call through the operating system or a kernel-mode driver to start executing work on the GPU. In some cases, the GPU software user-mode driver may submit work directly to the GPU, but this is less common and may not be supported by all devices or operating systems.

When the results of work executed on a GPU are consumed by the host processor or another accelerator, the GPU must issue a signal to indicate that work is complete. The steps involved in work completion are very similar to the steps for work submission, executed in reverse: the GPU may signal the operating system or kernel-mode driver that it has finished execution, then the user-mode driver will be informed, and finally the runtime library will observe that work has completed via GPU software API calls.

Each of these steps introduces latency, and in many cases, the runtime library and the GPU software are making a trade-off between lower latency and higher throughput. For example, submitting work to the GPU more frequently may reduce latency, but submitting frequently may also reduce throughput due to per-submission overheads. Collecting large batches of work increases latency but amortizes submission overheads over more work and introduces more opportunities for parallel execution. The runtime and drivers are tuned to make the right trade-off and usually do a good job, but if we suspect that driver heuristics are submitting work inefficiently, we should consult documentation to see if there are ways to override the default driver behavior using API-specific or even implementation-specific mechanisms. The techniques described in Chapter 20 to interact directly with an API backend can be useful to tune GPU submission policies.

Beware the Cost of Offloading!

Although SYCL implementations and GPU vendors are continually innovating and optimizing to reduce the cost of offloading work to a GPU, there will always be overhead involved both when starting work on a GPU and observing results on the host or another device. When choosing where to execute an algorithm, consider both the benefit of executing an algorithm on a device and the cost of moving the algorithm and any data that it requires to the device. In some cases, it may be most efficient to perform a parallel operation using the host processor—or to execute a serial part of an algorithm inefficiently on the GPU—to avoid the overhead of moving an algorithm from one processor to another.

Consider the performance of our algorithm as a whole—it may be most efficient to execute part of an algorithm inefficiently on one device than to transfer execution to another device!

Transfers to and from Device Memory

On GPUs with dedicated memory, be especially aware of transfer costs between dedicated GPU memory and memory on the host or another device. Figure 15-16 shows typical memory bandwidth differences between different memory types in a system.

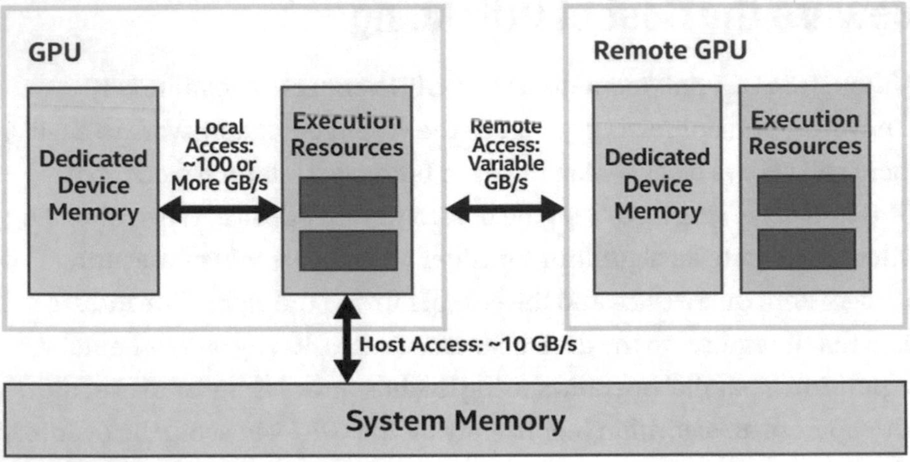

Figure 15-16. *Typical differences between device memory, remote memory, and host memory*

Recall from Chapter 3 that GPUs prefer to operate on dedicated device memory, which can be faster by an order of magnitude or more, instead of operating on host memory or another device's memory. Even though accesses to dedicated device memory are significantly faster than accesses to remote memory or system memory, if the data is not already in dedicated device memory, then it must be copied or migrated.

So long as the data will be accessed frequently, moving it into dedicated device memory is beneficial, especially if the transfer can be performed asynchronously while the GPU execution resources are busy processing another task. When the data is accessed infrequently or unpredictably though, it may be preferable to save transfer costs and operate on the data remotely or in system memory, even if per-access costs are higher. Chapter 6 describes ways to control where memory is allocated and different techniques to copy and prefetch data into dedicated device memory. These techniques are important when optimizing program execution for GPUs.

GPU Kernel Best Practices

The previous sections described how the dispatch parameters passed to a `parallel_for` affect how kernels are assigned to GPU processor resources and the software layers and overheads involved in executing a kernel on a GPU. This section describes best practices when a kernel is executing on a GPU.

Broadly speaking, kernels are either *memory bound*, meaning that their performance is limited by data read and write operations into or out of the execution resources on the GPU, or are *compute bound*, meaning that their performance is limited by the execution resources on the GPU. A good first step when optimizing a kernel for a GPU—and many other processors!—is to determine whether our kernel is memory bound or compute bound, since the techniques to improve a memory-bound kernel frequently will not benefit a compute-bound kernel and vice versa. GPU vendors often provide profiling tools to help make this determination.

Different optimization techniques are needed depending on whether our kernel is memory bound or compute bound!

Because GPUs tend to have many processors and wide SIMD widths, kernels tend to be memory bound more often than they are compute bound. If we are unsure where to start, examining how our kernel accesses memory is a good first step.

Accessing Global Memory

Efficiently accessing global memory is critical for optimal application performance because almost all data that a work-item or work-group operates on originates in global memory. If a kernel operates on global memory inefficiently, it will almost always perform poorly. Even though

GPUs often include dedicated hardware *gather* and *scatter* units for reading and writing arbitrary locations in memory, the performance of accesses to global memory is usually driven by the *locality* of data accesses. If one work-item in a work-group is accessing an element in memory that is adjacent to an element accessed by another work-item in the work-group, the global memory access performance is likely to be good. If work-items in a work-group instead access memory that is strided or random, the global memory access performance will likely be worse. Some GPU documentation describes operating on nearby memory accesses as *coalesced* memory accesses.

Recall that for our somewhat-parallel matrix multiplication kernel in Figure 15-5, we had a choice whether to process a row or a column of the result matrix in parallel, and we chose to operate on rows of the result matrix in parallel. This turns out to be a poor choice: if one work-item with `id` equal to `m` is grouped with a neighboring work-item with id equal to `m-1` or `m+1`, the indices used to access `matrixB` are the same for each work-item, but the indices used to access `matrixA` differ by `K`, meaning the accesses are highly strided. The access pattern for `matrixA` is shown in Figure 15-17.

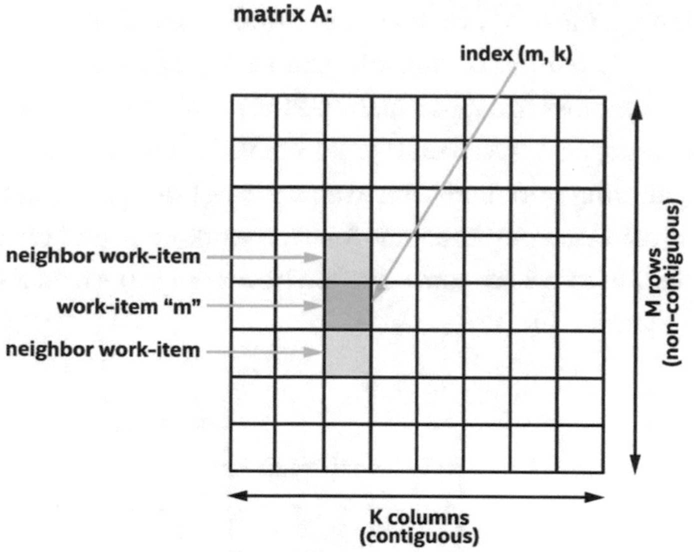

***Figure 15-17.** Accesses to `matrixA` are highly strided and inefficient*

If, instead, we choose to process columns of the result matrix in parallel, the access patterns have much better locality. The kernel in Figure 15-18 is structurally very similar to that in Figure 15-5 with the only difference being that each work-item in Figure 15-18 operates on a column of the result matrix, rather than a row of the result matrix.

```
h.parallel_for(N, [=](item<1> idx) {
   int n = idx[0];

   for (int m = 0; m < M; m++) {
     T sum = 0;
     for (int k = 0; k < K; k++) {
       sum += matrixA[m * K + k] * matrixB[k * N + n];
     }
     matrixC[m * N + n] = sum;
   }
 });
```

***Figure 15-18.** Computing columns of the result matrix in parallel, not rows*

Even though the two kernels are structurally very similar, the kernel that operates on columns of data will significantly outperform the kernel that operates on rows of data on many GPUs, purely due to the more efficient memory accesses: if one work-item with id equal to `n` is grouped with a neighboring work-item with id equal to `n-1` or `n+1`, the indices used to access `matrixA` are now the same for each work-item, and the indices used to access `matrixB` are consecutive. The access pattern for `matrixB` is shown in Figure 15-19.

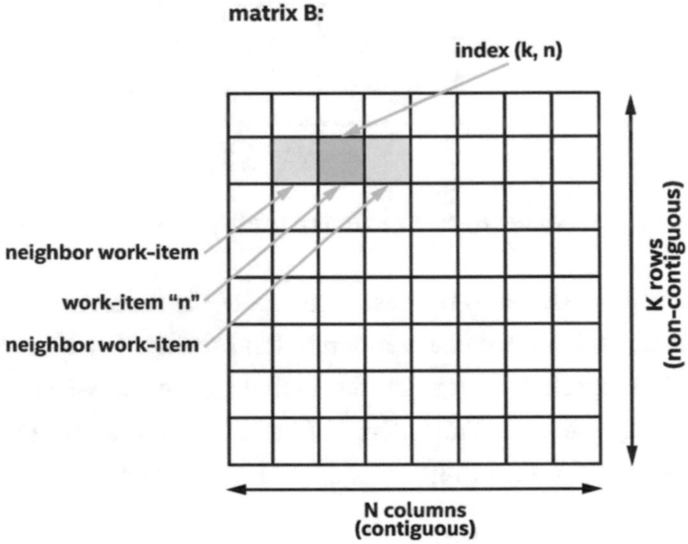

Figure 15-19. *Accesses to `matrixB` are consecutive and efficient*

Accesses to consecutive data are usually very efficient. A good rule of thumb is that the performance of accesses to global memory for a group of work-items is a function of the number of GPU cache lines accessed. If all accesses are within a single cache line, the access will execute with peak performance. If an access requires two cache lines, say by accessing every other element or by starting from a cache-misaligned address, the access may operate at half performance. When each work-item in the group accesses a unique cache line, say for a very strided or random accesses, the access is likely to operate at lowest performance.

PROFILING KERNEL VARIANTS

For matrix multiplication, choosing to parallelize along one dimension clearly results in more efficient memory accesses, but for other kernels, the choice may not be as obvious. For kernels where it is important to achieve the best performance, if it is not obvious which dimension to parallelize, it is sometimes worth developing and profiling different kernel variants that parallelize along each dimension to see what works better for a device and data set.

Accessing Work-Group Local Memory

In the previous section, we described how accesses to global memory benefit from *locality*, to maximize cache performance. As we saw, in some cases we can design our algorithm to efficiently access memory, such as by choosing to parallelize in one dimension instead of another. This technique isn't possible in all cases, however. This section describes how we can use work-group local memory to efficiently support more memory access patterns.

Recall from Chapter 9 that work-items in a work-group can cooperate to solve a problem by communicating through work-group local memory and synchronizing using work-group barriers. This technique is especially beneficial for GPUs, since typical GPUs have specialized hardware to implement both barriers and work-group local memory. Different GPU vendors and different products may implement work-group local memory differently, but work-group local memory frequently has two benefits compared to global memory: local memory may support higher bandwidth and lower latency than accesses to global memory, even when the global memory access hits a cache, and local memory is often divided into different memory regions, called *banks*. So long as each work-item in a group accesses a different bank, the local memory access executes with full performance. Banked accesses allow local memory to support far more access patterns with peak performance than global memory.

Many GPU vendors will assign consecutive local memory addresses to different banks. This ensures that consecutive memory accesses always operate at full performance, regardless of the starting address. When memory accesses are strided, though, some work-items in a group may access memory addresses assigned to the same bank. When this occurs, it is considered a *bank conflict* and results in serialized access and lower performance.

For maximum global memory performance, minimize the number of cache lines accessed.

For maximum local memory performance, minimize the number of bank conflicts!

A summary of access patterns and expected performance for global memory and local memory is shown in Figure 15-20. Assume that when `ptr` points to global memory, the pointer is aligned to the size of a GPU cache line. The best performance when accessing global memory can be achieved by accessing memory consecutively starting from a cache-aligned address. Accessing an unaligned address will likely lower global memory performance because the access may require accessing additional cache lines. Because accessing an unaligned local address will not result in additional bank conflicts, the local memory performance is unchanged.

The strided case is worth describing in more detail. Accessing every other element in global memory requires accessing more cache lines and will likely result in lower performance. Accessing every other element in local memory may result in bank conflicts and lower performance, but only if the number of banks is divisible by two. If the number of banks is odd, this case will operate at full performance also.

When the stride between accesses is very large, each work-item accesses a unique cache line, resulting in the worst performance. For local memory though, the performance depends on the stride and the number of banks. When the stride `N` is equal to the number of banks, each access results in a bank conflict, and all accesses are serialized, resulting in the worst performance. If the stride `M` and the number of banks share no common factors, however, the accesses will run at full performance. For this reason, many optimized GPU kernels will pad data structures in local memory to choose a stride that reduces or eliminates bank conflicts.

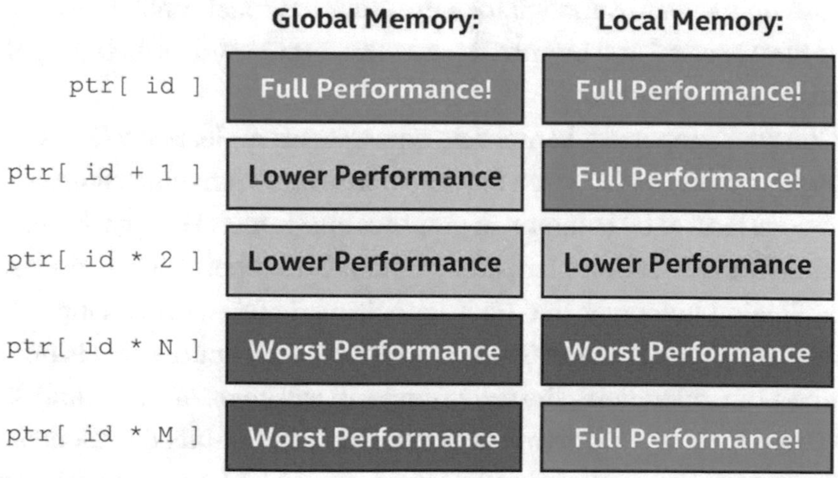

Figure 15-20. *Possible performance for different access patterns, for global and local memory*

Avoiding Local Memory Entirely with Sub-Groups

As discussed in Chapter 9, sub-group collective functions are an alternative way to exchange data between work-items in a group. For many GPUs, a sub-group represents a collection of work-items processed by a single instruction stream. In these cases, the work-items in the sub-group can inexpensively exchange data and synchronize without using work-group local memory. Many of the best-performing GPU kernels use sub-groups, so for expensive kernels, it is well worth examining if our algorithm can be reformulated to use sub-group collective functions.

Optimizing Computation Using Small Data Types

This section describes techniques to optimize kernels after eliminating or reducing memory access bottlenecks. One very important perspective to keep in mind is that GPUs have traditionally been designed to draw pictures on a screen. Although the pure computational capabilities of GPUs have evolved and improved over time, in some areas their graphics heritage is still apparent.

Consider support for kernel data types, for example. Many GPUs are highly optimized for 32-bit floating-point operations since these operations tend to be common in graphics and games. For algorithms that can cope with lower precision, many GPUs also support a lower-precision 16-bit floating-point type that trades precision for faster processing. Conversely, although many GPUs do support 64-bit double-precision floating-point operations, the extra precision will come at a cost, and 32-bit operations usually perform much better than their 64-bit equivalents.

The same is true for integer data types, where 32-bit integer data types typically perform better than 64-bit integer data types and 16-bit integers may perform even better still. If we can structure our computation to use smaller integers, our kernel may perform faster. One area to pay careful attention to are addressing operations, which typically operate on 64-bit `size_t` data types, but can sometimes be rearranged to perform most of the calculation using 32-bit data types. In some local memory cases, 16 bits of indexing is sufficient, since most local memory allocations are small.

Optimizing Math Functions

Another area where a kernel may trade off accuracy for performance involves SYCL built-in functions. SYCL includes a rich set of math functions with well-defined accuracy across a range of inputs. Most GPUs do not support these functions natively and implement them using a long sequence of other instructions. Although the math function implementations are typically well optimized for a GPU, if our application can tolerate lower accuracy, we should consider a different implementation with lower accuracy and higher performance instead. Please refer to Chapter 18 for more information about SYCL built-in functions.

For commonly used math functions, the SYCL library includes `fast` or `native` function variants with reduced or implementation-defined accuracy requirements. For some GPUs, these functions can be an order of magnitude faster than their precise equivalents, so they are well worth considering if they have enough precision for an algorithm. For example, many image postprocessing algorithms have well-defined inputs and can tolerate lower accuracy and hence are good candidates for using `fast` or `native` math functions.

If an algorithm can tolerate lower precision, we can use smaller data types or lower-precision math functions to increase performance!

Specialized Functions and Extensions

One final consideration when optimizing a kernel for a GPU is specialized instructions that are common in many GPUs. As one example, nearly all GPUs support a `mad` or `fma` multiply-and-add instruction that performs two operations in a single clock. GPU compilers are generally very good at identifying and optimizing individual multiplies and adds to use a single instruction instead, but SYCL also includes `mad` and `fma` functions that can be called explicitly. Of course, if we expect our GPU compiler to optimize multiplies and adds for us, we should be sure that we do not prevent optimizations by disabling floating-point contractions!

Other specialized GPU instructions may only be available via compiler optimizations, extensions to the SYCL language, or by interacting directly with a low-level GPU backend. For example, some GPUs support a specialized dot-product-and-accumulate instruction that compilers will try to identify and optimize for, or that may be called directly. Refer to Chapter 12 for more information on how to query the extensions that are supported by a GPU implementation and to Chapter 20 for information about backend interoperability.

Summary

In this chapter, we started by describing how typical GPUs work and how GPUs are different than traditional CPUs. We described how GPUs are optimized for large amounts of data, by trading processor features that accelerate a single instruction stream for additional processors.

We described how GPUs process multiple data elements in parallel using wide SIMD instructions and how GPUs use predication and masking to execute kernels with complex flow control using SIMD instructions. We discussed how predication and masking can reduce SIMD efficiency and decrease performance for kernels that are highly divergent and how choosing to parallelize along one dimension vs. another may reduce SIMD divergence.

Because GPUs have so many processing resources, we discussed how it is important to give GPUs enough work to keep occupancy high. We also described how GPUs use instruction streams to hide latency, making it even more crucial to give GPUs lots of work to execute.

Next, we discussed the software and hardware layers involved in offloading a kernel to a GPU and the costs of offloading. We discussed how it may be more efficient to execute an algorithm on a single device than it is to transfer execution from one device to another.

Finally, we described best practices for kernels once they are executing on a GPU. We described how many kernels start off memory bound and how to access global memory and local memory efficiently or how to avoid local memory entirely by using sub-group operations. When kernels are compute bound instead, we described how to optimize computation by trading lower precision for higher performance or using custom GPU extensions to access specialized instructions.

For More Information

There is much more to learn about GPU programming, and this chapter just scratched the surface!

GPU specifications and white papers are a great way to learn more about specific GPUs and GPU architectures. Many GPU vendors provide very detailed information about their GPUs and how to program them.

At the time of this writing, relevant reading about major GPUs can be found on software.intel.com, devblogs.nvidia.com, and amd.com.

Some GPU vendors have open source drivers or driver components. When available, it can be instructive to inspect or step through driver code, to get a sense for which operations are expensive or where overheads may exist in an application.

This chapter focused entirely on traditional accesses to global memory via buffer accessors or Unified Shared Memory, but most GPUs also include a fixed-function texture sampler that can accelerate operations on images. For more information about images and samplers, please refer to the SYCL specification.

CHAPTER 16

Programming for CPUs

Kernel programming originally became popular as a way to program GPUs. As kernel programming is generalized, it is important to understand how kernel style of programming affects the mapping of our code to a CPU.

The CPU has evolved over the years. A major shift occurred around 2005 when performance gains from increasing clock speeds diminished. Parallelism arose as the favored solution—instead of increasing clock speeds, CPU producers introduced multicore chips. Computers became more effective in performing multiple tasks at the same time!

While multicore prevailed as the path for increasing hardware performance, realizing that gain in software required nontrivial effort. Multicore processors required developers to come up with different algorithms so the hardware improvements could be noticeable, and this was not always easy. The more cores that we have, the harder it is to keep them busy efficiently. SYCL is one of the programming languages that address these challenges, with many constructs that help to exploit various forms of parallelism on CPUs (and other architectures).

This chapter discusses some particulars of CPU architectures, how CPU hardware typically executes SYCL applications and offers best practices when writing a SYCL code for a CPU platform.

J. Reinders et al., *Data Parallel C++*, https://doi.org/10.1007/978-1-4842-9691-2_16

Performance Caveats

SYCL paves a portable path to parallelize our applications or to develop parallel applications from scratch. The performance of an application, when run on CPUs, is largely dependent upon the following factors:

- The underlying performance of the launch and execution of kernel code
- The percentage of the program that runs in a parallel kernel and its scalability
- CPU utilization, effective data sharing, data locality, and load balancing
- The amount of synchronization and communication between work-items
- The overhead introduced to create, resume, manage, suspend, destroy, and synchronize any threads that work-items execute on, which is impacted by the number of serial-to-parallel or parallel-to-serial transitions
- Memory conflicts caused by shared memory (including falsely shared memory)
- Performance limitations of shared resources such as memory, write combining buffers, and memory bandwidth

In addition, as with any processor type, CPUs may differ from vendor to vendor or even from product generation to product generation. The best practices for one CPU may not be best practices for a different CPU and configuration.

To achieve optimal performance on a CPU, understand as many characteristics of the CPU architecture as possible!

The Basics of Multicore CPUs

Emergence and rapid advancements in multicore CPUs have driven substantial acceptance of shared memory parallel computing platforms. CPUs offer parallel computing platforms at laptop, desktop, and server levels, making them ubiquitous and exposing performance almost everywhere. The most common form of CPU architecture is cache-coherent non-uniform memory access (cc-NUMA), which is characterized by memory access times not being completely uniform. Many small dual-socket general-purpose CPU systems have this kind of memory system. This architecture has become dominant because the number of cores in a processor, as well as the number of sockets, continues to increase.

In a cc-NUMA CPU system, each socket connects to a subset of the total memory in the system. A cache-coherent interconnect glues all the sockets together and provides a single system memory view for programmers. Such a memory system is scalable, because the aggregate memory bandwidth scales with the number of sockets in the system. The benefit of the interconnect is that an application has transparent access to all the memory in the system, regardless of where the data resides. However, there is a cost: the latency to access data from memory is no longer consistent (i.e., we no longer have fixed access latency). The latency instead depends on where that data is stored in the system. In a good case, data comes from memory directly connected to the socket where code runs. In a bad case, data has to come from a memory connected to a socket far away in the system, and that cost of memory access can increase due to the number of hops in the interconnect between sockets on a cc-NUMA CPU system.

In Figure 16-1, a generic CPU architecture with cc-NUMA memory is shown. This is a simplified system architecture containing cores and memory components found in contemporary, general-purpose, multi-socket systems today. Throughout the remainder of this chapter, the figure will be used to illustrate the mapping of corresponding code examples.

To achieve optimal performance, we need to be sure to understand the characteristics of the cc-NUMA configuration of a specific system. For example, recent servers from Intel make use of a mesh interconnect architecture. In this configuration, the cores, caches, and memory controllers are organized into rows and columns. Understanding the connectivity of processors with memory can be critical when working to achieve peak performance of the system.

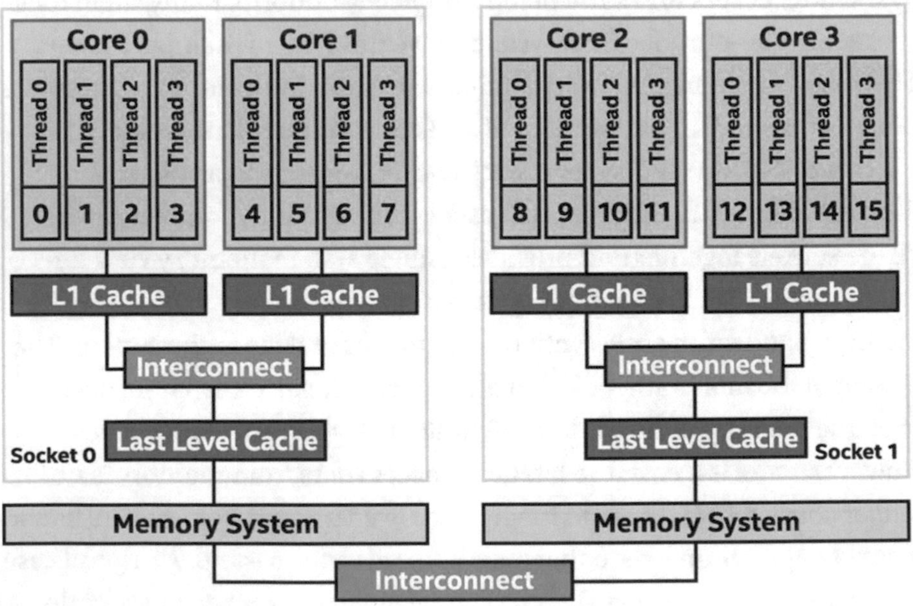

Figure 16-1. *Generic multicore CPU system*

The system in Figure 16-1 has two sockets, each of which has two cores with four hardware threads per core. Each core has its own level 1 (L1) cache. L1 caches are connected to a shared last-level cache, which is connected to the memory system on the socket. The memory access latency within a socket is uniform, meaning that it is consistent and can be predicted with accuracy.

The two sockets are connected through a cache-coherent interconnect. Memory is distributed across the system, but all the memory may be transparently accessed from anywhere in the system. The memory read and write latency is non-uniform when accessing memory that isn't in the socket where the code making the access is running, which means it imposes a potentially much longer and inconsistent latency when accessing data from a remote socket. A critical aspect of the interconnect, though, is coherency. We do not need to worry about inconsistent views of data in memory across the system and can instead focus on the performance impact of how we are accessing the distributed memory system. More advanced optimizations (e.g., atomic operation with a relaxed memory order) can enable operations that no longer require as much hardware memory consistency, but when we want the consistency, the hardware provides it for us.

Hardware threads in CPUs are the execution vehicles. These are the units that execute instruction streams. The hardware threads in Figure 16-1 are numbered consecutively from 0 to 15, which is a notation used to simplify discussions on the examples in this chapter. Unless otherwise noted, all references to a CPU system in this chapter are to the reference cc-NUMA system shown in Figure 16-1.

The Basics of SIMD Hardware

In 1996, a widely deployed SIMD instruction set was MMX extensions on top of the x86 architecture. Many SIMD instruction set extensions have since followed both on Intel architectures and more broadly across the industry. A CPU core carries out its job by executing instructions, and the specific instructions that a core knows how to execute are defined by the instruction set (e.g., x86, x86_64, AltiVec, NEON) and instruction set extensions (e.g., SSE, AVX, AVX-512) that it implements. Many of the operations added by instruction set extensions are focused on SIMD.

SIMD instructions allow multiple calculations to be carried out simultaneously on a single core by using registers and hardware bigger than the fundamental unit of data being processed. For example, using 512-bit registers we can perform eight 64-bit calculations with a single machine instruction.

This example shown in Figure 16-2 could, in theory, give us up to an eight times speed-up. In reality, it is likely to be somewhat curtailed as a portion of the eight times speed-up serves to remove one bottleneck and expose the next, such as memory throughput. In general, the performance benefit of using SIMD varies depending on the specific scenario, and in a few cases such as extensive branch divergence, gather/scatter for non-unit-stride memory access, and cache-line split for SIMD loads and stores, it can even perform worse than simpler non-SIMD equivalent code. That said, considerable gains are achievable on today's processors when we know when and how to apply (or have the compiler apply) SIMD. As with all performance optimizations, programmers should measure the gains on a typical target machine before putting it into production. There are more details on expected performance gains in the following sections of this chapter.

```
h.parallel_for(range(1024),
               [=](id<1> k) { z[k] = x[k] + y[k]; });
```

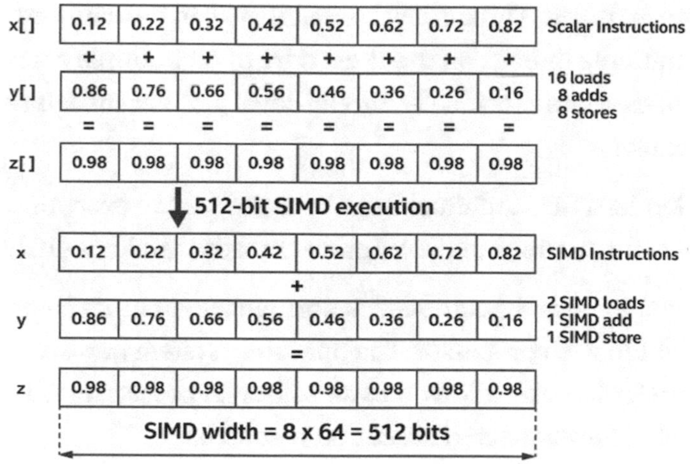

***Figure 16-2.** SIMD execution in a CPU hardware thread*

The cc-NUMA CPU architecture with SIMD units forms the foundation of a multicore processor, which can exploit a wide spectrum of parallelism starting from instruction-level parallelism in at least the five different ways as shown in Figure 16-3.

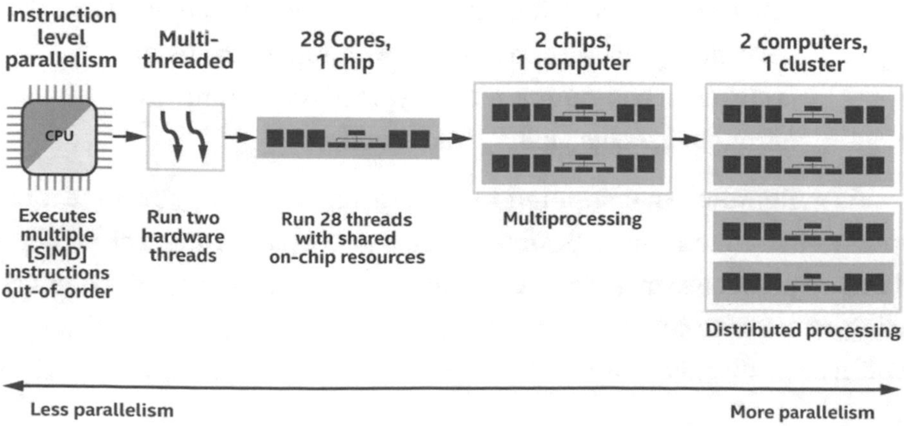

***Figure 16-3.** Five ways for executing instructions in parallel*

In Figure 16-3, instruction-level parallelism can be achieved through both out-of-order execution of scalar instructions and SIMD parallelism within a single thread. Thread-level parallelism can be achieved through executing multiple threads on the same core or on multiple cores at different scales. More specifically, thread-level parallelism can be exposed from the following:

- Modern CPU architectures allow one core to execute the instructions of two or more threads simultaneously.
- Multicore architectures that contain two or more *cores* within each processor. The operating system perceives each of its execution cores as a discrete processor, with all of the associated execution resources.
- Multiprocessing at the processor (chip) level, which can be accomplished by executing separate threads of code. As a result, the processor can have one thread running from an application and another thread running from an operating system, or it can have parallel threads running from within a single application.
- Distributed processing, which can be accomplished by executing processes consisting of multiple threads on a cluster of computers, which typically communicate through message passing frameworks.

As multiprocessor computers and multicore technology become more and more common, it is important to use parallel processing techniques as standard practice to increase performance. Later sections of this chapter will introduce the coding methods and performance-tuning techniques within SYCL that allow us to achieve peak performance on multicore CPUs.

Like other parallel processing hardware (e.g., GPUs), it is important to give the CPU a sufficiently large set of data elements to process. To demonstrate the importance of exploiting multilevel parallelism to handle a large set of data, consider a simple C++ STREAM Triad program, as shown in Figure 16-4.

```
// C++ STREAM Triad workload
// __restrict is used to denote no memory aliasing among
// arguments
template <typename T>
double triad(T* __restrict VA, T* __restrict VB,
             T* __restrict VC, size_t array_size,
             const T scalar) {
  double ts = timer_start();
  for (size_t id = 0; id < array_size; id++) {
    VC[id] = VA[id] + scalar * VB[id];
  }
  double te = timer_end();
  return (te - ts);
}
```

Figure 16-4. *STREAM Triad C++ loop*

A NOTE ABOUT STREAM TRIAD WORKLOAD

The STREAM Triad workload (`www.cs.virginia.edu/stream`) is an important and popular benchmark workload that CPU vendors use to demonstrate memory bandwidth capabilities. We use the STREAM Triad kernel to demonstrate code generation of a parallel kernel and the way that it is scheduled to achieve significantly improved performance through the techniques described in this chapter. STREAM Triad is a relatively simple workload but is sufficient to show many of the optimizations in an understandable way. There is a STREAM implementation from the University of Bristol, called BabelStream, that includes a C++ with SYCL version.

The STREAM Triad loop may be trivially executed on a CPU using a single CPU core for serial execution. A good C++ compiler will perform loop vectorization to generate SIMD code for the CPU that has hardware to exploit instruction-level SIMD parallelism. For example, for an Intel Xeon processor with AVX-512 support, the Intel C++ compiler generates SIMD code as shown in Figure 16-5. Critically, the compiler's transformation of the code reduced the number of loop iterations by doing more work per loop iteration (using SIMD instructions and loop unrolling).

```
# %bb.0:                          # %entry
vbroadcastsd    %xmm0, %zmm0      # broadcast "scalar" to SIMD reg zmm0
movq    $-32, %rax
.p2align        4, 0x90
.LBB0_1:                          # %loop.19
                                  # =>This Loop Header: Depth=1
vmovupd 256(%rdx,%rax,8), %zmm1 # load 8 elements from memory to zmm1
vfmadd213pd     256(%rsi,%rax,8), %zmm0, %zmm1 # zmm1=(zmm0*zmm1)+mem
                                  # perform SIMD FMA for 8 data elements
                                  # VC[id:8] = scalar*VB[id:8]+VA[id:8]
vmovupd %zmm1, 256(%rdi,%rax,8) # store 8-element result to mem from zmm1
                                  # This SIMD loop body is unrolled by 4
vmovupd 320(%rdx,%rax,8), %zmm1
vfmadd213pd     320(%rsi,%rax,8), %zmm0, %zmm1 # zmm1=(zmm0*zmm1)+mem
vmovupd %zmm1, 320(%rdi,%rax,8)

vmovupd 384(%rdx,%rax,8), %zmm1
vfmadd213pd     384(%rsi,%rax,8), %zmm0, %zmm1 # zmm1=(zmm0*zmm1)+mem
vmovupd %zmm1, 384(%rdi,%rax,8)

vmovupd 448(%rdx,%rax,8), %zmm1
vfmadd213pd     448(%rsi,%rax,8), %zmm0, %zmm1 # zmm1=(zmm0*zmm1)+mem
vmovupd %zmm1, 448(%rdi,%rax,8)
addq    $32, %rax
cmpq    $134217696, %rax          # imm = 0x7FFFFE0
jb      .LBB0_1
```

Figure 16-5. *AVX-512 assembly code for STREAM Triad C++ loop*

As shown in Figure 16-5, the compiler was able to exploit instruction-level parallelism in two ways. First is by using SIMD instructions, exploiting instruction-level data parallelism, in which a single instruction can process eight double-precision data elements simultaneously in parallel (per instruction). Second, the compiler applied loop unrolling to get the out-of-order execution effect of these instructions that have no dependences between them, based on hardware multiway instruction scheduling.

If we try to execute this function on a CPU, it will probably run well for small array sizes—not great, though, since it does not utilize any multicore or threading capabilities of the CPU. If we try to execute this function with a large array size on a CPU, however, it will likely perform very poorly because the single thread will only utilize a single CPU core and will be bottlenecked when it saturates the memory bandwidth of that core.

Exploiting Thread-Level Parallelism

To improve the performance of the STREAM Triad kernel, we can compute on a range of data elements that can be processed in parallel, by converting the loop to a `parallel_for` kernel.

The body of this STREAM Triad SYCL parallel kernel looks exactly like the body of the STREAM Triad loop that executes in serial C++ on the CPU, as shown in Figure 16-6.

```
constexpr int num_runs = 10;
constexpr size_t scalar = 3;

double triad(const std::vector<float>& vecA,
             const std::vector<float>& vecB,
             std::vector<float>& vecC) {
  assert(vecA.size() == vecB.size() &&
         vecB.size() == vecC.size());
  const size_t array_size = vecA.size();
  double min_time_ns = std::numeric_limits<double>::max();

  queue q{property::queue::enable_profiling{}};
  std::cout << "Running on device: "
            << q.get_device().get_info<info::device::name>()
            << "\n";

  buffer<float> bufA(vecA);
  buffer<float> bufB(vecB);
  buffer<float> bufC(vecC);

  for (int i = 0; i < num_runs; i++) {
    auto Q_event = q.submit([&](handler& h) {
      accessor A{bufA, h};
      accessor B{bufB, h};
      accessor C{bufC, h};

      h.parallel_for(array_size, [=](id<1> idx) {
        C[idx] = A[idx] + B[idx] * scalar;
      });
    });

    double exec_time_ns =
        Q_event.get_profiling_info<
            info::event_profiling::command_end>() -
        Q_event.get_profiling_info<
            info::event_profiling::command_start>();

    std::cout << "Execution time (iteration " << i
              << ") [sec]: "
              << (double)exec_time_ns * 1.0E-9 << "\n";
    min_time_ns = std::min(min_time_ns, exec_time_ns);
  }

  return min_time_ns;
}
```

Figure 16-6. *SYCL STREAM Triad* `parallel_for` *kernel code*

Even though the parallel kernel is very similar to the STREAM Triad function written as serial C++ with a loop, it runs much faster because the `parallel_for` enables different *elements* of the array to be processed on multiple cores in parallel. Figure 16-7 shows how this kernel could be mapped to a CPU. Assume that we have a system with one socket, four cores, and two hardware threads per core (for a total of eight threads) and that the implementation processes data in work-groups containing 32 work-items each. If we have 1024 double-precision data elements to be processed, we will have 32 work-groups. The work-group scheduling can be done in a round-robin order, that is, *thread-id* = *work-group-id* mod 8. Essentially, each thread will execute four work-groups. Eight work-groups can be executed in parallel for each round. Note that, in this case, the work-group is a set of work-items that is implicitly formed by the SYCL compiler and runtime.

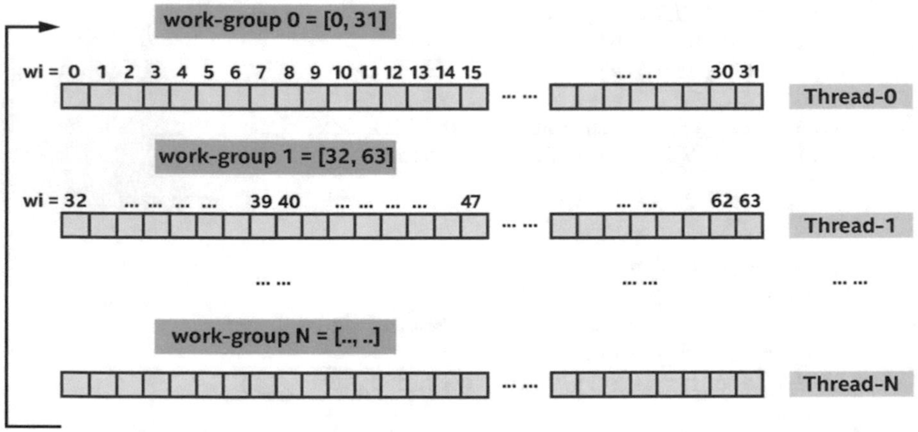

***Figure 16-7.** A mapping of a STREAM Triad parallel kernel*

Note that in the SYCL program, the exact way that data elements are partitioned and assigned to different processor cores (or threads) is not specified. This gives a SYCL implementation flexibility to choose how best to execute a parallel kernel on a specific CPU. With that said, an implementation may provide some level of control to programmers to enable performance tuning (e.g., via compiler options or environment variables).

While a CPU may impose a relatively expensive thread context switch and synchronization overhead, having more software threads resident on a processor core may be beneficial because it gives each processor core a choice of work to execute. If one software thread is waiting for another thread to produce data, the processor core can switch to a different software thread that is ready to run without leaving the processor core idle.

CHOOSING HOW TO BIND AND SCHEDULE THREADS

Choosing an effective scheme to partition and schedule the work among threads is important to tune an application on CPUs and other device types. Subsequent sections will describe some of the techniques.

Thread Affinity Insight

Thread affinity designates the CPU cores on which specific threads execute. Performance can suffer if a thread moves around among cores—for instance, if threads do not execute on the same core, cache locality can become an inefficiency if data ping-pongs between different cores.

The DPC++ compiler's runtime library supports several schemes for binding threads to cores through the environment variables `DPCPP_CPU_CU_AFFINITY`, `DPCPP_CPU_PLACES`, `DPCPP_CPU_NUM_CUS`, and `DPCPP_CPU_SCHEDULE`, which are not defined by SYCL. Other implementations may expose similar environment variables.

The first of these is the environment variable `DPCPP_CPU_CU_AFFINITY`. Tuning using these environment variable controls is simple and low cost but can have large impact for many applications. The description of this environment variable is shown in Figure 16-8.

DPCPP_CPU_CU_AFFINITY	Description
spread	Bind successive threads to distinct sockets starting with socket 0 in a round-robin order
close	Bind successive threads to distinct hardware threads starting with thread 0 in a round-robin order

Figure 16-8. *DPCPP_CPU_CU_AFFINITY environment variable*

When the environment variable DPCPP_CPU_CU_AFFINITY is specified, a software thread is bound to a hardware thread through the following formula:

$$spread: boundHT = (tid \bmod numHT) + (tid \bmod numSocket) \times numHT)$$
$$close: boundHT = tid \bmod (numSocket \times numHT)$$

where

- tid denotes a software thread identifier
- boundHT denotes a hardware thread (logical core) that thread tid is bound to
- numHT denotes the number of hardware threads per socket
- numSocket denotes the number of sockets in the system

Assume that we run a program with eight threads on a dual-core dual-socket system—in other words, we have four cores with a total of eight threads to program. Figure 16-9 shows examples of how threads can map to the hardware threads and cores for different DPCPP_CPU_CU_AFFINITY settings.

DPCPP_CPU_CU_AFFINITY	socket0		socket1	
	core0	core1	core2	core3
spread	<T0, T4>	<T2, T6>	<T1, T5>	<T3, T7>
close	<T0, T1>	<T2, T3>	<T4, T5>	<T6, T7>

Figure 16-9. *Mapping threads to cores with hardware threads*

In conjunction with the environment variable `DPCPP_CPU_CU_AFFINITY`, there are other environment variables that support CPU performance tuning:

- `DPCPP_CPU_NUM_CUS = [n]`, which sets the number of threads used for kernel execution. Its default value is the number of hardware threads in the system.
- `DPCPP_CPU_PLACES = [ sockets | numa_domains | cores | threads ]`, which specifies the places that the affinity will be set similar to `OMP_PLACES` in OpenMP 5.1. The default setting is `cores`.
- `DPCPP_CPU_SCHEDULE = [ dynamic | affinity | static ]`, which specifies the algorithm for scheduling work-groups. Its default setting is `dynamic`.

  `dynamic`: Enable the `auto_partitioner`, which usually performs sufficient splitting to balance the load among worker threads.

  `affinity`: Enable the `affinity_partitioner`, which improves cache affinity and uses proportional splitting when mapping subranges to worker threads.

  `static`: Enable the `static_partitioner`, which distributes iterations among worker threads as uniformly as possible.

When running on CPUs using Intel's OpenCL CPU runtime, work-group scheduling is handled by the Threading Building Blocks (TBB) library. Using `DPCPP_CPU_SCHEDULE` determines which TBB partitioner is used. Note that the TBB partitioner also uses a grain size to control work splitting, with a default grain size of 1 which indicates that all work-groups can be executed independently. More information can be found at tinyurl.com/oneTBBpart.

A lack of thread affinity tuning does not necessarily mean lower performance. Performance often depends more on how many total threads are executing in parallel than on how well the thread and data are related and bound. Testing the application using benchmarks is one way to be certain whether the thread affinity has a performance impact or not. The STREAM Triad code, as shown in Figure 16-1, started with a lower performance without thread affinity settings. By controlling the affinity setting and using static scheduling of software threads through the environment variables (exports shown in the following for Linux), performance improved:

```
export DPCPP_CPU_PLACES=numa_domains
export DPCPP_CPU_CU_AFFINITY=close
```

By using `numa_domains` as the places setting for affinity, the TBB task arenas are bound to NUMA nodes or sockets, and the work is uniformly distributed across task arenas. In general, the environment variable `DPCPP_CPU_PLACES` is recommended to be used together with `DPCPP_CPU_CU_AFFINITY`. These environment variable settings help us to achieve a ~30% performance gain on an Intel Xeon server system with 2 sockets, 28 cores per socket, and 2 hardware threads per core, running at 2.5 GHz. However, we can still do better to further improve the performance on this CPU.

Be Mindful of First Touch to Memory

Memory is stored where it is first touched (used). Since the initialization loop in our example is executed by the host thread serially, all the memory is associated with the socket that the host thread is running on. Subsequent access by other sockets will then access data from memory attached to the initial socket (used for the initialization), which is clearly undesirable for performance. We can achieve a higher performance on the STREAM Triad kernel by parallelizing the initialization loop to control the first touch effect across sockets, as shown in Figure 16-10.

```
template <typename T>
void init(queue& deviceQueue, T* VA, T* VB, T* VC,
          size_t array_size) {
  range<1> numOfItems{array_size};

  buffer<T, 1> bufferA(VA, numOfItems);
  buffer<T, 1> bufferB(VB, numOfItems);
  buffer<T, 1> bufferC(VC, numOfItems);

  auto queue_event = deviceQueue.submit([&](handler& cgh) {
    auto aA = bufA.template get_access<sycl_write>(cgh);
    auto aB = bufB.template get_access<sycl_write>(cgh);
    auto aC = bufC.template get_access<sycl_write>(cgh);

    cgh.parallel_for<class Init<T>>(numOfItems, [=](id<1> wi) {
      aA[wi] = 2.0;
      aB[wi] = 1.0;
      aC[wi] = 0.0;
    });
  });

  queue_event.wait();
}
```

Figure 16-10. *STREAM Triad parallel initialization kernel to control first touch effects*

Exploiting parallelism in the initialization code improves performance of the kernel when run on a CPU. In this instance, we achieve a ~2x performance gain on an Intel Xeon processor system.

The recent sections of this chapter have shown that by exploiting thread-level parallelism, we can utilize CPU cores and threads effectively. However, we need to exploit the SIMD vector-level parallelism in the CPU core hardware as well, to achieve peak performance.

SYCL parallel kernels benefit from thread-level parallelism across cores and hardware threads!

SIMD Vectorization on CPU

While a well-written SYCL kernel without cross-work-item dependences can run in parallel effectively on a CPU, implementations can also apply vectorization to SYCL kernels to leverage SIMD hardware similar to the GPU support described in Chapter 15. Essentially, CPU processors may optimize memory loads, stores, and operations using SIMD instructions by leveraging the fact that most data elements are often in contiguous memory and take the same control flow paths through a data-parallel kernel. For example, in a kernel with a statement `a[i] = a[i] + b[i]`, each data element executes with the same instruction stream *load, load, add,* and *store* by sharing hardware logic among multiple data elements and executing them as a group, which may be mapped naturally onto a hardware's SIMD instruction set. Specifically, multiple data elements can be processed simultaneously by a single instruction.

The number of data elements that are processed simultaneously by a single instruction is sometimes referred to as the vector length (or SIMD width) of the instruction or processor executing it. In Figure 16-11, our instruction stream runs with four-way SIMD execution.

Serial execution				*SIMD execution*
work-0	*work-1*	*work-2*	*work 3*	*vector sub-group*
load r0, a[0]	load r0, a[1]	load r0, a[2]	load r0, a[3]	simdload vr0, a[0...3]
load r1, b[0]	load r1, b[1]	load r1, b[2]	load r1, b[3]	simdload vr1, b[0...3]
add r0, r1	add r0, r1	add r0, r1	add r0, r1	simdadd vr0, vr1
store a[0], r0	store a[1], r0	store a[2], r0	store a[3], r0	simdstore a[0...3], vr0

Figure 16-11. *Instruction stream for SIMD execution*

CPU processors are not the only processors that implement SIMD instruction sets. Other processors such as GPUs implement SIMD instructions to improve efficiency when processing large sets of data. A key difference with Intel Xeon CPU processors, compared with other processor types, is having three fixed-size SIMD register widths 128-bit XMM, 256-bit YMM, and 512-bit ZMM instead of a variable length of SIMD width. When we write SYCL code with SIMD parallelism using sub-group or vector types (see Chapter 11), we need to be mindful of SIMD width and the number of SIMD vector registers in the hardware.

Ensure SIMD Execution Legality

Semantically, the SYCL execution model ensures that SIMD execution can be applied to any kernel, and a set of work-items in each work-group (i.e., a sub-group) may be executed concurrently using SIMD instructions. Some implementations may instead choose to execute loops within a kernel using SIMD instructions, but this is possible if and only if all original data dependences are preserved, or data dependences are resolved by the compiler based on privatization and reduction semantics. Such implementation would likely report a sub-group size of one.

A single SYCL kernel execution can be transformed from processing a single work-item to a set of work-items using SIMD instructions within the work-group. Under the ND-range model, the fastest-growing (unit-stride) dimension is selected by the compiler vectorizer on which to generate SIMD code. Essentially, to enable vectorization given an ND-range, there should be no cross-work-item dependences between any two work-items in the same sub-group, or the compiler needs to preserve cross-work-item forward dependences in the same sub-group.

When the kernel execution of work-items is mapped to threads on CPUs, fine-grained synchronization is known to be costly, and the thread context switch overhead is high as well. It is therefore an important performance optimization to eliminate dependences between work-items within a work-group when writing a SYCL kernel for CPUs. Another effective approach is to restrict such dependences to the work-items within a sub-group, as shown for the read-before-write dependence in Figure 16-12. If the sub-group is executed under a SIMD execution model, the sub-group barrier in the kernel can be treated by the compiler as a no-op, and no real synchronization cost is incurred at runtime.

```
const int n = 16, w = 16;

queue q;
range<2> G = {n, w};
range<2> L = {1, w};

int *a = malloc_shared<int>(n * (n + 1), q);

for (int i = 0; i < n; i++)
  for (int j = 0; j < n + 1; j++) a[i * n + j] = i + j;

q.parallel_for(
     nd_range<2>{G, L},
     [=](nd_item<2> it) [[sycl::reqd_sub_group_size(w)]] {
       // distribute uniform "i" over the sub-group with
       // 16-way redundant computation
       const int i = it.get_global_id(0);
       sub_group sg = it.get_sub_group();

       for (int j = sg.get_local_id()[0]; j < n; j += w) {
         // load a[i*n+j+1:16] before updating a[i*n+j:16]
         // to preserve loop-carried forward dependency
         auto va = a[i * n + j + 1];
         group_barrier(sg);
         a[i * n + j] = va + i + 2;
       }
       group_barrier(sg);
     })
    .wait();
```

***Figure 16-12.** Using a sub-group to vectorize a loop with a forward dependence*

The kernel is vectorized (with a vector length of *8* as an illustration), and its SIMD execution is shown in Figure 16-13. A work-group is formed with a group size of (1, 8), and the loop iterations inside the kernel are distributed over these sub-group work-items and executed with eight-way SIMD parallelism.

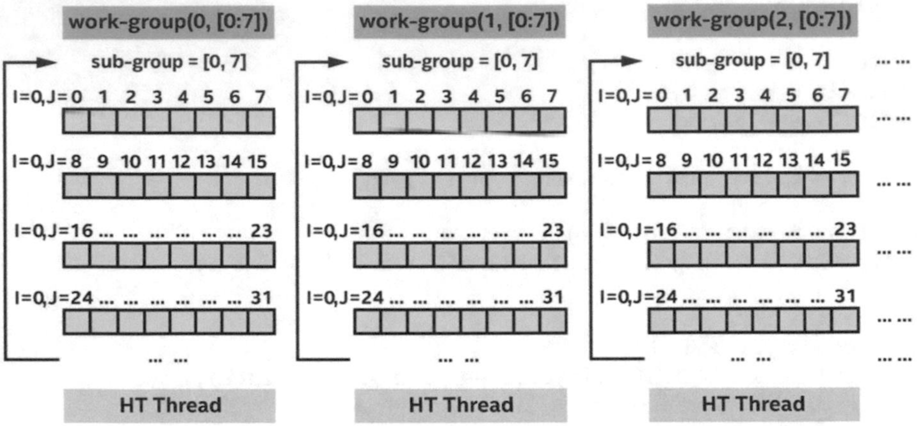

Figure 16-13. *SIMD vectorization for a loop with a forward dependence*

In this example, if the loop in the kernel dominates the performance, allowing SIMD vectorization across the sub-group will result in a significant performance improvement.

The use of SIMD instructions that process data elements in parallel is one way to let the performance of the kernel scale beyond the number of CPU cores and hardware threads.

SIMD Masking and Cost

In real applications, we can expect conditional statements such as an `if` statement, conditional expressions such as `a = b > a? a: b`, loops with a variable number of iterations, `switch` statements, and so on. Anything that is conditional may lead to scalar control flows not executing the same code paths and just like on a GPU (Chapter 15) can lead to decreased performance. A SIMD mask is a set of bits with the value `1` or `0`, which is generated from conditional statements in a kernel. Consider an example with `A={1, 2, 3, 4}`, `B={3, 7, 8, 1}` and the comparison expression `a < b`. The comparison returns a mask with four values `{1, 1, 1, 0}` that can be stored in a hardware mask register, to dictate which lanes of later SIMD instructions should execute the code that was guarded (enabled) by the comparison.

If a kernel contains conditional code, it is vectorized with masked instructions that are executed based on the mask bits associated with each data element (lane in the SIMD instruction). The mask bit for each data element is the corresponding bit in a mask register.

Using masking may result in lower performance than corresponding non-masked code. This may be caused by

- An additional mask blend operation on each load
- Dependence on the destination

Masking has a cost, so use it only when necessary. When a kernel is an ND-range kernel with explicit groupings of work-items in the execution range, care should be taken when choosing an ND-range work-group size to maximize SIMD efficiency by minimizing masking cost. When a work-group size is not evenly divisible by a processor's SIMD width, part of the work-group may execute with masking for the kernel.

Figure 16-14 shows how using merge masking creates a dependence on the destination register:

- With no masking, the processor executes two multiplies (`vmulps`) per cycle.
- With merge masking, the processor executes two multiplies every four cycles as the multiply instruction (`vmulps`) preserves results in the destination register as shown in Figure 16-17.
- Zero masking doesn't have a dependence on the destination register and therefore can execute two multiplies (`vmulps`) per cycle.

No Masking	Merge Masking	Zero Masking
vmulps zmm0, zmm6, zmm8 vmulps zmm1, zmm7, zmm8	vmulps zmm0{k1}, zmm6, zmm8 vmulps zmm1{k1}, zmm7, zmm8	vmulps zmm0{k1}{z}, zmm6, zmm8 vmulps zmm1{k1}{z}, zmm7, zmm8
Baseline	Slowdown 4x	Slowdown 1x

***Figure 16-14.** Three masking code generations for masking in kernel*

Accessing cache-aligned data gives better performance than accessing nonaligned data. In many cases, the address is not known at compile time or is known and not aligned. When working with loops, a peeling on memory accesses may be implemented, to process the first few elements using masked accesses, up to the first aligned address, and then to process unmasked accesses followed by a masked remainder, through multiversioning techniques. This method increases code size, but improves data processing overall. When working with parallel kernels, we as programmers can improve performance by employing similar techniques by hand, or by ensuring that allocations are appropriately aligned to improve performance.

Avoid Array of Struct for SIMD Efficiency

AOS (Array-of-Struct) structures lead to gathers and scatters, which can both impact SIMD efficiency and introduce extra bandwidth and latency for memory accesses. The presence of a hardware gather–scatter mechanism does not eliminate the need for this transformation—gather-scatter accesses commonly need significantly higher bandwidth and latency than contiguous loads. Given an AOS data layout of `struct {float x; float y; float z; float w;} a[4]`, consider a kernel operating on it as shown in Figure 16-15.

```
cgh.parallel_for<class aos<T>>(numOfItems,[=](id<1> wi) {
  x[wi] = a[wi].x;  // lead to gather x0, x1, x2, x3
  y[wi] = a[wi].y;  // lead to gather y0, y1, y2, y3
  z[wi] = a[wi].z;  // lead to gather z0, z1, z2, z3
  w[wi] = a[wi].w;  // lead to gather w0, w1, w2, w3
});
```

***Figure 16-15.** SIMD gather in a kernel*

When the compiler vectorizes the kernel along a set of work-items, it leads to SIMD gather instruction generation due to the need for non-unit-stride memory accesses. For example, the stride of `a[0].x`, `a[1].x`, `a[2].x`, and `a[3].x` is 4, not a more efficient unit-stride of 1.

w_3	z_3	y_3	x_3	w_2	z_2	y_2	x_2	w_1	z_1	y_1	x_1	w_0	z_0	y_0	x_0

In a kernel, we can often achieve a higher SIMD efficiency by eliminating the use of memory gather–scatter operations. Some code benefits from a data layout change that converts data structures written in an Array-of-Struct (AOS) representation to a Structure-of-Arrays (SOA) representation, that is, having separate arrays for each structure field to keep memory accesses contiguous when SIMD vectorization is performed. For example, consider a SOA data layout of `struct {float x[4]; float y[4]; float z[4]; float w[4];} a;` as shown here:

w_3	w_2	w_1	w_0	z_3	z_2	z_1	z_0	y_3	y_2	y_1	y_0	x_3	x_2	x_1	x_0

A kernel can operate on the data with unit-stride (contiguous) vector loads and stores as shown in Figure 16-16, even when vectorized!

```
cgh.parallel_for<class aos<T>>(numOfItems,[=](id<1> wi) {
  x[wi] = a.x[wi];  // lead to unit-stride vector load x[0:4]
  y[wi] = a.y[wi];  // lead to unit-stride vector load y[0:4]
  z[wi] = a.z[wi];  // lead to unit-stride vector load z[0:4]
  w[wi] = a.w[wi];  // lead to unit-stride vector load w[0:4]
});
```

Figure 16-16. *SIMD unit-stride vector load in a kernel*

The SOA data layout helps prevent gathers when accessing one field of the structure across the array elements and helps the compiler to vectorize kernels over the contiguous array elements associated with work-items. Note that such AOS-to-SOA or AOSOA data layout transformations are expected to be done at the program level (by us) considering all the places where those data structures are used. Doing it at just a loop level will involve costly transformations between the formats before and after the loop. However, we may also rely on the compiler to perform vector-load-and-shuffle optimizations for AOS data layouts with some cost. When a member of SOA (or AOS) data layout has a vector type, compiler vectorization may perform either horizontal expansion or vertical expansion based on underlying hardware to generate optimal code.

Data Type Impact on SIMD Efficiency

C++ programmers often use integer data types whenever they know that the data fits into a 32-bit signed type, often leading to code such as

```
int id = get_global_id(0); a[id] = b[id] + c[id];
```

However, given that the return type of the `get_global_id(0)` is `size_t` *(unsigned integer, often 64-bit)*, the conversion may reduce the optimization that a compiler can legally perform. This can then lead to SIMD gather/scatter instructions when the compiler vectorizes the code in the kernel, for example:

- Read of a[get_global_id(0)] may lead to a SIMD unit-stride vector load.
- Read of a[(int)get_global_id(0)] may lead to a non-unit-stride gather instruction.

This nuanced situation is introduced by the wraparound behavior (unspecified behavior and/or well-defined wraparound behavior in C++ standards) of data type conversion from size_t to int (or uint), which is mostly a historical artifact from the evolution of C-based languages. Specifically, overflow across some conversions is undefined behavior, which allows the compiler to assume that such conditions never happen and to optimize more aggressively. Figure 16-17 shows some examples for those wanting to understand the details.

get_global_id(0)	a[(int)get_global_id(0)]	get_global_id(0)	a((uint)get_global_id(0)]
0x7FFFFFFE	a[MAX_INT-1]	0xFFFFFFFE	a[MAX_UINT-1]
0x7FFFFFFF	a[MAX_INT (big positive)]	0xFFFFFFFF	a[MAX_UINT]
0x80000000	a[MIN_INT (big negative)]	0x100000000	a[0]
0x80000001	a[MIN_INT+1]	0x100000001	a[1]

Figure 16-17. *Examples of integer `type` `value` wraparound*

SIMD gather/scatter instructions are slower than SIMD unit-stride vector load/store operations. To achieve an optimal SIMD efficiency, avoiding gathers/scatters can be critical for an application regardless of which programming language is used.

Most SYCL get_*_id() family functions have the same detail, although many cases fit within MAX_INT because the possible return values are bounded (e.g., the maximum id within a work-group). Thus, whenever legal, SYCL compilers can assume unit-stride memory addresses across the chunk of neighboring work-items to avoid gathers/scatters. For cases that the compiler can't safely generate linear unit-stride vector memory loads/stores because of possible overflow from the value of global IDs and/or derivative value from global IDs, the compiler will generate gathers/scatters.

Under the philosophy of delivering optimal performance for users, the DPC++ compiler assumes no overflow, and captures the reality almost all of the time in practice, so the compiler can generate optimal SIMD code to achieve good performance. However, a compiler option `-fno-sycl-id-queries-fit-in-int` is provided by the DPC++ compiler for us to tell the compiler that there will be an overflow and that vectorized accesses derived from the id queries may not be safe. This can have large performance impact and should be used whenever unsafe to assume no overflow. The key takeaway is that a programmer should ensure the value of global ID fit in 32-bit int. Otherwise, the compiler option `-fno-sycl-id-queries-fit-in-int` should be used to guarantee program correctness, which may result in a lower performance.

SIMD Execution Using `single_task`

Under a single-task execution model, there are no work-items to vectorize over. Optimizations related to the vector types and functions may be possible, but this will depend on the compiler. The compiler and runtime are given a freedom either to enable explicit SIMD execution or to choose scalar execution within the `single_task` kernel, and the result will depend on the compiler implementation.

C++ compilers may map vector types occurring inside of a `single_task` to SIMD instructions when compiling to CPU. The vec load, store, and swizzle functions perform operations directly on vector variables, informing the compiler that data elements are accessing contiguous data starting from the same (uniform) location in memory and enabling us to request optimized loads/stores of contiguous data. As discussed in

Chapter 11, this interpretation of vec is valid—however, we should expect this functionality to be deprecated, eventually, in favor of a more explicit vector type (e.g., `std::simd`) once available.

```
queue q;

bool *resArray = malloc_shared<bool>(1, q);
resArray[0] = true;

q.single_task([=]() {
   sycl::vec<int, 4> old_v =
       sycl::vec<int, 4>(0, 100, 200, 300);
   sycl::vec<int, 4> new_v = sycl::vec<int, 4>();

   new_v.rgba() = old_v.abgr();
   int vals[] = {300, 200, 100, 0};

   if (new_v.r() != vals[0] || new_v.g() != vals[1] ||
       new_v.b() != vals[2] || new_v.a() != vals[3]) {
     resArray[0] = false;
   }
 }).wait();
```

Figure 16-18. *Using vector types and swizzle operations in the `single_task` kernel*

In the example shown in Figure 16-18, under single-task execution, a vector with three data elements is declared. A swizzle operation is performed with `old_v.abgr()`. If a CPU provides SIMD hardware instructions for some swizzle operations, we may achieve some performance benefits of using swizzle operations in applications.

SIMD VECTORIZATION GUIDELINES

CPU processors implement SIMD instruction sets with different SIMD widths. In many cases, this is an implementation detail and is transparent to the application executing kernels on the CPU, as the compiler can determine an efficient group of data elements to process with a specific SIMD size rather than requiring us to use the SIMD instructions explicitly. Sub-groups may be used to more directly express cases where the grouping of data elements should be subject to SIMD execution in kernels.

Given computational complexity, selecting the code and data layouts that are most amenable to vectorization may ultimately result in higher performance. While selecting data structures, try to choose a data layout, alignment, and data width such that the most frequently executed calculation can access memory in a SIMD-friendly manner with maximum parallelism, as described in this chapter.

Summary

To get the most out of thread-level parallelism and SIMD vector-level parallelism on CPUs, we need to keep the following goals in mind:

- Be familiar with all types of SYCL parallelism and the underlying CPU architectures that we wish to target.
- Exploit the right amount of parallelism—not more and not less—at a thread level that best matches hardware resources. Use vendor tooling, such as analyzers and profilers, to help guide our tuning work to achieve this.
- Be mindful of thread affinity and memory first touch impact on program performance.
- Design data structures with a data layout, alignment, and data width such that the most frequently executed calculations can access memory in a SIMD-friendly manner with maximum SIMD parallelism.
- Be mindful of balancing the cost of masking vs. code branches.

- Use a clear programming style that minimizes potential memory aliasing and side effects.
- Be aware of the scalability limitations of using vector types and interfaces. If a compiler implementation maps them to hardware SIMD instructions, a fixed vector size may not match the SIMD width of SIMD registers well across multiple generations of CPUs and CPUs from different vendors.

CHAPTER 17

Programming for FPGAs

Kernel-based programming originally became popular as a way to access GPUs. Since it has now been generalized across many types of accelerators, it is important to understand how our style of programming affects the mapping of code to an FPGA as well.

Field-programmable gate arrays (FPGAs) are unfamiliar to the majority of software developers, in part because most desktop computers don't include an FPGA alongside the typical CPU and GPU. But FPGAs *are* worth knowing about because they offer advantages in many applications. The same questions need to be asked as we would of other accelerators, such as "When should I use an FPGA?", "What parts of my applications should be offloaded to FPGA?", and "How do I write code that performs well on an FPGA?"

This chapter gives us the knowledge to start answering those questions, at least to the point where we can decide whether an FPGA is interesting for our applications, and to know which constructs are commonly used to achieve performance. This chapter is the launching point from which we can then read vendor documentation to fill in details for specific products and toolchains. We begin with an overview of how programs can map to spatial architectures such as FPGAs, followed by discussion of some properties that make FPGAs a good choice as an accelerator, and we finish by introducing the programming constructs used to achieve performance.

J. Reinders et al., *Data Parallel C++*, https://doi.org/10.1007/978-1-4842-9691-2_17

The "How to Think About FPGAs" section in this chapter is applicable to thinking about any FPGA. SYCL allows vendors to specify devices beyond CPUs and GPUs but does not specifically say how to support an FPGA. The specific vendor support for FPGAs described in this chapter is currently unique to DPC++, namely, FPGA selectors and pipes. FPGA selectors and pipes are the only DPC++ extensions used in this chapter. It is hoped that vendors will converge on similar or compatible means of supporting FPGAs, and this is encouraged by DPC++ as an open source project.

Performance Caveats

As with any processor or accelerator, FPGA devices differ from vendor to vendor or even from product generation to product generation; therefore, best practices for one device may not be best practices for a different device. The advice in this chapter is likely to benefit many FPGA devices, both now and in the future, however...

...to achieve optimal performance for a particular FPGA, always consult the vendor's documentation!

How to Think About FPGAs

FPGAs are commonly classified as a *spatial* architecture. They benefit from very different coding styles and forms of parallelism than devices that use an Instruction Set Architecture (ISA), including CPUs and GPUs, which are more familiar to most people. To get started forming an understanding of FPGAs, we'll briefly cover some ideas from ISA-based accelerators, so that we can highlight key differences.

For our purposes, an ISA-based accelerator is one where the device can execute many different instructions, one or a few at a time. The instructions are usually relatively primitive such as "load from memory at address A" or "add the following numbers." A chain of operations is strung together to form a program, and the processor conceptually executes one instruction after the other.

In an ISA-based accelerator, a single region of a chip (or the entire chip) executes a different instruction from the program in each clock cycle. The instructions execute on a fixed hardware architecture that can run different instructions at different times, such as shown in Figure 17-1. For example, the memory load unit feeding an addition is probably the same memory load unit used to feed a subtraction. Similarly, the same arithmetic unit is probably used to execute both the addition and subtraction instructions. Hardware on the chip is *reused* by different instructions as the program executes over time.

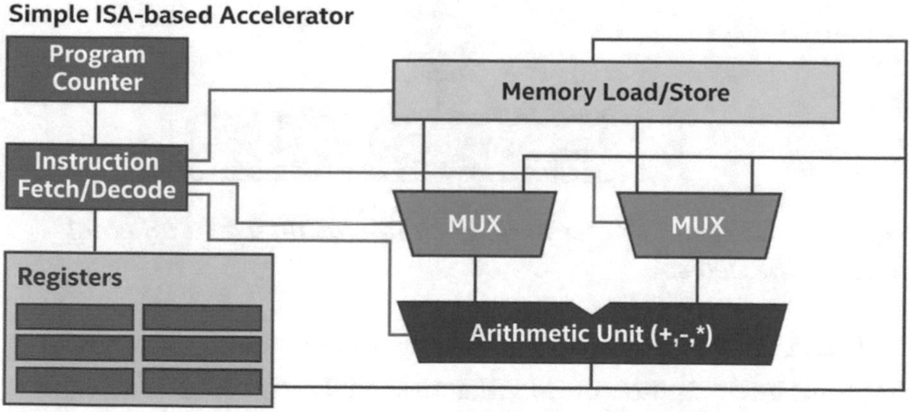

Figure 17-1. *Simple ISA-based (temporal) processing: reuses hardware (regions) over time*

Spatial architectures are different. Instead of being based around a machine that executes a variety of instructions on shared hardware, they start from the opposite perspective. Spatial implementations of a program conceptually take the entire program as a whole and lay it down *at once* on the device. Different regions of the device implement different instructions in the program. This is in many ways the opposite perspective from sharing hardware between instructions over time (e.g., ISA)—in spatial architectures, each instruction receives its own dedicated hardware that can execute simultaneously (same clock cycle) as the hardware implementing the other instructions. Figure 17-2 shows this idea which is a spatial implementation of an entire program (a very simple program in this example).

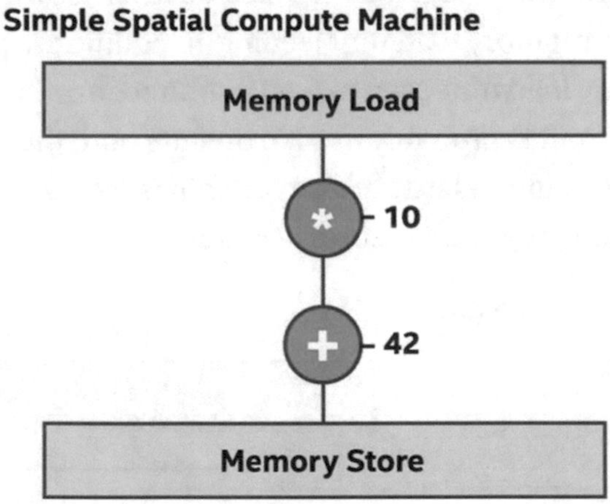

Figure 17-2. *Spatial processing: Each operation uses a different region of the device*

This description of a spatial implementation of a program is overly simplistic, but it captures the idea that in spatial architectures, different parts of the program execute on *different* parts of the device, as opposed to being issued over time to a shared set of more general-purpose hardware.

With different regions of an FPGA programmed to perform distinct operations, some of the hardware typically associated with ISA-based accelerators is unnecessary. For example, Figure 17-2 shows that we no longer need an instruction fetch or decode unit, program counter, or register file. Instead of storing data for future instructions in a register file, spatial architectures connect the output of one instruction to the input of the next, which is why spatial architectures are often called *data flow* architectures.

A few obvious questions arise from the mapping to FPGA that we've introduced. First, since each instruction in the program occupies some percentage of the spatial area of the device, what happens if the program requires more than 100% of the area? Some solutions provide resource sharing mechanisms to enable larger programs to fit at a performance cost, but FPGAs do have the concept of a program *fitting*. This is both an advantage and a disadvantage:

- **The benefit**: If a program uses most of the area on the FPGA and there is sufficient work to keep all of the hardware busy every clock cycle, then executing a program on the device can be incredibly efficient because of the extreme parallelism. More general architectures may have significant unused hardware per clock cycle, whereas with an FPGA, the use of area can be perfectly tailored to a specific application without waste. This customization can allow applications to run faster through massive parallelism, usually with compelling energy efficiency.
- **The downside**: Large programs may have to be tuned and restructured to fit on a device. Resource sharing features of compilers can help to address this, but usually with some degradation in performance that reduces the benefit of using an FPGA. ISA-based accelerators are very efficient resource sharing implementations—FPGAs prove most valuable for compute primarily when an application can be architected to utilize most of the available area.

Taken to the extreme, resource sharing solutions on an FPGA lead to an architecture that looks like an ISA-based accelerator, but that is built in reconfigurable logic instead being optimized in fixed silicon. The reconfigurable logic leads to overhead relative to a fixed silicon design—therefore, FPGAs are not typically chosen as ways to implement ISAs. FPGAs are of prime benefit when an application is able to utilize the resources to implement efficient data flow algorithms more directly, which we cover in the coming sections.

Pipeline Parallelism

Another question that often arises from Figure 17-2 is how the spatial implementation of a program relates to a clock frequency and how quickly a program will execute from start to finish. In the example shown, it's easy to believe that data could be loaded from memory, have multiplication and addition operations performed, and have the result stored back into memory, quite quickly. As the program becomes larger, potentially with tens of thousands of operations across the FPGA device, it becomes apparent that for all of the instructions to operate one after the other (operations often depend on results produced by previous operations), it might take significant time given the processing delays introduced by each operation.

Intermediate results between operations are updated (propagated) over time in a spatial architecture as shown in Figure 17-3. For example, the load executes and then passes its result into the multiplier, whose result is then passed into the adder and so on. After some amount of time, the intermediate data has propagated all the way to the end of the chain of operations, and the final result is available or stored to memory.

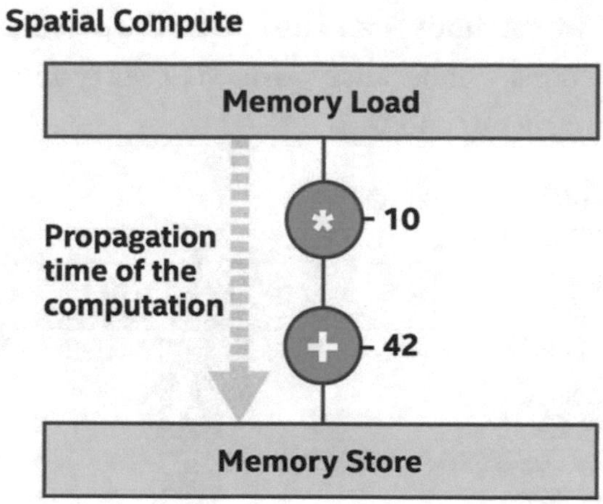

Figure 17-3. *Propagation time of a naïve spatial compute implementation*

A spatial implementation as shown in Figure 17-3 is quite inefficient, because most of the hardware is only doing useful work a small percentage of the time. Most of the time, an operation such as the multiply is either waiting for new data from the load or holding its output so that operations later in the chain can use its result. Most spatial compilers and implementations address this inefficiency by *pipelining*, which means that execution of a single program is spread across many clock cycles. This is achieved by inserting registers (a data storage primitive in the hardware) between some operations, where each register holds a binary value for the duration of a clock cycle. By holding the result of an operation's output so that the next operation in the chain can see and operate on that held value, the previous operation is free to work on a different computation without impacting the input to following operations.

The goal of algorithmic pipelining is to keep every operation (hardware unit) busy for the majority of every clock cycle. Figure 17-4 shows a pipelined implementation of the previous simple example. Keep in mind that the compiler does all of this pipelining and balancing for us! We cover this topic so that we can understand how to fill the pipeline with work in the coming sections, not because we need to worry about manually pipelining anything in our code.

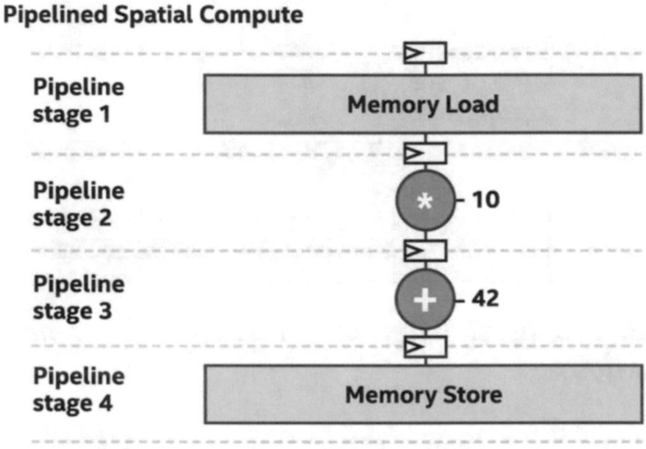

Figure 17-4. *Pipelining of a computation: Stages execute in parallel*

When a spatial implementation is pipelined, it becomes extremely efficient in the same way as a factory assembly line. Each pipeline stage performs only a small amount of the overall work, but it does so quickly and then begins to work on the next unit of work immediately afterward. It takes many clock cycles for a *single* computation to be processed by the pipeline, from start to finish, but the pipeline can compute *many* different instances of the computation on different data simultaneously.

When enough work starts executing in the pipeline, over enough consecutive clock cycles, then every single pipeline stage and therefore operation in the program can perform useful work during every clock cycle, meaning that the entire spatial device performs work simultaneously. This is one of the powers of spatial architectures—the entire device can execute work in parallel, all of the time. We call this *pipeline parallelism*.

Pipeline parallelism is the primary form of parallelism exploited on FPGAs to achieve performance.

PIPELINING IS AUTOMATIC

In the DPC++ implementation of SYCL for FPGAs, and in other high-level programming solutions for FPGAs, the pipelining of an algorithm is performed automatically by the compiler. It is useful to roughly understand the implementation on spatial architectures, as described in this section, because then it becomes easier to structure applications to take advantage of the pipeline parallelism. It should be made clear that pipeline register insertion and balancing is performed by the compiler and not manually by developers.

Real programs and algorithms often have control flow (e.g., if/else structures) that leaves some parts of the program inactive a certain percentage of the clock cycles. FPGA compilers typically perform optimizations that allow both sides of a branch to share the same hardware resources when it is possible, to minimize wasted spatial area and to maximize compute efficiency during control flow divergence. This makes control flow divergence much less expensive and less of a development concern than on other, especially vectorized architectures.

Kernels Consume Chip "Area"

In existing implementations, each kernel in a SYCL application generates a spatial pipeline that consumes some resources of the FPGA (we can think about this as *space* or *area* on the device), which is conceptually shown in Figure 17-5.

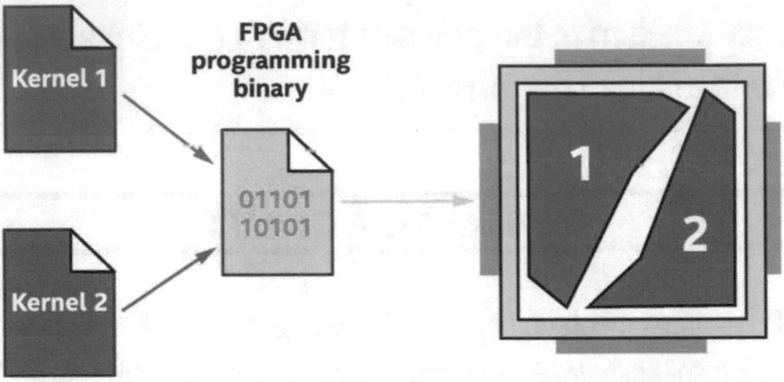

Figure 17-5. *Multiple kernels in the same FPGA binary: Kernels can run concurrently*

Since a kernel uses its own area on the device, different kernels can execute concurrently. If one kernel is waiting for something such as a memory access, other kernels on the FPGA can continue executing because they are independent pipelines elsewhere on the chip. This idea, more formally described as independent forward progress across kernels, is a critical property of FPGA spatial compute.

When to Use an FPGA

Like any accelerator architecture, predicting when an FPGA is the right choice of accelerator vs. an alternative often comes down to knowledge of the architecture, the application characteristics, and the system bottlenecks. This section describes some of the characteristics of an application to consider.

Lots and Lots of Work

Like most modern compute accelerators, achieving good performance requires a large amount of work to be performed. If computing a single result from a single element of data, then it may not be useful to leverage an accelerator at all (of any kind). This is no different with FPGAs. Knowing that FPGA compilers leverage pipeline parallelism makes this more apparent. A pipelined implementation of an algorithm has many stages, often thousands or more, each of which should have different work within it in any clock cycle. If there isn't enough work to occupy most of the pipeline stages most of the time, then efficiency will be low. We'll call the average utilization of pipeline stages over time *occupancy* of the pipeline. This is different from the definition of occupancy used when optimizing other architectures such as GPUs!

There are multiple ways to generate work on an FPGA to fill the pipeline stages, which we'll cover in coming sections.

Custom Operations or Operation Widths

FPGAs were originally designed to perform efficient integer and bitwise operations and to act as glue logic that could adapt interfaces of other chips to work with each other. Although FPGAs have evolved into computational powerhouses instead of just glue logic solutions, they are still very efficient at bitwise operations, integer math operations on custom data widths or types, and operations on arbitrary bit fields in packet headers, for example.

The fine-grained architecture of an FPGA, described at the end of this chapter, means that novel and arbitrary data types can be efficiently implemented. For example, if we need a 33-bit integer multiplier or a 129-bit adder, FPGAs can provide these custom operations with great efficiency. Because of this flexibility, FPGAs are commonly employed in rapidly evolving domains, such as recently in artificial intelligence, where the data widths and operations have been changing faster than can be built into ASICs.

Scalar Data Flow

An important aspect of FPGA spatial pipelines, apparent from Figure 17-4, is that the intermediate data between operations not only stays on-chip (is not stored to external memory), but that intermediate data between each pipeline stage has dedicated storage registers. FPGA parallelism often comes primarily from pipelining of computation such that many operations are being executed concurrently, each at a different stage of the pipeline. This results in scalar data flow being the common implementation (under the hood) even in arithmetically intense regions of a program and is fundamentally different from vector architectures where multiple computations are executed as lanes of a shared vector instruction.

The scalar nature of the parallelism in a spatial pipeline is important for many applications because it still applies even with tight data dependences across the units of work. These data dependences can be handled without loss of performance, as we will discuss later in this chapter when talking about loop-carried dependences. The result is that spatial pipelines, and therefore FPGAs, are a compelling architecture to target for algorithms where data dependences across units of work (such as work-items) can't be broken and fine-grained communication must occur. Many optimization techniques for other accelerators focus on breaking these dependences through various complex approaches or managing communication at controlled scales through features such as sub-groups. FPGAs can instead perform well with communication through tight dependences and should be on your mind when working with classes of algorithms where such patterns exist.

LOOPS ARE FINE!

A common misconception on data flow architectures is that loops with either fixed or dynamic iteration counts lead to poor data flow performance because they aren't simple feed-forward pipelines. At least with the Intel

FPGA toolchains, this is not true. Loop iterations can instead be a good way to produce high occupancy within the pipeline, and the compilers are built around the concept of allowing multiple loop iterations to execute in an overlapped way. Loops provide an easy mechanism to keep the pipeline busy with work!

Low Latency and Rich Connectivity

More conventional uses of FPGAs which take advantage of the rich input and output transceivers on the devices apply equally well for developers using SYCL. For example, as shown in Figure 17-6, some FPGA accelerator cards have network interfaces that make it possible to stream data directly into the device, process it, and then stream the result directly back to the network. Such systems are often sought when processing latency needs to be minimized and where processing through operating system network stacks is too slow or needs to be offloaded to free CPU processing cycles.

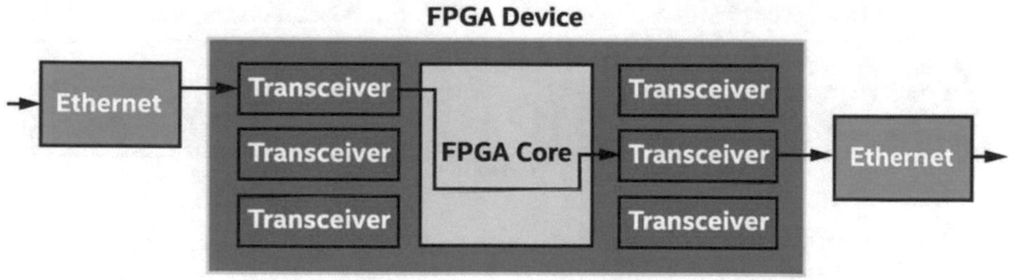

***Figure 17-6.** Low-latency I/O streaming: FPGA connects network data and computation tightly*

The opportunities are almost limitless when considering direct input/output through FPGA transceivers, but the options do come down to what is available on the circuit board that forms an accelerator. Because of the dependence on a specific accelerator card and variety of such uses, aside from describing the pipe language constructs in a coming section, this chapter doesn't dive into these applications. We should instead read the vendor documentation associated with a specific accelerator card or search for an accelerator card that matches our specific interface needs.

Customized Memory Systems

Memory systems on an FPGA, such as function private or work-group local memory, are built out of small blocks of on-chip memory. This is important because each memory system is custom built for the specific portion of an algorithm or kernel using it. FPGAs have significant on-chip memory bandwidth, and combined with the formation of custom memory systems, they can perform very well on applications that have atypical access patterns and structures. Figure 17-7 shows some of the optimizations that can be performed by the compiler when a memory system is implemented on an FPGA.

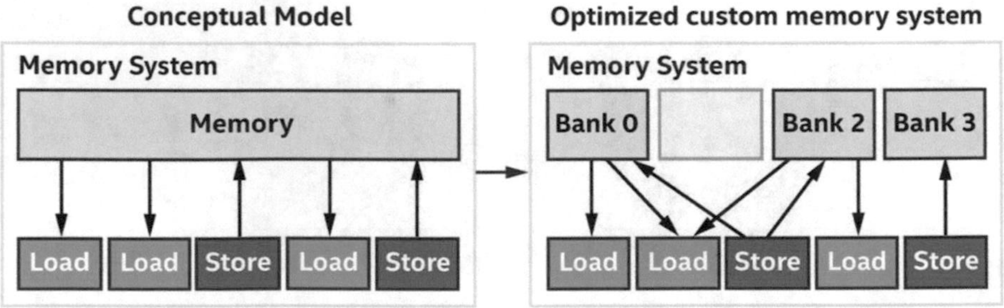

***Figure 17-7.** FPGA memory systems are customized by the compiler for our specific code*

Other architectures such as GPUs have fixed memory structures that are easy to reason about by experienced developers, but that can also be hard to optimize around in many cases. Many optimizations on other accelerators are focused on memory pattern modification to avoid bank conflicts, for example. If we have algorithms that would benefit from a custom memory structure, such as a different number of access ports per bank or an unusual number of banks, then FPGAs can offer immediate advantages. Conceptually, the difference is between writing code to use a fixed memory system efficiently (most other accelerators) vs. having the memory system custom designed by the compiler to be efficient with our specific code (FPGA).

Running on an FPGA

There are two steps to run a kernel on an FPGA (as with any ahead-of-time compilation accelerator):

- Compiling the source to a binary which can be run on our hardware of interest
- Selecting the correct accelerator that we are interested in at runtime

To compile kernels so that they can run on FPGA hardware, we can use the command line:

```
icpx -fsycl -fintelfpga my_source_code.cpp -Xshardware
```

This command tells the compiler to turn all kernels in `my_source_code.cpp` into binaries that can run on an Intel FPGA accelerator and then to package them within the host binary that is generated. When we execute the host binary (e.g., by running `./a.out` on Linux), the runtime will automatically program any attached FPGA as required, before executing the submitted kernels, as shown in Figure 17-8.

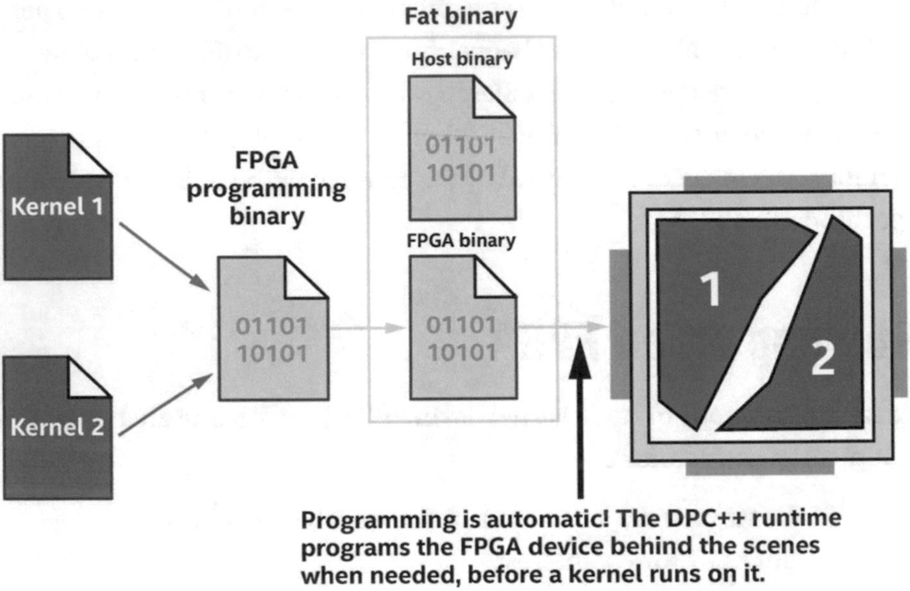

Figure 17-8. *FPGA programmed automatically at runtime*

FPGA programming binaries are embedded within the compiled DPC++ executable that we run on the host. The FPGA is automatically configured behind the scenes for us.

When we run a host program and submit the first kernel for execution on an FPGA, there might be a slight delay before the kernel begins executing, while the FPGA is programmed. Resubmitting kernels for additional executions won't see the same delay because the kernel is already programmed to the device and ready to run.

Selection of an FPGA device at runtime was covered in Chapter 2. We need to tell the host program where we want kernels to run because there are typically multiple accelerator options available, such as a CPU and GPU, in addition to the FPGA. To quickly recap one method to select an FPGA during program execution, we can use code like that in Figure 17-9.

```
#include <sycl/ext/intel/fpga_extensions.hpp>  // For fpga_selector_v
#include <sycl/sycl.hpp>
using namespace sycl;

void say_device(const queue& q) {
  std::cout << "Device : "
            << q.get_device().get_info<info::device::name>()
            << "\n";
}

int main() {
  queue q{ext::intel::fpga_selector_v};
  say_device(q);

  q.submit([&](handler& h) {
    h.parallel_for(1024, [=](auto idx) {
      // ...
    });
  });

  return 0;
}
```

Figure 17-9. *Choosing an FPGA device at runtime using the* `fpga_selector`

Compile Times

Rumors abound that compiling designs for an FPGA can take a long time, much longer than compiling for ISA-based accelerators. The rumors are true! The end of this chapter overviews the fine-grained architectural elements of an FPGA that lead to both the advantages of an FPGA and the computationally intensive compilation (place-and-route optimizations) that can take hours in some cases.

The compile time from source code to FPGA hardware execution is long enough that we don't want to develop and iterate on our code exclusively in hardware. FPGA development flows offer several stages that minimize the number of hardware compilations, to make us productive despite the hardware compile times. Figure 17-10 shows the typical stages, where most of our time is spent on the early steps that provide fast turnaround and rapid iteration.

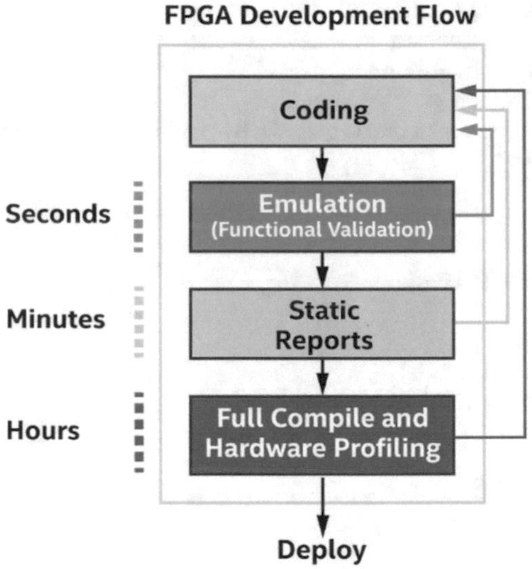

Figure 17-10. *Most verification and optimizations occur prior to lengthy hardware compilation*

Emulation and static reports from the compiler are the cornerstones of FPGA code development in DPC++. The emulator acts as if it was an FPGA, including supporting relevant extensions and emulating the execution model, but runs on the host processor. Compilation time is therefore the same as we would expect from compilation to a CPU device, although we won't see the performance boost that we would from execution on actual FPGA hardware. The emulator is great for establishing and testing functional correctness in an application.

Static reports, like emulation, are generated quickly by the toolchain. They report on the FPGA structures created by the compiler and on bottlenecks identified by the compiler. Both of these can be used to predict whether our design will achieve good performance when run on FPGA hardware and are used to optimize our code. Please read the vendor's documentation for information on the reports, which are often improved from release to release of a toolchain (see documentation for the latest and greatest features!). Extensive documentation is provided by vendors on how to interpret and optimize based on the reports. This information would be the topic of another book, so we can't dive into details in this single chapter.

The FPGA Emulator

Emulation is primarily used to functionally debug our application, to make sure that it behaves as expected and produces correct results. There is no reason to do this level of development on actual FPGA hardware where compile times are longer. The emulation flow is activated by removing the `-Xshardware` flag from the `icpx` compilation command and at the same time using `INTEL::fpga_emulator_selector_v` instead of `INTEL::fpga_selector_v` in our host code. We would compile using a command like

```
icpx -fsycl -fintelfpga my_source_code.cpp
```

By using `fpga_emulator_selector_v`, which uses the host processor to emulate an FPGA, we maintain a rapid development and debugging process before we have to commit to the lengthier compile for actual FPGA hardware. An example of using `INTEL::fpga_emulator_selector_v` instead of `INTEL::fpga_selector_v` is shown in Figure 17-11.

```
#include <sycl/ext/intel/fpga_extensions.hpp>  // For fpga_selector_v
#include <sycl/sycl.hpp>
using namespace sycl;

void say_device(const queue& q) {
  std::cout << "Device : "
            << q.get_device().get_info<info::device::name>()
            << "\n";
}

int main() {
  queue q{ext::intel::fpga_emulator_selector_v};
  say_device(q);

  q.submit([&](handler& h) {
    h.parallel_for(1024, [=](auto idx) {
      // ...
    });
  });

  return 0;
}
```

Figure 17-11. *Using `fpga_emulator_selector_v` for rapid development and debugging*

FPGA Hardware Compilation Occurs "Ahead-of-Time"

The *Full Compile and Hardware Profiling* stage in Figure 17-10 is an *ahead-of-time* compile in SYCL terminology. This means that the compilation of the kernel to a device binary occurs when we initially compile our program and not when the program is submitted to a device to be run. On an FPGA, this is particularly important because

- Compilation takes a length of time that we don't normally want to incur when running an application.
- DPC++ programs may be executed on systems that don't have a capable host processor. The compilation process to an FPGA binary benefits from a fast

processor with a good amount of attached memory. Ahead-of-time compilation lets us easily choose where the compile occurs, rather than having it run on systems where the program is deployed.

A LOT HAPPENS BEHIND THE SCENES WITH DPC++ ON AN FPGA!

Conventional FPGA design (not using a high-level language) can be very complicated. There are many steps beyond just writing our kernel, such as building and configuring the interfaces that communicate with off-chip memories and closing timing by inserting registers needed to make the compiled design run fast enough to communicate with certain peripherals. DPC++ solves all of this for us, so that we don't need to know anything about the details of conventional FPGA design to achieve working applications! The tooling treats our kernels as code to optimize and make efficient on the device and then automatically handles all of the details of talking to off-chip peripherals, closing timing, and setting up drivers for us.

Achieving peak performance on an FPGA still requires detailed knowledge of the architecture, just like any other accelerator, but the steps to move from code to a working design are much simpler and more productive with DPC++ than in traditional FPGA flows.

Writing Kernels for FPGAs

Once we have decided to use an FPGA for our application or even just decided to try one out, having an idea of how to write code to see good performance is important. This section highlights important concepts and covers a few topics that often cause confusion, to make getting started faster.

Exposing Parallelism

We have already looked at how pipeline parallelism is used to efficiently perform work on an FPGA. Another simple pipeline example is shown in Figure 17-12.

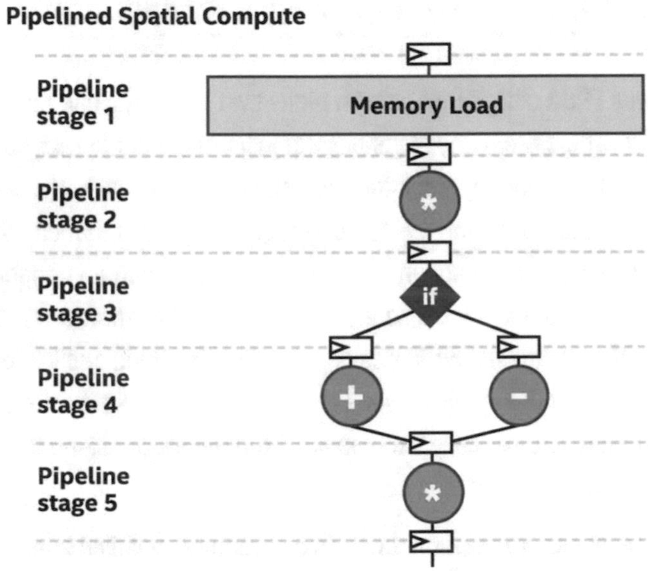

Figure 17-12. *Simple pipeline with five stages: six clock cycles to process an element of data*

In this pipeline, there are five stages. Data moves from one stage to the next once per clock cycle, so in this very simple example, it takes six clock cycles from when data enters into stage 1 until it exits from stage 5.

A major goal of pipelining is to enable multiple elements of data to be processed at different stages of the pipeline, simultaneously. To be sure that this is clear, Figure 17-13 shows a pipeline where there is not enough work (only one element of data in this case), which causes each pipeline stage to be unused during most of the clock cycles. This is an inefficient use of the FPGA resources because most of the hardware is idle most of the time.

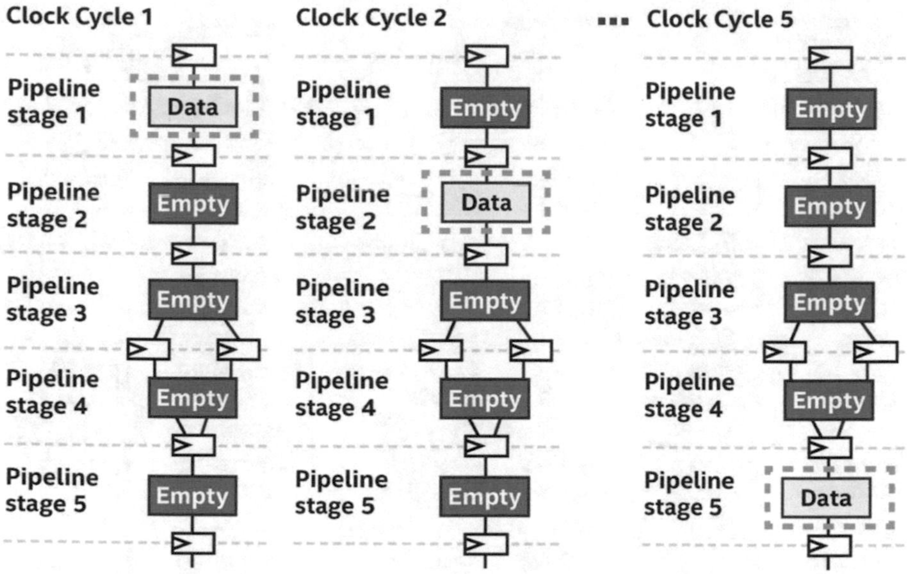

***Figure 17-13.** Pipeline stages are mostly unused if processing only a single element of work*

To keep the pipeline stages better occupied, it is useful to imagine a queue of un-started work waiting before the first stage, which *feeds* the pipeline. In each clock cycle, the pipeline can consume and start one more element of work from the queue, as shown in Figure 17-14. After some initial startup cycles, each stage of the pipeline is occupied and doing useful work every clock cycle, leading to efficient utilization of the FPGA resources.

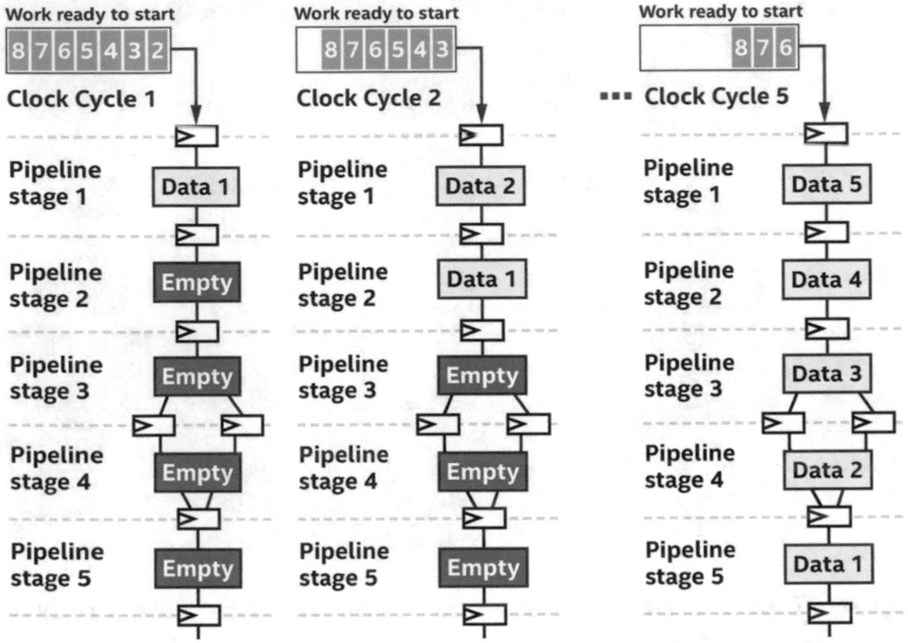

Figure 17-14. *Efficient utilization comes when each pipeline stage is kept busy*

The following two sections cover methods to keep the queue feeding the pipeline filled with work that is ready to start. We'll look at

1. ND-range kernels
2. Loops

Choosing between these options impacts how kernels that run on an FPGA should be fundamentally architected. In some cases, algorithms lend themselves well to one style or the other, and in other cases programmer preference and experience inform which method should be chosen.

Keeping the Pipeline Busy Using ND-Ranges

The ND-range hierarchical execution model was described in Chapter 4. Figure 17-15 illustrates the key concepts: an ND-range execution model where there is a hierarchical grouping of work-items, and where a work-item is the primitive unit of work that a kernel defines. This model was originally developed to enable efficient programming of GPUs where work-items may execute concurrently at various levels of the execution model hierarchy. To match the type of work that GPU hardware is efficient at, ND-range work-items do not frequently communicate with each other in most applications.

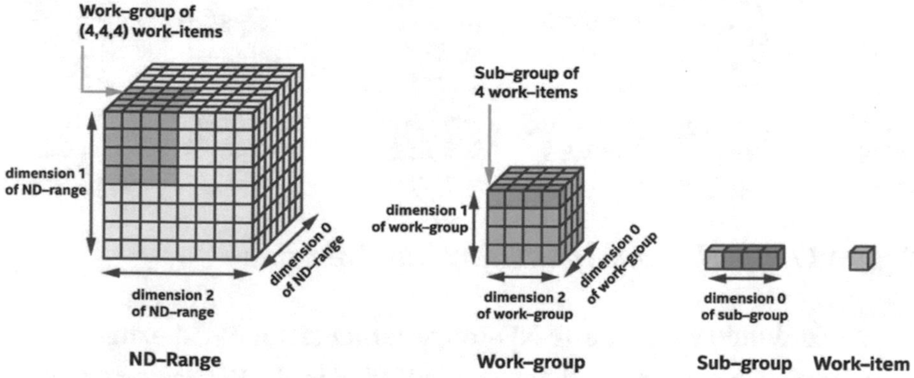

Figure 17-15. *ND-range execution model: a hierarchical grouping of work-items*

The FPGA spatial pipeline can be very efficiently filled with work using an ND-range. This programming style is fully supported on FPGA, and we can think of it as depicted in Figure 17-16 where on each clock cycle, a different work-item enters the first stage of the pipeline.

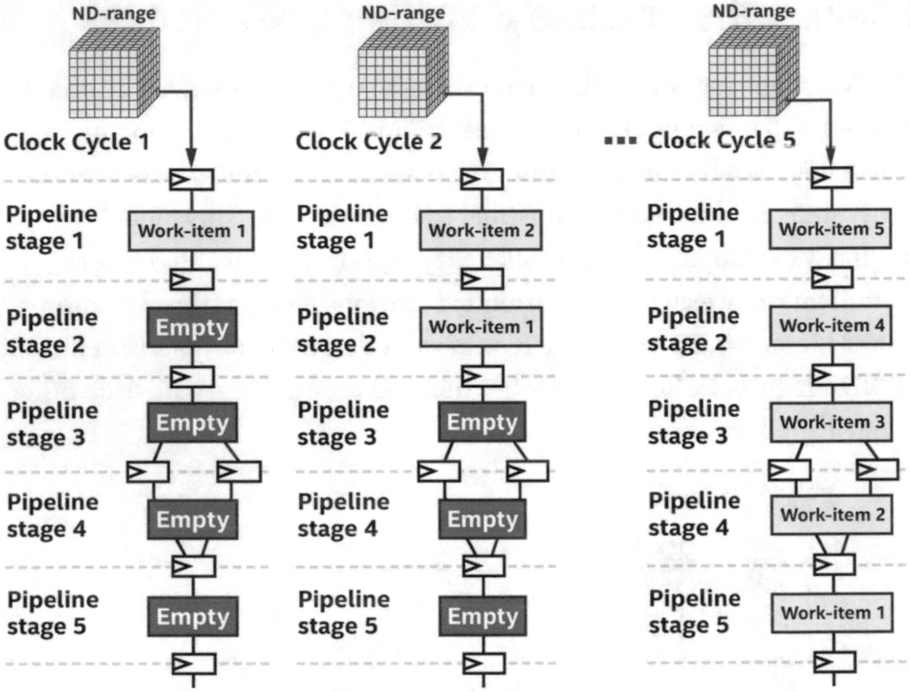

Figure 17-16. *ND-range feeding a spatial pipeline*

When should we create an ND-range kernel on an FPGA using work-items to keep the pipeline occupied? It's simple. Whenever we can structure our algorithm or application as independent work-items that don't need to communicate often (or ideally at all), we should use ND-range! If work-items do need to communicate often or if we don't naturally think in terms of ND-ranges, then loops (described in the next section) provide an efficient way to express our algorithm as well.

If we can structure our algorithm so that work-items don't need to communicate much (or at all), then ND-range is a great way to generate work to keep the spatial pipeline full!

A good example of a kernel that is efficient with an ND-range feeding the pipeline is a random number generator, with an algorithm where creation of numbers in the sequence is independent of the previous numbers generated.

Figure 17-17 shows an ND-range kernel that will call the random number generation function once for each work-item in the 16 × 16 × 16 range. Note how the random number generation function takes the work-item id as input.

```
h.parallel_for({16, 16, 16}, [=](auto I) {
  output[I] = generate_random_number_from_ID(I);
});
```

Figure 17-17. *Multiple work-item (16 × 16 × 16) invocation of a random number generator*

The example shows a `parallel_for` invocation that uses a `range`, with only a global size specified. We can alternately use the `parallel_for` invocation style that takes an `nd_range`, where both the global work size and local work-group sizes are specified. FPGAs can very efficiently implement work-group local memory from on-chip resources, so feel free to use work-groups whenever they make sense, either because we want work-group local memory or because having work-group IDs available simplifies our code.

PARALLEL RANDOM NUMBER GENERATORS

The example in Figure 17-17 assumes that generate_random_number_from_ID(I) is a random number generator which has been written to be safe and correct when invoked in a parallel way. For example, if different work-items in the parallel_for range execute the function, we expect different sequences to be created by each work-item, with each sequence adhering to whatever distribution is expected from the generator. Parallel random number generators are themselves a complex topic, so it is a good idea to use libraries or to learn about the topic through techniques such as block skip-ahead algorithms.

Pipelines Do Not Mind Data Dependences!

One of the challenges when programming vector architectures (e.g., GPUs) where some work-items execute together as lanes of vector instructions is structuring an algorithm to be efficient without extensive communication between work-items. Some algorithms and applications lend themselves well to vector hardware, and some don't. A common cause of a poor mapping is an algorithmic need for extensive sharing of data, due to data dependences with other computations that are in some sense neighbors. Sub-groups address some of this challenge on vector architectures by providing efficient communication between work-items in the same sub-group, as described in Chapter 14.

FPGAs play an important role for algorithms that can't be decomposed into independent work. FPGA spatial pipelines are not vectorized across work-items, but instead execute consecutive work-items across pipeline stages. This implementation of the parallelism means that fine-grained communication between work-items (even those in different work-groups) *can* be implemented easily and efficiently within the spatial pipeline!

One example is a random number generator where output N+1 depends on knowing what output N was. This creates a data dependence between two outputs, and if each output is generated by a work-item in an ND-range, then there is a data dependence between work-items that can require complex and often costly synchronization on some architectures. When coding such algorithms serially, one would typically write a loop, where iteration N+1 uses the computation from iteration N, such as shown in Figure 17-18. Each iteration depends on the state computed by the previous iteration. This is a very common pattern.

```
int state = 0;
for (int i = 0; i < size; i++) {
  state = generate_random_number(state);
  output[i] = state;
}
```

Figure 17-18. *Loop-carried data dependence (`state`)*

Spatial implementations can very efficiently communicate results backward in the pipeline to work that started in a later cycle (i.e., to work at an earlier stage in the pipeline), and spatial compilers implement many optimizations around this pattern. Figure 17-19 shows the idea of backward communication of data, from stage 5 to stage 4. Spatial pipelines are not vectorized across work-items. This enables efficient data dependence communication by passing results backward in the pipeline!

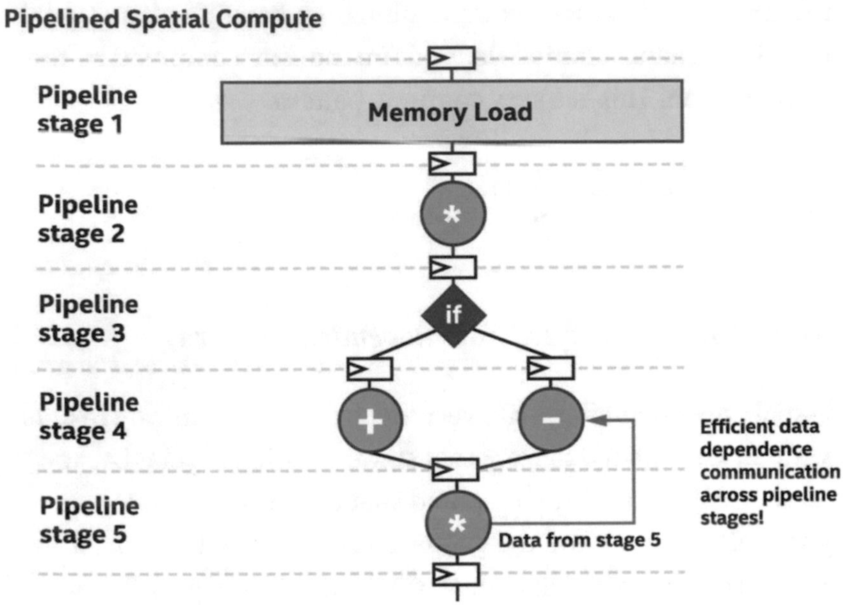

Figure 17-19. *Backward communication enables efficient data dependence communication*

The ability to pass data backward (to an earlier stage in the pipeline) is key to spatial architectures, but it isn't obvious how to write code that takes advantage of it. There are two approaches that make expressing this pattern easy:

1. Loops

2. Intra-kernel pipes with ND-range kernels

The second option is based on pipes that we describe later in this chapter, but it isn't nearly as common as loops so we mention it for completeness, but don't detail it here. Vendor documentation provides more details on the pipe approach, but it's easier to stick to loops which are described next unless there is a reason to do otherwise.

Spatial Pipeline Implementation of a Loop

A loop is a natural fit when programming an algorithm that has data dependences. Loops frequently express dependences across iterations, even in the most basic loop examples where the counter that determines when the loop should exit is carried across iterations (variable `i` in Figure 17-20).

```
int a = 0;
for (int i = 0; i < size; i++) {
  a = a + i;
}
```

Figure 17-20. *Loop with two loop-carried dependences (i.e., `i` and `a`)*

In the simple loop of Figure 17-20, it is understood that the value of `a`, which is on the right-hand side of `a= a + i`, reflects the value stored by the previous loop iteration or the initial value if it's the first iteration of the loop. When a spatial compiler implements a loop, iterations of the loop can be used to fill the stages of the pipeline as shown in Figure 17-21. Notice that the queue of work, which is ready to start, now contains loop iterations, not work-items!

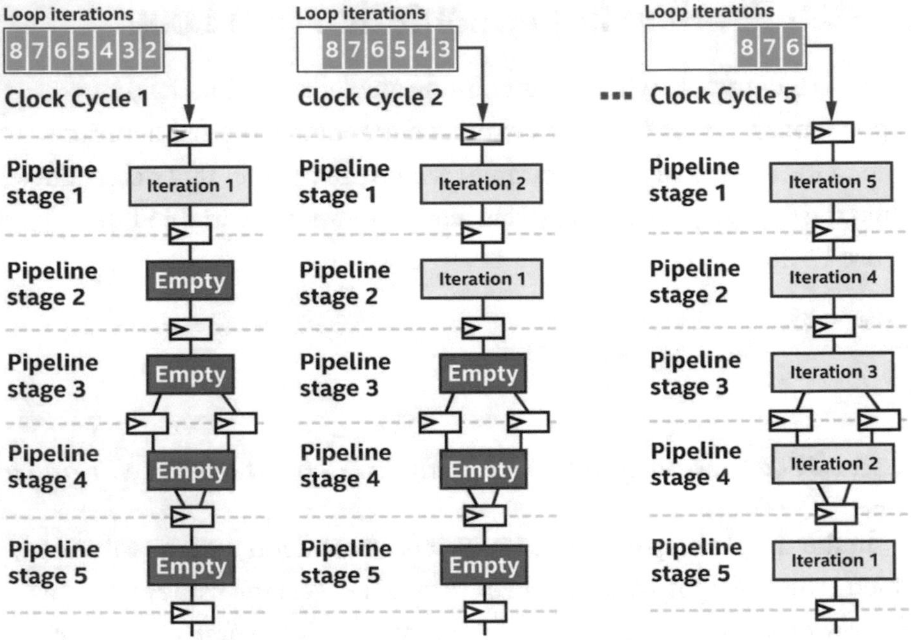

Figure 17-21. *Pipelines stages fed by successive iterations of a loop*

A modified random number generator example is shown in Figure 17-22. In this case, instead of generating a number based on the id of a work-item, as in Figure 17-17, the generator takes the previously computed value as an argument.

```
h.single_task([=]() {
  int state = seed;
  for (int i = 0; i < size; i++) {
    state = generate_incremental_random_number(state);
    output[i] = state;
  }
});
```

Figure 17-22. *Random number generator that depends on previous value generated*

The example uses `single_task` instead of `parallel_for` because the repeated work is expressed by a loop within the single task, so there isn't a reason to also include multiple work-items in this code (via `parallel_for`). The loop inside the `single_task` makes it much easier to express (programming convenience) that the previously computed value of `state` is passed to each invocation of the random number generation function.

In cases such as Figure 17-22, the FPGA can implement the loop efficiently. It can maintain a fully occupied pipeline in many cases or can at least tell us through reports what to change to increase occupancy. With this in mind, it becomes clear that this same algorithm would be much more difficult to describe if loop iterations were replaced with work-items, where the value generated by one work-item would need to be communicated to another work-item to be used in the incremental computation. The code complexity would rapidly increase, particularly if the work couldn't be batched so that each work-item was actually computing its own independent random number sequence.

Loop Initiation Interval

Conceptually, we probably think of iterations of a loop in C++ as executing one after another, as shown in Figure 17-23. That's the programming model and is the right way to think about loops. In implementation, though, compilers are free to perform many optimizations as long as most behavior (i.e., defined and race-free behavior) of the program doesn't observably change. Regardless of compiler optimizations, what matters is that the loop appears to execute *as if* Figure 17-23 is how it happened.

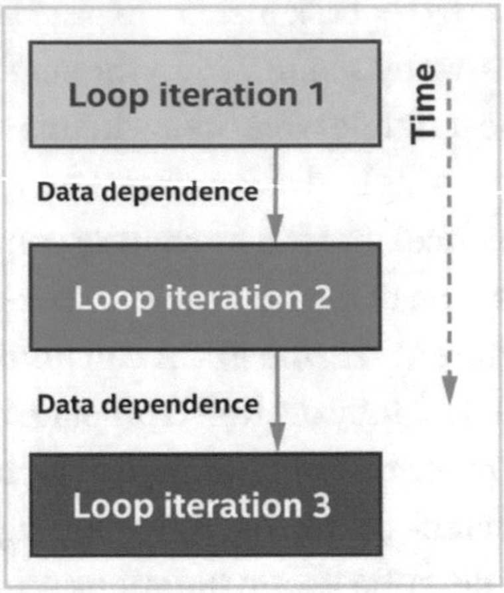

Figure 17-23. *Conceptually, loop iterations execute one after another*

Moving into the spatial compiler perspective, Figure 17-24 shows a loop pipelining optimization where the execution of iterations of a loop are overlapped in time. Different iterations will be executing different stages of the spatial pipeline from each other, and data dependences across stages of the pipeline can be managed by the compiler to ensure that the program appears to execute as if the iterations were sequential (except that the loop will finish executing sooner!).

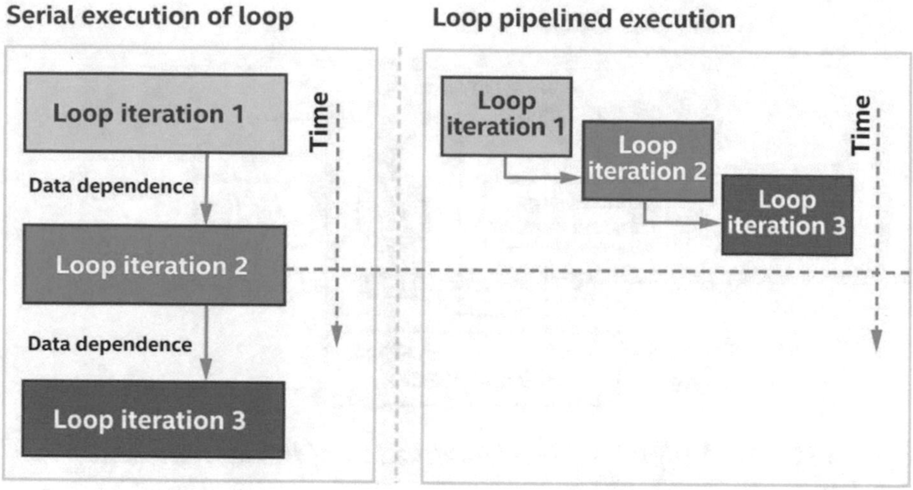

Figure 17-24. *Loop pipelining allows iterations of the loop to be overlapped across pipeline stages*

Loop pipelining is easy to understand with the realization that *many* results within a loop iteration may finish computation well before the loop iteration finishes *all* of its work and that, in a spatial pipeline, results can be passed to an earlier pipeline stage when the compiler decides to do so. Figure 17-25 shows this idea where the results of stage 1 are fed backward in the pipeline, allowing a future loop iteration to use the result early, before the previous iteration has completed.

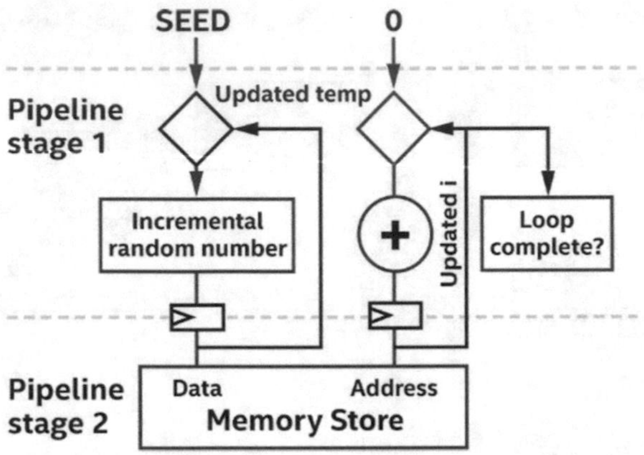

***Figure 17-25.** A pipelined implementation of the incremental random number generator*

With loop pipelining, it is possible for the execution of many iterations of a loop to overlap. The overlap means that even with loop-carried data dependences, loop iterations can still be used to fill the pipeline with work, leading to efficient utilization. Figure 17-26 shows how loop iterations might overlap their executions, even with loop-carried data dependences, within the same simple pipeline as was shown in Figure 17-25.

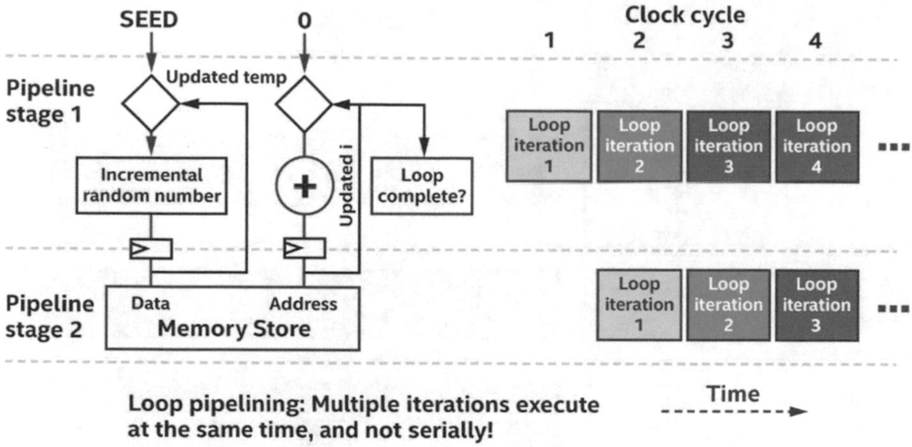

***Figure 17-26.** Loop pipelining simultaneously processes parts of multiple loop iterations*

In real algorithms, it is often not possible to launch a new loop iteration every single clock cycle, because a data dependence may take multiple clock cycles to compute. This often arises if memory lookups, particularly from off-chip memories, are on the critical path of the computation of a dependence. The result is a pipeline that can only initiate a new loop iteration every `N` clock cycles, and we refer to this as an *initiation interval* (`II`) of `N` cycles. An example is shown in Figure 17-27. A loop initiation interval (`II`) of two means that a new loop iteration can begin every second cycle, which results in suboptimal occupancy of the pipeline stages.

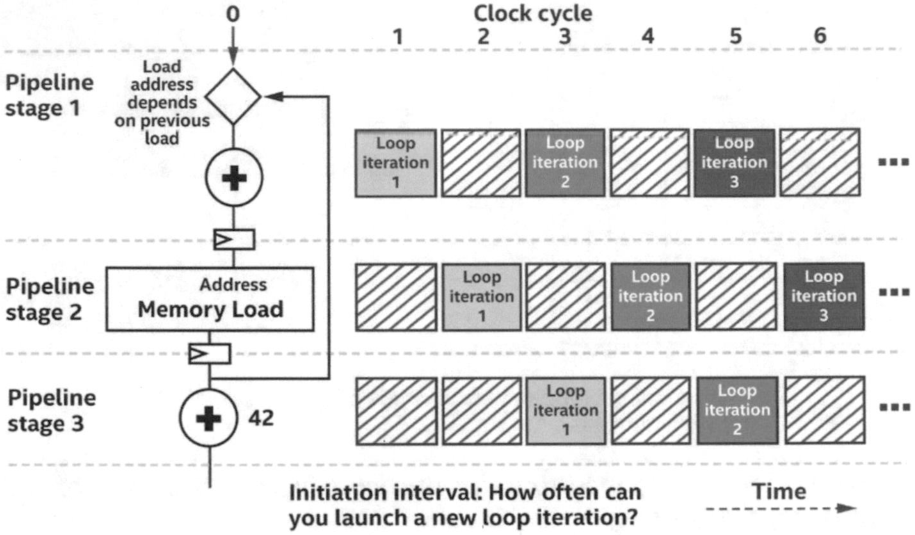

Figure 17-27. *Suboptimal occupancy of pipeline stages*

An II larger than one can lead to inefficiency in the pipeline because the average occupancy of each stage is reduced. This is apparent from Figure 17-27 where II=2 and pipeline stages are unused a large percentage (50%!) of the time. There are multiple ways to improve this situation.

The compiler performs extensive optimization to reduce II whenever possible, so its reports will also tell us what the initiation interval of each loop is and give us information on why it is larger than one, if that occurs. Restructuring the compute in a loop based on the reports can often reduce the II, particularly because as developers, we can make loop structural changes that the compiler isn't allowed to (because they would be observable). Read the compiler reports to learn how to reduce the II in specific cases.

An alternative way to reduce inefficiency from an II that is larger than one is through nested loops, which can fill all pipeline stages through interleaving of outer loop iterations with those of an inner loop that has II>1. Check vendor documentation and the compiler reports for details on using this technique.

Pipes

An important concept in spatial and other architectures is a first-in, first-out (FIFO) buffer. There are many reasons that FIFOs are important, but two properties are especially useful when thinking about programming:

1. There is **implicit control information carried alongside the data**. These signals tell us whether the FIFO is empty or full and can be useful when decomposing a problem into independent pieces.

2. FIFOs have **storage capacity**. This can make it easier to achieve performance in the presence of dynamic behaviors such as highly variable latencies when accessing memory.

Figure 17-28 shows a simple example of a FIFO's operation.

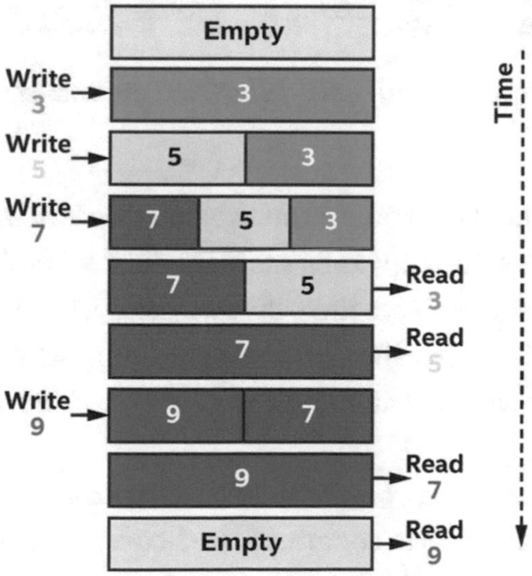

Figure 17-28. *Example operation of a FIFO over time*

FIFOs are exposed in DPC++ through a feature called *pipes*. The main reason that we should care about pipes when writing FPGA programs is that they allow us to decompose a problem into smaller pieces to focus on development and optimizations in a more modular way. They also allow the rich communication features of the FPGA to be harnessed. Figure 17-29 shows both of these graphically.

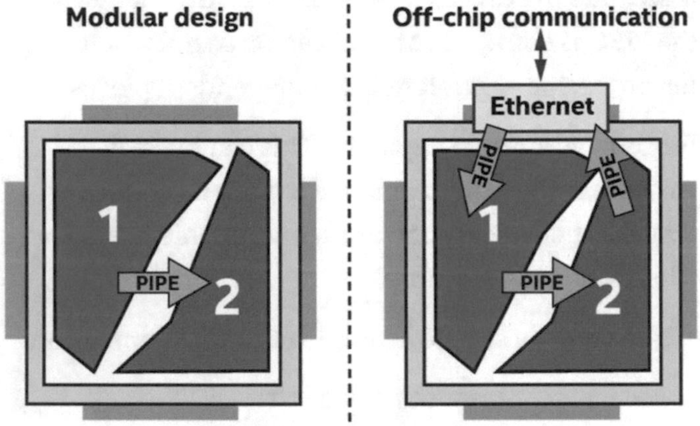

Figure 17-29. *Pipes simplify modular design and access to hardware peripherals*

Remember that FPGA kernels can exist on the device simultaneously (in different areas of the chip) and that in an efficient design, all parts of the kernels are active all the time, every clock cycle. This means that optimizing an FPGA application involves considering how kernels or parts of kernels interact with one another, and pipes provide an abstraction to make this easy.

Pipes are FIFOs that are implemented using on-chip memories on an FPGA, so they allow us to communicate between and within running kernels without the cost of moving data to off-chip memory. This provides inexpensive communication, and the control information that is coupled with a pipe (empty/full signals) provides a lightweight synchronization mechanism.

Do We Need Pipes? No. It is possible to write efficient kernels without using pipes. We can use all of the FPGA resources and achieve maximum performance using conventional programming styles without pipes. But it is easier for most developers to program and optimize more modular spatial designs, and pipes are a great tool to achieve this.

As shown in Figure 17-30, there are four general types of pipes available. In the rest of this section, we'll cover the first type (inter-kernel pipes), because they suffice to show what pipes are and how they are used. Pipes can also communicate within a single kernel and with the host or input/output peripherals. Please check vendor documentation for more information on those forms and uses of pipes that we don't have room to dive into here.

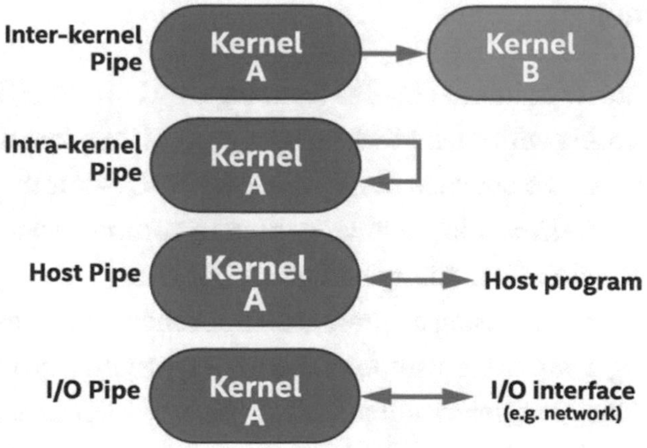

***Figure 17-30.** Types of pipe connectivity in DPC++*

A simple example is shown in Figure 17-31. In this case, there are two kernels that communicate through a pipe, with each read or write operating on a unit of an `int`.

```
// Create alias for pipe type to be consistent across uses
using my_pipe = ext::intel::pipe<class some_pipe, int>;

// ND-range kernel
q.submit([&](handler& h) {
  auto a = accessor(b_in, h);

  h.parallel_for(
      count, [=](auto idx) { my_pipe::write(a[idx]); });
});

// Single_task kernel
q.submit([&](handler& h) {
  auto a = accessor(b_out, h);

  h.single_task([=]() {
    for (int i = 0; i < count; i++) {
      a[i] = my_pipe::read();
    }
  });
});
```

Figure 17-31. *Pipe between two kernels: (1) ND-range and (2) single task with a loop*

There are a few points to observe from Figure 17-31. First, two kernels are communicating with each other using a pipe. If there are no accessor or event dependences between the kernels, the DPC++ runtime will execute both *at the same time,* allowing them to communicate through the pipe instead of full SYCL memory buffers or USM.

Pipes are identified using a type-based approach, where each is identified using a parameterization of the pipe type which is shown in Figure 17-32. The parameterization of the pipe type identifies a specific pipe. Reads or writes on the same pipe type are to the same FIFO. There are three template parameters that together define the type and therefore identity of a pipe.

```
template <typename name, typename dataT,
         size_t min_capacity = 0>
class pipe;
```

***Figure 17-32.** Parameterization of the pipe type*

It is recommended to use type aliases to define our pipe types, as shown in the first line of code in Figure 17-31, to reduce programming errors and improve code readability.

Use type aliases to identify pipes. This simplifies code and prevents accidental creation of unexpected pipes.

Pipes have a `min_capacity` parameter. It defaults to 0 which is *automatic selection*, but if specified, it guarantees that at least that number of words can be written to the pipe without any being read out. This parameter is useful when

- Two kernels communicating with a pipe do *not* run at the same time, and we need enough capacity in the pipe for a first kernel to write all of its outputs before a second kernel starts to run and reads from the pipe.
- If kernels generate or consume data in bursts, then adding capacity to a pipe can provide isolation between the kernels, decoupling their performance from each other. For example, a kernel producing data can continue to write (until the pipe capacity becomes full), even if a kernel consuming that data is busy and not ready to consume anything yet. This provides flexibility in execution of kernels relative to each other, at the cost only of some memory resources on the FPGA.

Blocking and Non-blocking Pipe Accesses

Like most FIFO interfaces, pipes have two styles of interface: *blocking* and *non-blocking*. Blocking accesses wait (block/pause execution!) for the operation to succeed, while non-blocking accesses return immediately and set a Boolean value indicating whether the operation succeeded.

The definition of success is simple: If we are reading from a pipe and there was data available to read (the pipe wasn't empty), then the read succeeds. If we are writing and the pipe wasn't already full, then the write succeeds. Figure 17-33 shows both forms of access member functions of the pipe class. We see the member functions of a pipe that allow it to be written to or read from. Recall that accesses to pipes can be blocking or non-blocking.

```
// Blocking
T read();
void write(const T &data);

// Non-blocking
T read(bool &success_code);
void write(const T &data, bool &success_code);
```

Figure 17-33. *Member functions of a pipe that allow it to be written to or read from*

Both blocking and non-blocking accesses have their uses depending on what our application is trying to achieve. If a kernel can't do any more work until it reads data from the pipe, then it probably makes sense to use a blocking read. If instead a kernel wants to read data from any one of a set of pipes and it is not sure which one might have data available, then reading from pipes with a non-blocking call makes more sense. In that case, the kernel can read from a pipe and process the data if there was any, but if the pipe was empty, it can instead move on and try reading from the next pipe that potentially has data available.

For More Information on Pipes

We could only scratch the surface of pipes in this chapter, but we should now have an idea of what they are and the basics of how to use them. FPGA vendor documentation has a lot more information and many examples of their use in different types of applications, so we should look there if we think that pipes are relevant for our particular needs.

Custom Memory Systems

When programming for most accelerators, much of the optimization effort tends to be spent making memory accesses more efficient. The same is true of FPGA designs, particularly when input and output data pass through off-chip memory.

There are two main reasons that memory accesses on an FPGA can be worth optimizing:

- To reduce required bandwidth, particularly if some of that bandwidth is used inefficiently
- To modify access patterns on a memory that is leading to unnecessary stalls in the spatial pipeline

It is worth talking briefly about *stalls* in the spatial pipeline. The compiler builds in assumptions about how long it will take to read from or write to specific types of memories, and it optimizes and balances the pipeline accordingly, hiding memory latencies in the process. But if we access memory in an inefficient way, we can introduce longer latencies and as a by-product stalls in the pipeline, where earlier stages cannot make progress executing because they're blocked by a pipeline stage that is waiting for something (e.g., a memory access). Figure 17-34 shows such a situation, where the pipeline above the load is stalled and unable to make forward progress.

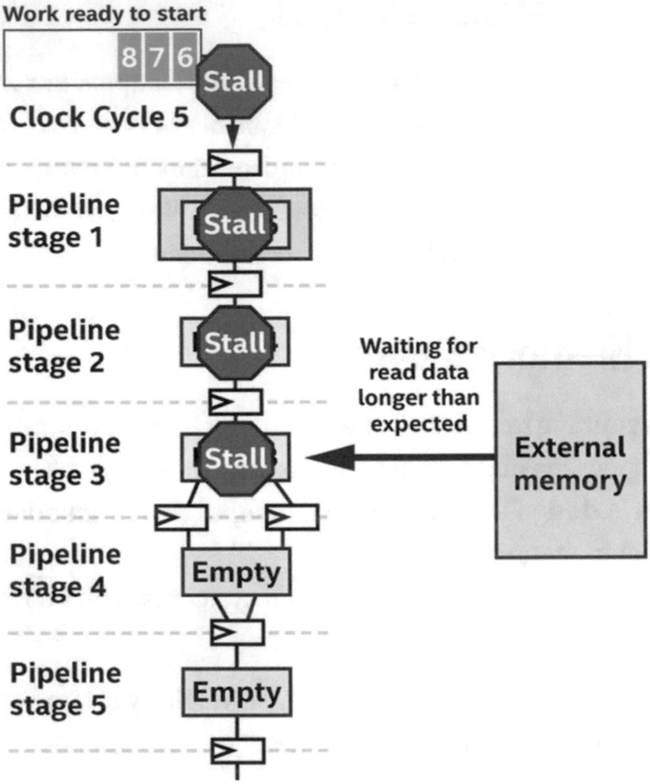

Figure 17-34. *How a memory stall can cause earlier pipeline stages to stall as well*

There are a few fronts on which memory system optimizations can be performed. As usual, the compiler reports are our primary guide to what the compiler has implemented for us and what might be worth tweaking or improving. We list a few optimization topics here to highlight some of the degrees of freedom available to us. Optimization is typically available both through explicit controls and by modifying code to allow the compiler to infer the structures that we intend. The compiler static reports and vendor documentation are key parts of memory system optimization, sometimes combined with profiling tools during hardware executions to capture actual memory behavior for validation or for the final stages of tuning. Some memory optimization considerations are as follows:

- **Static coalescing**: The compiler will combine memory accesses into a smaller number of wider accesses, where it can. This reduces the complexity of a memory system in terms of numbers of load or store units in the pipeline, ports on the memory system, the size and complexity of arbitration networks, and other memory system details. In general, we want to maximize static coalescing wherever possible, which we can confirm through the compiler reports. Simplifying addressing logic in a kernel can sometimes be enough for the compiler to perform more aggressive static coalescing, so always check in the reports that the compiler has inferred what we expect!
- **Memory access style**: The compiler creates load or store units for memory accesses, and these are tailored to both the memory technology being accessed (e.g., on-chip vs. DDR vs. HBM) and the access pattern inferred from the source code (e.g., streaming, dynamically coalesced/widened, or likely to benefit from a cache of a specific size). The compiler reports tell us what the compiler has inferred and allow us to modify or add controls to our code, where relevant, to improve performance.
- **Memory system structure**: Memory systems (both on- and off-chip) can have banked structures and numerous optimizations implemented by the compiler. There are many controls and mode modifications that can be used to control these structures and to tune specific aspects of the spatial implementation.

Some Closing Topics

When talking with developers who are getting started with FPGAs, we find that it often helps to understand at a high level the components that make up the device and also to mention clock frequency which seems to be a point of confusion. We close this chapter with these topics.

FPGA Building Blocks

To help with an understanding of the tool flows (particularly compile time), it is worth mentioning the building blocks that make up an FPGA. These building blocks are abstracted away through DPC++ and SYCL, and knowledge of them plays no part in typical application development (at least in the sense of making code functional). Their existence does, however, factor into development of an intuition for spatial architecture optimization and tool flows, and occasionally in advanced optimizations such as choosing the ideal data types for our application, for example.

A very simplified view of a modern FPGA device consists of five basic elements:

1. **Look-up tables**: Fundamental blocks that have a few binary input wires and produce a binary output. The output relative to the inputs is defined through the entries programmed into a look-up table. These are extremely primitive blocks, but there are many of them (millions) on a typical modern FPGA used for compute. These are the basis on which much of our design is implemented!

2. **Math engines**: For common math operations such as addition or multiplication of single-precision floating-point numbers, FPGAs have specialized hardware to make those operations very efficient.

A modern FPGA has thousands of these blocks, such that at least these many floating-point primitive operations can be performed in parallel *every clock cycle*! Most FPGAs name these math engines *digital signal processors* (DSPs).

3. **On-chip memory**: This is a distinguishing aspect of FPGAs vs. other accelerators, and memories come in two flavors (more actually, but we won't get into those here): (1) registers that are used to pipeline between operations and some other purposes and (2) block memories that provide small random-access memories spread across the device. A modern FPGA can have on the order of millions of register bits and more than 10,000 20 Kbit RAM memory blocks. Since each of those can be active every clock cycle, the result is significant on-chip memory capacity and bandwidth, when used efficiently.

4. **Interfaces to off-chip hardware**: FPGAs have evolved in part because of their very flexible transceivers and input/output connectivity that allows communications with almost anything ranging from off-chip memories to network interfaces and beyond.

5. **Routing fabric between all of the other elements**: There are many of each element mentioned previously on a typical FPGA, and the connectivity between them is not fixed. A complex programmable routing fabric allows signals to pass between the fine-grained elements that make up an FPGA.

Given the numbers of blocks on an FPGA of each specific type (some blocks are counted in the millions) and the fine granularity of those blocks such as look-up tables, the compile times seen when generating FPGA configuration bitstreams may make more sense. Not only does functionality need to be assigned to each fine-grained resource but routing needs to be configured between them. Much of the compile time comes from finding a first legal mapping of our design to the FPGA fabric, before optimizations even start! The extensive configurability of an FPGA is how a spatial implementation of your algorithms can achieve compelling performance.

Clock Frequency

FPGAs are extremely flexible and configurable, and that configurability comes with some cost to the frequency that an FPGA runs at compared with an equivalent design hardened into a CPU or any other fixed compute architecture. But this is not a problem! The spatial architecture of an FPGA more than makes up for the clock frequency because there are so many independent operations occurring simultaneously, spread across the area of the FPGA. Simply put, the frequency of an FPGA is lower than other architectures because of the configurable design, but more happens per clock cycle which balances out the frequency. We should compare compute throughput (e.g., in operations per second) and not raw frequency when benchmarking and comparing accelerators.

This said, as we approach 100% utilization of the resources on an FPGA, operating frequency may start to decrease. This is primarily a result of signal routing resources on the device becoming overused. There are ways to remedy this, typically at the cost of increased compile time. But it's best to avoid using more than 80–90% of the resources on an FPGA for most applications unless we are willing to dive into details to counteract frequency decrease.

RECOMMENDATION

Try not to exceed 90% of any resources on an FPGA and certainly not more than 90% of multiple resources. Exceeding these thresholds may lead to exhaustion of routing resources which leads to lower operating frequencies unless we are willing to dive into lower-level FPGA details to counteract this.

Summary

In this chapter, we have introduced how the compiler maps an algorithm to the FPGA's spatial architecture. We have also covered concepts that can help us to decide whether an FPGA is useful for our applications and that can help us get up and running developing code faster. From this starting point, we should be in good shape to browse vendor programming and optimization manuals and to start writing FPGA code! FPGAs provide performance and enable applications that don't map well to other accelerators, so we should keep them near the front of our mental toolbox!

CHAPTER 18

Libraries

We have spent the entire book promoting the art of *writing our own code*. Now we finally acknowledge that some great programmers have already written code that we can just use. Libraries are the best way to get our work done. This is not a case of being lazy—it is a case of having better things to do than reinvent the work of others.

This chapter covers three different sets of library functionality:

1. Built-in functions defined by the SYCL specification
2. The C++ standard library
3. C++17 parallel algorithms, supported by the oneAPI DPC++ Library (oneDPL)

SYCL defines a rich set of built-in functions that provide common functions shared by host and device code. All SYCL implementations support these functions, and so we can rely on key math libraries being available on all SYCL devices.

The C++ standard library is not guaranteed to be supported in device code by all SYCL implementations. However, the DPC++ compiler (and other compilers) support this as an extension to SYCL, and so we briefly discuss the limitations of that extension here.

Finally, the oneAPI DPC++ Library (oneDPL) provides a set of algorithms based on the C++17 algorithms, implemented in SYCL, to provide a high-productivity solution for SYCL programmers. This can

J. Reinders et al., *Data Parallel C++*, https://doi.org/10.1007/978-1-4842-9691-2_18

minimize programming effort across CPUs, GPUs, and FPGAs. Although oneDPL is not part of SYCL 2020, since it is implemented on top of SYCL, it should be compatible with any SYCL 2020 compiler.

Built-In Functions

SYCL provides a rich set of built-in functions with support for various data types. These built-in functions are available in the `sycl` namespace on host and device and can be classified as in the following:

- **Floating-point math functions**: `asin`, `acos`, `log`, `sqrt`, `floor`, etc.
- **Integer functions**: `abs`, `max`, `min`, etc.
- **Common functions**: `clamp`, `smoothstep`, etc.
- **Geometric functions**: `cross`, `dot`, `distance`, etc.
- **Relational functions**: `isequal`, `isless`, `isfinite`, etc.

The documentation for this extensive collection of functions can be found in the SYCL 2020 specification, and the online documentation at registry.khronos.org/SYCL/specs/sycl-2020/html/sycl-2020.html in sections 4.17.5 through 4.17.9.

Some compilers may provide options to control the precision of these functions. For example, the DPC++ compiler provides several such options, including `-mfma`, `-ffast-math`, and `-ffp-contract=fast`. It is important to check the documentation of a SYCL implementation to understand the availability of similar options (and their default values).

Several of the SYCL built-in functions have equivalents in the C++ standard library (e.g., `sycl::log` and `std::log`). SYCL implementations are not required to support calling C++ standard library functions within device code, but some implementations (e.g., DPC++) do.

Figure 18-1 demonstrates the usage of both the C++ `std::log` function and SYCL built-in `sycl::log` function in device code. Using DPC++ compiler implementation, both functions produce the same numeric results. In the example, the built-in relational function `sycl::isequal` is used to compare the results of `std::log` and `sycl::log`.

```
constexpr int size = 9;
std::array<float, size> a;
std::array<float, size> b;

bool pass = true;

for (int i = 0; i < size; ++i) {
  a[i] = i;
  b[i] = i;
}

queue q;

range sz{size};

buffer<float> bufA(a);
buffer<float> bufB(b);
buffer<bool> bufP(&pass, 1);

q.submit([&](handler &h) {
  accessor accA{bufA, h};
  accessor accB{bufB, h};
  accessor accP{bufP, h};

  h.parallel_for(size, [=](id<1> idx) {
    accA[idx] = std::log(accA[idx]);
    accB[idx] = sycl::log(accB[idx]);
    if (!sycl::isequal(accA[idx], accB[idx])) {
      accP[0] = false;
    }
  });
});
```

Figure 18-1. *Using `std::log` and `sycl::log`*

Note that the SYCL 2020 specification does not mandate that a SYCL math function implementation must produce the exact same numeric result as its corresponding C and C++ standard math function for a given hardware target. The specification allows for certain variations in the implementation to account for the characteristics and limitations of different hardware platforms. Therefore, it is possible for a SYCL implementation to produce matching results in practice, as demonstrated in the code example shown in Figure 18-1.

Use the `sycl::` Prefix with Built-In Functions

We strongly recommend invoking the SYCL built-in functions with an explicit `sycl::` prepended to the name. Calling just `sqrt()` is not guaranteed to invoke the SYCL built-in on all implementations even if "`using namespace sycl;`" has been used.

SYCL built-in functions should always be invoked with an explicit `sycl::` in front of the built-in name. Failure to follow this advice may result in strange and non-portable results.

When writing portable code, we recommend avoiding `using namespace sycl;` completely, in favor of explicitly using `std::` and `sycl::` namespaces. By being explicit, we remove the possibility of encountering unresolvable conflicts within certain SYCL implementations. This may also make code easier to debug in the future (e.g., if an implementation provides different precision guarantees for math functions in the `std::` and `sycl::` namespaces).

The C++ Standard Library

As mentioned previously, the SYCL specification does not guarantee that functions from the C++ standard library will be supported in device code. However, there are several compilers that *do* support these functions: this simplifies the offloading of existing C++ code to SYCL devices and makes it easier to write libraries that use SYCL as an implementation detail (e.g., a user passing a function into a library can write that function without using any SYCL-specific features).

YOUR MILEAGE MAY VARY

Since support in device code for functions from the `std::` namespace varies across SYCL implementations, we cannot be sure that kernels employing the C++ standard library will be portable across multiple SYCL compilers and implementations.

The DPC++ compiler is compatible with a set of tested C++ standard APIs—we simply need to include the corresponding C++ header files and use the `std` namespace. All these APIs can be employed in device kernels the way they are employed in a typical C++ host application. Figure 18-2 shows an example of how to use `std::swap` in device code.

```
int main() {
  std::array<int, 2> arr{8, 9};
  buffer<int> buf{arr};

  {
    host_accessor host_A(buf);
    std::cout << "Before: " << host_A[0] << ", "
              << host_A[1] << "\n";
  } // End scope of host_A so that upcoming kernel can
    // operate on buf

  queue q;
  q.submit([&](handler &h) {
    accessor a{buf, h};
    h.single_task([=]() {
      // Call std::swap!
      std::swap(a[0], a[1]);
    });
  });

  host_accessor host_B(buf);
  std::cout << "After:  " << host_B[0] << ", " << host_B[1]
            << "\n";
  return 0;
}

Sample output:
8, 9
9, 8
```

Figure 18-2. *Using `std::swap` in device code*

Figure 18-3 lists C++ standard APIs with “Y” to indicate those that have been tested for use in SYCL kernels for CPU, GPU, *and* FPGA devices, at the time of writing. A blank indicates incomplete coverage (not all three device types) at the time of publication for this book.

C++ Standard API	libstdc++	libc++	MSVC
std::abs	Y	Y	Y
std::acos	Y	Y	Y
std::acosh	Y	Y	Y
std::add const	Y	Y	Y
std::add cv	Y	Y	Y
std::add volatile	Y	Y	Y
std::alignment of	Y	Y	Y
std::all of	Y	Y	Y
std::any of	Y	Y	Y
std::arg	Y	Y	Y
std::array	Y	Y	Y
std::asin	Y	Y	Y
std::asinh	Y	Y	Y
std::assert	Y	Y	Y
std::atan	Y	Y	Y
std::atan2	Y	Y	Y
std::atanh	Y	Y	Y
std::binary negate	Y	Y	Y
std::binary search	Y	Y	Y
std::bit and	Y	Y	Y
std::bit not	Y	Y	Y
std::bit or	Y	Y	Y
std::bit xor	Y	Y	Y
std::cbrt	Y	Y	Y
std::ceil	Y	Y	Y
std::common type	Y	Y	Y
std::complex	Y	Y	Y
std::conditional	Y	Y	Y
std::conj	Y	Y	Y
std::copy	Y	Y	Y
std::copy backward	Y	Y	Y
std::copy if	Y	Y	Y
std::copy n	Y	Y	Y
std::copysign	Y	Y	Y
std::copysignf	Y	Y	Y
std::cos	Y	Y	Y
std::cosh	Y	Y	Y
std::count	Y	Y	Y
std::count if	Y	Y	Y
std::decay	Y	Y	Y
std::declval	Y	Y	Y
std::divides	Y	Y	Y
std::enable if	Y	Y	Y
std::equal range	Y	Y	Y
std::equal to	Y	Y	Y
std::erf	Y	Y	Y
std::erfc	Y	Y	Y
std::exp	Y	Y	Y
std::exp	Y	Y	Y
std::exp2	Y	Y	Y
std::expm1	Y	Y	Y
std::extent	Y	Y	Y
std::fabs	Y	Y	Y
std::fdim	Y	Y	Y
std::fill	Y	Y	Y
std::fill n	Y	Y	Y
std::find	Y	Y	Y
std::find if	Y	Y	Y
std::find if not	Y	Y	Y
std::floor	Y	Y	Y
std::fmax	Y	Y	Y
std::fmaxf	Y	Y	Y
std::fmin	Y	Y	Y
std::fminf	Y	Y	Y
std::fmod	Y	Y	Y
std::for each	Y	Y	Y

C++ Standard API	libstdc++	libc++	MSVC
std::for each n	Y	Y	Y
std::forward	Y	Y	Y
std::frexp	Y	Y	Y
std::generate	Y	Y	Y
std::generate n	Y	Y	Y
std::greater	Y	Y	Y
std::greater equal	Y	Y	Y
std::hypot	Y	Y	Y
std::ilogb	Y	Y	Y
std::imag	Y	Y	Y
std::initializer list	Y	Y	Y
std::integral constant	Y	Y	Y
std::is arithmetic	Y	Y	Y
std::is assignable	Y	Y	Y
std::is base of	Y	Y	Y
std::is base of union	Y	Y	Y
std::is compound	Y	Y	Y
std::is const	Y	Y	Y
std::is constructible	Y	Y	Y
std::is convertible	Y	Y	Y
std::is copy assignable	Y	Y	Y
std::is copy constructible	Y	Y	Y
std::is default constructible	Y	Y	Y
std::is destructible	Y	Y	Y
std::is empty	Y	Y	Y
std::is fundamental	Y	Y	Y
std::is heap	Y	Y	Y
std::is heap until	Y	Y	Y
std::is literal type	Y	Y	Y
std::is member pointer	Y	Y	Y
std::is move assignable	Y	Y	Y
std::is move constructible	Y	Y	Y
std::is object	Y	Y	Y
std::is permutation	Y	Y	Y
std::is pod	Y	Y	Y
std::is reference	Y	Y	Y
std::is same	Y	Y	Y
std::is scalar	Y	Y	Y
std::is signed	Y	Y	Y
std::is sorted	Y	Y	Y
std::is sorted until	Y	Y	Y
std::is standard layout	Y	Y	Y
std::is trivial	Y	Y	Y
std::is trivially assignable	Y	Y	Y
std::is trivially constructible	Y	Y	Y
std::is trivially copyable	Y	Y	Y
std::is unsigned	Y	Y	Y
std::is volatile	Y	Y	Y
std::isgreater	Y	Y	Y
std::isgreaterequal	Y	Y	Y
std::isinf	Y	Y	Y
std::isless	Y	Y	Y
std::islessequal	Y	Y	Y
std::isnan	Y	Y	Y
std::isunordered	Y	Y	Y
std::ldexp	Y	Y	Y
std::less	Y	Y	Y
std::less equal	Y	Y	Y
std::lgamma	Y	Y	Y
std::log	Y	Y	Y
std::log10	Y	Y	Y
std::log1p	Y	Y	Y
std::log2	Y	Y	Y
std::logb	Y	Y	Y
std::logical and	Y	Y	Y
std::logical not	Y	Y	Y

C++ Standard API	libstdc++	libc++	MSVC
std::logical or	Y	Y	Y
std::lower bound	Y	Y	Y
std::make heap	Y	Y	Y
std::max	Y	Y	Y
std::min	Y	Y	Y
std::minus	Y	Y	Y
std::modf	Y	Y	Y
std::modulus	Y	Y	Y
std::move	Y	Y	Y
std::move	Y	Y	Y
std::move backward	Y	Y	Y
std::move if noexcept	Y	Y	Y
std::multiplies	Y	Y	Y
std::nan	Y	Y	Y
std::nanf	Y	Y	Y
std::nearbyint	Y	Y	Y
std::nearbyintf	Y	Y	Y
std::negate	Y	Y	Y
std::nextafter	Y	Y	Y
std::none of	Y	Y	Y
std::norm	Y	Y	Y
std::not equal to	Y	Y	Y
std::not1/2	Y	Y	Y
std::numeric limits<T>::infinity	Y	Y	Y
std::numeric limits<T>::lowest	Y	Y	Y
std::numeric limits<T>::max	Y	Y	Y
std::numeric limits<T>::quiet NaN	Y	Y	Y
std::optional	Y	Y	Y
std::pair	Y	Y	Y
std::partial sort	Y	Y	Y
std::partial sort copy	Y	Y	Y
std::plus	Y	Y	Y
std::polar	Y	Y	Y
std::pop heap	Y	Y	Y
std::pow	Y	Y	Y
std::proj	Y	Y	Y
std::push heap	Y	Y	Y
std::rank	Y	Y	Y
std::ratio	Y	Y	Y
std::real	Y	Y	Y
std::reduce	Y	Y	Y
std::ref/cref	Y	Y	Y
std::reference wrapper	Y	Y	Y
std::remainder	Y	Y	Y
std::remove all extents	Y	Y	Y
std::remove const	Y	Y	Y
std::remove cv	Y	Y	Y
std::remove extent	Y	Y	Y
std::remove volatile	Y	Y	Y
std::remquo	Y	Y	Y
std::round	Y	Y	Y
std::roundf	Y	Y	Y
std::sin	Y	Y	Y
std::sinh	Y	Y	Y
std::sqrt	Y	Y	Y
std::swap	Y	Y	Y
std::tan	Y	Y	Y
std::tanh	Y	Y	Y
std::tgamma	Y	Y	Y
std::transform	Y	Y	Y
std::trunc	Y	Y	Y
std::truncf	Y	Y	Y
std::tuple	Y	Y	Y
std::unary negate	Y	Y	Y
std::upper bound	Y	Y	Y

Figure 18-3. *Library support with CPU/GPU/FPGA coverage (at time of book publication)*

The tested standard C++ APIs are supported in `libstdc++` (GNU) with `gcc` 7.5.0+ and `libc++` (LLVM) with `clang` 11.0+ and MSVC Standard C++ Library with Microsoft Visual Studio 2019+ for the host CPU as well.

On Linux, GNU `libstdc++` is the default C++ standard library for the DPC++ compiler, so no compilation or linking option is required. If we want to use `libc++`, use the compile options `-stdlib=libc++ -nostdinc++` to leverage `libc++` and to not include C++ std headers from the system. The DPC++ compiler has been verified using `libc++` in SYCL kernels on Linux, but the runtime needs to be rebuilt with `libc++` instead of `libstdc++`. Details are in `https://intel.github.io/llvm-docs/GetStartedGuide.html#build-dpc-toolchain-with-libc-library`. Because of these extra steps, `libc++` is not the recommended C++ standard library for us to use in general, without a specific reason to do so.

To achieve cross-architecture portability, if a `std::` function is not marked with "Y" in Figure 18-3, we need to be careful that we don't create functional incorrectness (or build failures) for our application as it runs on target devices that we haven't tested on!

---

oneAPI DPC++ Library (oneDPL)

C++17 introduced parallel versions of the algorithms defined in the C++ standard library. Unlike their serial counterparts, each of the parallel algorithms accepts an *execution policy* as its first argument—this execution policy denotes how an algorithm may execute.

Loosely speaking, an execution policy communicates to an implementation whether it can parallelize the algorithm using threads, SIMD instructions, or both. We can pass one of the values `seq`, `unseq`, `par`, or `par_unseq` as the execution policy, with meanings shown in Figure 18-4.

Execution Policy	Meaning
`seq`	Sequential execution.
`unseq`	Unsequenced SIMD execution. This policy requires that all functions provided are safe to execute in SIMD.
`par`	Parallel execution by multiple threads.
`par_unseq`	Combined effect of `unseq` and `par`.

Figure 18-4. *Execution policies*

oneDPL extends the standard execution policies to provide support for SYCL devices. These SYCL-aware execution policies specify not only *how* an algorithm should execute, but also *where* it should execute. A SYCL-aware policy inherits a standard C++ execution policy, encapsulates a SYCL device or queue, and allows us to set an optional kernel name. SYCL-aware execution policies can be used with all standard C++ algorithms that support execution policies according to the C++17 standard.

oneDPL is not tied to any single SYCL compiler, it is designed to support all SYCL compilers.

Before we can use oneDPL and its SYCL-aware execution policies, we need to add some additional header files. Which headers we include will depend on the algorithms we intend to use, some common examples include:

- `#include <oneapi/dpl/algorithm>`
- `#include <oneapi/dpl/numeric>`
- `#include <oneapi/dpl/memory>`

SYCL Execution Policy

Currently, only algorithms with the parallel unsequenced policy (`par_unseq`) can be safely offloaded to SYCL devices. This restriction stems from the forward progress guarantees provided by work-items in SYCL, which are incompatible with the requirements of other execution policies (e.g., `par`).

There are three steps to using a SYCL execution policy:

1. Add `#include <oneapi/dpl/execution>` into our code.
2. Create a policy object by providing a standard policy type, a class type for a unique kernel name

as a template argument (optional), and one of the following constructor arguments:

A SYCL queue

A SYCL dcvice

A SYCL device selector

An existing policy object with a different kernel name

3. Pass the created policy object to an algorithm.

A `oneapi::dpl::execution::dpcpp_default` object is a predefined `device_policy` created with a default kernel name and default queue. This can be used to create custom policy objects or passed directly when invoking an algorithm if the default choices are sufficient.

Figure 18-5 shows examples that assume use of the `using namespace oneapi::dpl::execution;` directive when referring to `policy` classes and functions.

```
auto policy_b = device_policy<parallel_unsequenced_policy,
                              class PolicyB>{
    sycl::device{sycl::gpu_selector{}}};
std::for_each(policy_b, …);
auto policy_c =
    device_policy<parallel_unsequenced_policy,
                  class PolicyC>{sycl::default_selector{}};
std::for_each(policy_c, …);
auto policy_d =
    make_device_policy<class PolicyD>(default_policy);
std::for_each(policy_d, …);
auto policy_e =
    make_device_policy<class PolicyE>(sycl::queue{});
std::for_each(policy_e, …);
```

Figure 18-5. *Creating execution policies*

Using oneDPL with Buffers

The algorithms in the C++ standard library are all based on iterators. To support passing SYCL buffers into these algorithms, oneDPL defines two special helper functions: `oneapi::dpl::begin` and `oneapi::dpl::end`.

These functions accept a SYCL buffer and return an object of an unspecified type that satisfies the following requirements:

- Is `CopyConstructible`, `CopyAssignable`, and comparable with operators == and !=.
- The following expressions are valid: `a + n`, `a - n`, and `a - b`, where `a` and `b` are objects of the type and `n` is an integer value.
- Has a `get_buffer` method with no arguments. The method returns the SYCL buffer passed to `oneapi::dpl::begin` and `oneapi::dpl::end` functions.

Note that using these helper functions requires us to add `#include <oneapi/dpl/iterator>` to our code. This functionality is not included by default, because these iterators are not required when using USM (which we will revisit shortly).

The code in Figure 18-6 shows how to use the `std::fill` function in conjunction with the begin/end helpers to fill a SYCL buffer. Note that the algorithm is in the `std::` namespace, and only the execution policy is in a nonstandard namespace—this is not a typo! The C++ standard library explicitly permits implementations to define their own execution policies to support coding patterns like this.

```
#include <oneapi/dpl/algorithm>
#include <oneapi/dpl/execution>
#include <oneapi/dpl/iterator>
#include <sycl/sycl.hpp>

int main() {
  sycl::queue q;
  sycl::buffer<int> buf{1000};

  auto buf_begin = oneapi::dpl::begin(buf);
  auto buf_end = oneapi::dpl::end(buf);

  auto policy = oneapi::dpl::execution::make_device_policy<
      class fill>(q);
  std::fill(policy, buf_begin, buf_end, 42);

  return 0;
}
```

Figure 18-6. *Using* `std::fill`

The code in Figure 18-7 shows an even simpler version of this code, using a default policy and ordinary (host-side) iterators. In this case, a temporary SYCL buffer is created, and the data is copied to this buffer. After processing of the temporary buffer on a device is complete, the data is copied back to the host. Working directly with existing SYCL buffers (where possible) is recommended to reduce data movement between the host and device and any unnecessary overhead of buffer creations and destructions.

```
#include <oneapi/dpl/algorithm>
#include <oneapi/dpl/execution>
#include <oneapi/dpl/iterator>
#include <sycl/sycl.hpp>

int main() {
  std::vector<int> v(100000);
  std::fill(oneapi::dpl::execution::dpcpp_default,
            v.begin(), v.end(), 42);

  if (v[788] == 42)
    std::cout << "passed" << std::endl;
  else
    std::cout << "failed" << std::endl;

  return 0;
}
```

Figure 18-7. *Using `std::fill` with default policy and host-side iterators*

Figure 18-8 shows an example which performs a binary search of the input sequence for each of the values in the search sequence provided. As the result of a search for the $\mathtt{i}^{th}$ element of the search sequence, a Boolean value indicating whether the search value was found in the input sequence is assigned to the $\mathtt{i}^{th}$ element of the result sequence. The algorithm returns an iterator that points to one past the last element of the result sequence that was assigned a result. The algorithm assumes that the input sequence has been sorted by the comparator provided. If no comparator is provided, then a function object that uses `operator<` to compare the elements will be used.

The complexity of the preceding description highlights that we should leverage library functions where possible, instead of writing our own implementations of similar algorithms which may take significant debugging and tuning time. Authors of the libraries that we can take advantage of are often experts in the internals of the device architectures we are targeting and may have access to information that we do not, so we should always leverage optimized libraries when they are available.

```
#include <oneapi/dpl/algorithm>
#include <iostream>
#include <oneapi/dpl/execution>
#include <oneapi/dpl/iterator>
#include <sycl/sycl.hpp>

using namespace sycl;

int main() {
  buffer<uint64_t, 1> kB{range<1>(10)};
  buffer<uint64_t, 1> vB{range<1>(5)};
  buffer<uint64_t, 1> rB{range<1>(5)};
  {
    host_accessor k{kB};
    host_accessor v{vB};

    // Initialize data, sorted
    k[0] = 0;
    k[1] = 5;
    k[2] = 6;
    k[3] = 6;
    k[4] = 7;
    k[5] = 7;
    k[6] = 8;
    k[7] = 8;
    k[8] = 9;
    k[9] = 9;

    v[0] = 1;
    v[1] = 6;
    v[2] = 3;
    v[3] = 7;
    v[4] = 8;
  }

  // create dpc++ iterators
  auto k_beg = oneapi::dpl::begin(kB);
  auto k_end = oneapi::dpl::end(kB);
  auto v_beg = oneapi::dpl::begin(vB);
  auto v_end = oneapi::dpl::end(vB);
  auto r_beg = oneapi::dpl::begin(rB);

  // create named policy from existing one
  auto policy = oneapi::dpl::execution::make_device_policy<
      class bSearch>(oneapi::dpl::execution::dpcpp_default);
```

***Figure 18-8.** Using binary_search*

```
// call algorithm
oneapi::dpl::binary_search(policy, k_beg, k_end, v_beg,
                           v_end, r_beg);

// check data
host_accessor r{rB};
if ((r[0] == false) && (r[1] == true) &&
    (r[2] == false) && (r[3] == true) && (r[4] == true)) {
  std::cout << "Passed. \nRun on "
            << policy.queue()
                   .get_device()
                   .get_info<info::device::name>()
            << "\n";
} else
    std::cout << "failed: values do not match.\n";

  return 0;
}
```

Figure 18-8. *(continued)*

The code example shown in Figure 18-8 demonstrates the three typical steps when using oneDPL in conjunction with SYCL buffers:

1. Create SYCL iterators from our buffers.
2. Create a named policy from an existing policy.
3. Invoke the parallel algorithm.

Using oneDPL with USM

In this section, we explore two ways to use oneDPL in combination with USM:

- Through USM pointers
- Through USM allocators

Unlike with buffers, we can directly use USM pointers as the iterators passed to an algorithm. Specifically, we can pass the pointers to the start and (one past the) end of the allocation to a parallel algorithm. It is important to be sure that the execution policy and the allocation itself were created for the same queue or context, to avoid undefined behavior at runtime. (Remember that this is not oneDPL specific, and we must always pay close attention to contexts when using USM!)

If the same USM allocation is to be processed by several algorithms, we can either use an in-order queue or explicitly wait for completion of each algorithm before using the same allocation in the next one (this is typical operation ordering when using USM). We should also be careful to ensure that we wait for completion before accessing the data on the host, as shown in Figure 18-9.

```
#include <oneapi/dpl/algorithm>
#include <oneapi/dpl/execution>
#include <sycl/sycl.hpp>

int main() {
  sycl::queue q;
  const int n = 10;
  int* h_head = sycl::malloc_host<int>(n, q);
  int* d_head = sycl::malloc_device<int>(n, q);
  std::fill(oneapi::dpl::execution::make_device_policy(q),
            d_head, d_head + n, 78);
  q.wait();

  q.memcpy(h_head, d_head, n * sizeof(int));
  q.wait();

  if (h_head[8] == 78)
    std::cout << "passed" << std::endl;
  else
    std::cout << "failed" << std::endl;

  sycl::free(h_head, q);
  sycl::free(d_head, q);
  return 0;
}
```

Figure 18-9. *Using oneDPL with a USM pointer*

Alternatively, we can use std::vector with a USM allocator as shown in Figure 18-10. With this approach, std::vector manages its own memory (as normal) but allocates any memory it needs via an internal call to sycl::malloc_shared. The begin() and end() member functions then return iterators that step through a USM allocation. This style of programming is very convenient, especially when migrating existing C++ code that already makes use of containers and algorithms.

```
#include <oneapi/dpl/algorithm>
#include <oneapi/dpl/execution>
#include <sycl/sycl.hpp>

int main() {
  sycl::queue q;
  const int n = 10;
  sycl::usm_allocator<int, sycl::usm::alloc::shared> alloc(
      q);
  std::vector<int, decltype(alloc)> vec(n, alloc);

  std::fill(oneapi::dpl::execution::make_device_policy(q),
            vec.begin(), vec.end(), 78);
  q.wait();

  return 0;
}
```

Figure 18-10. *Using oneDPL with a USM allocator*

Error Handling with SYCL Execution Policies

As detailed in Chapter 5, the SYCL error handling model supports two types of errors. With *synchronous* errors, the runtime throws exceptions, while *asynchronous* errors are only processed by an asynchronous error handler at specified times during program execution.

For algorithms executed with SYCL-aware execution policies, the handling of all errors (synchronous or asynchronous) is the responsibility of the caller. Specifically,

- No exceptions are thrown explicitly by algorithms.
- Exceptions thrown by the runtime on the host CPU, including SYCL synchronous exceptions, are passed through to the caller.
- SYCL asynchronous errors are not handled by oneDPL, so must be handled (if any handling is desired) by the caller using the usual SYCL asynchronous exception mechanisms.

Summary

We should use libraries wherever possible in our heterogeneous applications, to avoid wasting time rewriting and testing common functions and parallel patterns. We should leverage the work of others rather than writing everything ourselves, and we should use that approach wherever practical to simplify application development and (often) to realize superior performance.

This chapter has briefly introduced three sets of library functionality that we think every SYCL developer should be familiar with:

1. The SYCL built-in functions, for common math operations
2. The standard C++ library, for other common operations
3. The C++17 parallel algorithms (supported by oneDPL), for complete kernels

With any library, it is important to understand which devices, compilers, and implementations are tested and supported before relying upon them in production. This is not SYCL-specific advice, but worth remembering—the number of potential targets for a portable programming solution like SYCL is huge, and it is our responsibility as programmers to identify which libraries are aligned with our goals.

CHAPTER 19

Memory Model and Atomics

Memory consistency is not an esoteric concept if we want to be parallel programmers. It helps us to ensure that data is where we need it, when we need it, and that its values are what we are expecting. This chapter brings to light key things we need to master to ensure our program hums along correctly. This topic is not unique to SYCL.

Having a basic understanding of the memory (consistency) model of a programming language is necessary for *any* programmer who wants to allow concurrent updates to memory (whether those updates originate from multiple work-items in the same kernel, multiple devices, or both). This is true regardless of how memory is allocated, and the content of this chapter is equally important to us whether we choose to use buffers or USM allocations.

In previous chapters, we have focused on the development of simple kernels, where work-items either operate on completely independent data or share data using structured communication patterns that can be expressed directly using language and/or library features. As we move toward writing more complex and realistic kernels, we are likely to encounter situations where work-items may need to communicate in less structured ways—understanding how the memory model relates to SYCL language features and the capabilities of the hardware we are targeting is a necessary precondition for designing correct, portable, and efficient programs.

J. Reinders et al., *Data Parallel C++*, https://doi.org/10.1007/978-1-4842-9691-2_19

THREADS OF EXECUTION

C++17 introduced the concept of a "thread of execution" (often referred to simply as a "thread") to help describe the behaviors of library features related to parallelism and concurrency (e.g., the parallel algorithms). The C++ memory consistency model and execution model are defined entirely in terms of interactions between these "threads."

To simplify comparison between SYCL and C++, this chapter often uses the term "thread" to mean "thread of execution." A SYCL work-item is equivalent to a C++ thread of execution with weakly parallel forward progress guarantees, and so it is safe to use these terms interchangeably—occasionally, we may still use "work-item" to highlight when we are discussing SYCL-specific concepts.

The memory consistency model of C++ is sufficient for writing applications that execute entirely on the host, but it is modified by SYCL in order to address complexities that may arise when programming heterogeneous systems. Specifically, we need to be able to

- Reason about which types of memory allocation (buffers and USM) can be accessed by which devices in the system
- Prevent unsafe concurrent memory accesses (data races) during the execution of our kernels by using barriers and atomics
- Enable safe communication between work-items using barriers, fences, atomics, memory orders, and memory scopes

- Prevent optimizations that may unexpectedly alter the behavior of parallel applications—while still allowing other optimizations—using barriers, fences, atomics, memory orders, and memory scopes

Memory models are a complex topic, but for a good reason—processor architects care about making processors and accelerators execute our codes as efficiently as possible! We have worked hard in this chapter to break down this complexity and highlight the most critical concepts and language features. This chapter starts us down the path of not only knowing the memory model inside and out but also enjoying an important aspect of parallel programming that many people do not know exists. If questions remain after reading the descriptions and example codes here, we highly recommend visiting the websites listed at the end of this chapter or referring to the C++ and SYCL specifications.

What's in a Memory Model?

This section expands upon the motivation for programming languages to contain a memory model and introduces a few core concepts that parallel programmers should familiarize themselves with:

- Data races and synchronization
- Barriers and fences
- Atomic operations
- Memory ordering

Understanding these concepts at a high level is necessary to appreciate their expression and usage in C++ with SYCL. Readers with extensive experience in parallel programming, especially using C++, may wish to skip ahead.

Data Races and Synchronization

The *operations* that we write in our programs typically do not map directly to a single hardware instruction or micro-operation. A simple addition operation such as `data[i] += x` may be broken down into a sequence of several instructions or micro-operations:

- Load `data[i]` from memory into a temporary (register).
- Compute the result of adding `x` to `data[i]`.
- Store the result back to `data[i]`.

This is not something that we need to worry about when developing sequential applications—the three stages of the addition will be executed in the order that we expect, as depicted in Figure 19-1.

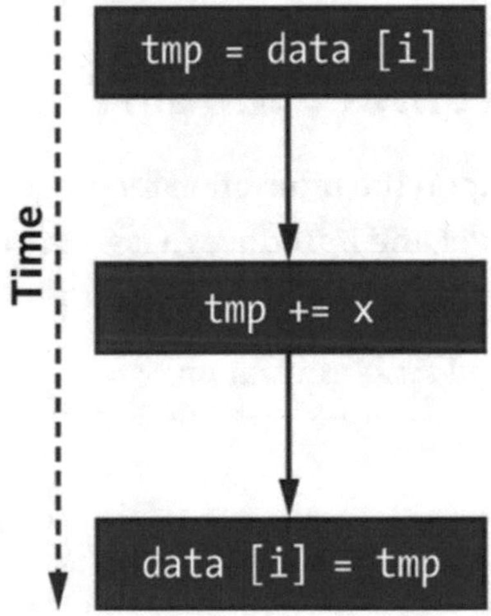

***Figure 19-1.** Sequential execution of `data[i] += x` broken into three separate operations*

Switching to parallel application development introduces an extra level of complexity: if we have multiple operations being applied to the same data concurrently, how can we be certain that their view of that data is consistent? Consider the situation shown in Figure 19-2, where two executions of `data[i] += x` have been interleaved on two threads. If the two threads use different values of `i`, the application will execute correctly. If they use the same value of `i`, both load the same value from memory, and one of the results is overwritten by the other! This is just one of many ways in which their operations could be scheduled, and the behavior of our application depends on which thread gets to which data first—our application contains a *data race*.

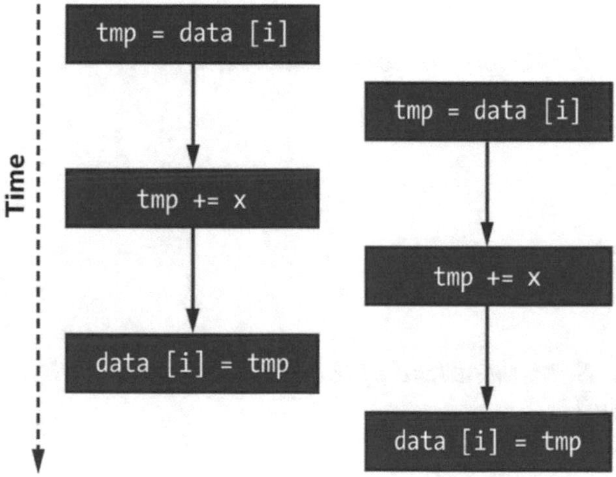

Figure 19-2. *One possible interleaving of* `data[i] += x` *executed concurrently*

The code in Figure 19-3 and its output in Figure 19-4 show how easily this can happen in practice. If `M` is greater than or equal to `N`, the value of `j` used by each thread is unique; if it is not, values of `j` will conflict, and updates may be lost. We say *may* be lost because a program containing a data race could still produce the correct answer some or all the time (depending on how work is scheduled by the implementation and hardware). Neither the compiler nor the hardware can possibly know what this program is *intended* to do or what the values of N and M may be at runtime—it is our responsibility as programmers to understand whether our programs may contain data races and whether they are sensitive to execution order.

```
int* data = malloc_shared<int>(N, q);
std::fill(data, data + N, 0);

q.parallel_for(N, [=](id<1> i) {
   int j = i % M;
   data[j] += 1;
 }).wait();

for (int i = 0; i < N; ++i) {
  std::cout << "data [" << i << "] = " << data[i] << "\n";
}
```

Figure 19-3. *Kernel containing a data race*

```
N = 2, M = 2:
data [0] = 1
data [1] = 1

N = 2, M = 1:
data [0] = 1
data [1] = 0
```

Figure 19-4. *Sample output of the code in Figure 19-3 for small values of* N *and* M

In general, when developing massively parallel SYCL applications, we should not concern ourselves with the exact order in which individual work-items execute—there are hopefully hundreds (or thousands!) of work-items in each of our kernels, and trying to impose a specific ordering upon them will negatively impact both scalability and performance. Rather, our focus should be on developing portable applications that execute correctly, which we can achieve by providing the compiler (and hardware) with information about when work-items share data, what guarantees are needed when sharing occurs, and which execution orderings are legal.

Massively parallel applications should not be concerned with the exact order in which individual work-items execute!

Barriers and Fences

One way to prevent data races between work-items in the same group is to introduce synchronization across different threads using work-group barriers and appropriate memory fences. We could use a work-group barrier to order our updates of `data[i]` as shown in Figure 19-5, and an updated version of our example kernel is given in Figure 19-6. Note that because a work-group barrier does not synchronize work-items in different groups, our simple example is only guaranteed to execute correctly if we limit ourselves to a single work-group!

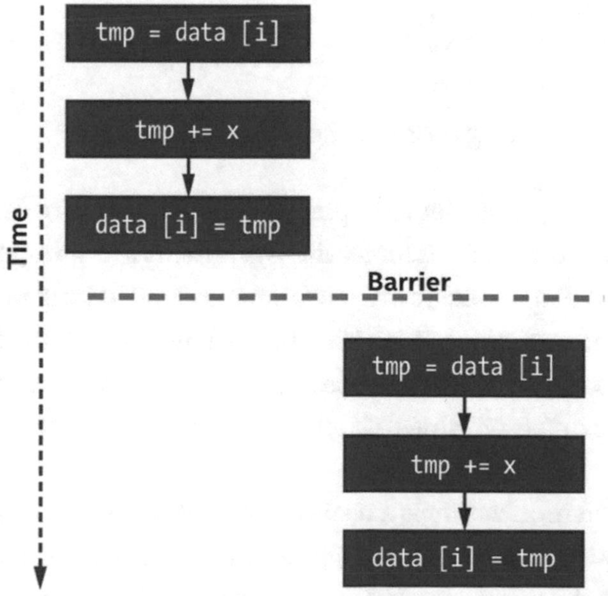

Figure 19-5. *Two executions of `data[i] += x` separated by a barrier*

```
int* data = malloc_shared<int>(N, q);
std::fill(data, data + N, 0);

// Launch exactly one work-group
// Number of work-groups = global / local
range<1> global{N};
range<1> local{N};

q.parallel_for(nd_range<1>{global, local},
               [=](nd_item<1> it) {
                 int i = it.get_global_id(0);
                 int j = i % M;
                 for (int round = 0; round < N; ++round) {
                   // Allow exactly one work-item update
                   // per round
                   if (i == round) {
                     data[j] += 1;
                   }
                   group_barrier(it.get_group());
                 }
               })
    .wait();

for (int i = 0; i < N; ++i) {
  std::cout << "data [" << i << "] = " << data[i] << "\n";
}
```

Figure 19-6. *Avoiding a data race using a barrier*

Although using a barrier to implement this pattern is possible, it is not typically encouraged—it forces the work-items in a group to execute sequentially and in a specific order, which may lead to long periods of inactivity in the presence of load imbalance. It may also introduce more synchronization than is strictly necessary—if the different work-items happen to use different values of `i`, they will still be forced to synchronize at the barrier.

Barrier synchronization is a useful tool for ensuring that all work-items in a work-group or sub-group complete some stage of a kernel before proceeding to the next stage, but is too heavy-handed for fine-grained (and potentially data-dependent) synchronization. For more general synchronization patterns, we must look to *atomic* operations.

Atomic Operations

Atomic operations enable concurrent access to a memory location without introducing a data race. When multiple atomic operations access the same memory, they are guaranteed not to overlap. Note that this guarantee does not apply if only some of the accesses use atomics and that it is our responsibility as programmers to ensure that we do not concurrently access the same data using operations with different atomicity guarantees.

Mixing atomic and non-atomic operations on the same memory location(s) at the same time results in undefined behavior!

If our simple addition is expressed using atomic operations, the result may look like Figure 19-8—each update is now an indivisible chunk of work, and our application will always produce the correct result. The corresponding code is shown in Figure 19-7—we will revisit the `atomic_ref` class and the meaning of its template arguments later in the chapter.

```
int* data = malloc_shared<int>(N, q);
std::fill(data, data + N, 0);

q.parallel_for(N, [=](id<1> i) {
   int j = i % M;
   atomic_ref<int, memory_order::relaxed,
              memory_scope::system,
              access::address_space::global_space>
       atomic_data(data[j]);
   atomic_data += 1;
 }).wait();

for (int i = 0; i < N; ++i) {
  std::cout << "data [" << i << "] = " << data[i] << "\n";
}
```

Figure 19-7. *Avoiding a data race using atomic operations*

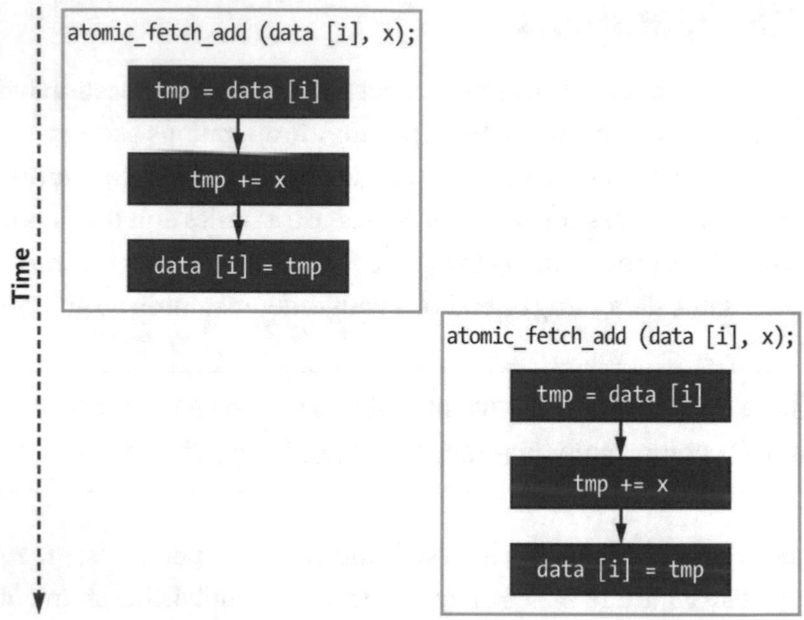

***Figure 19-8.** An interleaving of `data[i] += x` executed concurrently with atomic operations*

However, it is important to note that this is still only one possible execution order. Using atomic operations guarantees that the two updates do not overlap (if both threads use the same value of `i`), but there is still no guarantee as to which of the two threads will execute first. Even more importantly, there are no guarantees about how these atomic operations are ordered with respect to any *non-atomic* operations in different threads.

Memory Ordering

Even within a sequential application, optimizing compilers and the hardware are free to reorder operations if they do not change the observable behavior of an application. In other words, the application must behave *as if* it ran exactly as it was written by the programmer.

Unfortunately, this as-if guarantee is not strong enough to help us reason about the execution of parallel programs. We now have two sources of reordering to worry about: the compiler and hardware may reorder the execution of statements within each sequential thread, and the threads themselves may be executed in any (possibly interleaved) order. To design and implement safe communication protocols between threads, we need to be able to constrain this reordering. By providing the compiler with information about our desired *memory order*, we can prevent reordering optimizations that are incompatible with the intended behavior of our applications.

Three commonly available memory orderings are:

1. A *relaxed* memory ordering
2. An *acquire-release* or release-acquire memory ordering
3. A *sequentially consistent* memory ordering

Under a relaxed memory ordering, memory operations can be reordered without any restrictions. The most common usage of a relaxed memory model is incrementing shared variables (e.g., a single counter, an array of values during a histogram computation).

Under an acquire-release memory ordering, one thread *releasing* an atomic variable and another thread *acquiring* the same atomic variable acts as a synchronization point between those two threads and guarantees that any prior writes to memory issued by the releasing thread are visible to the acquiring thread. Informally, we can think of atomic operations releasing side effects from other memory operations to other threads or acquiring the side effects of memory operations on other threads. Such a memory model is required if we want to communicate values between pairs of threads via memory, which may be more common than we would think. When a program *acquires* a lock, it typically goes on to perform some additional calculations and modify some memory before eventually *releasing* the lock—only the lock variable is ever updated atomically, but we expect memory updates guarded by the lock to be protected from data races. This behavior relies on an acquire-release memory ordering for correctness, and attempting to use a relaxed memory ordering to implement a lock will not work.

Under a sequentially consistent memory ordering, the guarantees of acquire-release ordering still hold, but there additionally exists a single global order of all atomic operations. The behavior of this memory ordering is the most intuitive of the three and the closest that we can get to the original as-if guarantee we are used to relying upon when developing sequential applications. With sequential consistency, it becomes significantly easier to reason about communication between groups (rather than pairs) of threads, since all threads must agree on the global ordering of all atomic operations.

Understanding which memory orders are supported by a combination of programming model and device is a necessary part of designing portable parallel applications. Being explicit in describing the memory order required by our applications ensures that they fail predictably (e.g., at compile time) when the behavior we require is unsupported and prevents us from making unsafe assumptions.

The Memory Model

The chapter so far has introduced the concepts required to understand the memory model. The remainder of the chapter explains the memory model in detail, including

- How to express the memory ordering requirements of our kernels
- How to query the memory orders supported by a specific device

- How the memory model behaves with respect to disjoint address spaces and multiple devices
- How the memory model interacts with barriers, fences, and atomics
- How using atomic operations differs between buffers and USM

The memory model is based on the memory model of C++ but differs in some important ways. These differences reflect our long-term vision that SYCL should help inform the future of C++: the default behaviors and naming of classes are closely aligned with the C++ standard library and are intended to extend C++ functionality rather than to restrict it.

The table in Figure 19-9 summarizes how different memory model concepts are exposed as language features in C++ (C++11, C++14, C++17, C++20) vs. SYCL. The C++14, C++17, and C++20 standards additionally include some clarifications that impact implementations of C++. These clarifications should not affect the application code that we write, so we do not cover them here.

Feature	C++	SYCL
Atomic Objects	`std::atomic`	Not available.
Atomic References	`std::atomic_ref` (C++20 onwards)	`sycl::atomic_ref`

Memory Orders	`relaxed`
	`consume`
	`acquire`
	`release`
	`acq_rel`
	`seq_cst`
		`relaxed`
		
		`acquire`
		`release`
		`acq_rel`
		`seq_cst`

Memory Scopes	Not available.
	
	Behavior of atomics and fences matches SYCL `system` scope.
		`work_item`
		`sub_group`
		`work_group`
		`device`
		`system`

Fences	`std::atomic_thread_fence`	`sycl::atomic_fence`
Barriers	`std::barrier` (C++20 onwards)	`sycl::group_barrier`
Address Spaces	All memory is in a single (host) address space.	Host Device (Global) Device (Local) Device (Private) Shared (USM)

Figure 19-9. *Comparing C++ and SYCL memory models*

The `memory_order` Enumeration Class

The memory model exposes different memory orders through five values of the `memory_order` enumeration class (note: C++ "consume" is not part of SYCL), which can be supplied as arguments to fences and atomic operations. Supplying a memory order argument to an operation tells the compiler what memory ordering guarantees are required for all other memory operations (to any address) *relative to that operation,* as explained in the following:

- `memory_order::relaxed`

  Read and write operations can be reordered before or after the operation with no restrictions. There are no ordering guarantees.

- `memory_order::acquire`

  Read and write operations appearing after the operation in the program must occur after it (i.e., they cannot be reordered before the operation).

- `memory_order::release`

  Read and write operations appearing before the operation in the program must occur before it (i.e., they cannot be reordered after the operation), and preceding write operations are guaranteed to be visible to other work-items which have been synchronized by a corresponding acquire operation (i.e., an atomic operation using the same variable and `memory_order::acquire` or a barrier function).

- `memory_order::acq_rel`

  The operation acts as both an acquire and a release. Read and write operations cannot be reordered around the operation, and preceding writes must be made visible as previously described for `memory_order::release`.

- `memory_order::seq_cst`

  The operation acts as an acquire, release, or both depending on whether it is a read, write, or read–modify–write operation, respectively. All operations with this memory order are observed in a sequentially consistent order.

There are several restrictions on which memory orders are supported by each operation. The table in Figure 19-10 summarizes which combinations are valid.

Functions	Supported memory_order Values				
	relaxed	acquire	release	acq_rel	seq_cst
load	✓	✗	✗	✗	✓
store	✓	✗	✓	✗	✓
exchange compare_exchange_* fetch_*	✓	✓	✓	✓	✓
fence	✓	✓	✓	✓	✓

Figure 19-10. *Supporting atomic operations with `memory_order`*

Load operations do not write values to memory and are therefore incompatible with release semantics. Similarly, store operations do not read values from memory and are therefore incompatible with acquire semantics. The remaining read-modify-write atomic operations and fences are compatible with all memory orderings.

MEMORY ORDER IN C++

The C++ memory model additionally includes `memory_order::consume`, with similar behavior to `memory_order::acquire`. However, C++17 discourages its use, noting that its definition is being revised. Its inclusion in SYCL has therefore been left to consider for a future specification.

The `memory_scope` Enumeration Class

The C++ memory model assumes that applications execute on a single device with a single address space. Neither of these assumptions holds for SYCL applications: various parts of the application execute on different devices (i.e., a host and one or more accelerator devices); each device has multiple address spaces (i.e., private, local, and global); and the global address space of each device may or may not be disjoint (depending on USM support).

To address this, SYCL extends the C++ notion of memory order to include the *scope* of an atomic operation, denoting the minimum set of work-items to which a given memory ordering constraint applies. The set of scopes are defined by way of a `memory_scope` enumeration class:

- `memory_scope::work_item`

  The memory ordering constraint applies only to the calling work-item. This scope is only useful for image operations, as all other operations within a work-item are already guaranteed to execute in program order.

- `memory_scope::sub_group`, `memory_scope::work_group`

  The memory ordering constraint applies only to work-items in the same sub-group or work-group as the calling work-item.

- `memory_scope::device`

  The memory ordering constraint applies only to work-items executing on the same device as the calling work-item.

- `memory_scope::system`

  The memory ordering constraint applies to all work-items in the system.

Barring restrictions imposed by the capabilities of a device, all memory scopes are valid arguments to all atomic and fence operations. However, a scope argument may be automatically demoted to a narrower scope in one of three situations:

1. If an atomic operation updates a value in work-group local memory, any scope broader than `memory_scope::work_group` is narrowed (because local memory is only visible to work-items in the same work-group).

2. If a device does not support USM, specifying `memory_scope::system` is always equivalent to `memory_scope::device` (because buffers cannot be accessed concurrently by multiple devices).

3. If an atomic operation uses `memory_order::relaxed`, there are no ordering guarantees, and the memory scope argument is effectively ignored.

Querying Device Capabilities

To ensure compatibility with devices supported by previous versions of SYCL and to maximize portability, SYCL supports OpenCL 1.2 devices and other hardware that may not be capable of supporting the full C++ memory model (e.g., certain classes of embedded devices). SYCL provides device queries to help us reason about the memory order(s) and memory scope(s) supported by the devices available in a system:

- `atomic_memory_order_capabilities`

  Return a list of all memory orderings supported by atomic operations on a specific device. All devices are required to support at least `memory_order::relaxed`.

- `atomic_fence_order_capabilities`

  Return a list of all memory orderings supported by fence operations on a specific device. All devices are required to support at least `memory_order::relaxed`, `memory_order::acquire`, `memory_order::release`, and `memory_order::acq_rel`. Note that the minimum requirement for fences is stronger than the minimum requirement for atomic operations, since such fences are essential for reasoning about memory order in the presence of barriers.

- `atomic_memory_scope_capabilities`

  `atomic_fence_scope_capabilities`

  Return a list of all memory scopes supported by atomic and fence operations on a specific device. All devices are required to support at least `memory_order::work_group`.

It may be difficult at first to remember which memory orders and scopes are supported for which combinations of function and device capability. In practice, we can avoid much of this complexity by following one of the two development approaches outlined in the following:

1. **Develop applications with sequential consistency and system fences.**

   Only consider adopting less strict memory orders during performance tuning.

2. **Develop applications with relaxed consistency and work-group fences.**

   Only consider adopting more strict memory orders and broader memory scopes where required for correctness.

The first approach ensures that the semantics of all atomic operations and fences match the default behavior of C++. This is the simplest and least error-prone option but has the worst performance and portability characteristics.

The second approach is more aligned with the default behavior of previous versions of SYCL and languages like OpenCL. Although more complicated—since it requires that we become more familiar with the different memory orders and scopes—it ensures that the majority of the SYCL code we write will work on any device without performance penalties.

Barriers and Fences

All previous usages of barriers and fences in the book so far have ignored the issue of memory order and scope, by relying on default behavior.

By default, every group barrier in SYCL acts as an acquire-release fence to all address spaces accessible by the calling work-item and makes preceding writes visible to at least all other work-items in the same group (as defined by the group's `fence_scope` member variable). This ensures memory consistency within a group of work-items after a barrier, in line with our intuition of what it means to synchronize (and the definition of the *synchronizes-with* relation in C++). It is possible to override this default behavior by passing an explicit `memory_scope` argument to the `group_barrier` function.

The `atomic_fence` function gives us even more fine-grained control than this, allowing work-items to execute fences specifying both a memory order and scope.

Atomic Operations in SYCL

SYCL provides support for many kinds of atomic operations on a variety of data types. All devices are guaranteed to support atomic versions of common operations (e.g., loads, stores, arithmetic operators), as well as the atomic *compare-and-swap* operations required to implement lock-free algorithms. The language defines these operations for all fundamental integer, floating-point, and pointer types—all devices must support these operations for 32-bit types, but 64-bit-type support is optional.

The `atomic` Class

The `std::atomic` class from C++11 provides an interface for creating and operating on atomic variables. Instances of the atomic class own their data, cannot be moved or copied, and can only be updated using atomic operations. These restrictions significantly reduce the chances of using the class incorrectly and introducing undefined behavior. Unfortunately, they also prevent the class from being used in SYCL kernels—it is impossible to create atomic objects on the host and transfer them to the device! We are free to continue using `std::atomic` in our host code, but attempting to use it inside of device kernels will result in a compiler error.

ATOMIC CLASS DEPRECATED IN SYCL 2020

The SYCL 1.2.1 specification included a `cl::sycl::atomic` class that is loosely based on the `std::atomic` class from C++11. We say loosely because there are some differences between the interfaces of the two classes, most notably that the SYCL 1.2.1 version does not own its data and defaults to a relaxed memory ordering.

The `cl::sycl::atomic` class is deprecated in SYCL 2020. The `atomic_ref` class (covered in the next section) should be used in its place.

The atomic_ref Class

The std::atomic_ref class from C++20 provides an alternative interface for atomic operations which provides greater flexibility than std::atomic. The biggest difference between the two classes is that instances of std::atomic_ref do not own their data but are instead constructed from an existing non-atomic variable. Creating an atomic reference effectively acts as a promise that the referenced variable will only be accessed atomically for the lifetime of the reference. These are exactly the semantics needed by SYCL, since they allow us to create non-atomic data on the host, transfer that data to the device, and treat it as atomic data only after it has been transferred. The atomic_ref class used in SYCL kernels is therefore based on std::atomic_ref.

We say *based on* because the SYCL version of the class includes three additional template arguments as shown in Figure 19-11.

```
template <typename T, memory_order DefaultOrder,
          memory_scope DefaultScope,
          access::address_space AddressSpace>
class atomic_ref {
 public:
  using value_type = T;
  static constexpr size_t required_alignment =
      /* implementation-defined */;
  static constexpr bool is_always_lock_free =
      /* implementation-defined */;
  static constexpr memory_order default_read_order =
      memory_order_traits<DefaultOrder>::read_order;
  static constexpr memory_order default_write_order =
      memory_order_traits<DefaultOrder>::write_order;
  static constexpr memory_order
      default_read_modify_write_order = DefaultOrder;
  static constexpr memory_scope default_scope =
      DefaultScope;

  explicit atomic_ref(T& obj);
  atomic_ref(const atomic_ref& ref) noexcept;
};
```

Figure 19-11. *Constructors and static members of the atomic_ref class*

As discussed previously, the capabilities of different SYCL devices are varied. Selecting a default behavior for the atomic classes of SYCL is a difficult proposition: defaulting to C++ behavior (i.e., `memory_order::seq_cst`, `memory_scope::system`) limits code to executing only on the most capable of devices; on the other hand, breaking with C++ conventions and defaulting to the lowest common denominator (i.e., `memory_order::relaxed`, `memory_scope::work_group`) could lead to unexpected behavior when migrating existing C++ code. The design adopted by SYCL offers a compromise, allowing us to define our desired default behavior as part of an object's type (using the `DefaultOrder` and `DefaultScope` template arguments). Other orderings and scopes can be provided as runtime arguments to specific atomic operations as we see fit—the `DefaultOrder` and `DefaultScope` only impact operations where we do not or cannot override the default behavior (e.g., when using a shorthand operator like +=). The final (optional) template argument denotes the address space in which the referenced object is allocated. Note that if the final template argument is not specified, the referenced variable can be allocated in any address space—although specifying an address space here is optional, we recommend providing explicit address spaces (where possible) to give compilers more information and to avoid unwanted performance overheads.

An atomic reference provides support for different operations depending on the type of object that it references. The basic operations supported by all types are shown in Figure 19-12, providing the ability to atomically move data to and from memory.

```
void store(
    T operand, memory_order order = default_write_order,
    memory_scope scope = default_scope) const noexcept;
T operator=(
    T desired) const noexcept;  // equivalent to store

T load(memory_order order = default_read_order,
       memory_scope scope = default_scope) const noexcept;
operator T() const noexcept;  // equivalent to load

T exchange(
    T operand,
    memory_order order = default_read_modify_write_order,
    memory_scope scope = default_scope) const noexcept;

bool compare_exchange_weak(
    T &expected, T desired, memory_order success,
    memory_order failure,
    memory_scope scope = default_scope) const noexcept;

bool compare_exchange_weak(
    T &expected, T desired,
    memory_order order = default_read_modify_write_order,
    memory_scope scope = default_scope) const noexcept;

bool compare_exchange_strong(
    T &expected, T desired, memory_order success,
    memory_order failure,
    memory_scope scope = default_scope) const noexcept;

bool compare_exchange_strong(
    T &expected, T desired,
    memory_order order = default_read_modify_write_order,
    memory_scope scope = default_scope) const noexcept;
```

***Figure 19-12.** Basic operations with `atomic_ref` for all types*

Atomic references to objects of integral and floating-point types extend the set of available atomic operations to include arithmetic operations, as shown in Figure 19-13 and Figure 19-14. Devices are required to support atomic floating-point types irrespective of whether they feature native support for floating-point atomics in hardware, and many devices are expected to emulate atomic floating-point addition using an atomic compare exchange. This emulation is an important part of providing performance and portability in SYCL, and we should feel free to use floating-point atomics anywhere that an algorithm requires them—the resulting code will work correctly everywhere and will benefit from future improvements in floating-point atomic hardware without any modification!

```
Integral fetch_add(
    Integral operand,
    memory_order order = default_read_modify_write_order,
    memory_scope scope = default_scope) const noexcept;

Integral fetch_sub(
    Integral operand,
    memory_order order = default_read_modify_write_order,
    memory_scope scope = default_scope) const noexcept;

Integral fetch_and(
    Integral operand,
    memory_order order = default_read_modify_write_order,
    memory_scope scope = default_scope) const noexcept;

Integral fetch_or(
    Integral operand,
    memory_order order = default_read_modify_write_order,
    memory_scope scope = default_scope) const noexcept;

Integral fetch_min(
    Integral operand,
    memory_order order = default_read_modify_write_order,
    memory_scope scope = default_scope) const noexcept;

Integral fetch_max(
    Integral operand,
    memory_order order = default_read_modify_write_order,
    memory_scope scope = default_scope) const noexcept;

Integral operator++(int) const noexcept;
Integral operator--(int) const noexcept;
Integral operator++() const noexcept;
Integral operator--() const noexcept;
Integral operator+=(Integral) const noexcept;
Integral operator-=(Integral) const noexcept;
Integral operator&=(Integral) const noexcept;
Integral operator|=(Integral) const noexcept;
```

Figure 19-13. *Additional operations with `atomic_ref` only for integral types*

```
Floating fetch_add(
    Floating operand,
    memory_order order = default_read_modify_write_order,
    memory_scope scope = default_scope) const noexcept;

Floating fetch_sub(
    Floating operand,
    memory_order order = default_read_modify_write_order,
    memory_scope scope = default_scope) const noexcept;

Floating fetch_min(
    Floating operand,
    memory_order order = default_read_modify_write_order,
    memory_scope scope = default_scope) const noexcept;

Floating fetch_max(
    Floating operand,
    memory_order order = default_read_modify_write_order,
    memory_scope scope = default_scope) const noexcept;

Floating operator+=(Floating) const noexcept;
Floating operator-=(Floating) const noexcept;
```

Figure 19-14. *Additional operations with `atomic_ref` only for floating-point types*

Using Atomics with Buffers

As discussed in the previous section, there is no way in SYCL to allocate atomic data and move it between the host and device. To use atomic operations in conjunction with buffers, we must create a buffer of non-atomic data to be transferred to the device and then access that data through an atomic reference.

```
q.submit([&](handler& h) {
  accessor acc{buf, h};
  h.parallel_for(N, [=](id<1> i) {
    int j = i % M;
    atomic_ref<int, memory_order::relaxed,
               memory_scope::system,
               access::address_space::global_space>
        atomic_acc(acc[j]);
    atomic_acc += 1;
  });
});
```

Figure 19-15. *Accessing a buffer via an explicitly created* `atomic_ref`

The code in Figure 19-15 is an example of expressing atomicity in SYCL using an explicitly created atomic reference object. The buffer stores normal integers, and we require an accessor with both read and write permissions. We can then create an instance of `atomic_ref` for each data access, using the += operator as a shorthand alternative for the `fetch_add` member function.

This pattern is useful if we want to mix atomic and non-atomic accesses to a buffer within the same kernel, to avoid paying the performance overheads of atomic operations when they are not required. If we know that only a subset of the memory locations in the buffer will be accessed concurrently by multiple work-items, we only need to use atomic references when accessing that subset. Or, if we know that work-items in the same work-group only concurrently access local memory during one stage of a kernel (i.e., between two work-group barriers), we only need to use atomic references during that stage. When mixing atomic and non-atomic accesses like this, it is important to pay attention to object lifetimes—while any `atomic_ref` referencing a specific object exists, all accesses to that object must occur (atomically) via an instance of `atomic_ref`.

Using Atomics with Unified Shared Memory

As shown in Figure 19-16 (reproduced from Figure 19-7), we can construct atomic references from data stored in USM in exactly the same way as we could for buffers. Indeed, the only difference between this code and the code shown in Figure 19-15 is that the USM code does not require buffers or accessors.

```
q.parallel_for(N, [=](id<1> i) {
   int j = i % M;
   atomic_ref<int, memory_order::relaxed,
              memory_scope::system,
              access::address_space::global_space>
       atomic_data(data[j]);
   atomic_data += 1;
 }).wait();
```

Figure 19-16. *Accessing a USM allocation via an explicitly created* `atomic_ref`

Using Atomics in Real Life

The potential usages of atomics are so broad and varied that it would be impossible for us to provide an example of each usage in this book. We have included two representative examples, with broad applicability across domains:

1. Computing a histogram
2. Implementing device-wide synchronization

Computing a Histogram

The code in Figure 19-17 demonstrates how to use relaxed atomics in conjunction with work-group barriers to compute a histogram. The kernel is split by the barriers into three phases, each with their own atomicity requirements. Remember that the barrier acts both as a synchronization point and an acquire-release fence—this ensures that any reads and writes in one phase are visible to all work-items in the work-group in later phases.

The first phase sets the contents of some work-group local memory to zero. The work-items in each work-group update independent locations in work-group local memory by design—race conditions cannot occur, and no atomicity is required.

The second phase accumulates partial histogram results in local memory. Work-items in the same work-group may update the same locations in work-group local memory, but synchronization can be deferred until the end of the phase—we can satisfy the atomicity requirements using `memory_order::relaxed` and `memory_scope::work_group`.

The third phase contributes the partial histogram results to the total stored in global memory. Work-items in the same work-group are guaranteed to read from independent locations in work-group local memory, but may update the same locations in global memory—we no longer require atomicity for the work-group local memory and can satisfy the atomicity requirements for global memory using `memory_order::relaxed` and `memory_scope::system` as before.

```
q.submit([&](handler& h) {
  auto local = local_accessor<uint32_t, 1>{B, h};
  h.parallel_for(
      nd_range<1>{num_groups * num_items, num_items},
      [=](nd_item<1> it) {
        auto grp = it.get_group();

        // Phase 1: Work-items co-operate to zero local
        // memory
        for (int32_t b = it.get_local_id(0); b < B;
             b += it.get_local_range(0)) {
          local[b] = 0;
        }
        group_barrier(grp);  // Wait for all to be zeroed

        // Phase 2: Work-groups each compute a chunk of
        // the input. Work-items co-operate to compute
        // histogram in local memory
        const auto [group_start, group_end] =
            distribute_range(grp, N);
        for (int i = group_start + it.get_local_id(0);
             i < group_end; i += it.get_local_range(0)) {
          int32_t b = input[i] % B;
          atomic_ref<uint32_t, memory_order::relaxed,
                     memory_scope::work_group,
                     access::address_space::local_space>(local[b])++;
        }
        group_barrier(
            grp);  // Wait for all local histogram
                   // updates to complete

        // Phase 3: Work-items co-operate to update
        // global memory
        for (int32_t b = it.get_local_id(0); b < B;
             b += it.get_local_range(0)) {
          atomic_ref<uint32_t, memory_order::relaxed, memory_scope::system,
                     access::address_space::global_space>(histogram[b]) +=
              local[b];
        }
      });
 }).wait();
```

***Figure 19-17.** Computing a histogram using atomic references in different memory spaces*

Implementing Device-Wide Synchronization

Back in Chapter 4, we warned against writing kernels that attempt to synchronize work-items across work-groups. However, we fully expect several readers of this chapter will be itching to implement their own device-wide synchronization routines atop of atomic operations and that our warnings will be ignored.

Device-wide synchronization is currently not portable and is best left to expert programmers. Future versions of SYCL will address this.

The code discussed in this section is dangerous and should not be expected to work on all devices, because of potential differences in device hardware features and SYCL implementations. The memory ordering guarantees provided by atomics are orthogonal to forward progress guarantees, and, at the time of writing, work-group scheduling in SYCL is completely implementation-defined. Formalizing the concepts and terminology required to describe SYCL's ND-range execution model and the forward progress guarantees associated with work-items, sub-groups, and work-groups is currently an area of active academic research—future versions of SYCL are expected to build on this work to provide additional scheduling queries and controls. For now, these topics should be considered expert-only.

Figure 19-18 shows a simple implementation of a device-wide latch (a single-use barrier), and Figure 19-19 shows a simple example of its usage. Each work-group elects a single work-item to signal arrival of the group at the latch and await the arrival of other groups using a naïve spin-loop, while the other work-items wait for the elected work-item using a work-group barrier. It is this spin-loop that makes device-wide synchronization unsafe; if any work-groups have not yet begun executing or the currently executing work-groups are not scheduled fairly, the code may deadlock.

Relying on memory order alone to implement synchronization primitives may lead to deadlocks in the absence of sufficiently strong forward progress guarantees!

For the code to work correctly, the following three conditions must hold:

1. The atomic operations must use memory orders at least as strict as those shown, to guarantee that the correct fences are generated.
2. The elected leader of each work-group in the ND-range must make progress independently of the leaders in other work-groups, to avoid a single work-item spinning in the loop from starving other work-items that have yet to increment the counter.
3. The device must be capable of executing all work-groups in the ND-range simultaneously, with strong forward progress guarantees, in order to ensure that the elected leaders of every work-group in the ND-range eventually reach the latch.

```
struct device_latch {
  explicit device_latch(size_t num_groups)
      : counter(0), expected(num_groups) {}

  template <int Dimensions>
  void arrive_and_wait(nd_item<Dimensions>& it) {
    auto grp = it.get_group();
    group_barrier(grp);
    // Elect one work-item per work-group to be involved in
    // the synchronization. All other work-items wait at the
    // barrier after the branch.
    if (grp.leader()) {
      atomic_ref<size_t, memory_order::acq_rel,
                 memory_scope::device,
                 access::address_space::global_space>
          atomic_counter(counter);

      // Signal arrival at the barrier.
      // Previous writes should be visible to all work-items
      // on the device.
      atomic_counter++;

      // Wait for all work-groups to arrive.
      // Synchronize with previous releases by all
      // work-items on the device.
      while (atomic_counter.load() != expected) {
      }
    }
    group_barrier(grp);
  }

  size_t counter;
  size_t expected;
};
```

Figure 19-18. *Building a simple device-wide latch on top of atomic references*

```
// Allocate a one-time-use device_latch in USM
void* ptr = sycl::malloc_shared(sizeof(device_latch), q);
device_latch* latch = new (ptr) device_latch(num_groups);
q.submit([&](handler& h) {
   h.parallel_for(R, [=](nd_item<1> it) {
     // Every work-item writes a 1 to its location
     data[it.get_global_linear_id()] = 1;

     // Every work-item waits for all writes
     latch->arrive_and_wait(it);

     // Every work-item sums the values it can see
     size_t sum = 0;
     for (int i = 0; i < num_groups * items_per_group;
          ++i) {
       sum += data[i];
     }
     sums[it.get_global_linear_id()] = sum;
   });
 }).wait();
free(ptr, q);
```

Figure 19-19. *Using the device-wide latch from Figure 19-18*

Although this code is not guaranteed to be portable, we have included it here to highlight two key points: (1) SYCL is expressive enough to enable device-specific tuning, sometimes at the expense of portability; and (2) SYCL already contains the building blocks necessary to implement higher-level synchronization routines, which may be included in a future version of the language.

Summary

This chapter provided a high-level introduction to memory model and atomic classes. Understanding how to use (and how not to use!) these classes is key to developing correct, portable, and efficient parallel programs.

Memory models are an overwhelmingly complex topic, and our focus here has been on establishing a base for writing real applications. If more information is desired, there are several websites, books, and talks dedicated to memory models referenced in the following.

For More Information

- A. Williams, C++ Concurrency in Action: Practical Multithreading, Manning, 2012, 978-1933988771
- H. Sutter, "atomic<> Weapons: The C++ Memory Model and Modern Hardware", `herbsutter.com/2013/02/11/atomic-weapons-the-c-memory-model-and-modern-hardware/`
- H-J. Boehm, "Temporarily discourage memory_order_consume," `wg21.link/p0371`
- C++ Reference, "std::atomic," `en.cppreference.com/w/cpp/atomic/atomic`
- C++ Reference, "std::atomic_ref," `en.cppreference.com/w/cpp/atomic/atomic_ref`

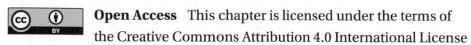

CHAPTER 20

Backend Interoperability

In this chapter we will learn about *backend interoperability*, a SYCL feature that can incrementally add SYCL to an application that is already using other data parallel techniques or APIs.

We will also learn how backend interoperability can be used by expert programmers familiar with low-level APIs to "peek behind the curtain" and use underlying data parallel APIs from SYCL programs directly. This provides direct access to API-specific features, when necessary, while retaining the portability and ease-of-use benefits of SYCL otherwise.

What Is Backend Interoperability?

So far in this book we have referred to SYCL programs running on SYCL devices, but in practice many SYCL implementations build upon lower-level APIs such as OpenCL, Level Zero, CUDA, or others to access the parallel hardware in a system. When a SYCL implementation is built upon a lower-level API, we refer to the target API as a *SYCL backend*. Figure 20-1 shows the relationship between SYCL backends, platforms, and devices. Most SYCL implementations can run SYCL programs on multiple SYCL backends simultaneously to utilize all the parallel hardware in a system.

J. Reinders et al., *Data Parallel C++*, https://doi.org/10.1007/978-1-4842-9691-2_20

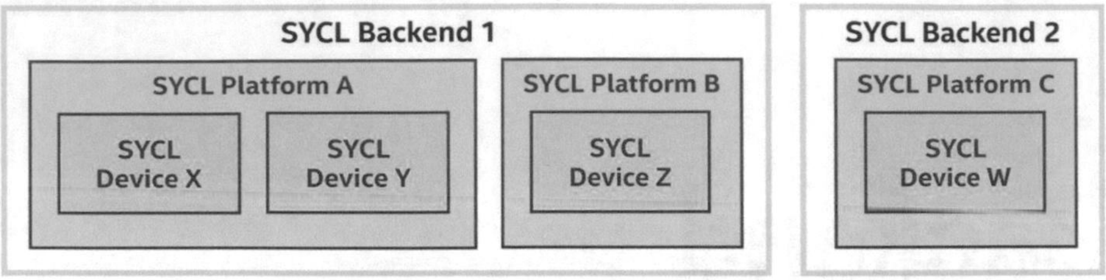

***Figure 20-1.** Relationship between SYCL backends, platforms, and devices*

We can query the SYCL backends in a system by first querying the SYCL platforms and then querying the SYCL backend associated with each platform, as shown in Figure 20-2. The output from this program will depend on the number and type of SYCL devices in a system. If the same device is supported by different SYCL backends, it may enumerate as a SYCL device for each backend.

```
#include <iostream>
#include <sycl/sycl.hpp>
using namespace sycl;

int main() {
  for (auto& p : platform::get_platforms()) {
    std::cout << "SYCL Platform: "
              << p.get_info<info::platform::name>()
              << " is associated with SYCL Backend: "
              << p.get_backend() << std::endl;
  }
  return 0;
}

Example Output:
SYCL Platform: Portable Computing Language is associated with SYCL Backend: opencl
SYCL Platform: Intel(R) OpenCL HD Graphics is associated with SYCL Backend: opencl
SYCL Platform: Intel(R) OpenCL is associated with SYCL Backend: opencl
SYCL Platform: Intel(R) FPGA Emulation Platform for OpenCL(TM) is associated with SYCL
Backend: opencl
SYCL Platform: Intel(R) Level-Zero is associated with SYCL Backend:
ext_oneapi_level_zero
SYCL Platform: NVIDIA CUDA BACKEND is associated with SYCL Backend: ext_oneapi_cuda
SYCL Platform: AMD HIP BACKEND is associated with SYCL Backend: ext_oneapi_hip
```

***Figure 20-2.** Querying the SYCL backend for a SYCL platform*

The associated backend can be queried for most SYCL objects, not just for SYCL platforms. For example, we can also query the associated backend for a SYCL device, a SYCL context, or a SYCL queue.

Backend interoperability lets us use knowledge of the associated backend to interact with and manipulate underlying *native backend objects* that represent SYCL objects for the associated backend.

When Is Backend Interoperability Useful?

Many SYCL programmers will never need to use backend interoperability. In fact, using backend interoperability may be undesirable; backend interoperability will frequently either make a program *more complex* because it requires multiple code paths for multiple SYCL backends, or it will make a program *less portable* because it will restrict execution to devices with a single associated backend.

Still, backend interoperability is a useful tool to have in our toolbox to solve some specific problems. In this section we will explore several common use cases where backend interoperability is useful.

BACKEND INTEROPERABILITY IS LIKE AN INLINE ASSEMBLER

A useful mental model for backend interoperability is that backend interoperability is to SYCL as inline assembler is to C++ host code: backend interoperability is not necessary for learning SYCL or being productive with SYCL, and backend interoperability is often undesirable because it increases complexity or decreases portability. Nevertheless, it is a useful tool to have in our toolbox to solve specific problems.

Adding SYCL to an Existing Codebase

The SYCL programs in this book are designed to teach specific SYCL concepts so they are intentionally straightforward and short. By contrast, most real-world software is large and complex, consisting of thousands or millions of lines of code, perhaps developed by many people over many years. Even if we wanted to do so, completely rewriting a large application to use SYCL may not be feasible.

One of the key benefits provided by backend interoperability is the ability to incrementally add SYCL to an existing codebase that is already using a low-level API, by creating SYCL objects from native backend objects for that API. For example, let's say we have a large OpenCL application that creates an OpenCL context and OpenCL memory objects. Backend interoperability has templated functions like `make_context` and `make_buffer` which let us seamlessly create SYCL objects from these OpenCL objects. After creating SYCL objects from the OpenCL objects, they can be used by SYCL queues and SYCL kernels just like any other SYCL object, as shown in Figure 20-3.

```
// Create SYCL objects from the native backend objects.
context c =
    make_context<backend::opencl>(openclContext);
device d = make_device<backend::opencl>(openclDevice);
buffer data_buf =
    make_buffer<backend::opencl, int>(openclBuffer, c);

// Now use the SYCL objects to create a queue and submit
// a kernel.
queue q{c, d};

q.submit([&](handler& h) {
   accessor data_acc{data_buf, h};
   h.parallel_for(size, [=](id<1> i) {
     data_acc[i] = data_acc[i] + 1;
   });
 }).wait();
```

Figure 20-3. *Creating SYCL objects from OpenCL objects*

The SYCL 2020 specification only defines interoperability with OpenCL backends, but SYCL implementations may provide interoperability with other backends via extensions. Figure 20-4 shows how SYCL objects may be created from Level Zero objects using the sycl_ext_oneapi_backend_level_zero extension.

```
// Create SYCL objects from the native backend objects.
device d = make_device<backend::ext_oneapi_level_zero>(
    level0Device);
context c =
    make_context<backend::ext_oneapi_level_zero>(
        {level0Context,
         {d},
         ext::oneapi::level_zero::ownership::keep});
buffer data_buf =
    make_buffer<backend::ext_oneapi_level_zero, int>(
        {level0Ptr,
         ext::oneapi::level_zero::ownership::keep},
        c);

// Now use the SYCL objects to create a queue and submit
// a kernel.
queue q{c, d};

q.submit([&](handler& h) {
   accessor data_acc{data_buf, h};
   h.parallel_for(size, [=](id<1> i) {
     data_acc[i] = data_acc[i] + 1;
   });
 }).wait();
```

Figure 20-4. *Creating SYCL objects from Level Zero objects*

Notice that the parameters that are passed to create the SYCL objects are slightly different for the Level Zero backend. This will generally be true for any supported backend interoperability because each backend may require different information to properly create the SYCL object. Otherwise, the same make_device, make_context, and make_buffer functions are used for both OpenCL and Level Zero backend interoperability.

Notice also that ownership is handled differently by each backend. For the OpenCL backend, the SYCL implementation uses the reference counting provided by OpenCL to manage the lifetimes of the native backend objects. For the Level Zero backend, the SYCL implementation must be explicitly told whether it should take ownership of the native backend object, or whether our application will keep ownership. If the SYCL implementation takes ownership of the native backend object, then the native backend object will be destroyed when the SYCL object is destroyed; otherwise, our application is responsible for freeing the native backend object directly.

Using Existing Libraries with SYCL

Backend interoperability can also be used to extract native backend objects from SYCL objects. This can be useful to use existing low-level libraries or other helper functions with our SYCL applications. There are two methods to do this: the first uses `get_native` free functions to get native backend objects from SYCL objects. The second uses a `host_task` and an `interop_handle` to get native backend objects from SYCL objects from code that is scheduled by the SYCL runtime.

Getting Backend Objects with Free Functions

For example, let's say we have an optimized OpenCL library that we would like to use with our SYCL application. We can call the backend interoperability `get_native` functions to get native OpenCL objects from our SYCL objects, which can then be used with the OpenCL library. For simplicity, the code in Figure 20-5 just performs a query and allocates some memory with the native OpenCL objects, but they could also be used to perform more complicated operations like creating command queues, compiling programs, and executing kernels.

```
cl_device_id openclDevice =
    get_native<backend::opencl>(d);
cl_context openclContext = get_native<backend::opencl>(c);

// Query the device name from OpenCL:
size_t sz = 0;
clGetDeviceInfo(openclDevice, CL_DEVICE_NAME, 0, nullptr,
                &sz);
std::string openclDeviceName(sz, ' ');
clGetDeviceInfo(openclDevice, CL_DEVICE_NAME, sz,
                &openclDeviceName[0], nullptr);
std::cout << "Device name from OpenCL is: "
          << openclDeviceName << "\n";

// Allocate some memory from OpenCL:
cl_mem openclBuffer = clCreateBuffer(
    openclContext, 0, sizeof(int), nullptr, nullptr);

// Clean up OpenCL objects when done:
clReleaseDevice(openclDevice);
clReleaseContext(openclContext);
clReleaseMemObject(openclBuffer);
```

Figure 20-5. *Extracting OpenCL objects from SYCL objects using `get_native` free functions*

The same `get_native` functions are also added for the Level Zero backend as part of the `sycl_ext_oneapi_backend_level_zero` extension, as shown in Figure 20-6.

```
ze_device_handle_t level0Device =
    get_native<backend::ext_oneapi_level_zero>(d);
ze_context_handle_t level0Context =
    get_native<backend::ext_oneapi_level_zero>(c);

// Query the device name from Level Zero:
ze_device_properties_t level0DeviceProps = {};
level0DeviceProps.stype =
    ZE_STRUCTURE_TYPE_DEVICE_PROPERTIES;

zeDeviceGetProperties(level0Device, &level0DeviceProps);

std::cout << "Device name from SYCL is: "
          << d.get_info<info::device::name>() << "\n";
std::cout << "Device name from Level Zero is: "
          << level0DeviceProps.name << "\n";

// Allocate some memory from Level Zero:
void* level0Ptr = nullptr;
ze_host_mem_alloc_desc_t level0HostAllocDesc = {};
level0HostAllocDesc.stype =
    ZE_STRUCTURE_TYPE_HOST_MEM_ALLOC_DESC;
zeMemAllocHost(level0Context, &level0HostAllocDesc,
               sizeof(int), 0, &level0Ptr);

// Clean up Level Zero objects when done:
zeMemFree(level0Context, level0Ptr);
```

Figure 20-6. *Extracting Level Zero objects from SYCL objects using `get_native` free functions*

Getting Backend Objects via an Interop Handle

Using the `get_native` free functions is an effective way to get backend-specific objects for large sections of code that will use backend APIs directly. In many cases, though, we only want to perform a specific operation in the SYCL task graph using a backend API. In these cases, we can perform the backend-specific operation using a SYCL `host_task` with a special `interop_handle` parameter. The interop_handle represents the state of the SYCL runtime when the host task is invoked and provides access to native backend objects representing the SYCL queue, device, context, and any buffers that were captured for the host task.

Figure 20-7 shows how to use the `interop_handle` to get native OpenCL objects from a `host_task` that is scheduled by the SYCL runtime. For simplicity, this sample also only performs some queries using the native OpenCL objects, but real application code would commonly enqueue a kernel or call into a library using the native OpenCL objects. Because these operations are performed from a host task, they will be properly scheduled with any other operations in the SYCL queue.

```
q.submit([&](handler& h) {
  accessor a{b, h};
  h.host_task([=](interop_handle ih) {
    // Get the OpenCL device from the interop handle:
    auto openclDevice =
        ih.get_native_device<backend::opencl>();

    // Query the device name from the OpenCL device:
    size_t sz = 0;
    clGetDeviceInfo(openclDevice, CL_DEVICE_NAME, 0,
                    nullptr, &sz);
    std::string openclDeviceName(sz, ' ');
    clGetDeviceInfo(openclDevice, CL_DEVICE_NAME, sz,
                    &openclDeviceName[0], nullptr);
    std::cout << "Device name from OpenCL is: "
              << openclDeviceName << "\n";

    // Get the OpenCL buffer from the interop handle:
    auto openclMem =
        ih.get_native_mem<backend::opencl>(a)[0];

    // Query the size of the OpenCL buffer:
    clGetMemObjectInfo(openclMem, CL_MEM_SIZE, sizeof(sz),
                       &sz, nullptr);
    std::cout << "Buffer size from OpenCL is: " << sz
              << " bytes\n";
  });
});
```

Figure 20-7. *Extracting OpenCL objects from SYCL objects using an `interop_handle`*

Notice that when getting native OpenCL objects for our accessor, the `get_native_mem` member function of the `interop_handle` returns a vector of `cl_mem` memory objects. This is a requirement in the SYCL 2020 specification, where the return type of member functions of the `interop_handle` must match the `get_native` free functions, but for the `interop_handle` usage we can simply use the first element of the vector.

As with the `get_native` free functions, similar functionality may also be provided for other SYCL backends via extensions. Figure 20-8 shows how to perform similar operations with the Level Zero backend using the `sycl_ext_oneapi_backend_level_zero` extension.

```
q.submit([&](handler& h) {
  accessor a{b, h};
  h.host_task([=](interop_handle ih) {
    // Get the Level Zero device from the interop handle:
    auto level0Device = ih.get_native_device<
        backend::ext_oneapi_level_zero>();

    // Query the device name from Level Zero:
    ze_device_properties_t level0DeviceProps = {};
    level0DeviceProps.stype =
        ZE_STRUCTURE_TYPE_DEVICE_PROPERTIES;
    zeDeviceGetProperties(level0Device,
                          &level0DeviceProps);
    std::cout << "Device name from Level Zero is: "
              << level0DeviceProps.name << "\n";

    // Get the Level Zero context and memory allocation
    // from the interop handle:
    auto level0Context = ih.get_native_context<
        backend::ext_oneapi_level_zero>();
    auto ptr =
        ih.get_native_mem<backend::ext_oneapi_level_zero>(
            a);

    // Query the size of the memory allocation:
    size_t sz = 0;
    zeMemGetAddressRange(level0Context, ptr, nullptr,
                         &sz);
    std::cout << "Buffer size from Level Zero is: " << sz
              << " bytes\n";
  });
});
```

Figure 20-8. *Extracting OpenCL objects from SYCL objects using an `interop_handle`*

Using Backend Interoperability for Kernels

This section describes how to use backend interoperability to compile kernels and manipulate kernel bundles. This is an area that was significantly redesigned in SYCL 2020 to increase robustness and to add the flexibility that is required to support different SYCL backends.

Earlier versions of SYCL supported two interoperability mechanisms for kernels. The first mechanism enabled creation of a kernel from an API-defined handle. The second enabled creation of a kernel from an API-defined source or intermediate representation, such as OpenCL C source or SPIR-V intermediate representation. These two mechanisms still exist in SYCL 2020, though the syntax for both mechanisms has been updated and now uses backend interoperability.

Interoperability with API-Defined Kernel Objects

With this form of interoperability, the kernel objects themselves are created using the low-level API and then imported into SYCL using backend interoperability. The code in Figure 20-9 shows how get an OpenCL context from a SYCL context, how to create an OpenCL kernel using this OpenCL context, and then how to create and use a SYCL kernel from the OpenCL kernel object.

```
// Get the native OpenCL context from the SYCL context:
auto openclContext = get_native<backend::opencl>(c);
const char* kernelSource =
    R"CLC(
        kernel void add(global int* data) {
            int index = get_global_id(0);
            data[index] = data[index] + 1;
        }
    )CLC";
// Create an OpenCL kernel using this context:
cl_program p = clCreateProgramWithSource(
    openclContext, 1, &kernelSource, nullptr, nullptr);
clBuildProgram(p, 0, nullptr, nullptr, nullptr,
               nullptr);
cl_kernel k = clCreateKernel(p, "add", nullptr);

// Create a SYCL kernel from the OpenCL kernel:
auto sk = make_kernel<backend::opencl>(k, c);

// Use the OpenCL kernel with a SYCL queue:
q.submit([&](handler& h) {
  accessor data_acc{data_buf, h};

  h.set_args(data_acc);
  h.parallel_for(size, sk);
});

// Clean up OpenCL objects when done:
clReleaseContext(openclContext);
clReleaseProgram(p);
clReleaseKernel(k);
```

Figure 20-9. *Kernel created from an OpenCL kernel object*

Because the SYCL compiler does not have visibility into a SYCL kernel that was created using the low-level API directly, any kernel arguments must explicitly be passed using the `set_arg()` or `set_args()` interface. Additionally, the SYCL runtime and the low-level API kernel must agree on a convention to pass objects as kernel arguments. This convention should be described as part of the backend interoperability specification. In this example, the accessor `data_acc` is passed as the global pointer kernel argument `data`.

The SYCL 2020 standard leaves the precise semantics of `set_arg()` and `set_args()` interfaces to be defined by each SYCL backend specification. This allows flexibility but is another way how the code using backend interoperability that we write is likely to be specific to the backends we target.

Interoperability with Non-SYCL Source Languages

With this form of interoperability, the contents of the kernel are described as source code or as an intermediate representation that is not defined by SYCL. This form of interoperability allows reuse of kernel libraries written in other source languages or use of domain-specific languages (DSLs) that generate code in an intermediate representation.

Previous versions of SYCL included functions like `build_with_source` to directly create a SYCL program from an API-defined source language but this functionality was removed in SYCL 2020. When a backend directly supports an API-defined source language, such as the OpenCL C kernel used by the OpenCL backend in Figure 20-9, this removal is not a problem, but what should we do if a backend does not directly support a specific source language?

Some SYCL implementations may provide an explicit *online compiler* to compile from a source language that cannot be used directly by a backend to a different format supported by a backend. Figure 20-10 shows how to use the experimental `sycl_ext_intel_online_compiler` extension to compile from OpenCL C source, which is not supported by the Level Zero backend, to SPIR-V intermediate representation, which is supported by the Level Zero backend. Using this method, a kernel can be used by any backend so long as it can be compiled by the online compiler into a format supported by the backend.

CAUTION, EXPERIMENTAL EXTENSION!

The `sycl_ext_intel_online_compiler` extension is an experimental extension, so it is subject to change or removal! We have included it in this book because it provides a way to achieve similar functionality as the previous SYCL `build_with_source` function and because it is a convenient way to demonstrate how domain-specific languages may interface with SYCL backends to execute kernels.

```
// Compile OpenCL C kernel source to SPIR-V intermediate
// representation using the online compiler:
const char* kernelSource =
    R"CLC(
        kernel void add(global int* data) {
            int index = get_global_id(0);
            data[index] = data[index] + 1;
        }
    )CLC";
online_compiler<source_language::opencl_c> compiler(d);
std::vector<byte> spirv =
    compiler.compile(kernelSource);

// Get the native Level Zero context and device:
auto level0Context =
    get_native<backend::ext_oneapi_level_zero>(c);
auto level0Device =
    get_native<backend::ext_oneapi_level_zero>(d);

// Create a Level Zero kernel using this context:
ze_module_handle_t level0Module = nullptr;
ze_module_desc_t moduleDesc = {};
moduleDesc.stype = ZE_STRUCTURE_TYPE_MODULE_DESC;
moduleDesc.format = ZE_MODULE_FORMAT_IL_SPIRV;
moduleDesc.inputSize = spirv.size();
moduleDesc.pInputModule = spirv.data();
zeModuleCreate(level0Context, level0Device, &moduleDesc,
               &level0Module, nullptr);

ze_kernel_handle_t level0Kernel = nullptr;
ze_kernel_desc_t kernelDesc = {};
kernelDesc.stype = ZE_STRUCTURE_TYPE_KERNEL_DESC;
kernelDesc.pKernelName = "add";
zeKernelCreate(level0Module, &kernelDesc,
               &level0Kernel);

// Create a SYCL kernel from the Level Zero kernel:
auto skb =
    make_kernel_bundle<backend::ext_oneapi_level_zero,
                       bundle_state::executable>(
        {level0Module}, c);
auto sk = make_kernel<backend::ext_oneapi_level_zero>(
    {skb, level0Kernel}, c);

// Use the Level Zero kernel with a SYCL queue:
q.submit([&](handler& h) {
  accessor data_acc{data_buf, h};

  h.set_args(data_acc);
  h.parallel_for(size, sk);
});
```

Figure 20-10. *Kernel created using SPIR-V and the online compiler*

In this example, the kernel source string is represented as a C++ raw string literal in the same file as the SYCL host API calls, but there is no requirement that this is the case, and some applications may read the kernel source string from a file or even generate it just-in-time.

As before, because the SYCL compiler does not have visibility into a SYCL kernel written in an API-defined source language, any kernel arguments must explicitly be passed using the `set_arg()` or `set_args()` interface.

Backend Interoperability Hints and Tips

This section describes practical hints and tips to effectively use backend interoperability.

Choosing a Device for a Specific Backend

The first requirement to properly use backend interoperability is to choose a SYCL device associated with the required SYCL backend. There are several ways to accomplish this.

The first is to integrate the required SYCL backend into existing custom device selection logic, by querying the associated backend while scoring each device. If our application is already using custom device selection logic, this should be a straightforward addition. This mechanism is also portable because it uses only standard SYCL queries.

For applications that do not already use custom device selection logic, we can write a short C++ lambda expression to iterate over all devices to find a device with the requested backend, as shown in Figure 20-11. Because this version of `find_device` does not request a specific device type, it is effectively a replacement for the standard `default_selector_v`.

```
#include <iostream>
#include <sycl/sycl.hpp>
using namespace sycl;

int main() {
  auto find_device = [](backend b,
                        info::device_type t =
                          info::device_type::all) {
    for (auto d : device::get_devices(t)) {
      if (d.get_backend() == b) {
        return d;
      }
    }
    throw sycl::exception(errc::runtime,
                          "Could not find a device with "
                          "the requested backend!");
  };

  try {
    device d{find_device(backend::opencl)};
    std::cout << "Found an OpenCL SYCL device: "
              << d.get_info<info::device::name>() << "\n";
  } catch (const sycl::exception &e) {
    std::cout << "No OpenCL SYCL devices were found.\n";
  }

  try {
    device d{find_device(backend::ext_oneapi_level_zero)};
    std::cout << "Found a Level Zero SYCL device: "
              << d.get_info<info::device::name>() << "\n";
  } catch (const sycl::exception &e) {
    std::cout << "No Level Zero SYCL devices were found.\n";
  }

  return 0;
}
```

```
Example Output:
Found an OpenCL SYCL device: pthread-12th Gen Intel(R) Core(TM) i9-12900K
Found a Level Zero SYCL device: Intel(R) UHD Graphics 770 [0x4680]
```

Figure 20-11. *Finding a SYCL device with a specific backend*

Finally, for fast prototyping some SYCL implementations can use external mechanisms, such as environment variables, to influence the SYCL devices they enumerate. As an example, the DPC++ SYCL runtime can use the ONEAPI_DEVICE_SELECTOR environment variable to limit enumerated devices to specific device types or associated device backends (refer to Chapter 13). This is not an ideal solution for production code because it requires external configuration, but it is a useful mechanism for prototype code to ensure that an application is using a specific device from a specific backend.

Be Careful About Contexts!

Recall from Chapters 6 and 13 that many SYCL objects, such as kernels and USM allocations, are generally not accessible by a SYCL context if they were created in a different SYCL context. This is still true when using backend interoperability; therefore, a backend-specific context created using a backend API generally will not have access to objects created in a different SYCL context (and vice versa) even if the SYCL context is associated with the same backend.

To safely share objects between SYCL and a backend, we should always either create our SYCL context from a native backend context using `make_context`, or we should get a native backend context from a SYCL context using `get_native`.

Always create a SYCL context from a native backend context or get a native backend context from a SYCL context to safely share objects between SYCL and a backend!

Access Low-Level API-Specific Features

Occasionally a cutting-edge feature will be available in a low-level API before it is available in SYCL, even as a SYCL extension. Some features may even be so backend-specific or so device-specific that they will never be exposed through SYCL. For example, some native backend APIs may provide access to queues with specific properties or unique kernel instructions for specific accelerator hardware. Although we hope and expect these cases to be rare, when these types of features exist, we may still gain access to them using backend interoperability.

Support for Other Backends

The examples in this chapter demonstrated backend interoperability with OpenCL and Level Zero backends, but SYCL is a growing ecosystem and SYCL implementations are regularly adding support for additional backends and devices. For example, several SYCL implementations supporting CUDA and HIP backends already have some support for interoperability with these backends. Check the documentation for a SYCL implementation to determine which SYCL backends are supported and whether they support backend interoperability!

Summary

In this chapter, we discovered how each SYCL object is associated with an underlying SYCL backend and how to query the SYCL backends in a system. We described how backend interoperability provides a mechanism for our SYCL application to directly interact with an underlying backend API. We discussed how this enables us to incrementally add SYCL to an application that is directly using a backend API, or to reuse libraries or utility functions written specifically for a backend API. We also discussed how backend interoperability reduces application portability, by restricting which SYCL devices the application will run on.

We specifically explored how backend interoperability for kernels provides similar functionality in SYCL 2020 that was present in earlier versions of SYCL. We examined how an online compiler extension can enable the use of some source languages for kernels, even if they are not directly understood by some SYCL backends.

Finally, we reviewed practical hints and tips to effectively use backend interoperability in our programs, such as how to choose a SYCL device for a specific SYCL backend, how to set up a SYCL context for backend interoperability, and how backend interoperability can provide access to features even if they have not been added to SYCL.

CHAPTER 21

Migrating CUDA Code

Many readers of this book have likely encountered data parallel code written in CUDA. Some readers may even be CUDA experts! In this chapter we will describe some of the similarities between CUDA and SYCL, some of the differences, and useful tools and techniques to help migrate CUDA code effectively and efficiently to C++ with SYCL.

Design Differences Between CUDA and SYCL

Before we dive into the details, it is first instructive to identify key design differences between CUDA and SYCL. This can provide useful background to inform why some differences exist, to understand which differences may disappear in time and which differences are likely to remain.

Multiple Targets vs. Single Device Targets

One of the biggest design differences between CUDA and SYCL is the universe of devices they are designed to support. CUDA is designed to support GPU devices from a single device vendor, so most CUDA devices look relatively similar. As an example, all CUDA devices currently include texture sampling hardware and all CUDA devices currently support the same maximum work-group size. This reduces complexity, but also reduces where a CUDA application may run.

J. Reinders et al., *Data Parallel C++*, https://doi.org/10.1007/978-1-4842-9691-2_21

By contrast, SYCL is designed to support a diverse set of heterogeneous accelerators, including different devices from different device vendors. This flexibility gives SYCL programs the freedom to take advantage of the computing resources in a modern heterogeneous system; however, this flexibility does come at a modest cost. For example, as SYCL programmers we may need to enumerate the devices in the system, examine their properties, and choose which device or devices are best suited to run different parts of our program.

Of course, if our SYCL program does not intend to utilize *all* the computing resources in our system, various shortcuts exist to reduce code verbosity, such as standard device selectors. Figure 21-1 shows a basic SYCL sample that uses a queue for the default device, chosen by the SYCL implementation.

```
// Declare an in-order SYCL queue for the default device
queue q{property::queue::in_order()};
std::cout << "Running on device: "
          << q.get_device().get_info<info::device::name>()
          << "\n";

int* buffer = malloc_host<int>(count, q);
q.fill(buffer, 0, count);

q.parallel_for(count, [=](auto id) {
   buffer[id] = id;
 }).wait();
```

Figure 21-1. *Running a kernel on the default SYCL device*

This SYCL code is very similar to the equivalent CUDA code, shown in Figure 21-2.

```
// The CUDA kernel is a separate function
__global__ void TestKernel(int* dst) {
  auto id = blockIdx.x * blockDim.x + threadIdx.x;
  dst[id] = id;
}

int main() {
  // CUDA uses device zero by default
  cudaDeviceProp deviceProp;
  cudaGetDeviceProperties(&deviceProp, 0);
  std::cout << "Running on device: " << deviceProp.name << "\n";

  int* buffer = nullptr;
  cudaMallocHost(&buffer, count * sizeof(int));
  cudaMemset(buffer, 0, count * sizeof(int));

  TestKernel<<<count / 256, 256>>>(buffer);
  cudaDeviceSynchronize();
  // ...
```

***Figure 21-2.** Running a kernel on the default CUDA device*

Real-world SYCL code is usually more complicated. For example, many SYCL applications will enumerate and choose a specific device or a combination of devices to run on (refer to Chapter 2) by searching for specific device characteristics (refer to Chapter 12). Concise options exist when this complexity is not needed or desired, though, and SYCL is well designed to support the additional complexity when it is required.

Aligning to C++ vs. Extending C++

Another important design difference between CUDA and SYCL is how they interact with other programming languages, especially C++. SYCL code *is* standard C++ code, without any language extensions. By learning to read, understand, and write C++ code, we are also able to read and understand SYCL code. Similarly, if a compiler can parse C++ code, it can also parse SYCL code.

CUDA made a different decision. Instead, CUDA *extends* C++ by adding new keywords and a special syntax to execute kernels. At times, the language extensions can be more concise, but they are also one more syntax to learn and remember, and the language extensions mean that CUDA code can only be compiled by a CUDA-enabled compiler.

To see this design difference in practice, notice how the SYCL example in Figure 21-1 uses a standard C++ lambda expression to represent the kernel code and a standard C++ function call to submit the kernel for execution. The CUDA example in Figure 21-2 instead uses a special `__global__` keyword to identify the kernel code and a special `<<< >>>` syntax to submit the kernel for execution.

Terminology Differences Between CUDA and SYCL

Now that we understand some of the key design differences between SYCL and CUDA we are almost ready to start examining specific similarities and differences. We have one more bit of background to take care of first, though: because CUDA and SYCL often use different terms for similar concepts, we need a decoder so we can meaningfully compare the two APIs, such as the summary in Figure 21-3.

Concept	SYCL Term	CUDA Term
A function that is executed in parallel on a device.	Kernel	Kernel
The N-dimensional parallel index space.	Range (generally), or ND-Range (with grouping)	Grid (always has grouping)
A kernel instance executing at a point in the parallel index space.	Work-Item	Thread
An application-defined group of kernel instances in the parallel index space that can communicate and synchronize.	Work-Group	Block
An implementation-defined group of kernel instances with additional communication and synchronization capabilities.	Sub-Group	Warp
Memory used to exchange data among instances in a group.	Local Memory	Shared Memory
Function used to synchronize instances in a group.	`group_barrier()`	`__syncthreads()`, `__syncwarp()`, `coop_group.sync()`
Object used to execute kernels or other work on a device.	Queue	Stream

Figure 21-3. *CUDA and SYCL decoder ring*

Unlike the rest of this book where SYCL terminology was used consistently, this chapter may use the CUDA terms and the SYCL terms interchangeably.

Similarities and Differences

This section describes some of the syntactic and behavioral similarities between SYCL and CUDA as well as places where SYCL and CUDA differ.

Execution Model

Fundamentally, both SYCL and CUDA use the same data-parallel kernel execution model introduced in Chapter 4 and described throughout this book. The terminology may be slightly different, for example, SYCL refers to an ND-range and CUDA refers to a grid, but we can use our decoder ring in Figure 21-3 to translate key concepts from SYCL to CUDA and vice versa.

In-Order vs. Out-of-Order Queues

Despite the many execution model similarities, several differences do exist. One difference is that CUDA streams are unconditionally *in-order*. This means that any kernel or memory operation submitted to a CUDA stream must complete before the next submitted kernel or memory copy operation can start. SYCL queues instead are *out-of-order* by default but may optionally be in-order by passing the `in_order` queue property when the SYCL queue is created (refer to Chapter 8).

An in-order CUDA stream is simpler because it does not require explicit scheduling or dependence management. This simplicity means that CUDA applications typically do not use mechanisms like `accessors` or `depends_on` to order operations in a stream. The in-order semantics also constrain execution, though, and do not offer any opportunity for overlapping execution of two commands in a single stream. Because a CUDA application cannot overlap execution of two commands in a single stream, when a CUDA application would like to (potentially) execute commands simultaneously, it will submit the commands to different CUDA streams, because commands in different CUDA streams may execute simultaneously.

This same pattern of submitting to multiple in-order queues to potentially execute kernels or memory operations simultaneously works in SYCL also, and many SYCL implementations and SYCL devices are optimized to handle this case. Out-of-order SYCL queues provide an alternative mechanism to overlap execution with just a single queue, though, and many SYCL implementations and SYCL devices are optimized to handle this case as well.

Ultimately, whether to use multiple in-order SYCL queues or fewer out-of-order SYCL queues is a matter of personal preference and programming style, and we can choose whichever option makes the most sense for our SYCL programs. The SYCL examples in this chapter create in-order SYCL queues to stay as close to the equivalent CUDA examples as possible.

Contiguous Dimension

Another difference that is likely to confuse novice and expert CUDA programmers alike concerns multidimensional SYCL ranges or CUDA grids: SYCL aligns its convention with multidimensional arrays in standard C++, so the last dimension is the *contiguous* dimension, also known as the *unit-stride* dimension or the *fastest moving* dimension. CUDA instead aligns to graphics conventions, so the first dimension is the contiguous dimension. Because of this difference, multidimensional SYCL ranges will appear to be transposed compared to the equivalent CUDA code, and the highest dimension of a SYCL `id` will correspond to the x-component of the comparable CUDA built-in variables, not the lowest dimension.

To demonstrate this difference, consider the CUDA example in Figure 21-4. In this example, each CUDA thread exchanges its value of `threadIdx.x` with its neighbor. Because the x-component is the fastest moving component in CUDA, we do not expect a CUDA thread's value to match its neighbor thread's value.

```
__global__ void ExchangeKernel(int* dst) {
  auto index = get_global_linear_id(); // helper function
  auto fastest = threadIdx.x;
  auto neighbor = __shfl_xor_sync(0xFFFFFFFF, fastest, 1);
  dst[index] = neighbor;
}
...
dim3 threadsPerBlock(16, 2);
ExchangeKernel<<<1, threadsPerBlock>>>(buffer);
cudaDeviceSynchronize();
```

Figure 21-4. *x-component is the contiguous dimension in CUDA*

The equivalent SYCL example is shown in Figure 21-5. Notice that in the SYCL example the ND-range is `{2, 16}` rather than `(16, 2)` in the CUDA example, so the parallel index space appears to be transposed. The SYCL example also describes the ND-range as a `{2, 16}` global range divided into work-groups of size `{2, 16}`, whereas the CUDA example describes a grid of one block with `(16, 2)` CUDA threads per block.

Additionally, notice that each SYCL work-item exchanges the value of its `item.get_local_id(1)` (not `item.get_local_id(0)`!) with its neighbor, because the last dimension is the fastest moving component in SYCL. In this SYCL example, we also do not expect a SYCL work-item's value to match its neighbor work-item's value.

```
q.parallel_for(nd_range<2>{{2, 16}, {2, 16}},
               [=](auto item) {
                 auto index = item.get_global_linear_id();
                 auto fastest = item.get_local_id(1);
                 auto sg = item.get_sub_group();
                 auto neighbor =
                     permute_group_by_xor(sg, fastest, 1);
                 buffer[index] = neighbor;
               })
    .wait();
```

Figure 21-5. *Last dimension is the contiguous dimension in SYCL*

Sub-Group Sizes (Warp Sizes)

There are a few more differences we can spot if we look carefully at these examples, specifically relating to the function used to exchange data with a neighbor.

The CUDA example uses the function `__shfl_xor_sync(0xFFFFFFFF, fastest, 1)` to exchange data with a neighbor. For this function, the first argument `0xFFFFFFFF` is a bitfield mask indicating the set of CUDA threads participating in the call. For CUDA devices, a 32-bit mask is sufficient, because the warp size is currently 32 for all CUDA devices.

The SYCL example uses the function `permute_group_by_xor(sg, fastest, 1)` to exchange data with its neighbor. For this function, the first argument describes the set of work-items participating in the call. In this case, `sg` represents the entire sub-group. Because the set of work-items is specified by a group object rather than a bitfield mask, it can represent sets of arbitrary sizes. This flexibility is desirable because the sub-group size may be less than or greater than 32 for some SYCL devices.

In this specific case, the CUDA example can be rewritten to use the more modern CUDA *cooperative groups* syntax rather than the older `__shfl_xor_sync` syntax. The CUDA cooperative groups equivalent is shown in Figure 21-6. This version looks a lot more like the SYCL kernel and is a good example how the later versions of CUDA and SYCL 2020 are growing even closer together.

```
__global__ void ExchangeKernelCoopGroups(int* dst) {
  namespace cg = cooperative_groups;
  auto index = cg::this_grid().thread_rank();
  auto fastest = threadIdx.x;
  auto warp = cg::tiled_partition<32>(cg::this_thread_block());
  auto neighbor = warp.shfl_xor(fastest, 1);
  dst[index] = neighbor;
}
```

Figure 21-6. *Exchanging data with CUDA cooperative groups*

Forward Progress Guarantees

We can find one more difference if we look very carefully at the examples in Figures 21-4 and 21-5, although this difference is more subtle. Once again, the difference is related to the `__shfl_xor_sync` function used to exchange data with a neighbor, and in this case the difference is implied by the `_sync` suffix on the function. The `_sync` suffix indicates this function is *synchronizing* the CUDA threads, though this naturally may lead us to ask, why may the CUDA threads be unsynchronized in the first place, before calling this function?

In Chapters 15 and 16, we developed a mental model for a data-parallel kernel executing on a CPU or GPU where a group of work-items is processed simultaneously, in lockstep, using SIMD instructions. While this is a useful mental model for CPUs and GPUs from many vendors, it is not the only way a data-parallel kernel may be executed using SYCL or CUDA, and one of the cases where this mental model breaks is for newer CUDA devices supporting a feature called *independent thread scheduling*.

For CUDA devices with independent thread scheduling, the individual CUDA threads make progress independently, rather than as a group. These additional forward progress guarantees enable code patterns to execute safely on a CUDA device that may not execute correctly on a SYCL device without the stronger forward progress guarantees. The `_sync` suffix on the `__shfl_xor_sync` function was added in CUDA to clearly indicate that the function requires synchronization and to specify the CUDA threads that are synchronizing using the 32-bit mask.

Forward progress guarantees are an active topic in the SYCL community, and it is very likely that a future version of SYCL will add queries to determine the forward progress capabilities of a device, along with properties to specify the forward progress requirements of a kernel. For now, though, we should be aware that a syntactically correct SYCL program that was ported from CUDA may not execute correctly on all SYCL devices due to independent thread scheduling.

Barriers

One final, subtle execution model difference we should be aware of concerns the CUDA `__syncthreads` function compared to the SYCL `group_barrier` equivalent. The CUDA `__syncthreads` function synchronizes all *non-exited* CUDA threads in the thread block, whereas the SYCL `group_barrier` function synchronizes *all* work-items in the work-group. This means that a CUDA kernel will run correctly if some CUDA threads early exit before calling `__syncthreads`, but there is no guarantee that a SYCL kernel like the one shown in Figure 21-7 will run correctly.

```
std::cout << "WARNING: May deadlock on some devices!\n";
q.parallel_for(nd_range<1>{64, 64}, [=](auto item) {
   int id = item.get_global_id(0);
   if (id >= count) {
     return;  // early exit
   }
   group_barrier(item.get_group());
   buffer[id] = id;
 }).wait();
```

Figure 21-7. *Possible SYCL barrier deadlock*

In this case, the fix is straightforward: the range check can be moved after the `group_barrier`, or in this specific case, the `group_barrier` can be removed entirely. This is not always the case though, and other kernels may require restructuring to ensure all work-items always reach or always skip a `group_barrier`.

Memory Model

Fundamentally, both CUDA and SYCL use a similar weakly-ordered memory model. Luckily there are only a few memory model differences we need to keep in mind when we are migrating a CUDA kernel to SYCL.

Barriers

By default, the CUDA __syncthreads barrier function and the SYCL group_barrier barrier function has the same effects on the memory model, assuming the group passed to the SYCL group_barrier is a work-group. Likewise, the CUDA __syncwarp barrier function has the same effects as the SYCL group_barrier barrier function, assuming the group passed to the SYCL group_barrier is a sub-group.

The SYCL group_barrier accepts an optional parameter to specify the fence_scope for the barrier, but in most cases, this can be omitted. A wider scope can be passed to group_barrier, such as memory_scope::device, but this usually is not required, and it may cause the SYCL group_barrier to be more expensive than the CUDA __syncthreads barrier.

```
q.parallel_for(nd_range<1>{16, 16}, [=](auto item) {
   // Equivalent of __syncthreads, or
   // this_thread_block().sync():
   group_barrier(item.get_group());

   // Equivalent of __syncwarp, or
   // tiled_partition<32>(this_thread_block()).sync():
   group_barrier(item.get_sub_group());
 }).wait();
```

Figure 21-8. *CUDA and SYCL barrier equivalents*

The code in Figure 21-8 shows the equivalent barrier syntax for CUDA and SYCL. Notice how the newer CUDA cooperative groups syntax using this_thread_block and tiled_partition has a sync function that is even closer to the SYCL group_barrier. This is another good example how later versions of CUDA and SYCL 2020 are becoming more and more similar.

Atomics and Fences

Both CUDA and SYCL support similar atomic operations, though as with barriers there are a few important differences we should be aware of. The most important difference concerns the default atomic *memory order*.

Many CUDA programs are written using an older C-like atomic syntax where the atomic function takes a pointer to memory, like `atomicAdd`. These atomic functions are *relaxed* atomics and operate at device scope. There are also suffixed versions of these atomic functions that operate at a different scope, such as `atomicAdd_system` and `atomicAdd_block`, but these are uncommon.

The SYCL atomic syntax is a little different and is based on `std::atomic_ref` from C++20 (refer to Chapter 19 for details about the SYCL `atomic_ref` class and how it compares to `std::atomic_ref`). If we want our SYCL atomic to be equivalent to the CUDA `atomicAdd` function, we will want to declare our SYCL `atomic_ref` to have a similar `memory_order::relaxed` memory order and `memory_scope::device` scope, as shown in Figure 21-9.

```
q.parallel_for(count, [=](auto id) {
  // The SYCL atomic_ref must specify the default order
  // and default scope as part of the atomic_ref type. To
  // match the behavior of the CUDA atomicAdd we want a
  // relaxed atomic with device scope:
  atomic_ref<int, memory_order::relaxed,
             memory_scope::device>
      aref(*buffer);

  // When no memory order is specified, the defaults are
  // used:
  aref.fetch_add(1);

  // We can also specify the memory order and scope as
  // part of the atomic operation:
  aref.fetch_add(1, memory_order::relaxed,
                 memory_scope::device);
});
```

Figure 21-9. *CUDA and SYCL atomic equivalents*

Newer CUDA code may use the `cuda::atomic_ref` class from the CUDA C++ Standard Library. The `cuda::atomic_ref` class looks more like the SYCL `atomic_ref` class, but there are some important differences to be aware of with it, also:

- The scope is optional for a CUDA `atomic_ref`, but defaults to the entire system if unspecified. The SYCL `atomic_ref` must specify an atomic scope in all cases.
- The default atomic order for a CUDA `atomic_ref` is unconditionally sequential consistency, whereas the SYCL `atomic_ref` may specify a different default atomic order. By specifying a default atomic order, our SYCL code can be more concise and use convenience operators like += even when the atomic order is something other than sequential consistency.

There is one final concern we need to keep in mind when our code or algorithm requires atomics: some atomic operations and atomic scopes are not required by the SYCL specification and may not be supported by all SYCL devices. This is also true for CUDA devices, but it is especially important to remember for SYCL due to the diversity of SYCL devices. Please refer to Chapter 12 for more detail on how to query properties of a SYCL device and to Chapter 19 for descriptions of the atomic capabilities that may be supported by a SYCL device or context.

Other Differences

This section describes a few other miscellaneous differences to keep in mind when we are porting CUDA code to SYCL.

Item Classes vs. Built-In Variables

One of the bigger stylistic differences between CUDA and SYCL is the way kernel instances identify their location in the N-dimensional parallel index space. Recall from Chapter 4 that every SYCL kernel must take an `item`, an `nd_item`, an `id`, or in some cases an integral argument identifying the work-item in the parallel index space. The `item` and `nd_item` classes can also be used to query information about the parallel index space itself, such as the global range, the local range, and the different groups that the work-item belongs to.

CUDA kernels do not include any arguments to identify the CUDA thread in the parallel index space. Instead, CUDA threads use built-in variables such as `blockIdx` and `threadIdx` to identify the location in the parallel index space and built-in variables such as `gridDim` and `blockDim` to represent information about the parallel index space itself. Newer CUDA kernels that use cooperative groups can also construct certain cooperative groups implicitly by calling built-in functions like `this_thread_block`.

This is usually only a syntactic difference that does not functionally affect the code we can write, though it does mean that SYCL kernels may pass an `item` or an `nd_item` to called functions in more cases, say if a called function needs to know the work-item index.

Contexts

Another conceptual difference between CUDA and SYCL is the idea of a SYCL context. Recall that a SYCL context is an object that stores the state of a SYCL application for a set of SYCL devices. As an example, a SYCL context may store information about memory allocations or compiled programs. Contexts are an important concept to a SYCL application because a single SYCL application may support devices from multiple vendors, perhaps using multiple backend APIs.

In most cases our SYCL programs can be blissfully unaware that contexts exist, and most of the example programs in this book do not create or manipulate contexts. If we do choose to create additional SYCL contexts in our programs though, either implicitly or explicitly, we need to be careful not to use context-specific SYCL objects from one context with a different SYCL context. At best, careless use of multiple contexts may cause our programs to run inefficiently, say if we end up compiling our SYCL kernels multiple times, once for each context. At worst, mixing SYCL objects across contexts may result in undefined behavior, causing our programs to become non-portable or executing improperly on some backends or devices.

For completeness, note that CUDA has a concept of contexts as well, though CUDA contexts are only exposed by the lower-level CUDA driver APIs. Most CUDA programs do not create or manipulate contexts, either.

Error Checking

One final difference to consider relates to error checking and error handling. Because of CUDA's C heritage, errors in CUDA are returned via error codes from CUDA function calls. For most CUDA functions, a failing error code indicates an error in the function returning the error, such as an incorrect parameter to the function. For some other CUDA functions though, like `cudaDeviceSynchronize`, the error value can also return asynchronous errors that occurred on the device.

SYCL also has synchronous and asynchronous errors, though both types of errors are reported using SYCL exceptions rather than return values from SYCL functions. Please refer to Chapter 5 for more information about error detection and error handling in SYCL.

Features in CUDA That Aren't In SYCL... Yet!

So far, we have described cases where features are in both CUDA and SYCL but are expressed differently. This section describes several features that are in CUDA but that do not (currently) have equivalents in SYCL. This is not an exhaustive list, but it is intended to describe some of the features that are commonly used by CUDA applications that may require more effort when migrating to SYCL.

Please note that vendor-specific features are an important part of the standardization process, regardless of whether they are extensions to a standard or defined in a completely vendor-specific API. Vendor-specific features provide important implementation experience and allow a feature to prove its value before it is refined and incorporated into a standard. Many of these features are already in active development for inclusion into the SYCL standard, and some may already be available as extensions to the standard.

GET INVOLVED!

Feedback from users and developers is another important part of the standardization process. If you have an idea for a new feature, or if you have found an extension or a feature from another API valuable, please consider becoming involved! SYCL is an open standard and many SYCL implementations are open source, making it easy to participate in the growing SYCL community.

Global Variables

Although programmers are told early on to never use global variables, sometimes a global variable is the right tool for the job. We might choose to use a global variable to store a useful constant, or a lookup table, or some other value that we would like to be accessible to all the work-items executing our data parallel kernel.

CUDA supports global variables in different address spaces and therefore with different lifetimes. For example, a CUDA program can declare a `__device__` global variable in the global memory space that is unique for each device. These global variables can be set by or read from the host and accessed by all the CUDA threads executing a kernel. A CUDA program can also declare a `__shared__` global variable in the CUDA shared memory space (remember, this is the equivalent of a variable declared in SYCL local memory) that is unique for every CUDA block and can only be accessed by the CUDA threads in that block.

SYCL does not support global variables in device code yet, though there are extensions in the works to provide similar functionality.

Cooperative Groups

As described earlier in this chapter, recent versions of CUDA support cooperative groups, which provide an alternative syntax for collective operations like barriers and shuffle functions. The SYCL group object and the SYCL group algorithms library have many similarities to CUDA cooperative groups, but some key differences remain.

The biggest difference is that the SYCL group functions currently work only on the predefined SYCL work-group and sub-group classes, whereas CUDA cooperative groups are more flexible. For example, a CUDA program may create fixed-size `tiled_partition` groups that divide an existing group into a set of smaller groups, or a CUDA program may represent the set of CUDA threads in a CUDA warp that are currently active as a `coalesced_group`.

A CUDA program may additionally create cooperative groups that are larger than a work-group. For example, a CUDA program may create a `grid_group` representing all the CUDA threads in the grid (equivalently, all the work-items in the global range), or a `cluster_group` representing all the CUDA threads in a *thread block cluster*. To effectively use these newer and larger groups, a CUDA kernel must be launched using special host API functions to ensure that all the CUDA threads in a grid may cooperate, or to specify the thread block cluster dimensions.

SYCL does not support all the cooperative group types in CUDA yet, though there are extensions in the works to add additional group types to SYCL. The introduction of the group object and group algorithms in SYCL 2020 has SYCL well positioned to support this functionality.

Matrix Multiplication Hardware

The final feature we will describe in this section is access to *matrix multiplication* hardware, also referred to as *matrix multiply and accumulate (MMA)* hardware, *tensor cores*, or *systolic arrays*. These are all different names for dedicated hardware engines that are purpose-built to accelerate the matrix multiplication operations that are key to many artificial intelligence (AI) workloads. If we want to customize these workloads, it is important that we have access to matrix multiplication hardware in our data parallel kernels to achieve peak performance.

CUDA provides access to matrix multiplication hardware via *warp matrix multiplication and accumulation (WMMA)* functions. These functions effectively allow the CUDA threads in a warp (equivalently, work-items in a sub-group) to cooperate to perform a matrix multiply and accumulate operation on smaller matrix tiles. The elements of these matrix tiles can be 32-bit `floats` or 64-bit `doubles` for some devices and algorithms, but more commonly use lower-precision types like as 8-bit `chars`, 16-bit `halfs`, or specialized AI types like `bfloat16s` (`bf16`).

Both CUDA and SYCL are actively evolving their support for matrix multiplication hardware. This is a good example of how different vendors will add support for their vendor-specific functionality via vendor-specific mechanisms initially, then a feature will be refined, and common best practices will be added to the standard.

Porting Tools and Techniques

Luckily, when we choose to migrate an application from CUDA to SYCL, it does not need to be a manual process, and we can use tools to automate parts of the migration. This section will describe one of these tools and techniques to assist with migration.

Migrating Code with dpct and SYCLomatic

In this section we will describe the DPC++ Compatibility Tool (`dpct`) and the related open source `SYCLomatic` tool. We will use `dpct` to automatically migrate a CUDA sample to SYCL, though the concepts described in this section apply equally well to `SYCLomatic`.

Figure 21-10 shows the important parts of the simple CUDA sample we will be migrating. This sample reverses blocks of a buffer. This is not a very useful sample in practice, but it has interesting cases that our auto-migration tool will need to handle, such as a CUDA shared memory global variable, a barrier, a device query, memory allocation and initialization, the kernel dispatch itself, and some basic error checking.

```
__shared__ int scratch[256];
__global__ void Reverse(int* ptr, size_t size) {
  auto gid = blockIdx.x * blockDim.x + threadIdx.x;
  auto lid = threadIdx.x;

  scratch[lid] = ptr[gid];
  __syncthreads();
  ptr[gid] = scratch[256 - lid - 1];
}

int main() {
  std::array<int, size> data;
  std::iota(data.begin(), data.end(), 0);

  cudaDeviceProp deviceProp;
  cudaGetDeviceProperties(&deviceProp, 0);
  std::cout << "Running on device: " << deviceProp.name << "\n";

  int* ptr = nullptr;
  cudaMalloc(&ptr, size * sizeof(int));
  cudaMemcpy(ptr, data.data(), size * sizeof(int),
             cudaMemcpyDefault);
  Reverse<<<size / 256, 256>>>(ptr, size);
  cudaError_t result = cudaDeviceSynchronize();
  if (result != cudaSuccess) {
    std::cout << "An error occurred!\n";
  }
  // ...
```

***Figure 21-10.** A simple CUDA program we will automatically migrate*

Running dpct

Because this is a simple example, we can simply invoke `dpct` and pass the CUDA source file we would like to migrate. For more complicated scenarios, `dpct` can be invoked as part of the application build process to identify the CUDA source files to migrate. Please refer to the links at the end of this chapter for more information and additional training material.

When we run dpct on our sample CUDA source file, we may see output like that shown in Figure 21-11. We can make several observations from this output. First, our file was processed successfully, which is great! There were a few warnings though, indicating cases that dpct was not able to able to migrate. For our example, all three warnings are due to the error checking differences between CUDA and SYCL. For our program, dpct was able to generate SYCL code that will behave correctly when the program does not generate an error, but it was not able to migrate the error checking.

The error checking warning is a good example how migration tools like dpct and SYCLomatic will not be able to migrate everything. We should expect to review and adjust the migrated code to address any migration issues, or to otherwise improve the migrated SYCL code for maintainability, portability, or performance.

```
$ dpct source_file.cu
NOTE: Could not auto-detect compilation database for file
'source_file.cu' in '/path/to/your/file' or any parent directory.
The directory "dpct_output" is used as "out-root"
Processing: /path/to/your/file/source_file.cu
/path/to/your/file/source_file.cu:38:5: warning: DPCT1001:0: The
statement could not be removed.
    std::cout << "An error occurred!\n";
    ^
/path/to/your/file/source_file.cu:37:3: warning: DPCT1000:1: Error
handling if-stmt was detected but could not be rewritten.
  if (result != cudaSuccess) {
  ^
/path/to/your/file/source_file.cu:36:24: warning: DPCT1003:2: Migrated
API does not return error code. (*, 0) is inserted. You may need to
rewrite this code.
  cudaError_t result = cudaDeviceSynchronize();
                       ^
Processed 1 file(s) in -in-root folder "/path/to/your/file"
```

Figure 21-11. *Sample dpct output when migrating this CUDA program*

For this example, though, we can use the migrated code as-is. Figure 21-12 shows how to compile our migrated code using the DPC++ compiler with NVIDIA GPU support and then shows successful execution of our migrated program on an Intel GPU, an Intel CPU, and an NVIDIA GPU. Note, if we were to run the migrated program on a different system with different devices, the output may look different, or it may fail to run if the selected device does not exist in the system.

```
$ icpx -fsycl -fsycl-targets=spir64,nvptx64-nvidia-cuda \
    migrated.cpp -o migrated
$ ./migrated
Running on device: Intel(R) UHD Graphics 770
Success.
$ ONEAPI_DEVICE_SELECTOR=opencl:cpu ./migrated
Running on device: 12th Gen Intel(R) Core(TM) i9-12900K
Success.
$ ONEAPI_DEVICE_SELECTOR=ext_oneapi_cuda:gpu ./migrated
Running on device: NVIDIA GeForce RTX 3060
Success.
```

Figure 21-12. *Compiling and running our migrated CUDA program*

Examining the dpct Output

If we examine the migrated output, we can see that `dpct` handled many of the differences described in this chapter. For example, in the generated SYCL kernel shown in Figure 21-13, we see that the `__shared__` global variable `scratch` was turned into a local memory accessor and passed into the kernel. We can also see that the built-in variables `blockIdx` and `threadIdx` were replaced by calls into an instance of the `nd_item` class and that the differing conventions for the contiguous dimension were properly handled, for example, by replacing the use of `threadIdx.x` with a call to `item_ct1.get_local_id(2)`.

```
void Reverse(int *ptr, size_t size,
             const sycl::nd_item<3> &item_ct1,
             int *scratch) {
  auto gid =
      item_ct1.get_group(2) * item_ct1.get_local_range(2) +
      item_ct1.get_local_id(2);
  auto lid = item_ct1.get_local_id(2);

  scratch[lid] = ptr[gid];
  item_ct1.barrier(sycl::access::fence_space::local_space);
  ptr[gid] = scratch[256 - lid - 1];
}
```

Figure 21-13. *SYCL kernel migrated from CUDA*

We can also see that dpct handled some of the host code differences by using several dpct utility functions, such as for the migrated device query shown in Figure 21-14. These helper functions are intended to be used by migrated code only. For portability and maintainability, we should prefer to use standard SYCL APIs directly for our additional development.

```
dpct::device_info deviceProp;
dpct::dev_mgr::instance().get_device(0).get_device_info(
    deviceProp);
std::cout << "Running on device: "
          << deviceProp.get_name() << "\n";
```

Figure 21-14. *SYCL device name query migrated from CUDA*

In general, though, the SYCL code that dpct generates is readable and the mapping between the CUDA code and the migrated SYCL code is clear. Even though additional hand-editing is often required, using automated tools like dpct or SYCLomatic can save time and reduce errors during migration.

Summary

In this chapter, we described how to migrate an application from CUDA to SYCL to enable an application to run on any SYCL device, including CUDA devices by using SYCL compilers with CUDA support.

We started by looking at the many similarities between CUDA and SYCL programs, terminology aside. We saw how CUDA and SYCL fundamentally use the same kernel-based approach to parallelism, with a similar execution model and memory model, making it relatively straightforward to migrate a CUDA program to SYCL. We also explored a few places where CUDA and SYCL have subtle syntactic or behavioral differences and are therefore good to keep in mind as we are migrating our CUDA applications to SYCL. We also described several features that are in CUDA but are not in SYCL (yet!), and we described how vendor-specific features are an important part of the standardization process.

Finally, we examined several tools to automate parts of the migration process and we used the `dpct` tool to automatically migrate a simple CUDA example to SYCL. We saw how the tool migrated most of the code automatically, producing functionally correct and readable code. We were able to run the migrated SYCL example on different SYCL devices after migration, even though additional reviewing and editing may be required for more complex applications.

For More Information

Migrating CUDA code to SYCL is a popular topic and there are many other resources available to learn more. Here are two resources the authors have found helpful:

- General information and tutorials showing how to migrate from CUDA to SYCL (tinyurl.com/cuda2sycl)
- Getting Started Guide for the DPC++ Compatibility Tool (tinyurl.com/startDPCpp)

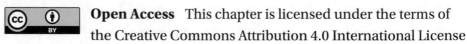

EPILOGUE

Future Direction of SYCL

Take a moment now to feel the peace and calm of knowing that we have covered programming using C++ with SYCL. All the pieces have fallen into place.

We've endeavored to ensure that the code samples in previous chapters use standard SYCL 2020 functionality and execute on a wide range of hardware, and the few places we used extensions (e.g., interoperability and FPGA-specific extensions), we call it out. However, the future-looking code shown in this epilogue does not compile with any compiler as of mid-2023.

In this epilogue, we speculate on the future. Our crystal ball can be a bit difficult to read—this epilogue comes without any warranty. Some of the predictions we made in the first edition of this book came true, but others did not.

This epilogue provides a sneak peek of upcoming SYCL features and DPC++ extensions that we are very excited about. We offer no guarantees that the code samples printed in this epilogue compile: some may already be compatible with a compiler released after the book, while others may compile only after some massaging of syntax. Some features may be released as extensions or incorporated into future versions of SYCL, while others may remain experimental features indefinitely. The code samples in the GitHub repository associated with this book may be updated to use new syntax as it evolves. Likewise, we will have an erratum for the

J. Reinders et al., *Data Parallel C++*, https://doi.org/10.1007/978-1-4842-9691-2

book, which may get additions made from time to time. We recommend checking for updates in these two places (code repository and book errata—links can be found early in Chapter 1).

Closer Alignment with C++11, C++14, and C++17

Maintaining close alignment between SYCL and C++ has two advantages. First, it enables SYCL to leverage the newest and greatest features of C++ to improve developer productivity. Second, it increases the chances of heterogeneous programming features introduced in SYCL successfully influencing the future direction of C++.

SYCL 1.2.1 was based on C++11, and many of the biggest improvements to the interfaces of SYCL 2020 are only possible because of language features introduced in C++14 (e.g., generic lambdas) and C++17 (e.g., class template argument deduction—CTAD). We expect SYCL and C++ to grow closer over time, and there are several exciting efforts already underway.

The C++ Standard Template Library (STL) contains several algorithms which correspond to the parallel patterns discussed in Chapter 17. The algorithms in the STL typically apply to sequences specified by pairs of iterators and—starting with C++17—support an *execution policy* argument denoting whether they should be executed sequentially or in parallel. The standard allows for implementations to define their own execution policies, too, and the oneAPI DPC++ Library (oneDPL) covered in Chapter 18 leverages such a custom execution policy to enable algorithms to execute on SYCL devices. The result is a high-productivity approach to programming heterogeneous devices—if an application can be expressed solely using functionality of the STL algorithms, oneDPL makes it possible to make use of the accelerators in our systems without writing a single line of SYCL kernel code! There are still open questions about how the STL algorithms should interact with certain SYCL concepts (e.g., buffers), and how to ensure that all the standard library classes we might want (e.g., `std::complex`, `std::atomic`) are available in device code, but oneDPL is the first step on a long path toward unifying our host and device code.

Adopting Features from C++20, C++23 and Beyond

The SYCL specification deliberately trails behind C++ to ensure that the features it uses have broad compiler support. However, SYCL committee members—many of whom are also involved in ISO C++ committees—are keeping a close eye on how future versions of C++ are developing.

Adopting C++ or SYCL features we discuss here that are not finalized yet into a specification could be a mistake—features may change significantly before making it into a standard. Nevertheless, there are a number of features under discussion that may change the way that future SYCL programs look and behave which are worth discussing.

Some of the features in SYCL 2020 were informed by C++20 (e.g., `std::atomic_ref`) and others were *pre-adopted* into the `sycl::` namespace (e.g., `std::bit_cast`, `std::span`). As we move toward the next official release of SYCL, we expect to align with C++20 more closely and incorporate the most useful parts of it. For example, C++20 introduced some additional thread synchronization routines in the form of `std::latch` and `std::barrier`; we already explored in Chapter 19 how similar interfaces could be used to define device-wide barriers, and it may make sense to reexamine sub-group and work-group barriers in the context of the new C++20 syntax as well.

One of the most exciting features in C++23 is `mdspan`, a non-owning view of data that provides both multidimensional array syntax for pointers and an `AccessorPolicy` as an extension point for controlling access to the underlying data. These semantics are very similar to those of SYCL accessors, and `mdspan` would enable accessor-like syntax to be used for both buffers and USM allocations, as shown in Figure EP-1.

```
queue q;
constexpr int N = 4;
constexpr int M = 2;
int* data = malloc_shared<int>(N * M, q);

stdex::mdspan<int, N, M> view{data};
q.parallel_for(range<2>{N, M}, [=](id<2> idx) {
   int i = idx[0];
   int j = idx[1];
   view(i, j) = i * M + j;
 }).wait();
```

Figure EP-1. *Attaching accessor-like indexing to a USM pointer using* `mdspan`

Hopefully it is only a matter of time until SYCL officially supports `mdspan`. In the meantime, we recommend that interested readers experiment with the open source production-quality reference implementation available as part of the Kokkos project.

Mixing SPMD and SIMD Programming

Another exciting, proposed feature for C++ is the `std::simd` class template, which seeks to provide a portable interface for explicit vector parallelism in C++. Adopting this interface would provide a clear distinction between the two different uses of vector types described in Chapter 11: uses of vector types for programmer convenience and uses of vector types by ninja programmers for low-level performance tuning. The presence of support for both SPMD and SIMD programming styles within the same language also raises some interesting questions: how should we declare which style a kernel uses, and should we be able to mix and match styles within the same kernel?

We have started to explore potential answers to this question in the form of a DPC++ extension (sycl_ext_oneapi_invoke_simd), which provides a new `invoke_simd` function (modelled on `std::invoke`) that allows developers to call explicitly vectorized (SIMD) code from within an SPMD kernel. The call to `invoke_simd` acts as a clear boundary between the two execution models implied by the two programming styles and defines how data should flow between them. The code in Figure EP-2 shows a very simple example of `invoke_simd`'s usage, calling out to a function that expects to receive a combination of scalar and vector (`simd`) arguments.

```
// Function expects one vector argument (x) and one scalar
// argument (n)
simd<float, 8> scale(simd<float, 8> x, float n) {
  return x * n;
}

q.parallel_for(..., sycl::nd_item<1> it)
    [[sycl::reqd_sub_group_size(8)]] {
  // In SPMD code, each work-item has its own x and n
  // variables
  float x = ...;
  float n = ...;

  // Invoke SIMD function (scale) using work-items in the
  // sub-group x values from each work-item are combined
  // into a simd<float, 8>
  // The value of n is defined to be the
  // same (uniform) across all work-items
  // Returned simd<float, 8> is unpacked
  sycl::sub_group sg = it.get_sub_group();
  float y = invoke_simd(sg, scale, x, uniform(n));
});
```

Figure EP-2. *A simple example of invoking a SIMD function from a SPMD kernel*

The approach taken by `invoke_simd` has several advantages. First, there can be no nasty surprises— functions with a different execution model are invoked explicitly, and the user is responsible for describing how to marshal data back and forth. Second, the mechanism allows for *fine-grained specialization*—it is possible to write just a few lines of explicitly vectorized code (e.g., for performance tuning) without having to throw away the rest of our SPMD code. Finally, it is straightforward to extend—`invoke_simd` itself can be extended to support new groups or new argument mappings via simple overloading, and similar `invoke_*` functions could be introduced to handle interoperability with different contexts (e.g., code written in a language that isn't SYCL).

Address Spaces

The introduction of generic address space support in SYCL 2020 has the potential to greatly simplify many codes, by allowing us to use regular C++ pointers without worrying about what kind of memory is being used. Many modern architectures provide hardware support for the generic address space, and so we can expect code using regular C++ pointers to work across a wide variety of machines and with minimal performance overhead.

However, there are some (older, or more special purpose) architectures on which generic address space support is a more complicated story. Some hardware may use different instructions to access different kinds of memory, requiring compilers to identify a concrete address space at compile time (i.e., to generate the correct instructions). There may also be SYCL backends incapable of representing a generic address space (e.g., OpenCL 1.2). SYCL 2020 makes allowances for such hardware and backends via a set of inference rules for deducing address spaces.

The address space deduction rules were inherited from SYCL 1.2.1, and the SYCL 2020 specification includes a note that the rules will be revisited in a future version of SYCL. Although it is unclear at the time of writing exactly how these rules will change, SYCL's long-term thinking is clear: in most cases, we should not be concerned with address space management and should trust the compiler and hardware to do the right thing.

Specialization Mechanism

There are plans to introduce compile-time queries enabling kernels to be specialized based on properties (*aspects*) of the targeted device (e.g., the device type, support for a specific extension, the size of work-group local memory, the sub-group size selected by the compiler). Such queries require a new kind of constant expression not currently present in C++—they are not necessarily `constexpr` when the host code is compiled but become `constexpr` when the target device becomes known.

The exact mechanism used to expose this "device-constant expression" concept is still being designed. We expect it to build on the specialization constants feature introduced in SYCL 2020 and to look and behave similarly to the code shown in Figure EP-3.

```
h.parallel_for(range{1}, [=](id<1> idx) {
  if_device_has<aspect::cpu>([&]() {
    /* Code specialized for CPUs */
    out << "On a CPU!" << endl;
  }).else_if_device_has<aspect::gpu>([&]() {
    /* Code specialized for GPUs */
    out << "On a GPU!" << endl;
  });
});
```

Figure EP-3. *Specializing kernel code based on device aspects at kernel compile time*

Compile-Time Properties

SYCL allows the behavior of certain classes (e.g., buffers, accessors) to be modified by passing a *property list* into the constructor. These properties are already very powerful, but their power is limited by the fact that the properties passed to a constructor are not known until runtime. Allowing for certain properties to be declared at compile time has the potential to significantly improve performance, by reducing the number of runtime checks and by enabling compilers to aggressively specialize both host and device code in the presence of specific properties.

The DPC++ compiler supports an experimental extension for compile-time properties (sycl_ext_oneapi_properties), and it already enables a wide variety of other extensions:

- Pointers annotated with information extending beyond just address spaces, which could inform the future of `sycl::multi_ptr` (sycl_ext_oneapi_annotated_ptr)
- Kernel configuration controls, which could replace C++ attributes and increase the capabilities of library-only SYCL implementations (sycl_ext_oneapi_kernel_properties)
- Descriptions of desired memory behavior and access controls (sycl_ext_oneapi_device_global, sycl_ext_oneapi_prefetch)

Our early experience with compile-time properties has been very positive, and we're finding more and more potential use cases for them all the time. Given their wide applicability, we are keen to see some version of compile-time properties adopted in a future SYCL specification.

Summary

There is already a lot of excitement around SYCL, and this is just the beginning! We (as a community) have a long path ahead of us, and it will take significant continued effort to distill the best practices for heterogeneous programming and to design new language features that strike the desired balance between performance, portability, and productivity.

We need your help! If your favorite feature of C++ (or any other programming language) is missing from SYCL, please reach out to us. Together, we can shape the future direction of SYCL and C++.

For More Information

- Khronos SYCL Registry, `www.khronos.org/registry/SYCL`
- H. Carter Edwards et al., "mdspan: A Non-Owning Multidimensional Array Reference," `wg21.link/p0009`
- D. Hollman et al., "Production-Quality mdspan Implementation," `github.com/kokkos/mdspan`
- Intel DPC++ Compiler Extensions, `tinyurl.com/syclextend`

Index

A

B

J. Reinders et al., *Data Parallel C++*, https://doi.org/10.1007/978-1-4842-9691-2

C

G

H

I

J

K

L

M

N

O

P

Q

R

W, X

Y, Z

Printed in the United States
by Baker & Taylor Publisher Services